# PRENTICE HALL
# WORLD STUDIES
# EUROPE and RUSSIA

# All in One

# Teaching Resources

PEARSON
Prentice
Hall

Needham, Massachusetts
Upper Saddle River, New Jersey

ISBN 0-13-128015-5

7 8 9 10 11 12 13    12 11 10 09 08

# Table of Contents

**Reading and Writing Skills Handbook**

Writing Skills: Four Purposes
for Writing........................7

Writing Skills: Writing to Describe.........8

Writing Skills: Writing the Conclusion......9

Writing Skills: Using the Revision
Checklist.........................10

Writing Skills: Writing to Persuade........11

Writing Skills: Structuring Paragraphs.....12

Writing Skills: Creating Paragraph
Outlines.........................13

Writing Skills: Writing to Inform
and Explain......................14

Writing Skills: Gathering Details..........15

Writing Skills: Writing a Cause
and Effect Essay..................16

Writing Skills: Writing a
Problem-and-Solution Essay..........17

Writing Skills: Choosing a Topic.........18

Writing Skills: Using the Library.........19

Writing Skills: Summarizing
and Taking Notes.................20

Writing Skills: Preparing Note Cards......21

Writing Skills: Writing an Introduction....22

Writing Skills: Writing the
Body of an Essay..................23

Writing Skills: Writing for Assessment.....24

Writing Skills: Writing a Letter..........25

Answer Key.........................26

**MapMaster Skills Handbook**

*The Five Themes of Geography*

MapMaster Skills: The Five Themes
of Geography.....................29

*Understanding Movements of the Earth*

MapMaster Skills: Understanding Movements
of the Earth......................30

Writing Skills: Doing Searches
on the Internet....................31

*Understanding Globes*

MapMaster Skills:
Understanding Hemispheres..........32

MapMaster Skills: Understanding
Latitude and Longitude..............33

DK Compact Atlas of the World
Activity: Understanding Latitude
and Longitude....................34

MapMaster Skills: Using Latitude
and Longitude....................35

MapMaster Skills: Understanding
Grids............................36

MapMaster Skills: Using a Grid..........37

MapMaster Skills: Comparing
Globes and Maps..................38

*Map Projections*

MapMaster Skills: Understanding
Projection........................39

MapMaster Skills: Great Circles
and Straight Lines.................40

MapMaster Skills: Maps with Accurate
Shapes: Conformal Maps.............41

MapMaster Skills: Maps with
Accurate Areas: Equal-Area Maps......42

MapMaster Skills: Maps with Accurate
Directions: Azimuthal Maps...........43

*How to Use a Map*

MapMaster Skills: Using the Map Key.....44

MapMaster Skills: Using the
Compass Rose....................45

DK Compact Atlas of the World Activity:
Using the Map Key.................46

DK Compact Atlas of the World Activity:
Using the Compass Rose.............47

DK Compact Atlas of the World Activity:
Using the Map Scale...............48

MapMaster Skills: Comparing Maps
of Different Scale..................49

MapMaster Skills: Maps with Accurate
Distances: Equidistant Maps..........50

*Political and Physical Maps*

MapMaster Skills: Reading
a Political Map....................51

DK Compact Atlas of the World
Activity: Reading a Political Map.......52

Outline Map 22: North Africa...........53

Outline Map 23: West and
Central Africa.....................54

Outline Map 24: East and
Southern Africa...................55

MapMaster Skills: Reading
a Physical Map . . . . . . . . . . . . . . . . . . . . 56

MapMaster Skills: Elevation
on a Map . . . . . . . . . . . . . . . . . . . . . . . . 57

DK Compact Atlas of the World
Activity: Reading a Physical Map . . . . . . . 58

MapMaster Skills: Relief on a Map . . . . . . . 59

MapMaster Skills: Maps of the
Ocean Floor . . . . . . . . . . . . . . . . . . . . . . 60

*Special-Purpose Maps*

MapMaster Skills: Reading
a Climate Map . . . . . . . . . . . . . . . . . . . . 61

MapMaster Skills: Reading
a Climate Graph . . . . . . . . . . . . . . . . . . . 62

MapMaster Skills: Reading a Natural
Vegetation Map . . . . . . . . . . . . . . . . . . . 63

Outline Map 26: South Asia: Political . . . . . . 64

MapMaster Skills: Reading a Time
Zone Map . . . . . . . . . . . . . . . . . . . . . . . 65

*Human Migration*

MapMaster Skills: Reading
a Historical Map . . . . . . . . . . . . . . . . . . . 66

MapMaster Skills: Analyzing
Statistics . . . . . . . . . . . . . . . . . . . . . . . . 67

*World Land Use*

MapMaster Skills: Reading an
Economic Activity Map . . . . . . . . . . . . . . 68

MapMaster Skills: Reading a Natural
Resources Map . . . . . . . . . . . . . . . . . . . . 69

Answer Key . . . . . . . . . . . . . . . . . . . . . . . . 70

## Book Projects

Changing Climates . . . . . . . . . . . . . . . . . . . 77

Tourism in Eastern Europe . . . . . . . . . . . . . 80

Olympic Cities . . . . . . . . . . . . . . . . . . . . . . 83

Folklore Corner . . . . . . . . . . . . . . . . . . . . . 86

Rubric for Assessing Student
Performance on a Project . . . . . . . . . . . . . 89

Rubric for Assessing Performance
of an Entire Group . . . . . . . . . . . . . . . . . 90

Rubric for Assessing Individual
Performance in a Group . . . . . . . . . . . . . . 91

Rubric for Assessing a Student
Portfolio . . . . . . . . . . . . . . . . . . . . . . . . . 92

## Regional Overview

Discovery Activities About Europe
and Russia . . . . . . . . . . . . . . . . . . . . . . . 93

Outline Map 13: Western Europe:
Physical . . . . . . . . . . . . . . . . . . . . . . . . . 96

Outline Map 14: Western Europe:
Political . . . . . . . . . . . . . . . . . . . . . . . . . 97

Outline Map 15: Northern Europe . . . . . . . . 98

Outline Map 16: Southern Europe . . . . . . . . 99

Outline Map 18: Eastern Europe
and Russia: Political . . . . . . . . . . . . . . . . 100

MapMaster Skills: Reading a
Population Density Map . . . . . . . . . . . . . 101

Writing Skills: Using the Library . . . . . . . . 102

Rubric for Assessing an Oral
Presentation . . . . . . . . . . . . . . . . . . . . . 103

Answer Key . . . . . . . . . . . . . . . . . . . . . . . 104

## Chapter and Section Support

Letter Home . . . . . . . . . . . . . . . . . . . . . . 105

**Europe and Russia: Physical Geography**
*Europe and Russia,* Chapter 1
*Eastern Hemisphere,* Chapter 6

Section 1: Lesson Plan . . . . . . . . . . . . . . . . 106

Section 1: Reading Readiness Guide . . . . . . 107

Section 1: Guided Reading and Review . . . . 108

Section 1: Quiz . . . . . . . . . . . . . . . . . . . . . 109

Section 2: Lesson Plan . . . . . . . . . . . . . . . . 110

Section 2: Reading Readiness Guide . . . . . . 111

Section 2: Guided Reading and Review . . . . 112

Section 2: Quiz . . . . . . . . . . . . . . . . . . . . . 113

Section 3: Lesson Plan . . . . . . . . . . . . . . . . 114

Section 3: Reading Readiness Guide . . . . . . 115

Section 3: Guided Reading and Review . . . . 116

Section 3: Quiz . . . . . . . . . . . . . . . . . . . . . 117

Target Reading Skill: Preview and
Set a Purpose . . . . . . . . . . . . . . . . . . . . 118

Target Reading Skill: Preview and
Predict . . . . . . . . . . . . . . . . . . . . . . . . . 119

Target Reading Skill: Preview and
Ask Questions . . . . . . . . . . . . . . . . . . . . 120

Word Knowledge . . . . . . . . . . . . . . . . . . . 121

Enrichment . . . . . . . . . . . . . . . . . . . . . . . 122

Skills for Life . . . . . . . . . . . . . . . . . . . . . . 123

Small Group Activity: Europe and
Russia Map and Climate Charts . . . . . . 124

Activity Shop Lab: Tracking the
Midnight Sun . . . . . . . . . . . . . . . . . . . . . . . 128

MapMaster Skills: Reading a
Natural Vegetation Map . . . . . . . . . . . . . . 130

Primary Sources and Literature Readings:
The Endless Steppe . . . . . . . . . . . . . . . . . 131

Writing Skills: Doing Searches
on the Internet . . . . . . . . . . . . . . . . . . . . . 133

Writing Skills: Preparing for
Presentations. . . . . . . . . . . . . . . . . . . . . . . 134

Vocabulary Development . . . . . . . . . . . . . . 135

Rubric for Assessing a Journal Entry. . . . . . 136

Rubric for Assessing a Writing
Assignment . . . . . . . . . . . . . . . . . . . . . . . . 137

Chapter Tests A and B . . . . . . . . . . . . . . . . . 138

Answer Key . . . . . . . . . . . . . . . . . . . . . . . . . 144

**Europe and Russia: Shaped by History**
*Europe and Russia,* **Chapter 2**
*Eastern Hemisphere,* **Chapter 7**

Section 1: Lesson Plan . . . . . . . . . . . . . . . . . 149

Section 1: Reading Readiness Guide . . . . . . 150

Section 1: Guided Reading and Review . . . 151

Section 1: Quiz. . . . . . . . . . . . . . . . . . . . . . . 152

Section 2: Lesson Plan . . . . . . . . . . . . . . . . . 153

Section 2: Reading Readiness Guide . . . . . . 154

Section 2: Guided Reading and Review . . . 155

Section 2: Quiz. . . . . . . . . . . . . . . . . . . . . . . 156

Section 3: Lesson Plan . . . . . . . . . . . . . . . . . 157

Section 3: Reading Readiness Guide . . . . . . 158

Section 3: Guided Reading and Review . . . 159

Section 3: Quiz. . . . . . . . . . . . . . . . . . . . . . . 160

Section 4: Lesson Plan . . . . . . . . . . . . . . . . . 161

Section 4: Reading Readiness Guide . . . . . . 162

Section 4: Guided Reading and Review . . . 163

Section 4: Quiz. . . . . . . . . . . . . . . . . . . . . . . 164

Section 5: Lesson Plan . . . . . . . . . . . . . . . . . 165

Section 5: Reading Readiness Guide . . . . . . 166

Section 5: Guided Reading and Review . . . 167

Section 5: Quiz. . . . . . . . . . . . . . . . . . . . . . . 168

Target Reading Skill: Reread or
Read Ahead. . . . . . . . . . . . . . . . . . . . . . . . 169

Target Reading Skill: Paraphrase . . . . . . . . .170

Target Reading Skill: Summarize . . . . . . . . .171

Word Knowledge . . . . . . . . . . . . . . . . . . . . .172

Enrichment . . . . . . . . . . . . . . . . . . . . . . . . . .173

Skills for Life . . . . . . . . . . . . . . . . . . . . . . . . .174

Small Group Activity: Castle Mural. . . . . . .175

Outline Map 14: Western Europe:
Political. . . . . . . . . . . . . . . . . . . . . . . . . . . .179

Outline Map 17: Eastern Europe:
Physical. . . . . . . . . . . . . . . . . . . . . . . . . . . .180

Outline Map 18: Eastern Europe
and Russia: Political . . . . . . . . . . . . . . . . .181

Primary Sources and Literature Readings:
A Spartan Reply . . . . . . . . . . . . . . . . . . . . .182

Primary Sources and Literature Readings:
Storm in the State . . . . . . . . . . . . . . . . . . .183

Primary Sources and Literature Readings:
Testing a Theory . . . . . . . . . . . . . . . . . . . . .184

Primary Sources and Literature Readings:
A Child in Prison Camp . . . . . . . . . . . . . .185

Primary Sources and Literature Readings:
A Letter from Napoleon's Army . . . . . . .188

Primary Sources and Literature Readings:
Lenin's Deathbed Words. . . . . . . . . . . . . .190

Primary Sources and Literature Readings:
Kampf. . . . . . . . . . . . . . . . . . . . . . . . . . . . .191

Primary Sources and Literature Readings:
The Endless Steppe. . . . . . . . . . . . . . . . . . .192

Primary Sources and Literature Readings:
Whose Falkland Islands Are They? . . . . .194

Primary Sources and Literature
Readings: Lords and Vassals . . . . . . . . . .197

Writing Skills: Writing Stories. . . . . . . . . . . .198

Vocabulary Development. . . . . . . . . . . . . . .199

Rubric for Assessing a Journal Entry . . . . . .200

Rubric for Assessing a Writing
Assignment . . . . . . . . . . . . . . . . . . . . . . . .201

Rubric for Assessing a Letter
to the Editor. . . . . . . . . . . . . . . . . . . . . . . .202

Chapter Tests A and B . . . . . . . . . . . . . . . . .203

Answer Key . . . . . . . . . . . . . . . . . . . . . . . . .209

**Cultures of Europe and Russia**
*Europe and Russia,* **Chapter 3**
*Eastern Hemisphere,* **Chapter 8**

Section 1: Lesson Plan . . . . . . . . . . . . . . . . . . 215

Section 1: Reading Readiness Guide . . . . . . 216

Section 1: Guided Reading and Review . . . 217

Section 1: Quiz. . . . . . . . . . . . . . . . . . . . . . . . 218

Section 2: Lesson Plan . . . . . . . . . . . . . . . . . . 219

Section 2: Reading Readiness Guide . . . . . . 220

Section 2: Guided Reading and Review . . . 221

Section 2: Quiz. . . . . . . . . . . . . . . . . . . . . . . . 222

Section 3: Lesson Plan . . . . . . . . . . . . . . . . . . 223

Section 3: Reading Readiness Guide . . . . . . 224

Section 3: Guided Reading and Review . . . 225

Section 3: Quiz. . . . . . . . . . . . . . . . . . . . . . . . 226

Target Reading Skill: Identify
Main Ideas. . . . . . . . . . . . . . . . . . . . . . . 227

Target Reading Skill: Identify
Supporting Details. . . . . . . . . . . . . . . . . 228

Target Reading Skill: Identify
Implied Main Ideas . . . . . . . . . . . . . . . . 229

Word Knowledge . . . . . . . . . . . . . . . . . . . . . 230

Enrichment. . . . . . . . . . . . . . . . . . . . . . . . . . 231

Skills for Life . . . . . . . . . . . . . . . . . . . . . . . . 232

Small Group Activity: European and
Russian Music. . . . . . . . . . . . . . . . . . . . 233

Primary Sources and Literature Readings:
Your Government Has
Returned to You! . . . . . . . . . . . . . . . . . . 237

Primary Sources and Literature Readings:
Lenin's Deathbed Words . . . . . . . . . . . . . 239

Primary Sources and Literature Readings:
Kampf . . . . . . . . . . . . . . . . . . . . . . . . . . 240

Primary Sources and Literature Readings:
Housekeeping in Russia Soon
After the Revolution . . . . . . . . . . . . . . . . 241

Writing Skills: Writing Plays . . . . . . . . . . . 242

Vocabulary Development . . . . . . . . . . . . . . . 243

Rubric for Assessing a Writing
Assignment. . . . . . . . . . . . . . . . . . . . . . . 244

Rubric for Assessing a Student Poster . . . . 245

Rubric for Assessing an Oral
Presentation . . . . . . . . . . . . . . . . . . . . . . 246

Chapter Tests A and B . . . . . . . . . . . . . . . . . 247

Answer Key. . . . . . . . . . . . . . . . . . . . . . . . . . 253

**Western Europe**
*Europe and Russia,* **Chapter 4**
*Eastern Hemisphere,* **Chapter 9**

Section 1: Lesson Plan. . . . . . . . . . . . . . . . . . 257

Section 1: Reading Readiness Guide . . . . . . 258

Section 1: Guided Reading and Review. . . . 259

Section 1: Quiz . . . . . . . . . . . . . . . . . . . . . . . 260

Section 2: Lesson Plan. . . . . . . . . . . . . . . . . . 261

Section 2: Reading Readiness Guide . . . . . . 262

Section 2: Guided Reading and Review. . . . 263

Section 2: Quiz . . . . . . . . . . . . . . . . . . . . . . . 264

Section 3: Lesson Plan. . . . . . . . . . . . . . . . . . 265

Section 3: Reading Readiness Guide . . . . . . 266

Section 3: Guided Reading and Review. . . . 267

Section 3: Quiz . . . . . . . . . . . . . . . . . . . . . . . 268

Section 4: Lesson Plan. . . . . . . . . . . . . . . . . . 269

Section 4: Reading Readiness Guide . . . . . . 270

Section 4: Guided Reading and Review. . . . 271

Section 4: Quiz . . . . . . . . . . . . . . . . . . . . . . . 272

Section 5: Lesson Plan. . . . . . . . . . . . . . . . . . 273

Section 5: Reading Readiness Guide . . . . . . 274

Section 5: Guided Reading and Review. . . . 275

Section 5: Quiz . . . . . . . . . . . . . . . . . . . . . . . 276

Target Reading Skill: Using Context
Clues: Definition and Description . . . . . . 277

Target Reading Skill: Using Context
Clues: Compare and Contrast. . . . . . . . . 278

Target Reading Skill: Using Context
Clues: General Knowledge . . . . . . . . . . . 279

Word Knowledge . . . . . . . . . . . . . . . . . . . . . 280

Enrichment . . . . . . . . . . . . . . . . . . . . . . . . . . 281

Skills for Life . . . . . . . . . . . . . . . . . . . . . . . . 282

Small Group Activity: Comparing
Types of Government. . . . . . . . . . . . . . . . 283

MapMaster Skills: Reading
a Circle Graph. . . . . . . . . . . . . . . . . . . . 287

MapMaster Skills: Reading a Table . . . . . . 288

MapMaster Skills: Reading
a Line Graph . . . . . . . . . . . . . . . . . . . . . 289

MapMaster Skills: Reading
a Bar Graph . . . . . . . . . . . . . . . . . . . . . 290

MapMaster Skills: Reading
a Timeline. . . . . . . . . . . . . . . . . . . . . . . . 291

Primary Sources and Literature Readings:
The Boy. . . . . . . . . . . . . . . . . . . . . . . . . . 292

Writing Skills: Writing to Inform and
  Explain. . . . . . . . . . . . . . . . . . . . . . . . . . 296
Vocabulary Development . . . . . . . . . . . . . . 297
Rubric for Assessing a Writing
  Assignment. . . . . . . . . . . . . . . . . . . . . . . 298
Rubric for Assessing a Journal Entry. . . . . . 299
Chapter Tests A and B. . . . . . . . . . . . . . . . 300
Answer Key. . . . . . . . . . . . . . . . . . . . . . . . 306

**Eastern Europe and Russia**
  *Europe and Russia,* **Chapter 5**
  *Eastern Hemisphere,* **Chapter 10**
Section 1: Lesson Plan . . . . . . . . . . . . . . . . 313
Section 1: Reading Readiness Guide . . . . . . 314
Section 1: Guided Reading and Review . . . 315
Section 1: Quiz. . . . . . . . . . . . . . . . . . . . . . 316
Section 2: Lesson Plan . . . . . . . . . . . . . . . . 317
Section 2: Reading Readiness Guide . . . . . . 318
Section 2: Guided Reading and Review . . . 319
Section 2: Quiz. . . . . . . . . . . . . . . . . . . . . . 320
Section 3: Lesson Plan . . . . . . . . . . . . . . . . 321
Section 3: Reading Readiness Guide . . . . . . 322
Section 3: Guided Reading and Review . . . 323
Section 3: Quiz. . . . . . . . . . . . . . . . . . . . . . 324
Section 4: Lesson Plan . . . . . . . . . . . . . . . . 325
Section 4: Reading Readiness Guide . . . . . . 326
Section 4: Guided Reading and Review . . . 327
Section 4: Quiz. . . . . . . . . . . . . . . . . . . . . . 328
Target Reading Skill: Compare and
  Contrast. . . . . . . . . . . . . . . . . . . . . . . . . 329
Target Reading Skill: Make
  Comparisons. . . . . . . . . . . . . . . . . . . . . . 330
Target Reading Skill: Identify
  Contrasts . . . . . . . . . . . . . . . . . . . . . . . . 331
Word Knowledge . . . . . . . . . . . . . . . . . . . . 332
Enrichment. . . . . . . . . . . . . . . . . . . . . . . . . 333
Skills for Life . . . . . . . . . . . . . . . . . . . . . . . 334
Small Group Activity: Chernobyl—
  Report on a Disaster . . . . . . . . . . . . . . . . 335
Activity Shop Interdisciplinary:
  Plan a New Railroad Line. . . . . . . . . . . . . 339
MapMaster Skills: Using
  the Map Key . . . . . . . . . . . . . . . . . . . . . . 341
MapMaster Skills: Reading a Table . . . . . . . 342
DK Compact Atlas of the World:
  Reading a Political Map . . . . . . . . . . . . . . 343

Outline Map 18: Eastern Europe and Russia:
  Political. . . . . . . . . . . . . . . . . . . . . . . . . . 344
Primary Sources and Literature Readings:
  Housekeeping in Russia Soon
  After the Revolution. . . . . . . . . . . . . . . . . 345
Vocabulary Development. . . . . . . . . . . . . . . 346
Rubric for Assessing a Bar Graph. . . . . . . . 347
Rubric for Assessing a Newspaper
  Article. . . . . . . . . . . . . . . . . . . . . . . . . . . 348
Rubric for Assessing a Timeline . . . . . . . . . 349
Rubric for Assessing a Writing
  Assignment . . . . . . . . . . . . . . . . . . . . . . . 350
Chapter Tests A and B . . . . . . . . . . . . . . . . 351
Answer Key . . . . . . . . . . . . . . . . . . . . . . . . 357

**Final Exams A and B . . . . . . . . . . 363**
Answer Key . . . . . . . . . . . . . . . . . . . . . . . . 369

**Europe and Russia Transparency
Planner . . . . . . . . . . . . . . . . . . . . . 375**

Reading and Writing Handbook

# Writing Skills

## Four Purposes for Writing

Why do we write? Before you answer, think about people throughout history and why they put their thoughts into writing.

We know that thousands of years ago, when writing was more difficult than it is today, people still found a way to record information. Why did they write? In Latin America, for example, the ancient Mayans carved symbols into stone to **inform** others about their history. The ancient Egyptians also carved or painted on stone to **explain** how they did things—from harvesting crops to preparing religious ceremonies.

Now think about when you write in your own life.

Perhaps you send a letter to a favorite aunt and uncle who live far away to **describe** a recent family party that they could not attend. Or you might write a notice in the school paper, trying to **persuade** students to volunteer for an after-school program.

As you can see from these examples, there are four general purposes for writing:

To **inform**—Provide specific facts and details, giving a clear understanding about something.

To **explain**—Tell why or how something takes place, giving the reasons or causes for things.

To **describe**—Create a picture in words, telling what someone or something is like.

To **persuade**—Try to convince another person to act, think, or believe in a particular way.

**Directions:** *Read the statements below. Identify why the writer wrote each sentence: to inform, to explain, to describe, or to persuade. Write your answers in the spaces provided.*

_____ **1.** The dog's fur felt soft beneath her fingers.

_____ **2.** To get to the playing field, take a left onto Marshall Road and a right onto Lowe Street.

_____ **3.** The test was delayed because Ms. Russo was out on Tuesday and didn't have time to go over the last lesson with the class.

_____ **4.** I believe that we should all get up by 7:30 a.m. to make sure we arrive at the field before the game starts at 8:15. That way, we'll get good seats.

Reading and Writing Handbook

# Writing Skills

## Writing to Describe

When you write to describe, you create a picture with words. You help someone experience an action, event, thing, or person simply through your words, rather than through their own five senses. Writing to describe appeals to your readers' senses to help them see, smell, taste, hear, or feel what you are writing about.

To write to describe, build lifelike images for your readers by using accurate adjectives and vivid verbs.

**Adjectives** are words that describe nouns. For example, you might read an advertisement that describes "sizzling" burgers (sense of hearing), or "finger-licking" chicken (sense of taste).

When writing to describe, also try to use vivid **verbs**, or action words. For instance, you might write, "he shuffled down the street," instead of "he went down the street," to paint a more precise picture of the man's attitude as he walked down the street. Think of descriptive verbs you hear in everyday life. A car "zoom zooms." A mouthwash "tingles your taste buds."

**Directions:** *Practice writing to describe by choosing one of the topics below or creating one of your own. Write one paragraph that gives your readers a complete and vivid image. First, fill in the spaces below with your chosen topic, purpose, audience, and ideas. Then write your paragraph on a separate sheet of paper.*

Possible topics:

- Describe for a friend the best meal you have ever eaten.
- For a grandparent, write a description of a recent school sporting event or activity.
- Write to a friend about the most memorable vacation you ever took.
- Describe for a teacher the most inspiring building or place in nature you have seen.

Your own idea: _____

Topic: _____

Purpose in writing: _____

Audience: _____

Ideas and images: _____

_____

_____

_____

Reading and Writing Handbook

# Writing Skills

## Writing the Conclusion

Why are "famous last words" so famous? It is usually because the last words spoken by a person—just like the concluding words in a good article, essay, or book—are often the most memorable. If carefully drafted, they stay with us the longest.

A strong conclusion reinforces and restates what the writer is trying to convey in the whole piece. It may offer a solution to a problem or challenge the reader to take some type of action. It may leave the reader with a thought-provoking message. How does it do that?

By **restating** the thesis statement, or main idea, from the introduction of the essay. (Restate the thesis statement in slightly different words, so that the conclusion is not boring or repetitious.)

By **summarizing** the key points from the body of the essay. (At this point, do not confuse the reader by bringing up new information.)

By **satisfying** the reader's sense of closure. (Write a creative "punch line" in the final sentence, as long as it is in keeping with the style and tone of the rest of the piece.)

**Directions:** *Read and compare the two concluding paragraphs below. Circle the one you think is a better conclusion. On the lines below, explain your selection.*

### Conclusion A

Unfortunately, the violence between Hindus and Sikhs persists today. The recent riots described here highlight the important role religion continues to play in South Asian life, culture, and politics. The riots also serve as a lesson in how easily religious zealots can control a situation. Whether the zealots' goal is to spread peace or to gain power will be revealed by the bloodshed they leave in their wake.

### Conclusion B

And so it seems that religion and political conflict have always gone hand in hand. As I have pointed out in this essay, this is particularly true in South Asia. It is also my opinion that this type of conflict is the most difficult to resolve.

_____

_____

_____

**Challenge:** You have just written an essay about Native Americans in the southwestern United States. Follow the guidelines above to create a concluding paragraph for that essay. Use a separate sheet of paper for your paragraph.

Reading and Writing Handbook

# Writing Skills

## Using the Revision Checklist

Every author needs an editor. Even famous authors rely on someone to review and revise their writing. Since most of us do not have a professional editor to check our work, we must learn how to do our own revisions.

So, how do you become your own best editor? Take an organized, disciplined approach. Use a revision checklist.

The checklist below lists questions that will guide you as you edit your essay. Since you probably know your own strengths and weaknesses as a writer, you may wish to add questions to this list.

### Revision Checklist

_____ Does your introductory paragraph spark interest, give necessary background, and include a thesis statement?

_____ Does your thesis statement present a clear main idea?

_____ Do the subtopics in the body of your essay support and develop the thesis statement?

_____ Are the subtopics presented in logical order throughout the essay?

_____ Does each paragraph in the body of the essay have a topic sentence?

_____ Have you used transitions to connect each paragraph to the next?

_____ Have you used appropriate language and tone for the intended audience?

_____ Does the concluding paragraph restate the main idea, summarize the key facts, and bring your essay to a memorable close?

_____ Are all your sources for quotations and facts cited within the essay or in footnotes?

_____ Have you correctly listed all your sources, including those for visuals, in the bibliography?

**Directions:** *Read an essay you have written aloud in front of a mirror. As you read, make a check mark at any points where you have to pause or stop. Often, these "stoppers" are places where phrasing is awkward, logic is unclear, or subtopics are inappropriate or out of place. Go through the revision checklist and revise your essay accordingly. Now, ask someone else—a fresh pair of eyes—to read the revised essay and point out any sections that need reworking.*

Reading and Writing Handbook

# Writing Skills

## Writing to Persuade

When you write to persuade, you try to convince people to agree with your opinion. You are surrounded by examples of persuasive writing every day. Look in a newspaper or a magazine. Advertisements try to persuade you to buy something. Movie reviews try to persuade you to do something. Editorial columns want you to believe something. Chances are that you often want to persuade others to your point of view, too.

What makes persuasive writing effective? In a persuasive essay, you state your point of view clearly and think about whom you are writing for. Then, gather evidence to support your argument and present the evidence in a convincing way. Also, consider the opposing viewpoint. That way, you can counter the arguments against your case—before they are even made.

**Directions:** *Practice writing to persuade by choosing one of the situations below, or use your own idea. Use the spaces provided to state your point of view, list the ideas that support your opinion, and list possible counter arguments. Then use a separate sheet to write your first draft.*

You're writing to a friend to persuade him or her to visit you during his or her vacation.

You're writing a speech that you will give to a class of fifth graders in which you will try to persuade them to wear protective biking gear.

You're writing an article for the school newspaper in which you want to persuade students to spend less time watching television and more time participating in school sports programs.

Your own idea: _____

Point of view to be expressed:

_____

_____

Ideas to support your point of view:

_____

_____

Possible counter arguments:

_____

_____

Reading and Writing Handbook

# Writing Skills

## Structuring Paragraphs

Knowing how to structure paragraphs is an important writing skill. Whatever your purpose for writing is, your writing will be made up of paragraphs.

All paragraphs have a topic and a main idea. A topic is the general subject that the paragraph is about. The topic should be something that can be covered in one paragraph. The main idea is the writer's point about the topic. The main idea is usually expressed in a topic sentence. The topic sentence often comes first and should clearly state the writer's point.

A paragraph also needs to have details that support the topic sentence. These sentences contain the **who, where, what, when, why, how many,** and **how much** details. These details show the reader examples and facts that prove the topic sentence.

Finally, a paragraph needs a concluding sentence. The concluding sentence may restate the topic sentence, it may summarize the supporting details, or it may give the reader something to think about.

**Directions:** *Read the following paragraph. Draw a line under the topic sentence. Then draw circles around the details, ideas, and facts that support the topic sentence. Finally, draw a dotted line under the concluding sentence.*

Gandhi used nonviolent resistance to challenge British control. He urged people

not to buy British goods, pay taxes, or serve in the British army. When threatened

with arrest or jail, he urged the people to submit. The number of those who

adopted his beliefs and actions grew over the years.

Reading and Writing Handbook

# Writing Skills

## Creating Paragraph Outlines

An outline is a good way to organize information. Organizing information before you write makes the writing process easier. It will also help you determine if the information you selected supports your topic sentence. A paragraph outline is very simple. Look at the following example.

I. Topic sentence

   A. Supporting detail

   B. Supporting detail

   C. Supporting detail

II. Concluding sentence

Suppose that you want to write a paragraph about the harsh environments in which some people live. You will need a topic sentence, some examples of people who live in harsh environments, and finally a concluding sentence. Perhaps your outline would look like the example below.

I. Some people live in harsh places.

   A. Inuit

   B. Sami

   C. Desert herders

II. People adapt.

A paragraph based on this example might turn out like this one:

Some people live in areas most of us would find uncomfortable. The Inuit and Sami people live in frozen Arctic regions. Herders in desert regions of Africa and Asia survive in places that would challenge most people. Over many generations, these people have developed ways of life suited to their environments.

**Directions:** *Select one section of your textbook and write a paragraph summarizing the information. Read the section you selected carefully, then determine what you will cover in your paragraph. On a separate sheet of paper develop your paragraph outline and then write the paragraph.*

Reading and Writing Handbook

# Writing Skills

## Writing to Inform and Explain

When you write to inform or explain a process, thing or event, you must base your writing on well-organized facts.

The best way to do that is to research your topic and organize your data. First, discover the **who, what, when, where, why,** and **how** of a subject. Then, report your findings to the reader in a clear, organized way.

For example, you might write an essay about an ancient culture. You discover that they played a kind of ball game in which the winner, not the loser, was sacrificed to the gods at the end of the game. A fascinating fact—a "**what**" in your essay. But why sacrifice the winner? And what other details—all the other "**Ws**" and the "**How**" listed above—can you provide to fully inform your reader?

The next step is to organize all the facts into logical sequence. If you are writing to explain a process, such as how to play a video game, for example, be sure to include all the steps in order. Leave out one, and your reader might not get past level one!

**Directions:** *Now practice writing to inform or explain by selecting one of the following topics or choosing one of your own. Do research, if necessary. Then, fill in the blanks below with your topic, purpose, audience, and key facts. On a separate sheet of paper, write your essay.*

- Write a summary of the best movie you saw this year, clearly explaining the plot.
- Explain to someone from out of town how to get from your home to your school.
- Write an informative article about an exciting vacation destination.
- Explain how to make your favorite dessert.

Your own idea: _____

Topic: _____

Purpose in writing: _____

Audience: _____

Facts/details to include:_____

_____

_____

_____

Reading and Writing Handbook

# Writing Skills

## Gathering Details

Writing is believable only if it includes accurate and compelling details. Two reliable sources for detailed information are the **library** and the **Internet.** At the library you can find magazine and newspaper articles, or entire books on virtually any subject. In the reference section you can locate compilations of data, such as the following:

**Almanacs,** usually updated annually, offer facts and statistics on a variety of subjects.

**Atlases** contain maps, as well as information on climate, population, vegetation, land use, and other geographic topics.

**Geographical dictionaries** identify locations and may provide brief economic, political, historical, or cultural information.

**Biographical dictionaries** provide information on prominent people, past and present.

**Encyclopedias** present articles on a wide range of subjects and may have yearly updates.

The Internet is a vast data resource. Try a "search engine" (such as Ask Jeeves, or Google) to find articles, Web sites, and more. Be sure to evaluate the reliability of your Internet sources carefully.

Finally, be sure to record all the details you have gathered, including the specifics about your information sources (titles, authors, dates, volume numbers, Internet Web sites, names and titles of interviewees, and so on).

**Directions:** *Name one or more sources you might use to find information on these topics:*

1. History of the Hudson's Bay Company _____

2. Name of the current political leader in Mexico _____

3. Population statistics for three Central American nations _____

4. Location of Inowroclaw, Poland _____

5. Location of mineral resources in North America _____

6. History of slavery in the Caribbean _____

7. U.S. imports and exports, by category, over a 10-year period _____

8. Explorations of Meriwether Lewis _____

9. Short history of Cuba _____

10. Profile of Francisco Pizarro _____

**Challenge:** Locate the reference section in your local library. Find four reference sources that might help you to write a paper on a geographic theme. On a sheet of paper, record the title, date, and volume number of each of these sources.

Reading and Writing Handbook

# Writing Skills

## Writing a Cause and Effect Essay

People want to know why things happen and what the impact will be.

A well-written cause and effect essay clearly explains the relationship among events. First, it states the thesis, or primary idea of the essay. Then it links the causes and effects, sometimes using transitional phrases, such as "because of" or "as a result of." The essay concludes by restating the thesis in a different way.

**Directions:** *Read the following essay. Then, answer the questions below.*

The fall of the Roman Empire was not caused by one single, terrible event. Rather, it occurred as a result of a series of political, military, and economic events that took place over hundreds of years.

One factor was failing political leadership. Corrupt emperors often stole from the empire to make themselves rich. Many emperors gained the throne through violence. This caused disorder in the government. Because of this turmoil, the government weakened.

The large size of the empire was another factor in the fall of Rome. The empire was so vast that it was extremely difficult to govern and control. Armies could not get to locations quickly and borders were exposed to enemy attack.

The Roman army itself was also a factor in the empire's decline. It was no longer made up of citizen soldiers but of foreign mercenaries, or soldiers for pay. These mercenaries would fight for the side that helped them the most. As a consequence, the army's loyalty was expensive and unreliable.

Finally, as Rome stopped conquering new lands, the Roman economy suffered. It no longer had the wealth and natural resources from new conquests. Taxes were increased. Many people throughout the empire were unemployed and discontent. Rome did not fall in one day, but spanned several hundred years. A weakened government, an unreliable army, and a fading economy slowly extinguished the glory that once was Rome.

1. What is the thesis statement?

   _____

2. Circle the causes mentioned in the body of the essay.

3. Underline the effects listed in the body of the essay.

4. List the connecting transitions in the essay.

   _____

   _____

Reading and Writing Handbook

# Writing Skills

## Writing a Problem-and-Solution Essay

Have a problem? No problem. You can learn to write a clear, effective problem-and-solution essay that presents the dilemma and offers feasible resolutions.

Some problem-and-solution essays take the form of news or opinion columns; others may be letters to politicians or e-mails to companies. In any case, to persuade your reader to review an issue and take action, you should:

**Be clear, logical, and objective** as you present the problem.

**Suggest multiple alternatives** to give your reader options.

**Write in a reasonable and respectful tone.**

**Directions:** *Read this problem-and-solution letter. Then, complete the tasks below.*

Dear State Senator Johnson,

As you are aware, our coastline has experienced rapid commercial growth in the last 10 years. While this is good in many ways, it also has caused major problems to the health and safety of our citizens.

This rapid growth of our community has increased traffic and put stress on our water and sewage systems. The construction of the new condominiums has created traffic and parking problems all along the coast. Our sewage and water systems have not been improved to keep up with the growing needs of the community.

Our committee would like to suggest that standards be set to limit future construction along the coastline. If that is not possible, then we would like to ask that limits be set on the height of new buildings to help slow the population growth. New building standards that provide parking spaces for the residents would help reduce parking problems and controlled access from parking lots to the main highway would help ease the traffic problems.

We also recommend that a state study of the water and sewer systems be conducted. This study may provide us with the state funding to improve these important systems that affect the health of our citizenry.

Thank you, Senator Johnson, for your serious consideration of these issues.

1. Underline the problems presented.

2. Circle the solutions offered.

3. Does the writer suggest a solution for each of the problems?

_____

_____

**Challenge:** Read about the problem of animal smuggling from the Brazilian rain forest. Then, write a problem-and-solution letter to the president of Brazil from the point of view of a concerned Brazilian citizen. Make sure you clearly state several specific problems related to smuggling and suggest solutions for each.

# Writing Skills

## Choosing a Topic

Skillful writing is as much about what you **leave out** as what you **put in.** By **limiting and focusing** your topic, you create a satisfying piece filled with interesting specifics.

Now think of a writing topic—say, the history and culture of South America. This choice is too general and unfocused for an essay. In fact, a series of books might be written about it. What about the history and culture of the Argentine pampas? That's still too broad. But narrow the topic to the role of the gaucho in Argentine culture, or even, the tools and traditions of the gaucho, and you gain focus.

Use these guidelines for choosing an appropriate topic for your writing:

Select a topic that interests you. You will enjoy the research and writing more.

Quickly determine how much information is available. You may find too little, leaving you scrambling for another topic to meet your deadline.

Narrow your topic choice. Too broad a subject may become so general that your essay loses focus.

**Directions:** *Review the groups of related topics below. In each group, which topic is best suited to a one-page essay? Circle the letter.*

1. **a.** The History of Mapmaking
   **b.** What Is a Landsat Image?
   **c.** The North American Landscape

2. **a.** Night Sounds in the Brazilian Rain Forest
   **b.** Explorers of the Brazilian Rain Forest
   **c.** Tourist Attractions in Brazil

3. **a.** The People and Culture of France
   **b.** France During World War I
   **c.** The Relative Location of France

4. **a.** Southwest Asia
   **b.** The Physical Geography of Iraq
   **c.** Religion in Southwest Asia

**Challenge:** Look through a newspaper or magazine or listen to a television or radio news report to choose three geography topics. Then limit each of the topics to ones you could easily write about in a one–page essay. List these three topic choices on a sheet of paper.

# Writing Skills

## Using the Library

The library of Alexandria, Egypt, was renowned throughout the ancient world. Experts believe it contained more than 700,000 scrolls, equivalent to perhaps 125,000 books today.

Today, we have access to a world of knowledge right around the corner—at community, school, and university libraries—and right at our fingertips—via computer. All we have to do is understand how to find the information we seek.

**Dewey Decimal System.** Used to organize most libraries, every book has a number, and the numbers are arranged in sequence around the library, grouped into 10 major categories:

| | | | |
|---|---|---|---|
| 000-099 | General Works | 500-599 | Pure Sciences |
| 100-199 | Philosophy | 600-699 | Applied Sciences/Technology |
| 200-299 | Religion | 700-799 | The Arts |
| 300-399 | Social Sciences | 800-899 | Literature |
| 400-499 | Language | 900-999 | Geography/History |

Each of these categories also has subcategories. Thus, books on similar subjects are grouped together.

**Library Catalog.** The catalog is a complete list of all the library's books, sorted alphabetically by title, author, and subject. Each entry in the catalog gives the book's Dewey Decimal number, so you can easily locate it on the shelves. Some libraries still use card catalogs, while other libraries have their catalog on computer (where you can search online by subject, author, or title).

**Other Resources.** Most libraries have newspapers, magazines, and pamphlets—some in printed form and some on film—with printed or computerized indexes to help you search for specific publication dates, subjects, or names.

**Directions:** *Visit your local or school library. Then, complete the activities below, using a separate sheet of paper for your responses.*

1. Draw a sketch of the general layout of your school or local library. Show the locations of each of the 10 major Dewey Decimal categories, as well as works of fiction, magazines and periodicals, reference books, books on computer, recorded books, and so on.

2. Briefly describe the library's catalog system. Is it a card or computer catalog? What do you need to know to use it?

3. Briefly explain how the magazines and periodicals are organized and indexed.

Reading and Writing Handbook

# Writing Skills

## Summarizing and Taking Notes

In a library, having a system of organization is very important. Otherwise, the large amount of information is in a jumble and not easily used. The same is true for gathering your own research. Where were those facts you found three days ago? What article gave such a good summary of your subject? Who was that expert you needed to quote? A system for summarizing and taking notes is essential to keep track of this information.

**Summarizing.** To summarize a long report—an encyclopedia article, for instance—start by identifying the thesis sentence in the introduction. Then paragraph by paragraph, write down the main ideas and supporting facts. In all cases, **use your own words to summarize.** If you use exact words from the source material, you must put them in quotation marks and jot down all the data (title, author, date, page, and so on) for a footnote in your report. If not, you will be committing plagiarism, a kind of literary theft of another's work.

**Taking Notes.** One convenient way to take notes is to use note cards, which can easily be sorted or rearranged to create a logical flow for your report. Here are some suggestions for creating useful note cards:

Place the citation information of each source (author, title, date) in the upper right-hand corner of each card.

Place a subject heading in the upper left-hand corner of the card.

Write down the ideas or facts found, noting the page number in the source.

Use one card for each new subject you find in each source.

Use quotation marks around exact quotes.

While you are researching, be sure to check for maps, graphs, charts, illustrations, or other graphic aids that might help you understand your subject and communicate it better to your audience. If you plan to include copies in your report, remember to note the source information to include in your footnotes.

**Directions:** *Using the guidelines above, complete the following tasks on a separate sheet of paper.*

1. Describe how you would summarize a long report or article.

2. List the information you should include on a note card.

3. Why is it important to use quotation marks around direct quotes from sources?

4. What kinds of graphic aids are useful for reports and why?

Reading and Writing Handbook

# Writing Skills

## Preparing Note Cards

Note cards are used to organize research data. Each card should contain a single source material and deal with one aspect of your topic. Each note card should include the following information:

A clear, brief **heading,** so you can sort all related topics together.

A **citation** of the information source to use as a footnote in the body or at the end of your text. Include the author, title, and page number, or other relevant source data.

A **paraphrase,** or summary of the information you need to use from the source.

Any **direct quotations** you want to use, in quotation marks, with all the words, punctuations, and spellings exactly as they appear in the original source.

**Directions:** *Use the information in the following two passages to prepare two note cards.*

### Passage A

In 1519 Spanish explorer Hernán Cortés and more than 500 Spaniards landed in eastern Mexico in search of land and gold…. Finding large amounts of gold and other treasure, and fearful that the Aztec would attack his vastly outnumbered Spanish force, Cortés seized Montezuma as a hostage.

The Spaniards melted down the intricate gold ornaments of the Aztec for shipment to Spain and forced Montezuma to swear allegiance to the king of Spain. The Spaniards remained in the city without opposition until about six months later, when, in Cortés' absence, [a] Spanish officer massacred 200 Aztec nobles…. After Cortés returned, the Aztec rebelled. Montezuma was killed during the revolt….

Microsoft Encarta online encyclopedia, listing Hernán Cortés

### Passage B

Hernán Cortés left Spain at the age of nineteen after a brief period studying law…. Later he impressed Governor Diego Velásquez and served as his clerk during the expedition to conquer and settle Cuba in 1511…. Cortés' ambition and personal magnetism made Velásquez suspect his loyalty…. Velásquez planned on removing him as the leader of the expedition. Cortés discovered this and cut short his preparations and set sail for the mainland on February 18, 1519.

With a few pieces of artillery, sixteen horsemen, and roughly 400 infantry soldiers recruited from the poor whites of Cuba, Cortés made for the Gulf coast. While there, Cortés renounced Velásquez' authority by founding his own city, Villa Rica de la Vera Cruz….

The European Voyages of Exploration site, University of Calgary; The Conquest of the Aztec Empire: Hernán Cortés [http://www.ucalgary.ca/applied_history/tutor/eurvoya/aztec.html]

Reading and Writing Handbook

# Writing Skills

## Writing an Introduction

The introduction to a research paper does important work. It "gets you off on the right foot" with your readers. When you write your introduction, remember to:

**Capture the reader's attention** with a fascinating fact, example, or quotation.

**Clearly state the thesis,** or main idea, of the paper.

**Provide brief background information** to support the thesis.

**Directions:** *Compare the following introductions for a research paper entitled, "The Himalayan Environment." Then respond to the questions that follow. (Use a separate sheet of paper, if necessary.)*

> **A.** At 11 o'clock on the morning of May 29, 1953, Edmund Hillary and Tenzing Norgay reached the summit of Mount Everest—about 5.5 miles above sea level. In Hillary's words, "In the distance I could see the pastel shades and fleecy clouds of Tibet…. [A] few more whacks of the ice ax, a few very weary steps, and we were on the summit of Everest."

> **B.** What mental images do the Himalaya Mountains bring to mind? Do you think of the world's highest peak? Or hear temple bells sounding from a remote monastery? One image gaining increasing significance is that of a vast laboratory for observing and studying plants and animals. Because of great differences in elevation, the Himalayan region contains almost every kind of climate to be found. In addition, the alignment of the mountains results in totally different conditions on the two opposing slopes. As a result, plant and animal habitats in this area are representative of habitats all around the world.

1. Which introduction do you think is most effective? Explain your choice.

_____

_____

For the introduction you selected as most effective, answer these questions:

2. How does the writer get the reader's attention?

_____

3. What will the main point of this paper be?

_____

4. What are some of the subtopics you might expect to find in this paper?

_____

_____

Reading and Writing Handbook

# Writing Skills

## Writing the Body of an Essay

Your research is done, and your facts are organized. You have written an engaging introduction. Now you must build the body of your essay. The body is the main part of the essay. It is composed of a series of related paragraphs that support, expand on and explain the thesis statement in the introduction.

Each of the paragraphs in the body of the essay should contain:

A **topic sentence,** or main idea, which elaborates on the essay's thesis.

Sentences that support the paragraph's topic sentence with **facts and details.**

**Transitional phrases** that link the paragraphs to each other or to the main thesis.

**Directions:** *Read the introductory paragraph and the paragraphs that make up the body of the essay below. Then, on the back of this page complete the activities that follow.*

It is an amazing thing that the Erie Canal should have been built at all. Its construction required clearing forests and battling disease-ridden swamps. It sprawled over 364 miles. Yet, once built, no one could deny the economic advantages it gave to the cities along its route. Its success led to a chain reaction of transportation projects in other states.

Jefferson had called the project to build the Erie Canal "little short of madness." Many states soon recognized that it was little short of madness *not* to build transportation systems, and they acted accordingly. Maryland built the Chesapeake and Ohio Canal. Soon South Carolina made plans to cross the Appalachians with a canal that would boost Charleston's economy.

Canals were not the only form of transportation that enjoyed a boom. Railroads were built, often funded by county and city dollars. Railroad promoters encouraged competition between communities, asking them to bid against one another. Railroad builders in some cities even asked for "donations" from communities to build connections, threatening to connect rival cities if the money was not provided.

Prentice Hall, *The American Nation*

1. Identify the thesis statement in the introduction.

2. Underline the topic sentences in the first two paragraphs of the body.

3. Do the other sentences in each paragraph support the topic sentence?

4. Circle the transitional statements in the first two paragraphs of the body. In what ways do the statements connect the paragraphs to each other?

5. Considering the thesis statement, what might the next paragraph of this essay be about?

Reading and Writing Handbook

# Writing Skills

## Writing for Assessment

Taking an essay test can be stressful. You will be assessed on your writing and logical thinking skills under pressure. But you can conquer that case of nerves when writing for assessment by following these logical steps:

**Read the essay question, or prompt, carefully.** What kind of essay are you being asked to write? Look for key words in the prompt, such as "compare," "contrast," "cause," "effect," "result," "summarize," "explain," or "persuade." These words will guide you in your writing

**Organize the information about the topic.** List the possible subtopics, facts, and examples. Then, select the ones that most clearly support the topic. Depending on the type of essay required, you will need to organize the information—by steps in a process (how-to), degree of persuasiveness (persuasion), key reasons and results (cause and effect), primary similarities and differences (compare-and-contrast), or most significant points (summary).

**Review the prompt and compare it with your notes.** Does your thesis statement reflect the prompt? Do each of your ideas, facts, or examples support the thesis?

**Write your essay.**

**Revise your essay.** Is the structure appropriate for the type of essay? Is the information organized clearly? Have you used the appropriate tone for your audience? Does the information support the thesis? Have you used precise vocabulary and varied sentence length?

**Proofread your essay.** Read your essay a final time to check for accuracy.

**Directions:** *From the following box, choose the type of essay you would use to answer each of the prompts listed below. Write your answer in the space provided. Then, underline the key word or words in each prompt that helped you decide which to select.*

| | | |
|---|---|---|
| compare-and-contrast | persuasion | summary |
| how-to | cause and effect | |

_____ **1.** What factors led up to the Great Depression and what has the United States government done to prevent them from happening again?

_____ **2.** Compare the foreign policies of President Kennedy with those of President Johnson.

_____ **3.** Explain the steps that champion bicyclist Lance Armstrong takes to train for the famous Tour de France race each year.

_____ **4.** Summarize the opening paragraphs of the Declaration of Independence.

Reading and Writing Handbook

# Writing Skills

## Writing a Letter

A business letter is a formal communication to someone in a company, organization or governmental body. Business letters request information, ask for action, express an opinion, or complete a transaction. Therefore, they should be respectful in tone and businesslike in appearance.

Business letters can follow several prescribed formats. But all should be typed or computer-printed on plain, white paper and include six elements: the **heading, inside address, salutation, body, closing,** and **signature**. Here is a sample business letter.

444 Morganville Road
Springdale, AZ 99999          **Heading**
December 1, 2004

Ms. Mary S. Zuniga, Director
National Museum of Native Heritage
1000 N. Main Street          **Inside Address**
Jackson, NM 77777

Dear Ms. Zuniga:

I am a social studies teacher at Springdale High School. As adviser to our school's history club, I am helping students plan next year's trip to several Native American sites in New Mexico. We would like to include your museum on our trip.

**Body**

We expect a large group of participants and would like to make arrangements with you in advance. We will be in Jackson, NM, on April 26–27, 2005. We would be happy to come to the museum on either of those days. We wondered if it would be possible to arrange for tour guides to accompany our group.

If you could contact me to discuss these plans further, it would be greatly appreciated. Thank you in advance for helping to make this trip an exciting and meaningful event for our students.

Sincerely,   ◄— **Closing**

Jason K. Albertson ◄— **Signature**

Jason K. Albertson

**Directions:** *On a separate sheet of paper, write a business letter to your local registrar of voters as a new resident in town, explaining your status and requesting information on how to register and where to vote in your community.*

# Answer Key

## Four Purposes for Writing

1. to describe
2. to inform
3. to explain
4. to persuade

## Writing to Describe

Answers will vary.

## Writing the Conclusion

Answers will vary.

## Using the Revision Checklist

Answers will vary.

## Writing to Persuade

Answers will vary depending on the situation chosen.

## Structuring Paragraphs

A line should be drawn beneath the first sentence in the paragraph. Student circles will vary, but should show an understanding of details, ideas, and facts that support the topic sentence. Dotted lines should be marked under the last sentence in the paragraph.

## Creating Paragraph Outlines

Answers will vary depending on selection chosen.

## Writing to Inform and Explain

Answers will vary, depending on the topic chosen.

## Gathering Details

Possible answers:
1. encyclopedia
2. almanac
3. almanac
4. atlas
5. atlas
6. encyclopedia
7. almanac
8. biographical dictionary
9. geographical dictionary
10. encyclopedia

## Writing a Cause and Effect Essay

1. The fall of the Roman Empire was not caused by one single, terrible event.
2. Possible answers: failing political leadership, large size of empire, type of army, a suffering economy
3. Possible answers: weakened government, exposed borders, nonloyal military, high taxes, unemployment, discontent citizens
4. Possible answers: as a result of, because of, as a consequence

## Writing a Problem-and-Solution Essay

1. Possible answers: increased traffic, stress on water and sewage systems
2. Possible answers: standards limiting future construction, limits to building height, building standards requiring parking spaces, controlled access to main highways, a study of the water and sewage system
3. Answers will vary.

## Choosing a Topic

1. b
2. a
3. c
4. b

## Using the Library

Answers will vary depending on the library visited.

## Summarizing and Taking Notes

Answers will vary.

## Preparing Note Cards

Answers will vary.

## *Answer Key* (continued)

## Writing an Introduction

Answers will vary.

## Writing the Body of an Essay

1. The success of the Erie Canal led to a chain reaction of transportation projects in other states.
2. Many states soon recognized that it was a little short of madness *not* to build transportation systems, and they acted accordingly. Canals were not the only form of transportation that enjoyed a boom.
3. yes
4. Circles should be made around the first sentence in the second and third paragraphs. The first transitional statement relates to the building of the Erie Canal mentioned in the introduction. The second relates to canals discussed in the first paragraph of the body.
5. Possible answer: other transportation systems such as roads

## Writing for Assessment

1. cause and effect
2. compare-and-contrast
3. how-to
4. summary

Key words will vary.

## Writing a Letter

Student letters will vary, but should include the standard format used for business letters.

MapMaster Skills Handbook

# MapMaster Skills: The Five Themes of Geography

The five themes of geography are location, regions, movement, place, and human-environment interaction. These five themes are tools that can help you organize information. You can use the five themes to gain additional insight about the people and places you are studying.

**Directions:** *Read the sentences below and decide which of the five themes of geography can be applied to each sentence. Then, write your answer in the blank space next to each sentence.*

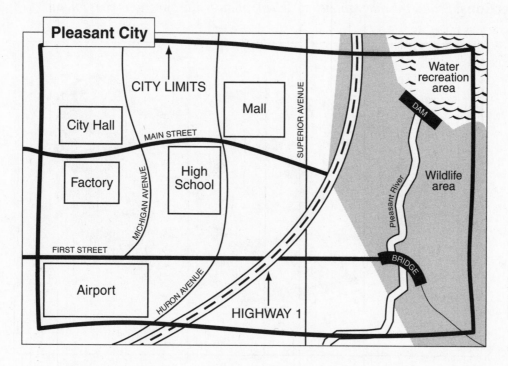

_____ **1.** Pleasant City is at 40°N and 100°W, about 400 miles west of the Mississippi River.

_____ **2.** People who live outside Pleasant City take Highway 1 to work in the factory.

_____ **3.** City Hall is located within the boundaries of Pleasant City.

_____ **4.** The residents of Pleasant City built a dam to protect the city from flooding. The dam also created a water recreation area.

_____ **5.** Pleasant City is known for the plants and animals that live along the river.

MapMaster Skills Handbook

# MapMaster Skills: Understanding Movements of the Earth

Earth, the planet where we live, is constantly moving. Earth spins on its axis (the invisible line that runs through the center of Earth) at the same time it orbits the sun. Earth is also tilted at an angle. As Earth moves around the sun, the parts of Earth that are tilted toward the sun experience more warmth. For example, summer in the Southern Hemisphere occurs when that half of Earth is tilted toward the sun. We experience day, night, and the changing seasons depending on where we live on Earth and where Earth is in relationship to the sun.

**Directions:** *Study the diagram below. Then, answer the questions that follow.*

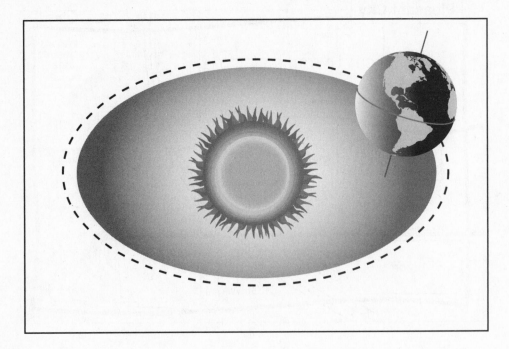

1. Which season is the Northern Hemisphere experiencing? _____

2. What season is it in the Southern Hemisphere? _____

3. Place an X on the dotted orbit line to show the position of Earth when it is summer in the United States.

4. What would happen to the seasons if Earth were not tilted on its axis?

_____

_____

MapMaster Skills Handbook

# Writing Skills

## Doing Searches on the Internet

Research on the Internet can provide information that may not be available anywhere else. Some information found on the Internet, however, may not be accurate and reliable. You may need to use several sources to verify your information. Information provided by professional businesses and organizations is generally more reliable than that provided by individuals.

**Directions:** *Read about World Wide Web search methods below. Then, use a computer with Internet access to complete the activities.*

**URL.** URL stands for Uniform Resource Locator, which is the "address" of a site on the Web. You can recognize the address (usually found at the top of your screen as "location") as a string of characters beginning with *http://* and ending with the specific characters that lead to that site. The easiest way to reach a site is to type in a known URL. For example, the URL *http://www.nasa.gov* will lead you directly to the NASA Space Center's Web site.

    **Search Engines.** Very often, you don't know the URL that will lead you to the information you need. When this happens, you need to use a "search engine." A search engine is a database on the Web that organizes Web sites according to key words in their files or titles. Some already have categories from which you can choose. In others, you simply enter key words relating to your topics and allow the engine to do the searching for you. This will generate a list of file names from which you can choose. Yahoo! at *http://www.yahoo.com* and Lycos at *http://www.lycos.com* are two examples of search engines.

    **Links.** Once you have found a site relating to your topic, through either its URL or a search engine, it may offer further information through the use of a link. Links are words in a Web document that are often underlined or highlighted in some other way. Choosing a particular link may lead you to another Web site offering more information on the same topic.

1. Once you are connected to the Internet, type in the URL for the Yahoo! search engine. Scroll down to the Web site directory. How many categories of links does the menu display?

2. Choose the link for "Regional." When you have connected to this link, choose the link for "Countries." Pick a foreign country, then click on its link. How many links are displayed for that country? Give two examples. Does the country's Web site have categories for its links, such as business or events?

3. Choose one of the links within that country's Web site. What is the purpose of the Web site you have chosen? Toward whom does it seem to be directed?

MapMaster Skills Handbook

# MapMaster Skills: Understanding Hemispheres

The word *hemisphere* means half of a sphere. The earth can be divided into hemispheres in two different ways. When it is divided along the Equator, the two hemispheres are the Northern Hemisphere and the Southern Hemisphere. When it is divided along the Prime Meridian from the North Pole to the South Pole, the two hemispheres are the Western Hemisphere and the Eastern Hemisphere.

**Directions:** *Study the illustrations of the earth's hemispheres below. Then, on a separate piece of paper, answer the questions that follow.*

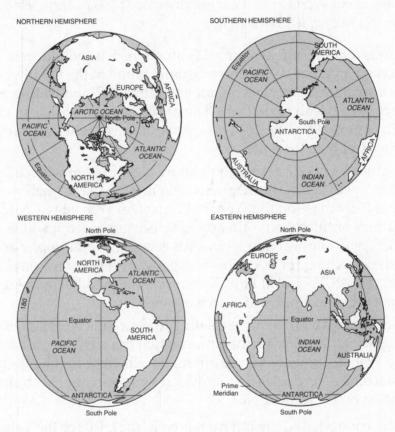

1. In which two hemispheres is the United States located?

2. What is the line that divides the Northern Hemisphere from the Southern Hemisphere?

3. In which two hemispheres is Australia located?

4. Which ocean is not found in the Western Hemisphere?

5. Which hemisphere is the only one in which Antarctica is not found?

# MapMaster Skills: Understanding Latitude and Longitude

Lines of latitude and longitude work somewhat like a map grid, but on a global scale. These two sets of imaginary lines circle the globe. Lines of latitude run east and west; lines of longitude run north and south. Together, they form a grid. Locations on these lines are stated in degrees. Each degree is divided into 60 minutes.

Lines of latitude are also called parallels because they are parallel to each other. The Equator is located at 0° latitude. All the other lines of latitude are said to be so many degrees north or south of the Equator.

Lines of longitude are also called meridians. All lines of longitude pass through the North Pole and the South Pole. The line for 0° longitude passes through Greenwich, England. It is called the Prime Meridian. All other lines of longitude are measured in degrees east or west of the Prime Meridian. East and west meridians meet at 180° in the Pacific Ocean.

**Directions:** *Study the illustrations of latitude and longitude below. Then, answer the questions that follow.*

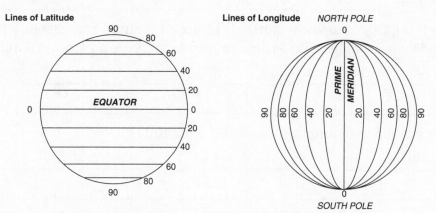

1. What are two names for the lines that run north to south?

   _____

2. What are two names for the lines that run east to west?

   _____

3. What would be the line of latitude for a place that is halfway between the Equator and the North Pole?

   _____

4. What would be the line of longitude for a place that is west of the Prime Meridian, halfway between the Prime Meridian and the 180° line of longitude?

   _____

MapMaster Skills Handbook

# DK Compact Atlas of the World Activity: Understanding Latitude and Longitude

Your teacher will provide you with the page number for the map to use in this activity. Use your map and learn more about latitude and longitude by completing the questions below.

1. What is the southernmost line of latitude on your map? _____

2. What is the northernmost line of latitude on your map? _____

3. Which lines are parallel, the lines of latitude or the lines of longitude?

   _____

4. Which lines meet at the poles? _____

5. What do you notice about the lines of longitude as they get closer to the Equator?

   _____

6. Do the degrees on lines of latitude get larger or smaller the farther they are from the Equator? _____

7. Why is it important to know north or south for latitude and east or west for longitude when using latitude and longitude to locate a place on a map?

   _____

   _____

8. What is unique to 0° longitude and 180° longitude?

   _____

   _____

## Outline Map Activity

Using the Outline Map provided by your teacher, highlight the Prime Meridian and label it. Do the same with the Equator. Locate and label the region of the world you are studying. At the base of the Outline Map, list the degrees of latitude and longitude surrounding the region you have labeled.

# MapMaster Skills: Using Latitude and Longitude

Every place on earth has two points, or coordinates, that mark its location. These coordinates are measured in degrees of latitude and degrees of longitude. Imagine that you want to find out where Beijing, China, is. You start with the index section of an atlas. This index gives you not only the page number of the map of China, but also the coordinates for Beijing: 40°N, 116°E. So you know that when you turn to the map of China, you will look for the line of latitude marked 40°N. Then, you will look in the area between 110°E and 120°E and you will find Beijing.

**Directions:** *The map of Australia below shows lines of latitude and lines of longitude, each labeled in degrees. Give the approximate locations of the cities listed below the map.*

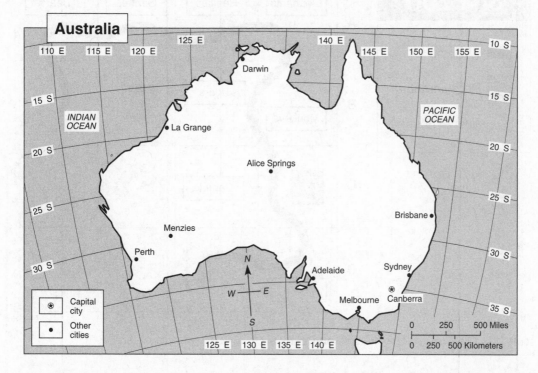

|            | Latitude | Longitude |
|------------|----------|-----------|
| **1. Canberra**  |          |           |
| **2. Melbourne** |          |           |
| **3. Darwin**    |          |           |
| **4. Perth**     |          |           |
| **5. Brisbane**  |          |           |

# MapMaster Skills: Understanding Grids

Maps often have grids drawn on them to help you find the exact location of a place. A grid is a system of horizontal and vertical lines that cross each other to form squares. The squares are labeled with numbers from left to right and with letters from top to bottom. That way, each square has its own number/letter combination. A grid map of a city zoo appears below.

**Directions:** *Study the map and the grid below. Then, answer the questions that follow.*

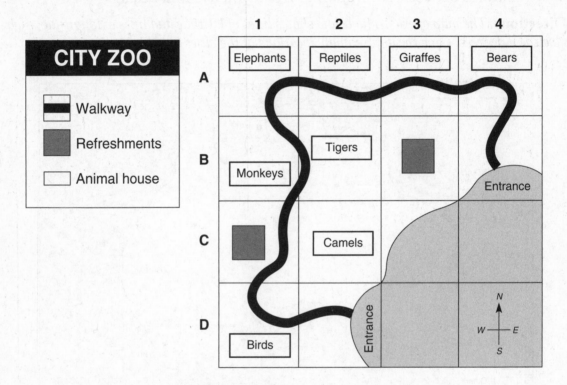

1. In what square are the bears located?

   _____

2. What animals are located in A3?

   _____

3. In what two squares are the zoo entrances?

   _____

4. If you were to follow the walkway from the west entrance to the elephant house, what squares would you pass through?

   _____

5. What squares would you pass through if you came in at the north entrance and followed the walkway to the elephant house?

   _____

Name _____  Date _____  Class _____

MapMaster Skills Handbook

# MapMaster Skills: Using a Grid

Map grids are very useful for locating places on a street map or a road map. Imagine that you arrive in a city you've never visited before and that you need to locate a particular street. You don't want to read all of the street names on the map to find the one you need. Instead, you use the map index. The map index will give the number and the letter of the square in which the street you want is located. Once you find the correct square, you will find the street in that square.

**Directions:** *Study the street map of Lima, Peru, and the index to some of its main buildings. Then, answer the questions that follow.*

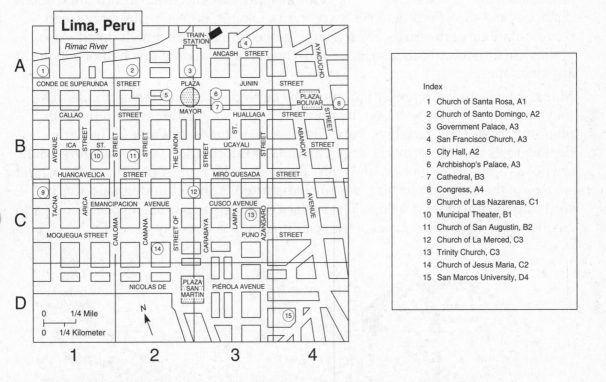

Index

1  Church of Santa Rosa, A1
2  Church of Santo Domingo, A2
3  Government Palace, A3
4  San Francisco Church, A3
5  City Hall, A2
6  Archbishop's Palace, A3
7  Cathedral, B3
8  Congress, A4
9  Church of Las Nazarenas, C1
10  Municipal Theater, B1
11  Church of San Augustin, B2
12  Church of La Merced, C3
13  Trinity Church, C3
14  Church of Jesus Maria, C2
15  San Marcos University, D4

<aside>MapMaster Skills Handbook</aside>

1. At the intersection of which two streets is the Church of Santa Rosa?

   _____

2. What is the grid location of San Marcos University?_____

3. If you were walking from the Church of La Merced to Trinity Church, what avenue would you walk along? _____

4. What street would you take to get from the Church of San Augustin to the Church of Jesus Maria?_____

5. If you were telling someone the location of the building where Congress meets, what two streets would you name?

   _____

# MapMaster Skills: Comparing Globes and Maps

Globes and maps are used frequently in geography. To make the best possible use of maps and globes, you need to understand how they relate to one another and what kind of information each can provide.

**Directions:** *Read the information about globes and maps below. Then, answer the questions that follow. Use a separate piece of paper for your answers.*

**Globes.** A globe is the most accurate way of showing the world's surface. It is a scale model of the earth, showing actual shapes, relative sizes, and locations of landmasses and bodies of water. A globe also provides accurate information about distances and directions between two points. Globes, however, are very small representations of the earth. Even a large globe cannot show much detail. Also, globes are difficult to carry around, and you can look at only one half of a globe at any one time.

**Maps.** Maps are flat representations of the curved surface of the earth. Because they are flat, they can be shown in a book. They can be folded up and used for planning trips. They can show very large areas or very small areas. They are flexible tools that can provide large amounts of information very efficiently. Maps are not as accurate as globes, however. To create a flat representation of the curved surface of the earth, something has to be distorted. You can understand this by studying the illustration below. The surface of the globe has been "peeled off" and cut along the lines of longitude. The resulting map is not easy to read.

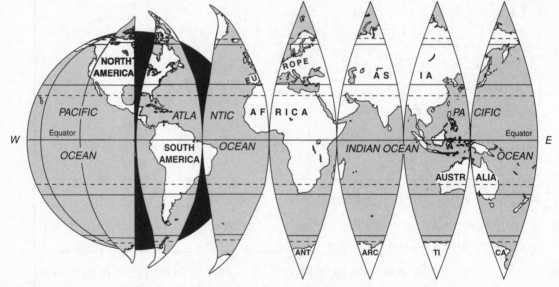

1. What advantage does a globe have over a flat map?

2. What are the main disadvantages of a globe?

3. What advantages do maps have over globes?

4. Why are maps less accurate than globes?

5. What does the illustration on this page tell you?

MapMaster Skills Handbook

# MapMaster Skills: Understanding Projection

The method used to show the curved surface of the earth as a flat map is called a projection. The three most common kinds of projections are based on different ways of placing a piece of paper around the globe and "pulling" the images off the globe and onto the paper. Other projections are based on mathematical formulas.

**Directions:** *Study the projections described and illustrated below. Then, answer the questions that follow. Use a separate piece of paper for your answers.*

**Cylindrical Projection.** This projection is made by placing a rectangular piece of paper around the globe so that it touches the Equator. Lines of longitude that meet at the poles on a globe are parallel. The areas near the poles are distorted and look much larger than they really are.

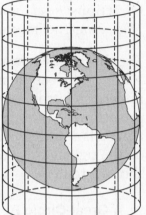

**Conic Projection.** Here, a cone-shaped piece of paper is placed over the globe. The areas where the paper touches the globe are most accurately represented. Those near the tip of the globe are most distorted.

**Flat-Plane Projection.** Here a flat piece of paper is placed against the globe. The map is accurate at the point of contact. Distortion increases as you move away from the center. Flat-plane projections are often used to show polar regions.

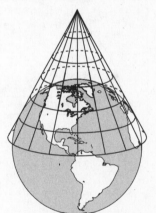

**Other Projections.** An example of a map based on a mathematical formula is the Robinson projection, which balances different kinds of distortion to make maps that are easy to read.

1. What is a map projection?

2. Which areas of the earth are most distorted on a cylindrical projection?

3. Which kind of projection is often used to show polar areas?

4. Which projection, based on mathematical formulas, balances different kinds of distortions?

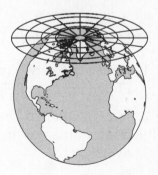

MapMaster Skills Handbook

# MapMaster Skills: Great Circles and Straight Lines

Travelers flying from London to New York are often surprised to hear the captain announce that they are flying over Nova Scotia in Canada. "Why aren't we going straight across the Atlantic?" they ask, thinking of the route they have seen on a flat map. The reason is the captain has taken the great-circle route: the shortest distance between the two cities.

**Directions:** *Read the information about great circles, and study the illustrations below. Then, complete the activities, and on the back of this page answer the questions.*

The shortest distance between any two points on a globe can be found by stretching a string between them. To find the shortest distance using maps, you need to understand projection and distortion. Look at the two maps below. The cylindrical projection on the left suggests that the shortest distance between Philadelphia and Beijing is a straight east-west line. Compare this with the flat-plane polar projection on the right. Here, you see that the great-circle route across the North Pole is the shortest route.

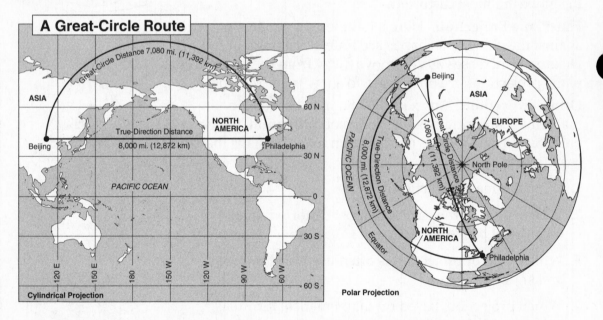

1. Which of the two maps would be more helpful to an airline pilot flying from Philadelphia to Beijing? Why?

2. Imagine that you are going to fly west from Moscow to San Francisco. Look at a political map of the world. Which countries does the map suggest you will fly over?

3. Now, use a globe and a piece of string to plot the straight-line, or great-circle, route between Moscow and San Francisco. Which countries would you actually fly over?

4. What does this activity reveal about maps?

MapMaster Skills Handbook

# MapMaster Skills: Maps with Accurate Shapes: Conformal Maps

**Directions:** *Read the information about conformal maps, and study the map below. Then, answer the questions that follow.*

Conformal maps are so named because the shapes of the landmasses conform to, or look like, the shapes that appear on the globe. Directions are also correct. However, distances and size are greatly distorted, especially in the polar regions. Lines of latitude and longitude cross at right angles. The lines of longitude that meet at the poles on a globe, however, are parallel on this map. The Mercator projection below is an example of a conformal map.

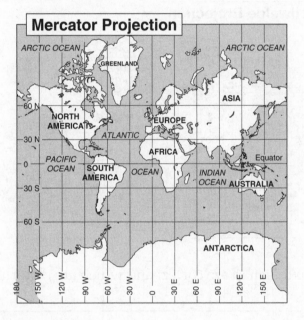

1. Use a globe to compare the size of Antarctica on this map with the size of that continent on the globe. What do you observe?

   _____

2. Look at the comparative sizes of Greenland and Africa on the map and on the globe. What do you observe?

   _____

3. Which aspects of this map are correct and which are distorted?

   _____

4. Why do you think this projection is often used for making navigational charts?

   _____

MapMaster Skills Handbook

# MapMaster Skills: Maps with Accurate Areas: Equal-Area Maps

**Directions:** *Read the information about equal-area maps, and study the map below. Then, answer the questions that follow.*

Equal-area maps show the correct sizes of landmasses in relation to other landmasses. A nation that is twice the size of another nation will appear that way on the map. However, in order to depict correct size, an equal-area map distorts both shape and direction. The Mollweide projection below is an example of an equal-area map.

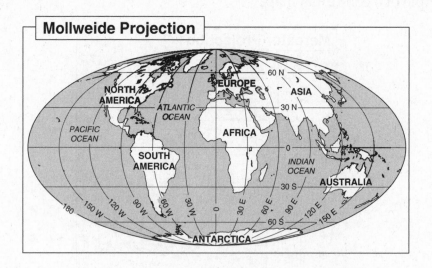

1. Which aspects of this map are correct and which are distorted?

   _____

   _____

2. Describe the lines of longitude on this map.

   _____

   _____

3. Compare the shape of North America on this map with the shape of North America on a globe. What do you observe?

   _____

   _____

   _____

MapMaster Skills Handbook

# MapMaster Skills: Maps with Accurate Directions: Azimuthal Maps

**Directions:** *Read the information about azimuthal maps, and study the map. Then, answer the questions that follow.*

Azimuthal maps show direction correctly. Shape and size are distorted, with the greatest distortions on the outer edges of the map. Azimuthal maps are circular and often have the North Pole or the South Pole as their central point. The azimuthal projection below has the North Pole as its central point.

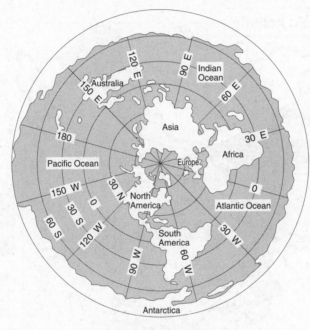

**Azimuthal Projection**

1. What does an azimuthal map show correctly?

   _____

2. What is distorted on this type of map?

   _____

3. Which continent on the map above is most distorted?

   _____

4. What direction would you take from the North Pole if you wanted to fly through the center of South America?

   _____

5. What direction would you take from the North Pole to reach Central America?

   _____

MapMaster Skills Handbook

# MapMaster Skills: Using the Map Key

A map key explains what the symbols, shading, and colors on a map represent. Symbols range from simple dots and circles that represent cities and capitals to tiny drawings that represent types of manufacturing and industry or agriculture. Shading and colors are used to show elevation, population density, political divisions, and so on. The map key for the map of China below uses a combination of shading and drawings to represent economic activity and resources.

**Directions:** *Study the map and the map key. Then, on a separate piece of paper, answer the questions that follow.*

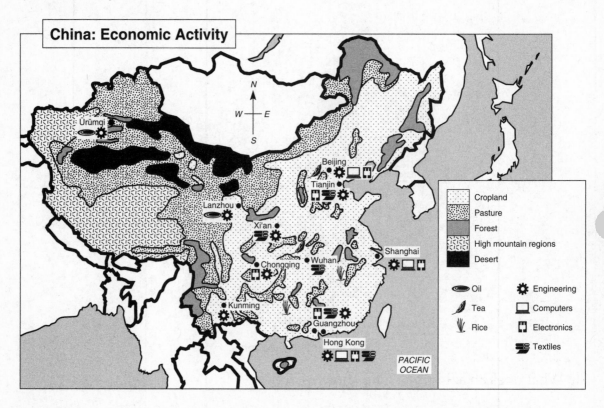

1. How many different types of shading are represented on the map key?

2. What symbol is used to represent oil?

3. Which part of China is least developed economically?

4. Describe the economic activity and resources around Beijing.

5. Based on the map, which city in China has the most varied manufacturing and industry?

6. Why does the map use a combination of shadings and drawings to show economic activity and resources?

# MapMaster Skills: Using the Compass Rose

Most maps include a symbol to tell you which direction on the map is north. On some maps the symbol is a single arrow pointing toward the letter *N*. The *N* stands for north, and the arrow is pointing toward the North Pole. You can figure out the other directions from that single arrow.

Other maps show the four main directions of the compass—north, east, south, and west. These are called the cardinal directions. However, some maps provide a compass rose that indicates intermediate directions as well as the cardinal directions. Intermediate directions are northeast, southeast, southwest, and northwest.

**Directions:** *Study the compass rose and the map of Madagascar beside it. Then, answer the questions that follow.*

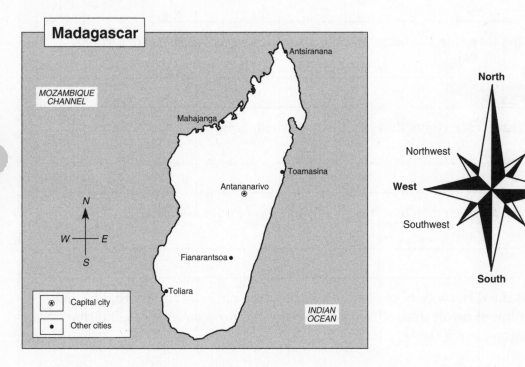

1. What is the direction from Fianarantsoa to Mahajanga? _____

2. In what direction would you travel to go from Toliara to Fianarantsoa?

   _____

3. Is the Mozambique Channel east or west of Madagascar? _____

4. On what coast is Antsiranana located? _____

5. If you flew from Antsiranana to Toliara, in what direction would you be traveling? _____

6. Which coast of Madagascar is closest to the capital? _____

# DK Compact Atlas of the World Activity:
# Using the Map Key

Review the Key to Map Symbols located at the front of your *Compact Atlas of the World*. Your teacher will provide you with the page number for the map to use in this activity. Then, use the Key to Map Symbols page with your regional map to complete the questions below.

1. What are the name and height of the highest mountain on your map?

_____

2. In what countries can you find volcanoes? What are the volcanoes called?

_____

_____

3. Name the three largest lakes and the countries in which they are located.

_____

_____

4. List at least three rivers that run through the largest country on your map.

_____

_____

5. List at least three cities that have a population of over 100,000.

_____

_____

6. What is the difference between the symbol for a national capital that has a population of fewer than 50,000 and the symbol for a national capital that has a population over 500,000?

_____

_____

7. What bodies of water border the region on your map?

_____

_____

## Outline Map Activity

Using the Outline Map provided by your teacher, label each country or state in the region you are studying. Locate and label the capital of each country or state and include the estimated population of the capital. Make sure to include a map key that identifies the symbols you are using on your map.

MapMaster Skills Handbook

# DK Compact Atlas of the World Activity:
# Using the Compass Rose

Your teacher will tell you which map in the *Compact Atlas of the World* to use for this activity. Find the compass rose on the map. Use the compass rose and the map to answer the questions below. Use a separate piece of paper to record your answers.

1. Describe the type of compass rose found on your map.

2. Describe the location of the compass rose using the directions of the compass. For example, if the compass rose is centrally located in the upper portion of the map, then the compass rose is north.

3. What cardinal directions are parallel to lines of latitude?

4. What cardinal directions are parallel to lines of longitude?

5. What point on the map is farthest north?

6. Describe the southwestern section of your map.

7. What are the grid locations running through the center of your map from east to west?

8. If you flew from the southernmost portion of the map toward the equator, in what direction would you be traveling?

9. Select a landform or city on your map and describe its location relative to other landforms or cities on the map. For example, Main City is south of Pleasant City, north of the wildlife center, east of the mountain range, and west of the lake.

## Outline Map Activity

Using the Outline Map provided by your teacher, locate the compass rose. Locate and label the countries that are the farthest north, east, south, and west in the region of the world that you are studying.

MapMaster Skills Handbook

MapMaster Skills Handbook

# DK Compact Atlas of the World Activity: Using the Map Scale

Your teacher will tell you which map in the *Compact Atlas of the World* to use for this activity. Use this map and a ruler to practice using a map scale by completing the questions below.

1. The scale on your map measures distance using two different units of distance. What are the two units of distance?

   _____

2. Find a mountain range on your map and measure its length in miles.

   _____

3. Find a river on your map and measure its length in kilometers.

   _____

4. Find the largest country on your map and measure the distance from the capital city to the next closest city. Record your answer in meters and kilometers.

   _____

5. Locate two capital cities on your map. Measure the distance in miles between the two cities. Write the name of both cities and the distance between them on the lines below.

   _____

6. Why might the actual distance between the cities you selected for question 5 be different than the distance you recorded?

   _____

7. If the scale on your map were changed from one inch equals 500 kilometers to one inch equals 250 kilometers, would there be more or less detail on the map?

   _____

## Outline Map Activity

Using the Outline Map provided by your teacher, label the countries or states, three major cities in each, and the major landforms within the region. Label the Map Key box *Distances*, and record in the box the distances between these key features of the map.

MapMaster Skills Handbook

# MapMaster Skills: Comparing Maps of Different Scale

The scale of a map shows you how a distance on the map relates to the actual distance on the earth's surface. A small-scale map shows a large area; a large-scale map shows a smaller area in greater detail. Map A below is a small-scale map of part of Southwest Asia; Map B is a large-scale map of Kuwait.

**Directions:** *Study the two maps below. Then answer the questions that follow.*

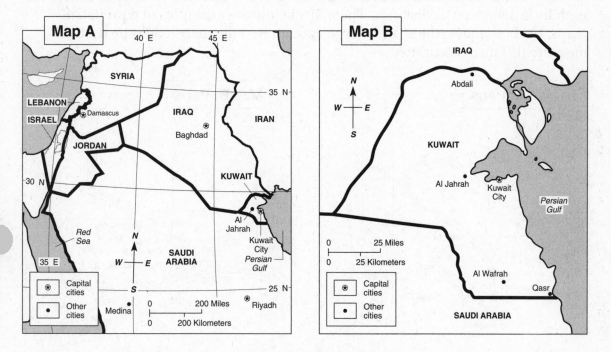

1. What does Map A tell you about Kuwait that Map B does not?

_____

2. What does Map B tell you about Kuwait that Map A does not?

_____

3. Which map would you use to describe Kuwait's position in relation to other countries of Southwest Asia?

_____

4. Which map would you use to determine the distance from Kuwait City to Al Wafrah?

_____

MapMaster Skills Handbook

# MapMaster Skills: Maps with Accurate Distances: Equidistant Maps

**Directions:** *Read the information about equidistant maps, and study the maps below. Then, answer the questions that follow. Use a separate piece of paper for your answers.*

Equidistant maps show the correct distance between places. Maps of the world can never show all distances accurately because it is not possible to show the correct lengths of all lines of latitude and longitude. Small areas, however, can be mapped with little distortion of distance. The maps below are examples of equidistant maps. On both maps, the scale is large enough that the maps could be used to measure distances accurately.

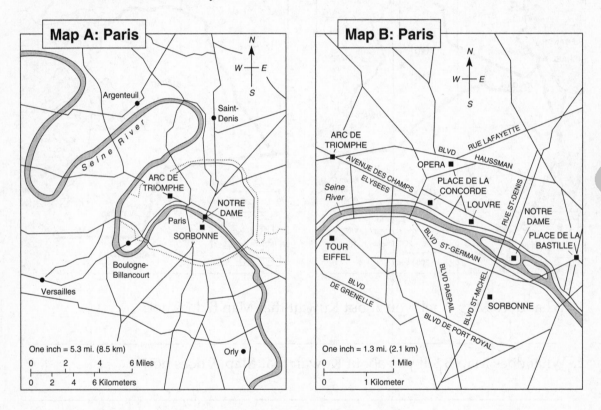

1. What does an equidistant map show correctly?

2. Why would it not be possible to have an equidistant map of the world?

3. What kinds of areas lend themselves to equidistant maps?

4. What kinds of distances could you measure on Map A above?

5. What kinds of distances could you measure on Map B?

# MapMaster Skills: Reading a Political Map

A political map shows political features such as national or state boundaries, capital cities and other major cities. Some political maps use color to differentiate countries or states. The map of Western Europe below is an example of a political map.

**Directions:** *Study the map and the key below. Then, answer the questions that follow.*

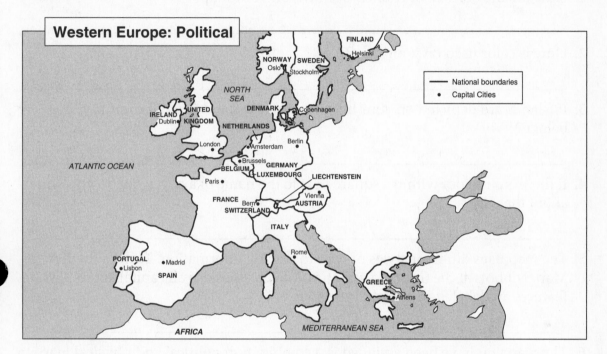

1. What does a solid black line on the map signify?

   _____

2. Which nations of Western Europe border on the Mediterranean Sea?

   _____

3. List the nations that share a border with Belgium.

   _____

4. What is the capital of Spain?

   _____

5. What is the capital of Germany?

   _____

6. Which western European country lies closest to the North African coast?

   _____

MapMaster Skills Handbook

# DK Compact Atlas of the World Activity: Reading a Political Map

Your teacher will tell you which map in the *Compact Atlas of the World* to use for this activity. Review the population key in the left-hand margin of the page. You may also wish to refer to the Key to Map Symbols at the front of the atlas.

1.  How are the borders of countries shown on your map?

    _____

2.  How is color used on your map?

    _____

3.  If islands are depicted on your map, how can you tell to what country they belong?

    _____

4.  If there is a red dot within a square next to the name of a city, what do you know about that city?

    _____

5.  The map uses different styles of type to convey information. Turn to the Key to Map Symbols at the front of your atlas. Which cities use all capital letters? What features are labeled in an *italic* type style?

    _____

6.  The map you have been assigned is a combination political and physical map. That means some features on your map belong to political maps and other features belong to physical maps. Which of the features on your map might not be found on a physical map?

## Outline Map Activity

Using the Outline Map provided by your teacher, label each country or state in the region you are studying. Locate and label the capital of each country or state, using symbols appropriate to the estimated population. Include other political features as necessary. Make sure to include a map key that identifies the symbols you are using on your map.

MapMaster Skills Handbook

# Outline Map 22: North Africa

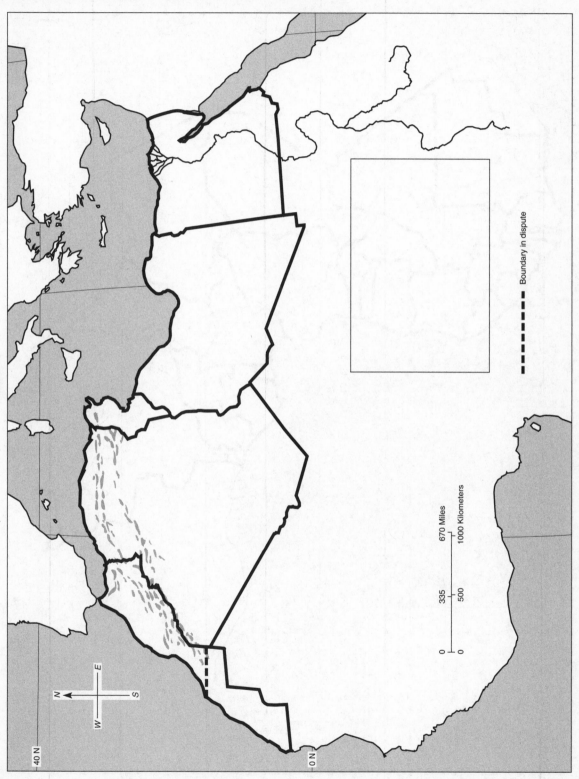

670 Miles

1000 Kilometers

335

500

0

0

Boundary in dispute

40 N

0 N

N
E
S
W

MapMaster Skills
Handbook

MapMaster Skills Handbook

# Outline Map 23: West and Central Africa

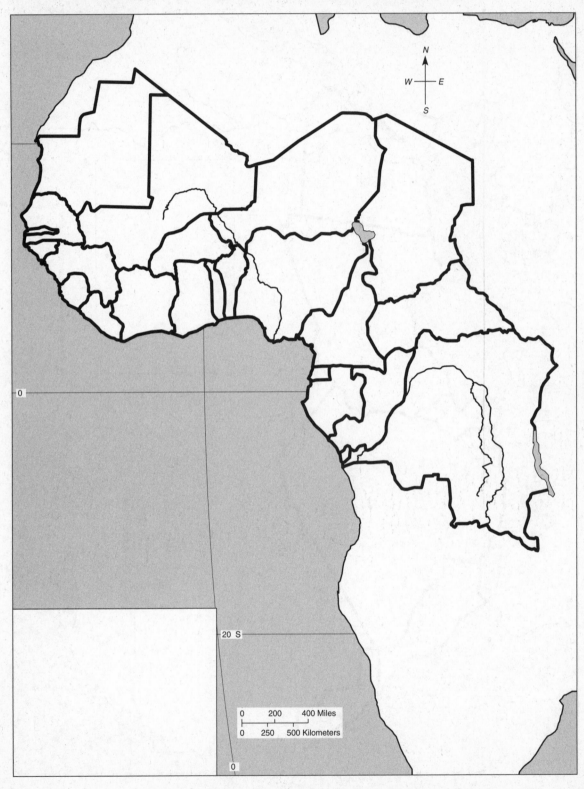

N
W ─┼─ E
S

0

20 S

0

| 0 | 200 | 400 Miles |
| 0 | 250 | 500 Kilometers |

0

MapMaster Skills Handbook

# Outline Map 24: East and Southern Africa

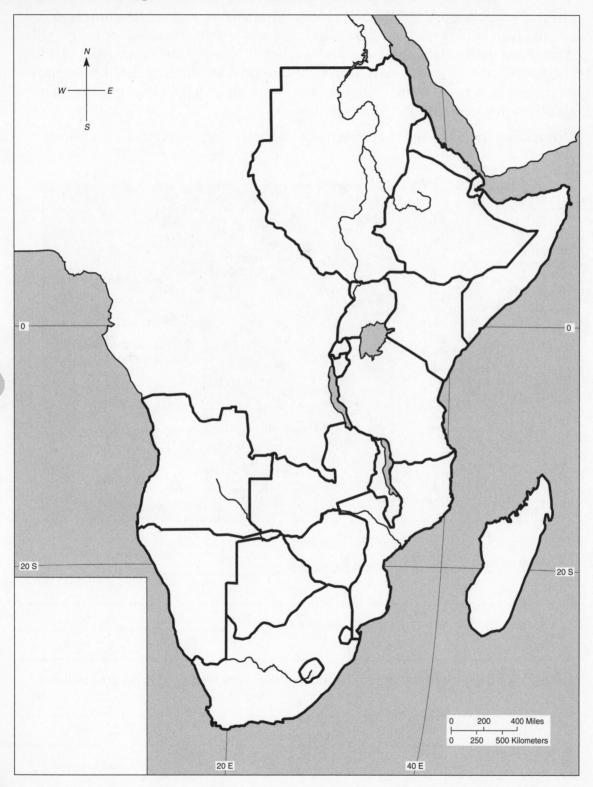

Name _____ Date _____ Class _____

# MapMaster Skills: Reading a Physical Map

Physical maps are usually colored or shaded to show a region's landforms and waterways. Color is often used on physical maps to show elevation or the height of land above sea level. Shading illustrates relief or how the land is uneven. Shading also helps give a physical map a three-dimensional appearance. Unlike political maps, physical maps show more than the boundaries of countries or states. They also show the geographic features of the land.

**Directions:** *Study the map of Ecuador below. Then, answer the questions that follow.*

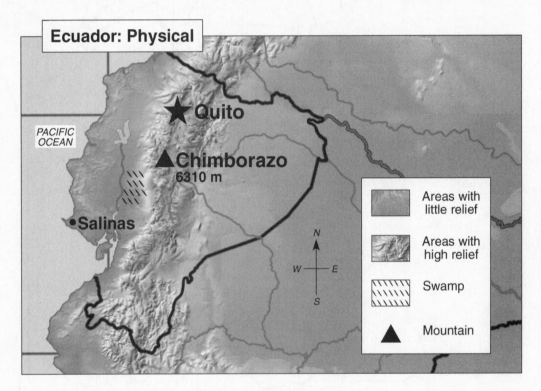

1. Where is the highest elevation located? _____

_____

2. Where can you find the largest area of flat land? _____

_____

3. Describe the physical features found between the cities of Quito and Salinas.

_____

_____

_____

_____

# MapMaster Skills: Elevation on a Map

Elevation refers to the height of land above sea level. Mountains are the landforms with the highest elevation. Elevation is shown on maps by different colors or different types of shading. On a color map, lower elevations are generally shown in different shades of green, while higher elevations are shown in shades of brown. On the map of Canada below, different elevations are indicated by different types of patterns. The lighter the pattern, the higher the elevation.

**Directions:** *Study the map and the map key below. Then, answer the questions.*

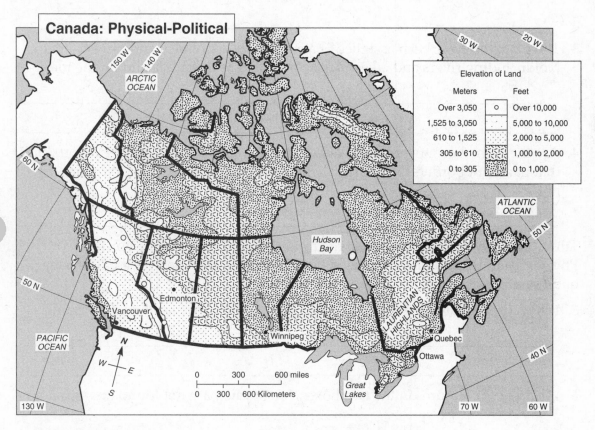

1. In which area of Canada are the highest elevations found?

   _____

2. What is the elevation of most of the land around Hudson Bay?

   _____

3. Which city is at a higher elevation, Quebec or Edmonton?

   _____

4. What kinds of landforms would you expect to find in the western part of Canada?

   _____

MapMaster Skills Handbook

# DK Compact Atlas of the World Activity: Reading a Physical Map

Your teacher will provide you with the page number to use in this activity. To learn more about physical maps, use the map on that page to answer the questions below.

1. Name at least three rivers found on your map.

_____

2. Name at least two lakes found on your map.

_____

3. The map you have been assigned is a combination political and physical map. Not including rivers and lakes, what physical features are found on the map?

_____

_____

4. Are there any borders or names of countries or states on the map? Do you think that names or borders are standard elements of a physical map? Why or why not?

_____

Turn to the Key to Map Symbols at the front of the atlas. Study the box labeled Physical Features and the box labeled Drainage Features to answer the following questions.

5. Which of the features in the two boxes you studied are found on your map?

_____

_____

6. Which of the features in the two boxes you studied are not found on your map?

_____

_____

## Outline Map Activity

Using the Outline Map provided by your teacher, locate and label all the major physical features in the region you are studying. Make sure to include a map key that identifies the symbols you are using on your map.

# MapMaster Skills: Relief on a Map

A relief map shows the location of major landforms. Some relief maps use shading and symbols to indicate different types of landforms. Others use a technique called shaded relief to show mountain ranges. With shaded relief, the location of mountains can be seen at a glance because the area they cover is shaded as if with a pencil. The relief map of Eastern Russia below uses shaded relief, the higher the elevation the lighter the shading.

**Directions:** *Study the map below. Then, answer the questions that follow.*

1. Describe the land where the city of Magadan is located.

   _____

2. Describe the region near the border of Mongolia and Russia.

   _____

3. How does Siberia differ from other areas of Eastern Russia?

   _____

4. What information does shaded relief provide, and what information is not provided?

   _____

MapMaster Skills Handbook

# MapMaster Skills: Maps of the Ocean Floor

Maps of the ocean floor show that there are mountains and valleys under the oceans as well as on land. Many small islands are actually the tops of underwater mountains. The map below shows the ocean floor of the Atlantic.

**Directions:** *Study the map below. Then, use an atlas to help you answer the questions.*

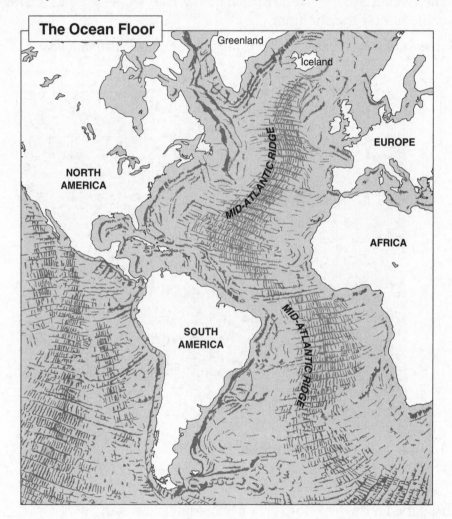

**The Ocean Floor**

1.  What is the name of the mountain range that runs through the Atlantic from north to south?_____

2.  Name three island groups off the northwest coast of Africa that are the tops of mountains. _____

3.  Circle and label the island of Cuba on the map above.

4.  Circle and label the Falkland Islands.

5.  Circle and label the Galápagos Islands.

# MapMaster Skills: Reading a Climate Map

Climate maps divide the world into climate regions. Each type of climate region has specific patterns of temperature, precipitation, and wind. The map below shows the climate regions of the British Isles and the Nordic nations.

**Directions:** *Study the map and the map key below. Then, answer the questions that follow.*

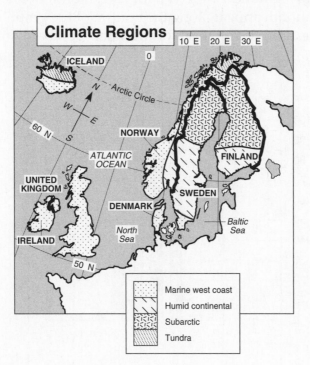

1. What is the climate region of the British Isles?

   _____

2. What three climate regions are found in Finland?

   _____

3. Which climate region is found in the northernmost parts of the area shown on the map?

   _____

4. If you were to travel from the west coast of Norway to the east coast of Sweden, at about 60°N latitude, which climate regions would you experience?

   _____

5. Which of the countries shown have a subarctic climate region?

   _____

MapMaster Skills Handbook

# MapMaster Skills: Reading a Climate Graph

A climate graph consists of a line graph and a bar graph that provide information on temperature and precipitation. The line on the graph below shows average temperature in degrees Fahrenheit. The scale for the line graph is on the left. The bars show average precipitation in inches. The scale for the bars is on the right. Temperature and precipitation are given for each month of the year. Letters representing each month appear along the bottom of the graph. This climate graph shows temperature and precipitation for Mumbai (Bombay), India.

**Directions:** *Study the climate graph. Then, answer the questions that follow.*

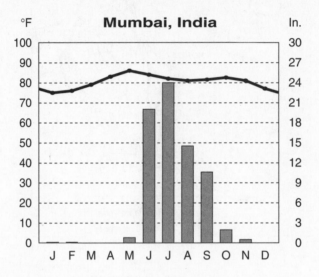

1. What information is presented in the climate graph?

   _____

2. Which is the rainiest month in Mumbai?

   _____

3. During which months does Mumbai receive less than 3 inches of rain?

   _____

4. During which months does Mumbai receive more than 12 inches of rain?

   _____

5. How would you describe the temperature pattern of Mumbai?

   _____

6. Do you think the temperatures in Mumbai affect the amount of rainfall? Why or why not?

   _____

# MapMaster Skills: Reading a Natural Vegetation Map

A natural vegetation map tells you what plants grow naturally in places that have not been altered significantly by human activity. The map below shows the natural vegetation regions of the mainland United States.

**Directions:** *Study the map and the map key below. Then, answer the questions that follow. You may wish to consult an atlas.*

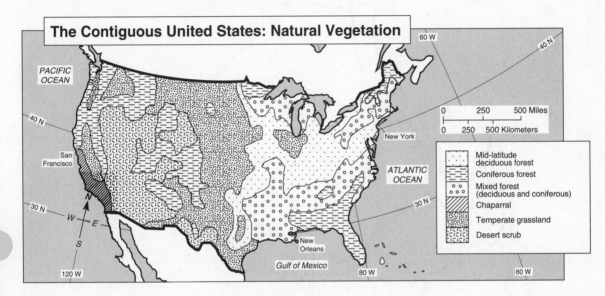

The Contiguous United States: Natural Vegetation

1. What is the natural vegetation of the area where you live?

   _____

2. What is the natural vegetation of the Great Plains?

   _____

3. If you were going to northern New England, what vegetation would you expect to find?

   _____

4. In the southern part of which state is chaparral the natural vegetation?

   _____

5. What kind of forest would you find in the Rocky Mountains?

   _____

6. What kinds of vegetation do the state of Washington and the state of Florida have in common?

   _____

MapMaster Skills Handbook

# Outline Map 26: South Asia: Political

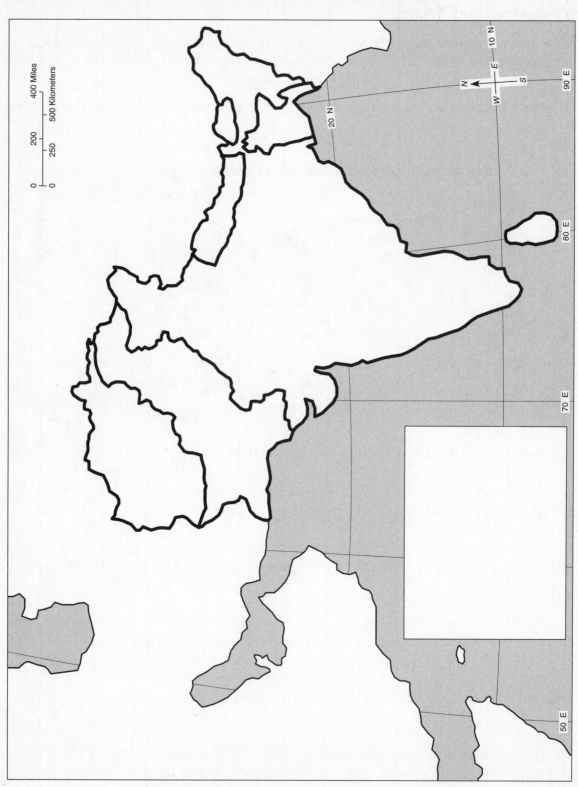

# MapMaster Skills: Reading a Time Zone Map

A time zone map helps you figure out what time it is in different parts of the world. There are 24 time zones altogether—one for each hour of the day. Four of the 24 time zones are shown in the map of North Africa below. The band across the top is a key to the actual time in each time zone. The band across the bottom tells you how many hours to add or subtract for each time zone. It shows that you add an hour for each time zone as you move from west to east.

**Directions:** *Study the map below. Then, answer the questions that follow.*

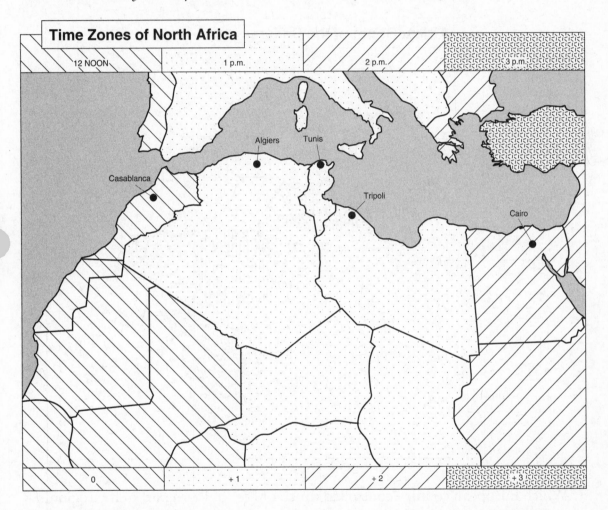

1. If it is 6 p.m. in Cairo, what time is it in a city two time zones to the west?

   _____

2. If it is 2 a.m. in Tunis, what time is it in Casablanca? _____

3. When it is 12 noon in Algiers, what time is it in Tripoli? _____

4. When it is midnight in Tunis, what time is it in Cairo?_____

5. When it is 5 p.m. in Tripoli, what time is it in the zone labeled + 3?_____

MapMaster Skills Handbook

# MapMaster Skills: Reading a Historical Map

A historical map tells you what was happening in a region at an earlier time in history. Comparing a historical map with a map of the present day can help you to understand the impact of history. The map below shows Africa south of the Sahara in 1914, when most parts of the continent were European colonies.

**Directions:** *Study the map and the map key below. Then, on the other side of this paper answer the questions that follow. You may wish to refer to a map of present-day Africa in an atlas to help you locate places.*

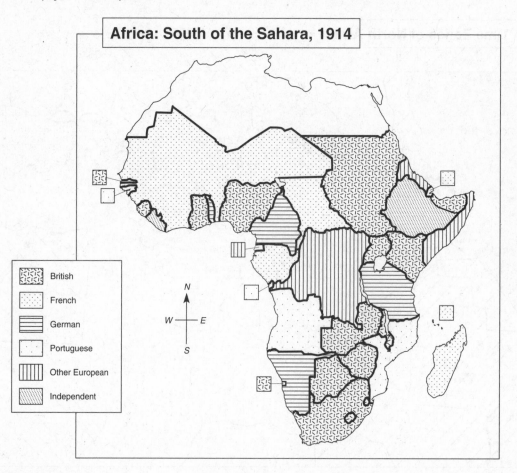

Africa: South of the Sahara, 1914

Key:
- British
- French
- German
- Portuguese
- Other European
- Independent

1. Which European country controlled much of the southern part of the region in 1914?

2. Which present-day countries were controlled by the Portuguese?

3. Which two countries remained independent in 1914?

4. Which European country controlled Madagascar and the Comoro Islands?

5. What do present-day Namibia, Cameroon, and Tanzania have in common?

MapMaster Skills Handbook

# MapMaster Skills: Analyzing Statistics

Social scientists use many different kinds of statistics to describe the characteristics of a region or a country. Such statistics are efficient ways of providing information, and they enable you to make quick comparisons. Some of the most commonly used statistics are described below.

**Directions:** *Study the definitions, and then complete the activities.*

**Birthrate.** This rate reflects the number of live births each year for each 1,000 people. A birthrate of 36 means that for every 1,000 people, 36 babies are born each year.

**Death Rate.** This rate means the number of deaths each year for every 1,000 people.

**Rate of Natural Increase.** This number tells the rate by which a population is growing: the birthrate minus the death rate, expressed as a percentage.

**Infant Mortality Rate.** This rate shows the number of infants out of every 1,000 born who die before their first birthday.

**Life Expectancy.** This figure is the average number of years a person is expected to live. Because men and women have different life expectancies, figures for both genders are often provided.

**Literacy Rate.** This rate is usually defined as the ability to read and write at the lower elementary school level. It is sometimes defined as the ability to read instructions necessary for a job.

**Gross National Product (GNP).** This number represents the total value of goods and services produced in a year.

**Per Capita GNP.** To find this figure, gross national product is divided by the country's population. This figure shows what each person's income would be if the country's income were divided equally. That is not usually the case.

1. Choose three countries that interest you, and find the statistics for each, as listed above. You will find the statistics you need in an almanac.

2. Prepare a table that will enable you to compare the statistics you find.

3. Write a brief description of your findings on the lines below.

_____

_____

_____

_____

_____

_____

# MapMaster Skills: Reading an Economic Activity Map

An economic activity map shows general information about how people make a living in different parts of a country or region. The map below shows economic activity in Somalia, a country in Northeast Africa.

**Directions:** *Study the map and the map key below. Then, on the back of this page answer the questions that follow.*

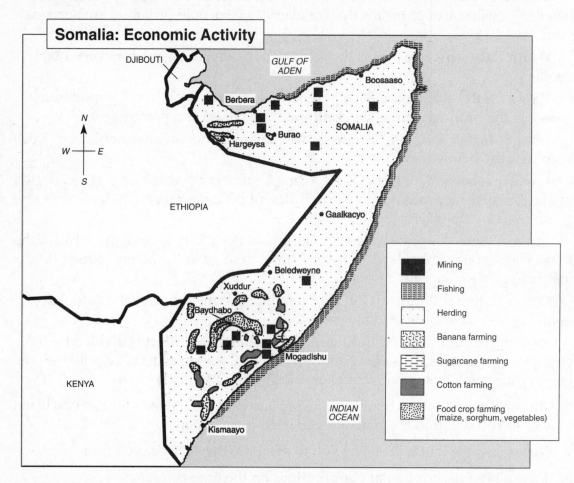

1. What is the main farming activity in the northwestern part of Somalia?

2. What economic activity is the most widespread within the country?

3. What part of the country is more fertile, the north or south?

4. What inland city is located the farthest from any mine?

5. What two farming activities take place in and around the city of Baydhabo?

6. What city is closest to the banana-growing region?

MapMaster Skills Handbook

# MapMaster Skills: Reading a Natural Resources Map

A natural resources map shows what kinds of resources are found in a place and where those resources are located. Some maps use symbols to represent different types of resources; others, like the one below, use letters, such as *G* for gold or *L* for lead.

**Directions:** *Study the map and the map key below. Then, answer the questions that follow. A political map of the United States will help you identify individual states.*

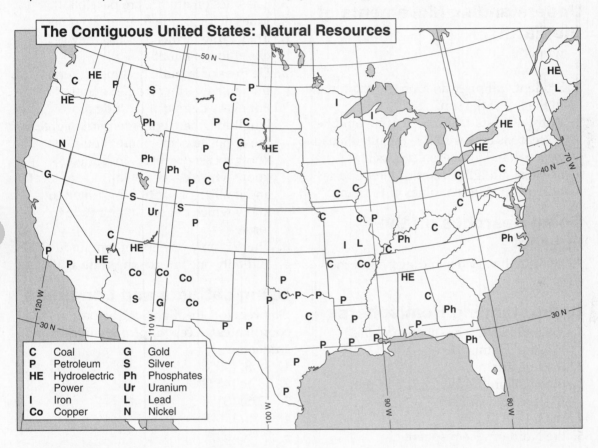

The Contiguous United States: Natural Resources

| | | | |
|---|---|---|---|
| **C** | Coal | **G** | Gold |
| **P** | Petroleum | **S** | Silver |
| **HE** | Hydroelectric | **Ph** | Phosphates |
| | Power | **Ur** | Uranium |
| **I** | Iron | **L** | Lead |
| **Co** | Copper | **N** | Nickel |

1. What is the symbol for coal? _____

2. Which area of the country, according to this map, is least rich in mineral deposits? _____

3. Which minerals listed are not found in the western half of the United States?

   _____

4. What landform do all the states with silver deposits have in common?

   _____

# Answer Key

## The Five Themes of Geography

1. location
2. movement
3. regions
4. human-environment interaction
5. place

## Understanding Movements of the Earth

1. winter
2. summer
3. Student will place an X on the orbit line to the left of the sun.
4. Without a tilt to the axis, there would be no seasons on Earth. It is the tilted axis which makes the seasons possible because sunlight strikes different parts of Earth at different times of the year.

## Doing Searches on the Internet

Answers will vary depending on Internet sites.

## Understanding Hemispheres

1. the Northern Hemisphere and the Western Hemisphere
2. the Equator
3. the Southern Hemisphere and the Eastern Hemisphere
4. the Indian Ocean
5. the Northern Hemisphere

## Understanding Latitude and Longitude

1. lines of longitude or meridians
2. lines of latitude or parallels
3. 45°N latitude
4. 90°W longitude

## DK Compact Atlas: Understanding Latitude and Longitude

1. Answers will vary depending on selected map.
2. Answers will vary depending on selected map.
3. The lines of latitude are parallel.
4. Lines of longitude meet at the poles.
5. They grow farther apart as they get closer to the Equator.
6. Degrees of latitude become larger as they move farther from the Equator.
7. For every degree of latitude or longitude, there is an identical degree in the opposite hemisphere. You must know if east or west is indicated to know which degree of latitude to locate and if north or south is indicated to know which degree of longitude to locate.
8. There is only one line of longitude at 0° and only one line of longitude at 180°.

## Using Latitude and Longitude

Answers to 1 through 5 are actual coordinates. Accept approximations from students.
1. 35°S, 149°E
2. 38°S, 145°E
3. 12°S, 131°E
4. 31°S, 116°E
5. 27°S, 153°E

## Understanding Grids

1. A4
2. giraffes
3. D2 and B4
4. D2, D1, C1, B1, B2, A1
5. B4, A4, A3, A2, A1

***Answer Key*** (*continued*)

## Using a Grid

1. Conde de Superunda Street and Tacna Avenue
2. D4
3. Cusco Avenue
4. Camana Street
5. Huallaga Street and Ayacucho Street

## Comparing Globes and Maps

1. A globe provides more accurate information on shape, size, location, distance, and direction than a flat map.
2. A globe cannot show much detail; it is difficult to carry around; you can see only half the world at any one time.
3. They can be shown in a book; they can be taken on trips; they can show small or large areas.
4. To be produced in a flat version, they have to be distorted.
5. It shows why map distortions occur.

## Understanding Projection

1. a method of showing the curved surface of the earth as a flat map
2. the areas near the poles
3. a flat-plane projection
4. the Robinson projection

## Great Circles and Straight Lines

1. the flat-plane polar projection; It would show the shortest distance more accurately as well as the route itself.
2. Possible answers: Belarus, Lithuania, Poland, Germany, Netherlands (or Belgium), France, United States
3. Finland, Sweden, Norway, Greenland, Canada, United States
4. that they are not always accurate representations of distance; that you should know what kind of projection you are looking at when using a map to plot routes or calculate distances

## Maps with Accurate Shapes: Conformal Maps

1. Antarctica appears to be much larger on the map than it is in reality.
2. Greenland and Africa are similar in size on the map. The globe shows that Greenland is many times smaller than Africa.
3. Shape and direction are correct; distance and size are distorted.
4. Possible answer: Directions are accurate on conformal maps, so they are useful for navigation. It is easier to measure angles because lines of latitude and longitude are straight.

## Maps with Accurate Areas: Equal-Area Maps

1. Sizes of landmasses in relation to other landmasses are correct; shape and direction are distorted.
2. Lines of longitude are curved so that they meet at the poles. The 180° line of longitude appears on both outside edges of the map.
3. The shape of North America on the map is distorted to curve inward toward the center of the map.

## Maps with Accurate Directions: Azimuthal Maps

1. direction
2. shape and size
3. Antarctica
4. You would fly south along the 60°W line of longitude.
5. You would go south along the 90°W line of longitude.

***Answer Key*** (*continued*)

## Using the Map Key

1. Five different shadings are represented on the map.
2. a pool of oil
3. The western half is least developed economically.
4. Answers may include that Beijing is near cropland and some pasture, tea is grown nearby, other activities include engineering, computers, and electronics.
5. Based on the map, Hong Kong has the most varied manufacturing and industry.
6. Shadings show large areas; drawings are better for smaller locations.

## Using the Compass Rose

1. north
2. northeast
3. west
4. north
5. southwest
6. east coast

## DK Compact Atlas: Using the Map Key

1. Answers will vary depending on selected map.
2. Answers will vary depending on selected map.
3. Answers will vary depending on selected map.
4. Answers will vary depending on selected map.
5. Answers will vary depending on selected map.
6. A national capital with a population of fewer than 50,000 would be shown as a red circle. A national capital with a population over 500,000 would be shown as a red circle inside a black square.
7. Answers will vary depending on selected map.

## DK Compact Atlas: Using the Compass Rose

1. The compass rose points to the four cardinal and four intermediate directions, but only north is identified.
2. Answers will vary depending on selected map.
3. east and west
4. north and south
5. Answers will vary depending on selected map.
6. Answers will vary depending on selected map.
7. Answers will vary depending on selected map.
8. Answers will vary depending on selected map.
9. Answers will vary depending on selected map.

## DK Compact Atlas: Using the Map Scale

1. kilometers and miles.
2. Answers will vary depending on selected map.
3. Answers will vary depending on selected map.
4. Answers will vary depending on selected map.
5. Answers will vary depending on selected map.
6. Answers will vary but may include that if the terrain is rugged, the actual distance would be longer, that scale is an estimate, and that accuracy depends on the person measuring.
7. There would be more detail on the map.

## *Answer Key* (continued)

## Comparing Maps of Different Scale

1. It shows Kuwait's location and size in relation to neighboring countries.
2. It shows the details of the shape of Kuwait as well as offshore islands and the location of major cities.
3. Map A
4. Map B

## Maps with Accurate Distances: Equidistant Maps

1. distances between places
2. because it is not possible to show the correct lengths of all lines of latitude and longitude
3. small areas such as parts of cities or towns
4. distances from Paris to some of the surrounding cities
5. distances between buildings and monuments within the city of Paris

## Reading a Political Map

1. a national boundary
2. Spain, France, Italy, Greece
3. France, Germany, Luxembourg, Netherlands
4. Madrid
5. Berlin
6. Spain

## DK Compact Atlas: Reading a Political Map

1. Borders are shown as gold lines.
2. Color is used to differentiate countries.
3. There may be a curved border or the country to which they belong may be identified within parentheses below the name of the island.
4. It is a national capital of more than 500,000 people.
5. A capital city is identified with capital letters. Physical features such as mountains, rivers, and deserts are labeled in italics.
6. Features that might not be found on physical maps include the use of color for different countries, names of cities, population symbols for cities, disputed borders, and sovereignty of islands.

## Reading a Physical Map

1. Mt. Chimborazo is the highest point in Ecuador. Highest elevations run north to south through the center of Ecuador.
2. The largest area of flat land is in the eastern portion of Ecuador.
3. Answers will vary but may include mountains giving way to flat land, a river, a swamp, a lake, small hills, and then finally the Pacific Ocean.

## Elevation on a Map

1. in the western part
2. 0 to 1,000 feet (0 to 305 m)
3. Edmonton
4. Students should suggest mountains or mountain ranges and narrow coastal plains.

## DK Compact Atlas: Reading a Physical Map

1. Answers will vary depending on selected map.
2. Answers will vary depending on selected map.
3. Answers will vary but may include volcanoes, mountains, depressions, tunnels, deserts, waterfalls, wetlands, oceans, seasonal lakes and rivers, and pack ice.
4. Answers will vary but should reflect the students' understanding that country or state names and borders are standard elements of a political map and not of a physical map.

## Answer Key *(continued)*

5. Answers will vary depending on selected map.
6. Answers will vary depending on selected map.

### Relief on a Map

1. It is a hilly peninsula. The city is located on the eastern side.
2. From Russia, the land slopes upward forming high mountains at the border.
3. Siberia is a high, flat plateau. It is surrounded by mountains on the east and south. North and west of Siberia are lower, more level areas.
4. Shaded relief can show you the contours of the land, but not the actual elevation.

### Maps of the Ocean Floor

1. the Mid-Atlantic Ridge
2. Canary Islands, Madeira Islands, Azores
3-5. Students should correctly identify the islands named.

### Reading a Climate Map

1. marine west coast
2. humid continental, subarctic, tundra
3. tundra
4. marine west coast and humid continental
5. Norway, Sweden, Finland

### Reading a Climate Graph

1. average monthly rainfall and temperatures in Mumbai
2. July
3. January, February, March, April, May, October, November, December
4. June, July, August
5. Temperatures are fairly steady throughout the year, ranging from a low of about 75°F to a high of about 85°F.
6. Possible answer: No. Temperatures fluctuate only 10° all year; rainfall ranges from 0 to 24 inches.

### Reading a Natural Vegetation Map

1. Answers will vary.
2. temperate grassland
3. coniferous forest
4. California
5. coniferous forests
6. Both have coniferous forests.

### Reading a Time Zone Map

1. 4 p.m.
2. 1 a.m.
3. 12 noon
4. 1 a.m.
5. 7 p.m.

### Reading a Historical Map

1. Great Britain
2. Angola, Mozambique, Guinea-Bissau
3. Liberia and Ethiopia
4. France
5. All were German colonies.

### Analyzing Statistics

Answers will vary, depending on the countries chosen. Encourage students to make comparisons and draw conclusions.

### Reading an Economic Activity Map

1. food crop farming
2. herding
3. the south
4. Gaalkacyo
5. cotton farming and food crop farming
6. Kismaayo

### Reading a Natural Resources Map

1. the letter C
2. the Midwest, especially Kansas, Indiana, Iowa, Nebraska, and Wisconsin
3. iron, lead
4. the Rocky Mountains

Book Projects

# Changing Climates

## A. Arctic Countries and Mediterranean Countries

Which European countries are near the Arctic? Which are near the Mediterranean? Look at an atlas or other books that contain maps of Europe. Begin by finding the Arctic Circle. Notice which countries it passes through. Then find the Mediterranean. List the European countries that border it.

You can use the chart below to record the names of European countries that are near the Arctic Circle or the Mediterranean. When you have completed the chart, you can choose one country for the guide you will write.

**Arctic and Mediterranean European Countries**

| European Countries Close to the Arctic | European Countries That Border the Mediterranean |
|---|---|
| | |

Book Projects

Book Projects

## *Changing Climates* (continued)

## B. Planning Your Guide

Now that you have chosen a country, you can plan your guide. Begin by finding information about the climate. What are the average temperatures and levels of precipitation? How does the climate change with the seasons? What are other important facts about the climate?

Then look for ways in which the climate affects how people live. What are houses and buildings like? What kinds of clothes do people wear? What foods do they eat? Remember to include information about preparing for a large climate change.

Use the chart below to record the climate and ways of life in the country you have chosen.

**Climate Facts and Information**

| Average Temperature and Precipitation | Types of Dwellings and Clothing | Common Foods | Recreational Activities | Other Important Facts |
|---|---|---|---|---|
|  |  |  |  |  |

You can use the information in the chart to help write your climate guide.

Name _____ Date _____ Class _____

Book Projects

## Changing Climates (continued)

## C. Writing a Newcomer's Climate Guide

When you have gathered information, choose the facts that you think are the most important. Remember that you are writing for a person who is moving from a very different place. Try to think of things that he or she would not consider in advance. For example, a person from the Mediterranean might not know about the long winter nights and long summer days in the Arctic.

Before you write the guide itself, jot down ideas you want to use. You can write them in the chart below. Include useful tips and ideas for a title. Use the chart to help organize your ideas and write the guide. You might check off each point as you use it.

**Notes for the Newcomer's Guide**

| Guide Subjects | Information, Tips, and Ideas |
|---|---|
| **Clothing**<br>Summer<br>Winter | |
| **Housing** | |
| **Food**<br>Summer<br>Winter | |
| **Recreation**<br>Summer<br>Winter | |
| **Outdoor Tips** | |
| **Indoor Tips** | |
| **Other** | |

Now write your climate guide, using the information on the chart.

Book Projects

# Tourism in Eastern Europe

## A. Choosing a Country

What places in Eastern Europe would you like to visit? In which countries do you think your family or friends might like to travel? Think about things that attract tourists. Most people like to look at beautiful scenery, such as mountains or seacoasts. Many enjoy going to large cities or historical landmarks. If you need ideas, try reviewing the text or looking at a map of Eastern Europe. What tourist attractions stand out for you?

You can begin to plan your travel destination by picking one or two countries. Be sure to choose places that will attract tourists. Use the chart below to record things in each country that will be interesting or exciting for tourists.

**Tourist Hot Spots in Eastern Europe**

| Country | Scenery | Cities | Cultural Events | Other Attractions |
|---------|---------|--------|-----------------|-------------------|
|         |         |        |                 |                   |
|         |         |        |                 |                   |

Use the information in the chart to choose a country for your travel advertisement.

Book Projects

## Tourism in Europe *(continued)*

## B. Gathering Information and Photos

Once you have chosen a country, look for more information that you can use in your brochure. You can use the library to find magazine articles and books. Be sure that they are up to date. The names and borders of countries in Eastern Europe have been changing a great deal in recent years. Photocopy illustrations that you might use.

You might also call a travel agent for help. Ask for brochures or posters that you can cut up for photographs. At the same time, you may get ideas for designing your own advertisement.

Use the chart below to keep a record of articles, information, and illustrations that you have found.

**Travel Advertisement Information and Photos**

| Article Subject | Photos and Illustrations | Source of Article | Tourist Information |
|---|---|---|---|
|  |  |  |  |
|  |  |  |  |
|  |  |  |  |

Use the information on the chart when you begin to write.

Book Projects

## Tourism in Europe *(continued)*

## C. Creating a Travel Advertisement

You have the information and images you need. Now you can create the advertisement itself. First decide on the form you want to use. You might make a poster or a brochure, or you may have other ideas. Remember, you want to make something simple and that attracts attention.

**Materials**

> paper
> glue
> paint and paintbrush
> tape
> scissors
> colored markers
> crayons

**Procedure**

1. Once you have chosen a form for your advertisement, gather the materials you will need. Look at the materials list above. Add items as you need them.

2. Begin by sketching a design for your advertisement. If you are doing a brochure that must be opened, be sure to plan eye-catching lettering and illustrations for the first page. Use colors that will attract attention.

3. Write the text for the advertisement. Use the facts that will make people want to visit your country. Remember that you are trying to persuade them to travel.

4. Put the text and illustrations together in a final form. When you have finished your advertisement, share it with the class. You might create a travel corner or bulletin board to display the advertisements. Notice which advertisements really catch your eye.

Book Projects

# Olympic Cities

## A. Olympic Qualities

Do you know any cities that have been used for the Olympics in recent years? Use an almanac or encyclopedia to find this information. You will discover that the summer Olympics are usually in large cities. These cities often have much to offer even without the Olympics. They have plenty of hotel space. And they have or are able to build indoor and outdoor arenas for the events. The winter Olympics must be in a cold climate, have excellent skiing, and have lots of hotel space.

As you read the text, keep track of cities that you think might make good Olympic sites. You can use the chart below to record your ideas. Include reasons why you think each place would make a good host city.

**Olympic Cities**

| Name | Size | Location | Why the City Would Make a Good Site |
|------|------|----------|-------------------------------------|
|      |      |          |                                     |
|      |      |          |                                     |
|      |      |          |                                     |

You can use the information on the page to choose one city as an Olympic site.

Book Projects

## *Olympic Cities* (continued)

## B. Gathering Information About an Olympic City

Once you have chosen a city for the Olympics, you can research information for your proposal. Remember that you want to be able to explain what the city has to offer to the Olympics. You will need background information about this place to do a good job. Use library books, articles, and encyclopedias as sources. As you gather information, look for pictures of the city to include.

You can use the chart below to record the city's strengths. Keep track of each source of information. Then if you need to check your source, you will know where to look.

### Record Your Research

| Size of City and Location | Sports Facilities | Number of Hotels | Cultural Attractions | Other | Information Sources |
|---|---|---|---|---|---|
|  |  |  |  |  |  |

Use the information on the chart to decide what points you want to include in your proposal.

## *Olympic Cities* (continued)

## C. Writing a Proposal

Before you begin to write, think about why you are writing. You are trying to persuade the Olympic committee that your city should be an Olympic site. Many other cities will compete for this honor. How can you best help your city?

Think about how you want your proposal to look. How many pages will it be? What kinds of graphics will it contain? Do you want to include a cover letter explaining what you want? Do you want to put it in a notebook? Once you have decided on the form, you can begin to work.

### Materials

paper

colored markers

crayons

pens or pencils

photographs or illustrations of the city

paint and paintbrush

glue

### Procedure

If you prefer, you can work in small groups. Divide the jobs that need to be done.

When you have finished, show your work to your teacher and classmates.

Book Projects

# Folklore Corner

## A. Finding Traditional Tales

You probably already know some stories from European countries. Many fairy tales that American children learn came from Europe. Look in the library for books of fairy or folk tales. Many of these tell which country a story comes from. You may also find books that have only tales from a specific country.

Try to find at least one story from each country you read about in the text. You may wish to work in small groups to share the work of locating stories. You can record the title of the story on the chart below. Be sure to record where you found each story. Since the stories you are looking for are quite old, newer countries like Slovenia or Slovakia may not be listed. You might look under Yugoslavia and Czechoslovakia for possible examples. While you are collecting stories, search for other good books as well as illustrations, objects, and photos that can be used in your display.

### Traditional Tales

| Country | Story Title | Source |
|---|---|---|
| Great Britain | | |
| France | | |
| Sweden | | |
| Italy | | |
| Germany | | |
| Poland | | |
| Bosnia and Herzegovina | | |
| Ukraine | | |
| Russia | | |

Use the information on the chart as a reference list of stories for your library.

## *Folklore Corner* (continued)

## B. When You Have Collected Stories

Think how each story reflects what you know about its country's culture. You may wish to work in small groups to read and talk about the stories. Think about the characters. Discuss how they dress, speak, and act. Try to imagine the setting. How does it reflect what you know about the geography of the area? What is the message of the story? How does it relate to life in the area it comes from?

Use the chart below to write your ideas about each story and the culture it represents.

### How Traditional Tales Reflect a Country's Culture

| Story Title | Country | Characters, Plot, and Setting | Culture of the Country |
|---|---|---|---|
|  |  |  |  |
|  |  |  |  |
|  |  |  |  |
|  |  |  |  |
|  |  |  |  |
|  |  |  |  |
|  |  |  |  |

Use the information on the chart to help plan your Folklore Corner display.

Book Projects

## *Folklore Corner* (continued)

## C. Creating a Folklore Display

Collect as many books of European and Russian folk tales as you can. Even if you did not use a story from a certain book, it can still make a good addition to your library. Gather all the objects, drawings, and photographs that you might use. Then work in small groups to create the display. Decide among yourselves how to divide the work.

### Materials
- books
- drawings
- paper
- colored markers
- scissors
- tape
- cultural objects
- photographs
- pens or pencils
- paint and paintbrush
- glue

### Procedure

1. Begin by choosing a good location for your display. It should be easy to see, but not in the way. Think about how much room you will need. Will the display be on one flat surface? Or will you have some of it on bookshelves? Could you use a bulletin board for some of the information?

2. Divide the jobs that need to be done. Be sure each person has a meaningful task. Some can arrange books. Some can choose and organize objects, illustrations, and photographs. Others can make labels and write any text that is to be included.

3. Meet as a class to decide when the display is to be completed. Brainstorm ideas for finishing the project. When you are finished, you might invite other classes to come to visit your Folklore Corner. You might read or tell one or two stories and explain where they are from and how they reflect that culture.

# Rubric for Assessing Student Performance on a Project

| Grading Criteria | Excellent | Acceptable | Minimal | Unacceptable |
|---|---|---|---|---|
| **Preparation and Research** | Prepares by investigating a wide range of primary and secondary sources. | Uses several appropriate resources. | Relies on only one or two sources of research. | Little evidence of preparation and research. |
| **Subject Matter** | Strong grasp and understanding of subject matter; meets project criteria completely and concisely. | Familiar with subject matter; meets project criteria. | Gaps in understanding of subject matter; not all project criteria met. | Little understanding of subject matter or project criteria evident. |
| **Presentation** | Demonstrates careful thought and initiative; uses innovative approaches to present original ideas. | Evidence of some creative thought present. | Contains one or two interesting ideas. | No original ideas or methods evident. |

Book Projects

Book Projects

# Rubric for Assessing Performance of an Entire Group

| Grading Criteria | Excellent | Acceptable | Minimal | Unacceptable |
|---|---|---|---|---|
| **Participation** | All group members make important contributions toward group goals. | All group members participate on some level. | Workload is unfairly distributed among group members. | One or two group members do all the work. |
| **Teamwork** | Group members develop enthusiasm and rapport and work extremely well together. | Group members work well together. | Some group members do too much work; others fail to follow through on assigned tasks. | Group members unable to work together to develop and complete goals. |
| **Presentation of Ideas or Project** | Organized and creative; makes excellent use of individual group members' skills and talents. | Fulfills assignment criteria; takes advantage of some group members' individual abilities. | Meets some assignment criteria; demonstrates some evidence of team effort. | Does not adhere to assignment criteria; shows lack of preparation and team effort. |

# Rubric for Assessing Individual Performance in a Group

| Grading Criteria | Excellent | Acceptable | Minimal | Unacceptable |
|---|---|---|---|---|
| **Participation** | Willingly contributes creative ideas; elicits contributions from other group members. | Contributes several good ideas. | Participates by agreeing with others' ideas; contributes no original ideas. | Makes few or irrelevant contributions. |
| **Teamwork** | Listens attentively to others' ideas; works cooperatively with all other group members. | Listens to others' ideas; works well with most group members. | Sometimes listens to others' ideas; has some difficulty working cooperatively. | Inattentive; allows other group members to do the bulk of the work. |
| **Leadership** | Takes on a leadership role; guides group in developing and completing goals. | Takes some initiative in guiding group toward completing goals. | Follows through on assigned tasks. | Fails to complete assigned tasks. |

# Rubric for Assessing a Student Portfolio

| Grading Criteria | Excellent | Acceptable | Minimal | Unacceptable |
|---|---|---|---|---|
| **Content** | Wide variety of written and visual materials showing student's skills and growth over a period of time. | Collection of written and visual materials showing student's abilities and progress. | Several pieces of work showing some of the student's abilities. | A few pieces of work that do not show the student's abilities and growth. |
| **Skills and Abilities** | Work shows much evidence of critical thinking and problem-solving skills and understanding of relationships among topics and concepts studied. | Work shows some evidence of critical thinking and problem-solving skills and understanding of relationships among topics and concepts studied. | Only minimal level of critical thinking and problem-solving skills shown. | Little evidence of critical thought or concept understanding. |
| **Presentation** | Items carefully selected and creatively arranged and presented; each item accompanied by an explanation of why it was included; portfolio includes table of contents. | Items dated and carefully arranged; portfolio is neat. | Some care taken in arranging materials; portfolio lacks table of contents and explanations. | Limited contents appear "thrown together." |

# Discovery Activities About Europe and Russia

**Directions:** *Use this sheet and the text and maps on pages 2–7 of your textbook to answer the following questions.*

1. **Investigate Europe and Russia's Location**

   Use the map on page 2 of your textbook to locate Europe, Russia, the United States, the Equator, and the Arctic Circle.

   **a.** If you lived on the west coast of the United States, in which direction would you travel to get to the east coast of Russia?

   _____

   **b.** Which is closer to Europe and Russia—the Equator or the Tropic of Cancer?

   _____

   **c.** Which is closer to the United States—the Equator or the Tropic of Cancer?

   _____

   **d.** Does any part of Europe and Russia touch the Arctic Circle?

   _____

   **e.** Does any part of the United States touch the Arctic Circle?

   _____

   **f.** Why do you think that the climates of the United States and Europe are similar?

   _____

2. **Estimate the Size of Europe and Russia**

   Use a ruler and the map on page 2 of your textbook to answer the following questions.

   **a.** How many times taller is Europe and Russia from north to south than the United States mainland?

   _____

   **b.** How many times wider is Europe and Russia from east to west than the United States mainland?

   _____

   **c.** How does just Europe compare in height from north to south with the United States?

   _____

## *Discovery Activities About Europe and Russia* (continued)

    **d.** How does just Europe compare in width from east to west with the United States?

_____

    **e.** If the United States is about 3,500,000 square miles (9,064,958 square kilometers), about how many square miles do you think Europe covers?

_____

**3. Investigate the Countries of Europe**

    Use the maps on page 3 of your textbook to answer the following questions.

    **a.** Name three of the smallest countries in Europe.

_____

    **b.** Name four countries that share a border with Germany.

_____

    **c.** What are the names of the oceans and seas that surround Europe?

_____

    **d.** What are the names of three countries in Europe that are landlocked (have no seacoast)?

_____

**4. Examine the Mountains of Europe and Russia**

    Use the maps on page 4 of your textbook to answer the following questions.

    **a.** Name four mountain ranges in Central and Southern Europe.

_____

    **b.** What mountain range separates France from Spain?

_____

    **c.** What mountain range is located the farthest east in Russia?

_____

**5. Compare Population Densities in Europe and Russia**

    Use the maps on page 5 of your textbook to answer the following questions.

    **a.** What color on the maps represent areas where many people live?

_____

    **b.** What color on the maps represent areas where few people live?

_____

## *Discovery Activities About Europe and Russia* (continued)

**c.** In general, which areas are more densely populated—northern areas or southern areas of Europe and Russia?

_____

**d.** In general, which area is more densely populated—Europe or Russia?

_____

## Practice Your Geography Skills

**Directions:** *Use the maps on pages 2–7 of your textbook to answer the following questions.*

**1.** You begin to explore Europe from its west coast. From Portugal you fly over the headwaters of the Danube and the Rhine rivers. In which direction are you flying?

_____

**2.** You board a train in Moscow and travel east. When you get to the furthest point in Siberia, you have gone about one third of the way around the world. What mountain range did you cross first?

_____

**3.** You are going to drive from Warsaw to Moscow. In what direction do you travel?

_____

## Bonus Questions

**1.** You are as close as you can get to Africa while you are still in Europe. What country are you in?

_____

**2.** With the exception of Iceland, which country of Europe is located the farthest west?

_____

**3.** One day you swam in the Bay of Biscay. The next, you stayed in the same country and traveled to the Mediterranean Sea to swim. You could be in one of two countries, which ones?

_____

**4.** You were traveling on the Scandinavian Peninsula and crossed a border directly into Russia. In which two countries might you have been?

_____

# Outline Map 13: Western Europe: Physical

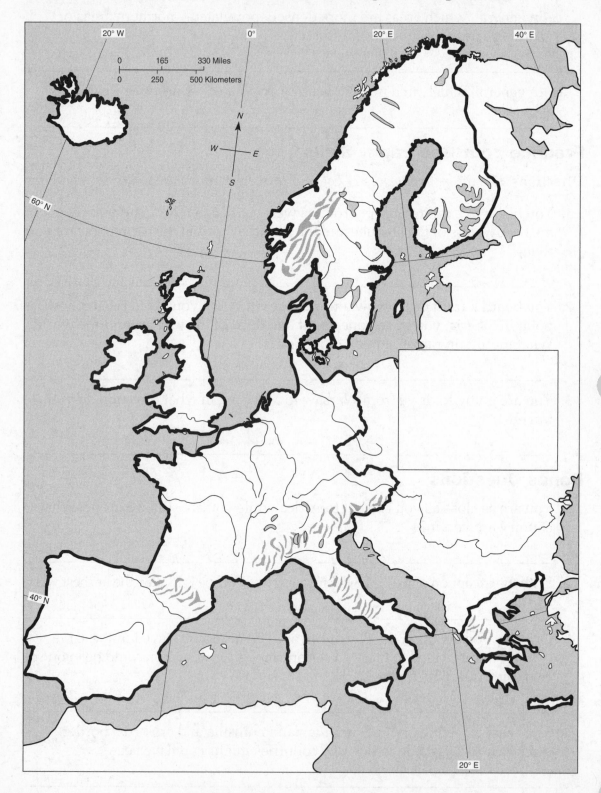

# Outline Map 14: Western Europe: Political

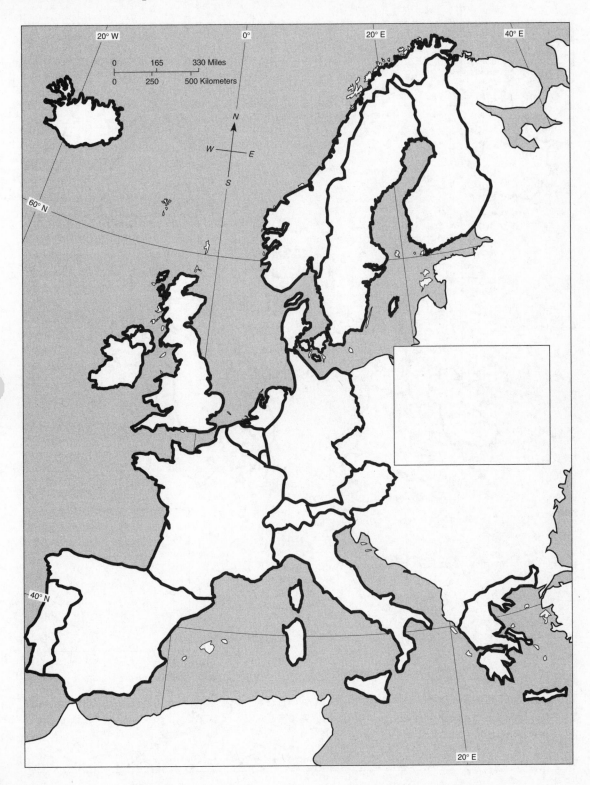

# Outline Map 15: Northern Europe

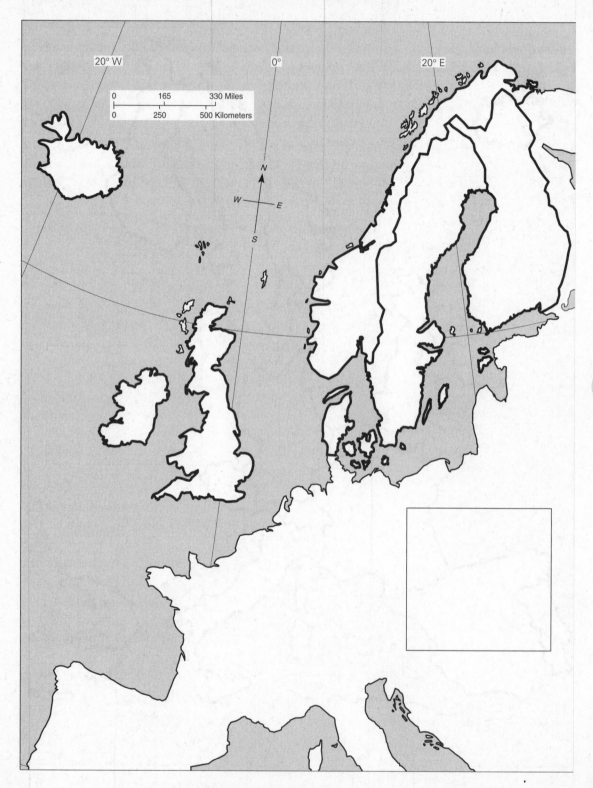

20° W          0°          20° E

| 0 | 165 | 330 Miles |
| 0 | 250 | 500 Kilometers |

N
W   E
S

# Outline Map 16: Southern Europe

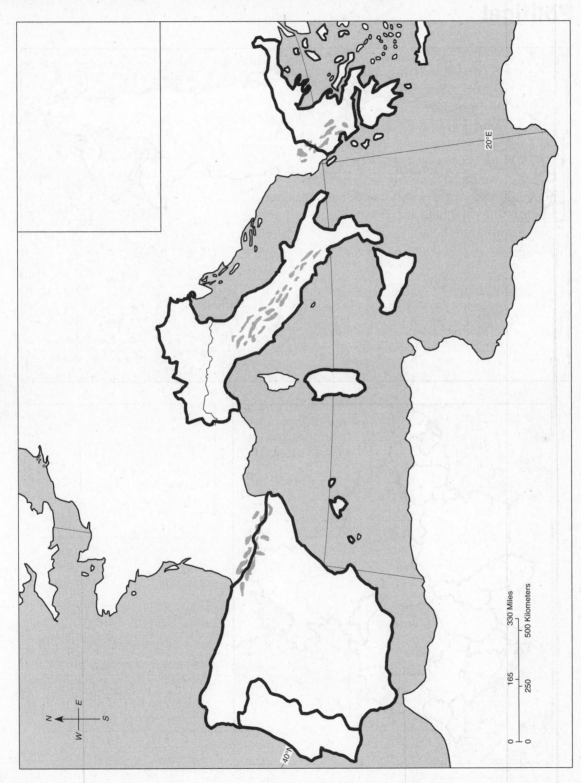

20°E

40°N

330 Miles

500 Kilometers

165

250

0

0

N
E
S
W

# Outline Map 18: Eastern Europe and Russia: Political

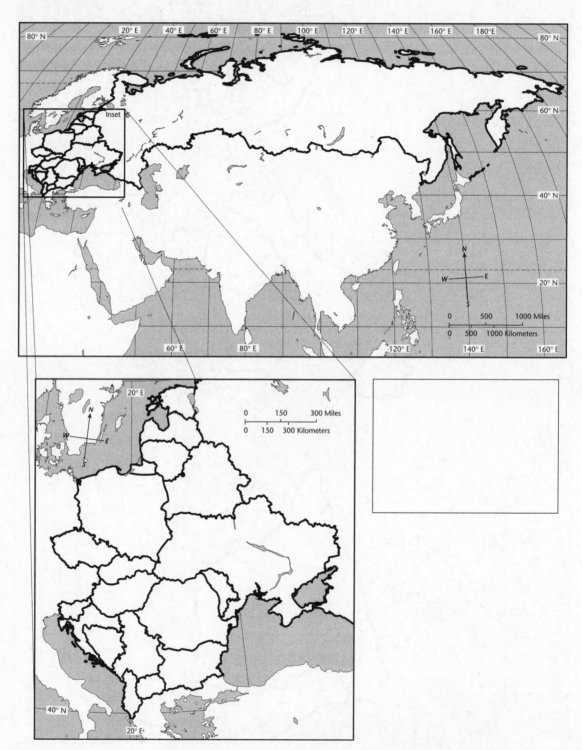

# MapMaster Skills

## Reading a Population Density Map

A type of map that uses isolines is a population density map. The isolines on a population density map outline the areas with similar population densities. A population density map shows which parts of a region are heavily populated and which parts are sparsely or lightly populated. The map key tells you how many people live in each square mile or square kilometer of the region shown. The map below shows the population density of Japan.

**Directions:** *Study the map and the map key below. Then, answer the questions that follow. You may need to use a physical map of Japan to help you answer some of the questions below.*

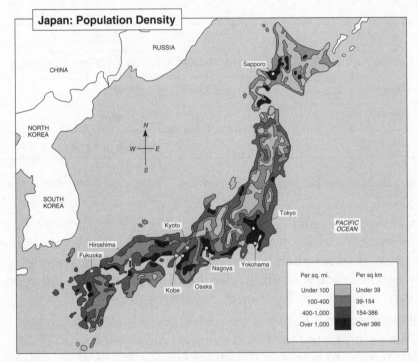

1. What is the highest number of people per square mile, as shown on the key?

_____

2. Identify the most densely populated cities indicated on the map.

_____

3. Which areas of Japan are the least populated?

_____

4. What reasons can you suggest for the population density of Japan's coasts?

_____

_____

Regional Overview

# Writing Skills

## Using the Library

The library of Alexandria, Egypt, was renowned throughout the ancient world. Experts believe it contained more than 700,000 scrolls, equivalent to perhaps 125,000 books today.

Today, we have access to a world of knowledge right around the corner—at community, school, and university libraries—and right at our fingertips—via computer. All we have to do is understand how to find the information we seek.

**Dewey Decimal System.** Used to organize most libraries, every book has a number, and the numbers are arranged in sequence around the library, grouped into 10 major categories:

| 000–099 | General Works | 500–599 | Pure Sciences |
|---------|---------------|---------|---------------|
| 100–199 | Philosophy | 600–699 | Applied Sciences/Technology |
| 200–299 | Religion | 700–799 | The Arts |
| 300–399 | Social Sciences | 800–899 | Literature |
| 400–499 | Language | 900–999 | Geography/History |

Each of these categories also has subcategories. Thus, books on similar subjects are grouped together.

**Library Catalog.** The catalog is a complete list of all the library's books, sorted alphabetically by title, author, and subject. Each entry in the catalog gives the book's Dewey Decimal number, so you can easily locate it on the shelves. Some libraries still use card catalogs, while other libraries have their catalog on computer (where you can search online by subject, author, or title).

**Other Resources.** Most libraries have newspapers, magazines, and pamphlets—some in printed form and some on film—with printed or computerized indexes to help you search for specific publication dates, subjects, or names.

**Directions:** *Visit your local or school library. Then, complete the activities below, using a separate sheet of paper for your responses.*

1. Draw a sketch of the general layout of your school or local library. Show the locations of each of the 10 major Dewey Decimal categories, as well as works of fiction, magazines and periodicals, reference books, books on computer, recorded books, and so on.

2. Briefly describe the library's catalog system. Is it a card or computer catalog? What do you need to know to use it?

3. Briefly explain how the magazines and periodicals are organized and indexed.

# Rubric for Assessing an Oral Presentation

| Grading Criteria | Excellent | Acceptable | Minimal | Unacceptable |
|---|---|---|---|---|
| **Preparation** | Gathers information from varied sources; makes note cards to use as cues during the presentation; creates attractive visual aids to illustrate the presentation. | Gathers information from three or four sources; prepares notes and visual aids to use during presentation. | Gathers information from one or two sources; writes presentation word-for-word as it will be given. | Gathers information from only one source; may not be able to complete task because of lack of preparation. |
| **Content** | Abundance of material clearly related to topic; points clearly made; varied use of materials. | Adequate information about the topic; many good points made; some variation in use of materials. | Some information not connected to the topic. | Information included has little connection to topic. |
| **Organization** | Information is well organized and logically ordered; argument easy to follow; conclusion clear. | Most information presented in logical order; argument generally clear and easy to follow. | Ideas loosely connected; organization and flow choppy and somewhat difficult to follow. | No apparent logical order of information in presentation. |
| **Speaking Skills** | Enthusiastic, poised, and confident during the presentation; uses complete sentences; speaks clearly. | Engaged during presentation; speaks mostly in complete sentences. | Little or no expression; enunciation not always clear; speaks mostly in sentence fragments. | Appears disinterested during presentation; hard to understand. |

# Answer Key

## Discovery Activities About Europe and Russia

**1a.** west

**1b.** the Tropic of Cancer

**1c.** the Tropic of Cancer

**1d.** yes, portions of northern Scandinavia and northern Russia

**1e.** yes, Alaska

**1f.** because they are in about the same latitudes (same distance from the Equator and Arctic Circle)

**2a.** about 1.5 times as tall from north to south

**2b.** almost 3 times as wide from east to west

**2c.** they are about the same

**2d.** Europe is about 1.25 times wider from east to west

**2e.** Students' answers will vary. Estimates might range from 4,000,000 to 5,000,000 square miles (actual area is 3,998,000 square miles).

**3a.** Answers may vary, but should include three of the following: Andorra, Liechtenstein, Luxembourg, Malta, Monaco, San Marino, Vatican City

**3b.** Answers may vary, but should include four of the following: France, Belgium, Luxembourg, Netherlands, Switzerland, Austria, Czech Republic, Poland, Denmark

**3c.** Arctic Ocean, Atlantic Ocean, Barents Sea, Norwegian Sea, Baltic Sea, North Sea, Bay of Biscay, Mediterranean Sea, Black Sea

**3d.** Answers may vary, but should include three of the following: Austria, Hungary, Slovakia, Czech Republic, Luxembourg, Switzerland, Moldova, Macedonia

**4a.** Answers may vary, but should include four of the following: Pyrenees, Apennines, Alps, Transylvanian Alps, Dinaric Alps, Balkan Mountains, Kjolen Mountains, Carpathian Mountains

**4b.** Pyrenees

**4c.** East Siberian Mountains

**5a.** dark purple

**5b.** yellow

**5c.** southern areas of Europe and Russia

**5d.** Europe

### Practice Your Geography Skills

1. northeast
2. Ural Mountains
3. northeast

### Bonus Questions

1. Spain
2. Ireland
3. France or Spain
4. Finland or Norway

## MapMaster Skills: Reading a Population Density Map

1. over 1000 per sq. mi.
2. Sapporo, Tokyo, Yokohama, Nagoya, Osaka
3. in general, the central areas of each island
4. Answers will vary but may include that the flattest land (suitable for farming) is near the coasts. Large cities are located near protected bays. Fishing is more accessible from the coast.

## Writing Skills: Using the Library

Answers will vary depending on the library visited.

# Letter Home

Dear Family,

For the next few weeks, our social studies class will be studying Europe and Russia. Along the way, students will learn about the physical geography, history, and cultures of the countries that make up this region.

First, we will study the land, water, climate, vegetation, and natural resources of Europe and Russia. We will explore the great variety of climates and vegetation, as well as the areas' rich natural resources. You might take this opportunity to look at an atlas with your child and compare the latitudes of different locations in the United States, Europe, and Russia.

Next, we will focus on how Europe and Russia have been shaped by history, beginning with ancient Greece. We will continue through the Middle Ages, the Renaissance, and the Industrial Revolution. Finally, we will explore the history of Imperial Russia and the Soviet Union, as well as the formation of the European Union.

We will then explore the cultures of Europe and Russia. Students will learn about the region's different ethnic groups and how they influence culture. Students will also learn about different centers of culture, such as Paris, London, and St. Petersburg. Tell your child that European and Russian cultures have played a large role in the culture and arts of the United States.

From Russia, we will return to Western Europe and take a closer look at five key countries: the United Kingdom, France, Sweden, Italy, and Germany. If you have relatives or friends with close ties to these or other European countries, ask them to share what they know with your child. Our class will also be studying the unique political systems of these five countries. With your child, you might like to compare the system of government in the United States with the different systems in Western European countries.

We will close our study of Europe and Russia with a closer look at Poland, five Balkan nations, Ukraine, and Russia. Students will learn how Poland, the Balkan nations, and Ukraine were recently formed. We will also study the great changes these countries are undergoing as they move from communism to capitalism. If you have friends or relatives from any of these countries, encourage them to talk with your child about history, ways of life, and the changes taking place today.

In the weeks ahead, your child may be talking about many of the projects he or she is working on. Please take the time to support your child's learning experience through discussion and involvement.

Sincerely,

Europe and Russia: Physical Geography
SECTION 1 Lesson Plan

# Land and Water

**Key**
**L1** Basic to Average
**L2** For All Students
**L3** Average to Advanced
**ELL** English Language Learners

⏱ *1.5 periods, .75 block*

## Section Objectives

1. Learn about the size, location, and population of Europe.
2. Examine the major landforms of Europe and Russia.
3. Find out about the waterways of Europe and Russia.

## Vocabulary

• population density • peninsula • plateau
• tributary • navigable

## Local Standards

## Reading/Language Arts Objective

Set a purpose for reading in order to focus on important ideas.

---

## PREPARE TO READ

**Build Background Knowledge**
Ask students to preview the section and predict the geographic features they will learn about.
**Set a Purpose for Reading**
Have students evaluate statements on the *Reading Readiness Guide.*
**Preview Key Terms**
Teach the section's Key Terms.
**Target Reading Skill**
Introduce the section's Target Reading Skill of **setting a purpose for reading.**

## Targeted Resources

❑ **All in One Europe and Russia Teaching Resources**
 • Reading Readiness Guide, p. 107 **L2**
 • Preview and Set a Purpose, p. 118 **L2**
❑ **Spanish Reading and Vocabulary Study Guide,** Section 1, pp. 7–8 **ELL** **L1**

---

## INSTRUCT

**Size, Location, and Population**
Discuss how the size and location of Europe and Russia affect their climates and populations.
**Major Landforms**
Discuss the land regions of Europe and Russia.
**Waterways of Europe and Russia**
Discuss the Rhine and the Volga rivers.
**Target Reading Skill**
Review **setting a purpose for reading.**

## Targeted Resources

❑ **All in One Europe and Russia Teaching Resources,** Guided Reading and Review, p. 108 **L2**
❑ **Europe and Russia Transparencies,** Section Reading Support Transparency ER 32 **L2**
❑ **Teacher's Edition**
 • For Advanced Readers, p. 14 **L3**
 • For English Language Learners, p. 15 **L1**
❑ **Spanish Support,** Guided Reading and Review, p. 4 **ELL** **L2**

---

## ASSESS AND RETEACH

**Assess Progress**
Evaluate student comprehension with the section assessment and section quiz.
**Reteach**
Assign the Reading and Vocabulary Study Guide to help struggling students
**Extend**
Assign a Small Group Activity.

## Targeted Resources

❑ **All in One Europe and Russia Teaching Resources**
 • Section Quiz, p. 109 **L2**
 • Small Group Activity, pp. 124–127 **L3**
❑ **Reading and Vocabulary Study Guide,** Section 1, pp. 6–8 **L1**
❑ **Spanish Support,** Section Quiz, p. 5 **ELL** **L2**

---

Name _____ Date _____ Class _____

Section 1: Land and Water
Europe and Russia: Physical Geography

# Reading Readiness Guide

## Anticipation Guide

How much do you think you know about the major landforms and rivers of
Europe and Russia? As your teacher reads the statements, mark whether you think
each statement is true (T) or false (F) in the Me column. Then discuss your answers
with your group and mark the group's decision in the Group column. As you read,
look for information that will clarify whether the statements are true or false.

After you read the section, read the statements again and mark the After
Reading column to indicate whether they are true or false.

| Before Reading | | Statements | After Reading |
|---|---|---|---|
| Me | Group | | |
| | | 1. Europe and Russia are parts of Eurasia, the world's largest landmass. | |
| | | 2. Europe is a large continent with 47 different countries. | |
| | | 3. Russia is the largest country in the world. | |
| | | 4. There are many physical barriers between Russia and the countries of Europe, so movement between these two regions has always been difficult. | |
| | | 5. The North European Plain covers more than half of Europe and has the most productive farmland, as well as the largest cities, in Europe. | |
| | | 6. The region known as Siberia makes up about 75 percent of Russian territory, but very few people live there because of the harsh climate. | |
| | | 7. The longest river in Europe is the Rhine River. | |

Section 1: Land and Water
Europe and Russia: Physical Geography

# Guided Reading and Review

## A. As You Read

**Directions:** *As you read Section 1, answer the following questions in the spaces provided.*

1. Russia stretches over which two continents?

   _____

2. How does the latitude of most of Europe and Russia compare with that of the United States?

   _____

3. How large is Europe? How large is Russia?

   _____

   _____

4. What type of landform does the continent of Europe form?

   _____

5. How do people use the land in southern Europe's Central Uplands?

   _____

6. Where are most of Russia's industries located?

   _____

7. How is the Volga River linked to the Baltic Sea and other seas?

   _____

## B. Reviewing Key Terms

**Directions:** *Write the key terms for the following definitions in the blanks provided.*

8. the average number of people living in a square mile or a square kilometer
   _____

9. a land area nearly surrounded by water _____

10. a large raised area of mostly level land bordered on one or more sides by steep slopes or cliffs _____

11. a river or stream that flows into a larger river _____

12. wide and deep enough for ships to travel through _____

Section 1: Land and Water
Europe and Russia: Physical Geography

# Section Quiz

## A. Key Terms

**Directions:** *Read the statements below. If a statement is true, write T in the blank provided. If it is false, write F. Rewrite false statements on the back of this page to make them true.*

_____   1. A large raised area of mostly level land is a plateau.

_____   2. The average number of people living in an area is the population distribution.

_____   3. A peninsula is nearly surrounded by land.

_____   4. A river or stream that flows into a larger river is a tributary.

_____   5. A navigable river is one that is not usable for ship travel.

## B. Main Ideas

**Directions:** *Write the letter of the correct answer in each blank.*

_____   6. Why does Russia have a low population density?

    **a.** All the cities have small populations.

    **b.** The population of eastern Russia is very small.

    **c.** Few people can live in the western section of the country.

    **d.** There are too few natural resources to support a large population.

_____   7. Why have Western European countries become leaders in the shipping industry?

    **a.** Europe is on a peninsula in the Arctic Ocean.

    **b.** Europe is on a peninsula in the Atlantic Ocean.

    **c.** Europe is one of the world's largest continents.

    **d.** Europe is located on a large plateau near the Volga River.

_____   8. What is one important landform shared by Europe and western Russia?

    **a.** the Alpine Mountains

    **b.** the Ural Mountains

    **c.** the North European Plain

    **d.** the Central Uplands

_____   9. Only 20 percent of Russia's people live in Siberia because of

    **a.** the yearly floods.

    **b.** the lack of resources.

    **c.** the harsh climate.

    **d.** the high taxes.

_____   10. Which statement describes the Volga River in Russia?

    **a.** It is used as a trade route the entire year.

    **b.** It enables ships to travel to the Arctic Ocean.

    **c.** It enables ships to travel to the Atlantic Ocean.

    **d.** It is not navigable for part of the year because of ice.

Chapter and Section Support

Europe and Russia: Physical Geography
SECTION 2 Lesson Plan

# Climate and Vegetation

**Key**
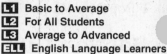
**L1** Basic to Average
**L2** For All Students
**L3** Average to Advanced
**ELL** English Language Learners

*2 periods, 1 block (includes Skills for Life)*

## Section Objectives

1. Find out about the wide range of climates in Europe and Russia.
2. Learn about the major climate regions of Europe and Russia.
3. Examine the natural vegetation regions of Europe and Russia.

## Vocabulary

• rain shadow • steppes • tundra • permafrost

## Local Standards

## Reading/Language Arts Objective

Make predictions about the text to help set a purpose for reading and remember what you have read.

### PREPARE TO READ

**Build Background Knowledge**
Have students compare the climates of Barcelona and Irkutsk to that of their own region.
**Set a Purpose for Reading**
Have students evaluate statements on the *Reading Readiness Guide*.
**Preview Key Terms**
Teach the section's Key Terms.
**Target Reading Skill**
Introduce the section's Target Reading Skill of **predicting**.

### Targeted Resources

❏ **All in One** **Europe and Russia Teaching Resources**
• Reading Readiness Guide, p. 111 **L2**
• Preview and Predict, p. 119 **L2**
❏ **Spanish Reading and Vocabulary Study Guide,** Section 2, pp. 9–10 **ELL** **L1**

### INSTRUCT

**A Wide Range of Climates**
Discuss how oceans and location affect the climates of Europe and Russia.
**Target Reading Skill**
Review **predicting**.
**Major Climate Regions**
Discuss the different climate regions in Europe and Russia.
**Natural Vegetation Regions**
Discuss different types of vegetation native to Europe and Russia.

### Targeted Resources

❏ **All in One** **Europe and Russia Teaching Resources**
• Guided Reading and Review, p. 112 **L2**
• Book Project, pp. 77–79 **L3**
❏ **Europe and Russia Transparencies,**
Section Reading Support Transparency ER 33 **L2**
❏ **Teacher's Edition**
• For Gifted and Talented, p. 22 **L3**
• For Less Proficient Readers, p. 22 **L1**

### ASSESS AND RETEACH

**Assess Progress**
Evaluate student comprehension with the section assessment and section quiz.
**Reteach**
Assign the Reading and Vocabulary Study Guide to help struggling students.
**Extend**
Extend the lesson by assigning an Enrichment activity.

### Targeted Resources

❏ **All in One** **Europe and Russia Teaching Resources**
• Section Quiz, p. 113 **L2**
• Enrichment, p. 122 **L3**
❏ **Reading and Vocabulary Study Guide,** Section 2, pp. 9–11 **L1**
❏ **Spanish Support,** Section Quiz, p. 7 **ELL** **L2**

Section 2: Climate and Vegetation
Europe and Russia: Physical Geography

# Reading Readiness Guide

## Anticipation Guide

How much do you think you know about the climates and vegetation in Europe and Russia? As your teacher reads the statements, mark whether you think each statement is true (T) or false (F) in the Me column. Then discuss your answers with your group and mark the group's decision in the Group column. As you read, look for information that will clarify whether the statements are true or false.

After you read the section, read the statements again and mark the After Reading column to indicate whether they are true or false.

| Before Reading | | Statements | After Reading |
|---|---|---|---|
| Me | Group | | |
| | | 1. Warm waters and winds bring mild weather to much of northwestern Europe. | |
| | | 2. Four climate regions are common to Europe and Russia. | |
| | | 3. The northernmost areas of Europe and Russia have a semiarid climate. | |
| | | 4. In the Mediterranean climate, summers are hot and dry, and winters are mild and rainy. | |
| | | 5. The natural vegetation for much of Europe is tundra. | |
| | | 6. Located in northern Europe, the largest forest in the world covers more than 4 million square miles. | |
| | | 7. The grasslands of Russia, called steppes, are similar to the Great Plains of the United States. | |

Section 2: Climate and Vegetation
Europe and Russia: Physical Geography

# Guided Reading and Review

## A. As You Read

**Directions:** *As you read Section 2, complete the following chart with information about climate and vegetation in Europe and Russia. Write supporting details for each main idea in the spaces below.*

| **Main Idea A**<br>Four examples of European or Russian climate regions and their locations are: |
| --- |
| 1. |
| 2. |
| 3. |
| 4. |

| **Main Idea B**<br>Four types of vegetation found in Europe or Russia and their locations are: |
| --- |
| 5. |
| 6. |
| 7. |
| 8. |

## B. Reviewing Key Terms

**Directions:** *Complete these sentences by writing the correct key terms in the blanks provided.*

9. An area on the dry, sheltered side of a mountain that receives little rain is called a _____.

10. Russian grasslands, or _____, have fertile soil for farming, and are similar to the Great Plains of the United States.

11. A cold, dry, treeless region that is covered with snow for most of the year is known as a(n) _____.

12. During the brief season when the top surface of the _____ thaws, grasses, mosses, and other plant life quickly grow.

Section 2: Climate and Vegetation
Europe and Russia: Physical Geography

# Section Quiz

## A. Key Terms

**Directions:** *Define each of the following key terms. Write your definitions on the back of this page.*

1. permafrost

2. tundra

3. rain shadow

4. steppes

## B. Main Ideas

**Directions:** *Write the letter of the correct answer in each blank.*

_____ 5. How does the North Atlantic Current affect weather in northwestern Europe?

    **a.** It carries warm water and cold winds.

    **b.** It carries warm water and warm winds.

    **c.** It carries cold water and cold winds.

    **d.** It carries cold water and snow and ice.

_____ 6. In Europe, areas to the west of mountains receive

    **a.** no rainfall.

    **b.** little rainfall.

    **c.** heavy snow.

    **d.** heavy rainfall.

_____ 7. In southern Europe, the climate is described as

    **a.** Mediterranean.

    **b.** cold.

    **c.** tropical.

    **d.** Arctic.

_____ 8. The natural vegetation for much of Europe is

    **a.** tundra.

    **b.** permafrost.

    **c.** forest.

    **d.** plains.

_____ 9. The largest forest in the world is called the

    **a.** tundra.

    **b.** steppe.

    **c.** taiga.

    **d.** pelmeny.

_____ 10. Much of the Russian steppes are used for

    **a.** mining.

    **b.** forestry.

    **c.** manufacturing.

    **d.** farming.

Chapter and Section Support

Europe and Russia: Physical Geography
SECTION 3 Lesson Plan

# Resources and Land Use

*3.5 periods, 1.75 blocks (includes Chapter Review and Assessment)*

## Section Objectives

1. Learn about the resources of Western Europe.
2. Find out about the natural resources of Eastern Europe.
3. Examine Russia's natural resources.

## Vocabulary

• loess • hydroelectric power • fossil fuel

## Local Standards

## Reading/Language Arts Objective

Preview and ask questions to help you remember important ideas in the section.

### PREPARE TO READ

**Build Background Knowledge**
Discuss the importance of soil, water, and fuel.
**Set a Purpose for Reading**
Have students evaluate statements on the *Reading Readiness Guide*.
**Preview Key Terms**
Teach the section's Key Terms.
**Target Reading Skill**
Introduce the section's Target Reading Skill of **previewing and asking questions**.

### Targeted Resources

❑ **All in One Europe and Russia Teaching Resources**
• Reading Readiness Guide, p. 115 **L2**
• Preview and Ask Questions, p. 120 **L2**
❑ **Spanish Reading and Vocabulary Study Guide,** Section 3, pp. 11–12, **ELL L1**

### INSTRUCT

**Resources of Western Europe**
Discuss natural resources and where they are found in Western Europe.
**Resources of Eastern Europe**
Discuss the benefits of having a variety of natural resources, and compare the resources of Eastern and Western Europe.
**Resources of Russia**
Discuss the challenge of collecting the natural resources of Russia.
**Target Reading Skill**
Review **previewing and asking questions**.

### Targeted Resources

❑ **All in One Europe and Russia Teaching Resources,** Guided Reading and Review, p. 116 **L2**
❑ **Europe and Russia Transparencies,** Section Reading Support Transparency ER 34 **L2**
❑ **Teacher's Edition**
• For Less Proficient Readers, p. 30 **L1**
• For Advanced Readers, p. 31 **L3**

### ASSESS AND RETEACH

**Assess Progress**
Evaluate student comprehension with the section assessment and section quiz.
**Reteach**
Assign the Reading and Vocabulary Study Guide to help struggling students.
**Extend**
Extend the lesson by assigning an Internet activity.

### Targeted Resources

❑ **All in One Europe and Russia Teaching Resources**
• Section Quiz, p. 117 **L2**
• Chapter Tests A and B, pp. 138–143 **L2**
❑ **Reading and Vocabulary Study Guide,** Section 3, pp. 12–14 **L1**
❑ **Spanish Support**
• Section Quiz, p. 9 **ELL L2**
• Chapter Summary, p. 10 **ELL L2**
• Vocabulary Development, p. 11 **ELL L2**

Section 3: Resources and Land Use
Europe and Russia: Physical Geography

# Reading Readiness Guide

## Anticipation Guide

How much do you think you know about the natural resources of Western and Eastern Europe and Russia? As your teacher reads the statements, mark whether you think each statement is true (T) or false (F) in the Me column. Then discuss your answers with your group and mark the group's decision in the Group column. As you read, look for information that will clarify whether the statements are true or false.

After you read the section, read the statements again and mark the After Reading column to indicate whether they are true or false.

| Before Reading: | | Statements | After Reading |
|---|---|---|---|
| Me | Group | | |
| | | 1. Western Europe has a rich supply of natural resources, including fertile soil, water, and fuels. | |
| | | 2. Water is used to create electric power in many countries in Western Europe. | |
| | | 3. An abundance of coal and iron gave Western European industries a head start in the 1800s, when industries grew rapidly. | |
| | | 4. The natural resources of Eastern Europe are very different from those of Western Europe. | |
| | | 5. Coal deposits are the most important resource in Ukraine, a large country in Eastern Europe. | |
| | | 6. Russia has a huge variety of natural resources, which they have used to become one of the richest countries. | |
| | | 7. Russia has the world's largest reserves of iron and the world's largest forest reserves. | |

Section 3: Resources and Land Use
Europe and Russia: Physical Geography

# Guided Reading and Review

## A. As You Read

**Directions:** *As you read Section 3, complete the following table with information about natural resources in Europe and Russia.*

## Natural Resources

| Western Europe | 1. |
| --- | --- |
| | 2. |
| | 3. |
| | 4. |
| Eastern Europe and Russia | 5. |
| | 6. |
| | 7. |
| | 8. |

## B. Reviewing Key Terms

**Directions:** *Write the definitions for the following key terms in the blanks provided.*

9. loess _____

10. hydroelectric power _____

11. fossil fuel _____

Section 3: Resources and Land Use
Europe and Russia: Physical Geography

# Section Quiz

## A. Key Terms

**Directions:** *Read the statements below. If a statement is true, write T in the blank provided. If it is false, write F. Rewrite false statements on the back of this page to make them true.*

_____ **1.** Loess is a type of poor, sandy soil.

_____ **2.** Fossil fuels are an energy source that developed from the remains of ancient plants and animals.

_____ **3.** Hydroelectric power is generated by windmills.

## B. Main Ideas

**Directions:** *Write the letter of the correct answer in each blank.*

_____ **4.** Europe's most important natural resources include fuels,

    **a.** water, and timber.    **c.** fertile soil, and water.

    **b.** solar energy, and manufactured goods.    **d.** agricultural products, and manufactured goods.

_____ **5.** Why has the Ruhr been one of Western Europe's most important industrial regions?

    **a.** It has access to Asia and Africa.    **c.** It has many shipping routes.

    **b.** It has fuel resources.    **d.** It has agricultural resources.

_____ **6.** Russia has not developed its natural resources to the degree that Western Europe has because of its

    **a.** annual flooding.    **c.** distance from the United States.

    **b.** harsh climate, huge size, and few navigable rivers.    **d.** huge size, warm climate, and location.

_____ **7.** How are oil and natural gas carried from Siberia to European Russia?

    **a.** by tanker ships    **c.** by tank trucks

    **b.** by railroads    **d.** by pipelines

_____ **8.** Some of the worst cases of pollution are found in

    **a.** France.    **c.** Russia.

    **b.** Germany.    **d.** Serbia.

Chapter and Section Support

Europe and Russia: Physical Geography

# Target Reading Skill: Using the Reading Process

## Preview and Set a Purpose

Previewing is a key part of the reading process. It is the first step you should take when you read a textbook. Begin reading your text by previewing the chapter and section titles. Then, preview the headings in the section. These help you pinpoint what you are going to be reading. Ask yourself how the section title and the headings are related. Next, look at the map titles, the photographs, and other illustrations. What do these tell you about the content?

Setting a purpose before you begin to read is another key part of the reading process. Whenever you read you set a purpose for your reading. When you read a novel, you are probably reading for pleasure. When you read the sports section of the newspaper, your purpose may be to learn which team won a game. The main purpose for reading a textbook is to learn about the subject you are studying. Textbooks are organized in a special way to help you learn. You need to read them in a special way to take advantage of the way they are set up.

Previewing the section of a textbook will raise questions that will help you set a purpose for your reading. Take note of the objectives listed for each section. The objectives will help you identify core content and also help you set a purpose for your reading.

**Directions:** *Examine this section of your text. Then, on a separate sheet of paper, answer the following questions.*

1. What is the chapter title?

2. What unites Americans as one people?

3. What are the headings within the section?

4. Are there maps in the section? If so, what are their titles?

5. Look at the chapter preview and the objectives listed at the beginning of the section. What questions do they raise in your mind? What information should you look for as you read to answer these questions? What information should you look for to address the objectives?

6. What is your purpose for reading this section?

7. What do you expect to learn?

# Target Reading Skill: Using the Reading Process

## Preview and Predict

Previewing and predicting content are essential parts of the reading process. As you begin to read each section of your textbook, making predictions about the content will help you set a purpose for reading. Making predictions will also help you stay actively engaged in your reading. Predicting will also help you remember what you have read.

Predicting is a way of applying what you are learning as you learn. You might predict how one fact, such as the climate in a region, might affect another fact, such as the types of crops grown in that area.

In order to predict what will be covered in the section, you should examine the section title, the objectives, and the headings in the section. Look at the maps, illustrations, and the photographs. They are clues that will help you predict what you will learn as you read the text. Predict the facts that you will learn as you read, and then check your predictions. Were you correct? Look for proof in the paragraphs.

**Directions:** *Examine this section of your textbook. Look at the section title, the headings, and the illustrations. Then, make predictions about what you will learn as you read. After you have made your predictions, read the section and revise your answers.*

1. Based on the objectives for the section, what do you expect to learn? Write your predictions on the lines below.

   _____

   _____

2. What headings in the section address the objectives for this section? List those headings on the lines below.

   _____

   _____

3. Choose two of the headings that you have listed. Predict what you will learn in those two parts of this section.

   _____

4. Read the two parts you selected. Were your predictions correct? If not, what steps can you take to make better predictions?

   _____

5. Do the maps, charts, and illustrations in the section support your predictions? If so, in what ways? If not, how might you change your predictions?

   _____

Europe and Russia: Physical Geography

# Target Reading Skill: Using the Reading Process

## Preview and Ask Questions

Previewing and then asking yourself questions before and as you read a section will help you set a purpose for reading. Before you read this section, preview the headings, the maps, and the illustrations to see what the section is about. What do you think are the most important concepts in this section?

**Directions:** *Examine the section, read the section objectives and the key terms. Look at the headings, the illustrations, and the maps that appear in the section. Then, ask yourself questions that you believe are central to the section. On the lines below, write the headings and subheadings that appear in the section. Then, write one question for each heading and subheading.*

*After you have written your questions, read the section. When you have finished, check to see if your question was answered. If it was, write the answer to your question. If your question was not answered, rephrase the question so it can be answered.*

**Section Title** _____

 **Main Heading:** _____

 **Your question:** _____

 Answer: _____


 **Subheading:** _____

 **Your question:** _____

 Answer: _____


 **Subheading:** _____

 **Your question:** _____

 Answer: _____

Name _____ Date _____ Class _____

Europe and Russia: Physical Geography

# Word Knowledge

**Directions:** *As your teacher reads the words, think about what each word might mean and mark the appropriate number in the Before Reading column.*

①= Know it   ②= Kind of know it   ③= Don't know it

After you have read and discussed the chapter, rate the words again in the After Reading column. Then write a definition or example for each word to help you clarify and remember the words.

| | Word | Rating | | Definition or Example |
|---|---|---|---|---|
| | | **Before Reading** | **After Reading** | |
| **Section 1** | landmass, *n.* | | | |
| | enable, *v.* | | | |
| | level, *adj.* | | | |
| | link, *v.* | | | |
| **Section 2** | dramatic, *adj.* | | | |
| | overlap, *v.* | | | |
| | brief, *adj.* | | | |
| **Section 3** | deposit, *v.* | | | |
| | nourish, *v.* | | | |
| | element, *n.* | | | |
| | transport, *v.* | | | |

Europe and Russia: Physical Geography

# Enrichment

## Acid Rain: A Threat to Europe's Remaining Forests

**Directions:** *Most of Europe's natural forests were cut down long ago. Now the remaining forests face a different threat: acid rain. Read the following passage. Then, choose one of the research activities to complete. Present your findings in a written, oral, or visual report.*

"The familiar fir-clad slopes of the Bavarian Alps may become a barren, treeless wilderness in as little as 15 years unless immediate action is taken to stop acid rain." That is the conclusion of a report by the German Alpine Society, which claims that "78 percent of the Alpine forest in Germany is dead or dying. . . ." Not only will the landscape change, the report concluded there will be avalanches in towns and villages built on mountainsides if the trees disappear. Ski resorts will be forced to close, and it will be impossible to drive on miles of mountain roads. People who work with the environment fear the politicians won't be able to solve the problem of acid rain. The report also stated, "[It is very discouraging that] young trees planted on the slopes disappear rapidly into the mouths of goats and deer, which are deprived of their normal food sources by the death of mature tree stands."

"Disaster," said one of the report's scientists, "is just around the corner."

From *National Review Magazine*, September 12, 1986. Copyright © 1986 by National Review, Inc. Reprinted by permission.

## Activities

- Research the causes of acid rain and its effects on forests and lakes throughout Europe.
- Investigate solutions to the problem of acid rain.
- Search the Internet and other sources for the latest information about the status of Germany's forests.

Name _____ Date _____ Class _____

Europe and Russia: Physical Geography

# Skills for Life

## Using a Precipitation Map

**Directions:** *Study the following precipitation map. Then, in the lines provided, write answers to the questions that follow.*

1. What does the map show? _____

2. What units of measurement for precipitation are shown in the key?

   _____

3. What is the average annual precipitation in Moscow?

   _____

4. Compare the average annual precipitation in Moscow with Vladivostok.

   _____

5. Identify two cities on the map that receive 10 to 19 inches of precipitation per year.

   _____

6. The largest area in Russia that receives less than 10 inches of rain per year is north, east, south, or west of Magadan?

   _____

Europe and Russia: Physical Geography

# Small Group Activity

## Europe and Russia Map and Climate Charts

Europe and Russia include a wide variety of climates. There are the Mediterranean regions of the south, where hot, dry summers alternate with rainy, mild winters. There are high alpine mountains, coastal marine areas, and tundra in the north. In this activity, your group will make a mural that shows the climates for four locations in Europe and Russia. You will use information and graphics from the text and other references as well.

### Background

You know from reading the text that there are many factors affecting the European and Russian climate. Much of Europe's climate is strongly influenced by the Atlantic Ocean and the Mediterranean Sea. Though most of Europe is farther north than the United States, warm ocean currents create a mild climate in many areas. Even some northern ports in Europe are free from ice in winter. East of the European Alps, there is much less rainfall than along the coast. The tall mountains catch moisture and create a dry side, known as a rain shadow. In the northernmost parts of Europe and Russia there are cold areas where the ground stays frozen all year. These places are not warmed by an ocean current, and they border the Arctic region. Other inland areas have both a long, cold winter and a very hot summer.

### Procedure

1. **Research information.** Read all the steps in this project. Then meet with your group to decide who will do each job. Begin by choosing the four locations you will study. Try choosing places that have different climates. Look in the text as well as atlases, almanacs, and encyclopedias for information. Find out about average temperature, precipitation, and snow levels. Explore factors that influence the climate in each place. They could include latitude, nearness to oceans, and elevation.

2. **Create a map.** When your group has gathered information, have some members create the map. If possible, use an overhead projector to sketch the outlines of Europe and Russia onto a large piece of paper. Or you can work together to copy another map. You don't have to include all country borders, but clearly mark and label each location you have chosen. Be sure to leave room on the map for climate charts.

Name _____ Date _____ Class _____

Europe and Russia: Physical Geography

## *Small Group Activity* (continued)

3. **Make the climate charts.** While some members are creating the map, others can be organizing and writing climate charts. These should include facts and information about the climate. Be sure all the information is clearly written and easy to understand. You can use the space below or another sheet of paper to sketch your charts.

Decide as a group how to use the charts. You might attach them to the edge of the map and connect them to a location with a line. You can also create illustrations of one or two scenes from each location. Illustrations can show what the climate is like at a certain time of year. For example, you could draw someone lying on a warm Italian beach in summer, or someone bundled up against the Arctic cold of a Siberian winter.

4. **Display your mural.** When your mural is done, display it in the classroom. Compare the different locations on each mural. Talk about how each group has chosen to present its information. Note the strong points about each mural and ways in which each one might be improved.

# Small Group Activity: Teacher Page

## Europe and Russia Maps and Climate Charts

### Content Objectives

- Students will learn about the climates of different locations in Europe and Russia.
- Students will gain a deeper understanding of the factors that influence European and Russian climates.

### Skill Objectives

- Writing for a purpose—explanation
- Locating information
- Organizing information

### Advance Preparation

Gather the following materials:

- large sheets of paper for maps
- pencils, markers, pens, paints, scissors, and glue

**Suggested group size:** six students

**Suggested time:** 40 minutes for researching information and beginning to plan the maps; 40 minutes for creating the maps and climate charts; 40 minutes for presenting and discussing the maps

### Procedure

Divide the class into groups. Distribute the student pages and have students begin research. You may wish to give a copy of the rubric for maps and climate charts to each group.

Students can begin by sharing the research. Once they have gathered information, they can divide the remaining work. Some students in each group can be preparing the climate charts while others can be working on the map. Students might enjoy painting or drawing a scene from each location that illustrates some aspect of the climate.

When students have finished their maps, discuss the maps with the class. You can use these questions to start discussion:

- What conclusions might you draw about the vegetation in each location you chose?
- What kinds of clothing might people wear in the winter? In the summer?
- Which location on your map has the climate that is most similar to where you live?
- How well would you say your group worked together?

# Small Group Activity: Teacher Page

Maps and climate charts will be evaluated according to the following rubric.

## Rubric for Maps and Climate Charts

| Grading Criteria | Excellent | Admirable | Acceptable |
|---|---|---|---|
| **Research** | Students locate a great deal of information about the climates in different locations; they learn the factors that influence climate in each place; they use many different sources. | Students locate a great deal of information about each location's climate. | Students locate some information about each location's climate. |
| **Making the Maps** | Maps are accurate, neatly drawn, and illustrated; they show country borders, major cities, and scenes that illustrate the climate. | Maps are accurate, neat, and easy to read. | Maps show the four locations in Europe and Russia. |
| **Making the Climate Charts** | Charts include accurate and interesting facts and information, including factors that influence climate; they are written neatly and are clearly related to the locations on the maps. | Charts are accurate and easy to read; they are clearly related to the locations on the maps. | Charts are fairly accurate; they contain basic climate information; some are hard to relate to a location on the maps. |
| **Teamwork** | Group members work well together; they help each other with research, drawing the map, and creating the chart. | Members of the group work well together on different parts of the project. | Some members work harder and show more enthusiasm than others. |

Europe and Russia: Physical Geography

# Activity Shop Lab

## Tracking the Midnight Sun

In Hammerfest, Norway, people who are outside in the middle of a December afternoon see a dark sky full of stars. In the summer, people who go to bed at midnight can see the sun shining through their windows.

All around the world, the length of daylight changes throughout the year. The amount of change in daylight is greatest in areas near the North or South Poles. Because Hammerfest is in the Arctic, near the North Pole, there is a huge difference in the number of light hours during winter and summer days.

### Purpose

The length of daylight changes as Earth makes its yearly orbit around the sun. Because of the tilt of Earth's axis, the Northern Hemisphere faces away from the sun during winter. It faces toward the sun during summer. In this activity, you will make a model that shows why Arctic Scandinavia and Russia have dark days in winter and midnight sun in summer.

### Materials

- unshaded lamp
- tangerine or orange
- masking tape
- marker
- pencil
- metric tape measure

### Procedure

### Step One

**Make a model of Earth.** Hold your tangerine or orange around its middle and push your pencil down through the fruit's core. The fruit represents Earth and the pencil represents Earth's axis, or the imaginary line around which Earth turns. The point where the pencil emerges represents the North Pole. With your marker, draw a line all the way around the fruit, midway between the two ends of the pencil. This circle represents the Equator. Next, measure the distance in centimeters between the "Equator" and the "North Pole." Then, use your marker to draw another circle around the fruit approximately seven ninths of the distance from the "Equator" to the "North Pole." This circle represents the 70° latitude. Areas north of the 70° latitude are considered Arctic areas. Make a dot just above this line to represent Hammerfest, Norway.

Europe and Russia: Physical Geography

Chapter and Section Support

**Step Two**

**Make a model of Earth's path around the sun.** Place the unshaded lamp on the floor. With the masking tape, mark a circle on the floor with the lamp at its center. This line represents Earth's orbit. Next, mark the tape at four points equally spaced around the orbit. Label the points "Arctic spring," "Arctic summer," "Arctic autumn," and "Arctic winter." Turn on the lamp.

**Step Three**

**Show what happens when it is summer in the Arctic.** Hold the fruit at the level of the lamp's lightbulb and place it above the spot on the floor labeled "Arctic summer." Make sure to tilt "Earth's'" axis correctly. Earth turns on its axis once every 24 hours, or once each day. Where Earth faces the sun, it is daytime. Where Earth faces away from the sun, it is night. Slowly turn "Earth" on its axis. Notice where the lamp's light hits the fruit. Notice what parts of the fruit are in shadow. Study the amount of light and shadow in the Arctic.

1. How much light does Hammerfest receive in summer? _____

**Step Four**

**Show what happens when it is winter in the Arctic.** Hold the fruit at the level of the lamp's lightbulb and place it above the spot on the floor labeled "Arctic winter." Line up the axis as before. Slowly turn the fruit on its axis. Study the amount of light and shadow that hits the Arctic.

2. How much light does Hammerfest receive in winter? Why?

_____

_____

**Directions:** *Use a separate sheet of paper to answer the following questions.*

**Observations**

3. In the Arctic, is the length of daylight more affected by Earth's rotation or the tilt of Earth's axis? Explain your answer.

4. During the summer, how much of the day is light in Hammerfest? How much is light during winter? Why?

**Analysis and Conclusion**

5. If Earth were not tilted on its axis, how do you think life in the Arctic would be different? Explain your answer.

6. Suppose Earth orbited around the sun, but never rotated on its axis. How much daylight would Hammerfest receive during the summer? Autumn? Winter? Spring? Explain your answer.

Europe and Russia: Physical Geography

# MapMaster Skills

## Reading a Natural Vegetation Map

A natural vegetation map tells you what plants grow naturally in places that have not been altered significantly by human activity. The map below shows the natural vegetation regions of the mainland United States.

**Directions:** *Study the map and the map key below. Then, answer the questions that follow. You may wish to consult an atlas.*

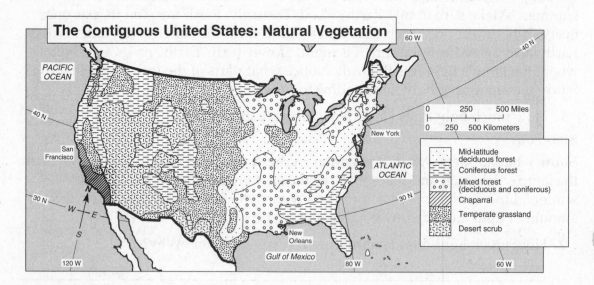

1. What is the natural vegetation of the area where you live?

   _____

2. What is the natural vegetation of the Great Plains?

   _____

3. If you were going to northern New England, what vegetation would you expect to find?

   _____

4. In the southern part of which state is chaparral the natural vegetation?

   _____

5. What kind of forest would you find in the Rocky Mountains?

   _____

6. What kinds of vegetation do the state of Washington and the state of Florida have in common?

   _____

Europe and Russia: Physical Geography

# Primary Sources and Literature Readings

## The Endless Steppe

by Esther Hautzig

**Esther Hautzig was born and spent her early years in Vilna, Poland. In 1939, the Soviet army, which was then fighting in World War II alongside the Germans, invaded Vilna. Esther and her family were exiled to Siberia, along with many others. Here, Esther describes the harsh lands to which they were sent.**

My first glimpse of Rubtsovsk was of a frontier village built around a large open square in straight lines, as if the muddy paths were laid out for ticktacktoe. Immediately surrounding the square were the market stalls, open wooden sheds. These were empty that day. Once again the loud-speaker crackled with authority; this time we were ordered to arrange ourselves in family groups in the square and await further instructions. Since families had clung to each other, this was done with dispatch.

The square was even hotter than the road, the sun being reflected from its cobblestones of all sizes and shapes. I stepped closer to my mother.

The flatness of this land was awesome. There wasn't a hill in sight; it was an enormous, unrippled sea of parched and lifeless grass.

"Tata, why is the earth so flat here?"

"These must be steppes, Esther."

"Steppes? But steppes are in Siberia."

"This is Siberia," he said quietly.

If I had been told that I had been transported to the moon, I could not have been more stunned.

"Siberia?" My voice trembled. "But Siberia is full of snow."

"It will be," my father said.

Siberia! Siberia was the end of the world, a point of no return. Siberia was for criminals and political enemies, where the punishment was unbelievably cruel, and where people died like flies. Summer or no summer—and who had ever talked about hot Siberia?—Siberia was the tundra and mountainous drifts of snow. Siberia was *wolves*.

I had been careless. I had neglected to pray to God to save us from a gypsum mine in Siberia.

From *The Endless Steppe,* by Esther Hautzig. Copyright © 1968 by Esther Hautzig, published by HarperKeypoint, an imprint of HarperCollins Publishers.

## Primary Sources and Literature Readings (continued)

**Vocabulary Builder**

| | |
|---|---|
| Tata | Papa or Father |
| steppes | flat, treeless plains |
| tundra | far northern lands, treeless and with permanently frozen subsoil |
| gypsum | a mineral used in making plaster |

### Think It Over

1. What might it feel like to live in a place with no trees or hills?

   _____

   _____

   _____

   _____

2. Why was Esther so surprised to find it was hot in Siberia?

   _____

   _____

   _____

   _____

Europe and Russia: Physical Geography

# Writing Skills

## Doing Searches on the Internet

Research on the Internet can provide information that may not be available anywhere else. Some information found on the Internet, however, may not be accurate and reliable. You may need to use several sources to verify your information. Information provided by professional businesses and organizations is generally more reliable than that provided by individuals.

**Directions:** *Read about World Wide Web search methods below. Then, use a computer with Internet access to complete the activities.*

**URL.** URL stands for Uniform Resource Locator, which is the "address" of a site on the Web. You can recognize the address (usually found at the top of your screen as "location") as a string of characters beginning with *http://* and ending with the specific characters that lead to that site. The easiest way to reach a site is to type in a known URL. For example, the URL *http://www.nasa.gov* will lead you directly to the NASA Space Center's Web site.

**Search Engines.** Very often, you don't know the URL that will lead you to the information you need. When this happens, you need to use a "search engine." A search engine is a database on the Web that organizes Web sites according to key words in their files or titles. Some already have categories from which you can choose. In others, you simply enter key words relating to your topics and allow the engine to do the searching for you. This will generate a list of file names from which you can choose. Yahoo! at *http://www.yahoo.com* and Lycos at *http://www.lycos.com* are two examples of search engines.

**Links.** Once you have found a site relating to your topic, through either its URL or a search engine, it may offer further information through the use of a link. Links are words in a Web document that are often underlined or highlighted in some other way. Choosing a particular link may lead you to another Web site offering more information on the same topic.

1. Once you are connected to the Internet, type in the URL for the Yahoo! search engine. Scroll down to the Web site directory. How many categories of links does the menu display?

2. Choose the link for "Regional." When you have connected to this link, choose the link for "Countries." Pick a foreign country, then click on its link. How many links are displayed for that country? Give two examples. Does the country's Web site have categories for its links, such as business or events?

3. Choose one of the links within that country's Web site. What is the purpose of the Web site you have chosen? Toward whom does it seem to be directed?

Europe and Russia: Physical Geography

# Writing Skills

## Preparing for Presentations

You've done your research, and you've prepared an outline and a report. Now, you have to present your findings to the class. The keys to making effective presentations are planning and practice. The better prepared you are ahead of time, the more likely your presentation will go smoothly.

**Directions:** *Study the tips below for preparing and presenting a report. Then, complete the activities that follow.*

- Organize your main facts and ideas on note cards, using just a few words that will remind you at a glance of what you want to say.

- Prepare a brief, lively introduction that will catch your listeners' attention and give them a framework for listening to your report.

- Prepare a conclusion that rounds off your speech nicely. As with a written report, sum up your ideas in brief, interesting sentences that will help your listeners remember your main points.

- You may want to prepare a graphic to reinforce an important or complicated point. Be sure it can be seen from the back of the room.

- Practice your report at home in front of a mirror. Speak slowly and clearly. Remember that you know your material well, but the audience will hear it for the first time. Vary your tone of voice. Use appropriate hand and facial expressions.

- On the day of your presentation, relax. Refer to your notes to keep your talk flowing smoothly, but do *not* read your cards to the class. Strive to maintain eye contact with your audience. Speak clearly and confidently.

- When you have finished, offer to answer questions.

To prepare you for giving your own oral report, remember times when you have been in the audience yourself. Then, complete the activity that follows on a separate sheet of paper.

1. Think of a time when you listened intently to every word a speaker was saying. List some of the reasons you were interested in the speaker's presentation.

2. Think of a time when a speaker nearly lulled you to sleep. List some reasons you lost interest in the presentation.

   **Challenge:** Practice your speaking skills at home. Select a passage from your textbook, a newspaper, or a magazine. Read it aloud in front of a mirror. Pay special attention to speaking slowly and clearly and to giving meaning to the words with your voice. Also, watch your eye contact, facial expressions, and body language. Try to see and hear yourself as others will.

Name _____ Date _____ Class _____

Europe and Russia: Physical Geography

# Vocabulary Development

**Directions:** *Match the key terms in the box with the definitions below. Write the correct letter in each blank. Then, write a sentence in the space provided using that term or the plural form of the term. If necessary, look up the terms in your textbook glossary.*

| | |
|---|---|
| **a.** population density | **g.** tundra |
| **b.** peninsula | **h.** permafrost |
| **c.** plateau | **i.** steppes |
| **d.** tributary | **j.** loess |
| **e.** navigable | **k.** hydroelectric power |
| **f.** rain shadow | **l.** fossil fuel |

_____ 1. a type of rich, dust-like soil

_____

_____ 2. wide and deep enough for ships to travel through

_____

_____ 3. the average number of people living in a square mile or square kilometer

_____

_____ 4. a source of energy that forms from the remains of ancient plants and animals

_____

_____ 5. the grasslands of fertile soil suitable for farming in Russia

_____

_____ 6. a river or stream that flows into a larger river

_____

_____ 7. the power generated by water-driven turbines

_____

_____ 8. a large raised area of mostly level land bordered on one or more sides by steep slopes or cliffs

_____

_____ 9. a permanently frozen layer of ground below the top layer of soil

_____

_____ 10. the area on the dry, sheltered side of a mountain that receives little rainfall

_____

_____ 11. a land area nearly surrounded by water

_____

_____ 12. a cold, dry, treeless region covered with snow for most of the year

_____

# Rubric for Assessing a Journal Entry

| Grading Criteria | Excellent | Acceptable | Minimal | Unacceptable |
|---|---|---|---|---|
| **Content** | Response to assigned topic thorough and well written, with varied sentence structure and vocabulary; opinions always supported with facts. | Response thoughtful and fairly well written; most opinions supported with facts. | Response adequately addresses some aspects of the assigned topic; opinions sometimes based on incorrect information. | Response consists of unsupported opinions only marginally related to topic. |
| **Idea Development** | Excellent use of examples and details to explore and develop ideas and opinions. | Good reliance upon examples and details to illustrate and develop ideas and opinions. | Incomplete development of ideas; details and examples not always relevant. | Ideas not clearly stated or developed. |
| **Organization** | Very logically organized; contains introduction, development of main idea (or ideas), and conclusion. | Contains introduction, some development of ideas, and conclusion. | Topics and ideas discussed somewhat randomly; entry may lack clearly defined introduction or conclusion. | Entry is unstructured. |
| **Mechanics** | Flawless spelling and punctuation. | Few or no spelling errors; some minor punctuation mistakes. | Several spelling and punctuation errors. | Many instances of incorrect spelling and punctuation. |

# Rubric for Assessing a Writing Assignment

| Grading Criteria | Excellent | Acceptable | Minimal | Unacceptable |
|---|---|---|---|---|
| Content | Clearly focused introduction; idea development interesting and sophisticated; supporting evidence detailed, accurate, and convincing; perceptive conclusion. | Introduction gives assignment direction; idea development clear; supporting evidence accurate; strong conclusion. | Introduction unclear; idea development uneven and simplistic; supporting evidence uneven; conclusion summarizes information in assignment. | Introduction incomplete, ineffective; idea development ineffective; supporting evidence vague, inaccurate, or missing; conclusion incomplete or missing. |
| Organization | Paragraph order reinforces content; strong topic sentences make content easy to follow; effective and varied transitions. | Logical paragraph order; clear topic sentences; clear and functional transitions. | Ineffective paragraph order; narrow or inaccurate topic sentences; few clear transitions. | Inconsistent paragraph order; topic sentences and transitions missing. |
| Mechanics | Flawless punctuation and spelling; varied and interesting sentence structure. | Few spelling and punctuation errors; sentence structure correct. | Some careless spelling and punctuation errors; some errors in sentence structure. | Many spelling and punctuation errors; many sentence fragments and run-ons. |

Europe and Russia: Physical Geography

# Test A

## A. Key Terms

**Directions:** *Fill in the blanks in Column I by writing the letter of the correct term from Column II. You will not use all the terms. (15 points)*

**Column I**

_____ 1. A _____ is a river or stream that flows into a larger river.

_____ 2. When a river is blocked by ice, it is not _____, or clear enough for ships to travel.

_____ 3. A treeless plain where grasses and mosses grow is a _____.

_____ 4. A permanently frozen layer of ground below the top layer of soil is known as _____.

_____ 5. In Europe, winds have deposited a type of rich, dust-like soil known as _____.

**Column II**

a. hydroelectric power

b. loess

c. navigable

d. peninsula

e. permafrost

f. population density

g. rain shadow

h. tributary

i. tundra

## B. Key Concepts

**Directions:** *Write the letter of the correct answer in each blank. (45 points)*

_____ 6. How do the population densities of Europe and Russia compare?

a. Europe's population density is greater than most of the world's, and Russia's is lower.

b. Europe and Russia have very low population densities.

c. Russia's population density is greater than most of the world's, and Europe's is lower.

d. Europe and Russia have very high population densities.

Europe and Russia: Physical Geography

## Test A *(continued)*

_____ 7. Western Europe's peninsulas and bays have enabled the countries there to become leaders in

    **a.** culture.

    **b.** manufacturing.

    **c.** the mining industry.

    **d.** the shipping industry.

_____ 8. More than half of Europe is covered by a landform called the

    **a.** Central Uplands.

    **b.** Alpine Mountain System.

    **c.** North European Plain.

    **d.** Northwestern Highlands.

_____ 9. How does Siberia's harsh climate affect life in that region?

    **a.** Few people live there.

    **b.** Many people live there.

    **c.** It is a major transportation center.

    **d.** Many major cities are located there.

_____ 10. The North Atlantic Current affects northwestern Europe by

    **a.** carrying cold water and ice.

    **b.** bringing stormy weather and snow.

    **c.** bringing warm water and winds.

    **d.** carrying snow and ice.

_____ 11. Areas of Europe that are west of the mountains receive

    **a.** no rainfall.

    **b.** little sunlight.

    **c.** heavy rainfall.

    **d.** mostly clouds.

_____ 12. The three great vegetation regions of Russia are

    **a.** the rain forests, the prairies, and the grasslands.

    **b.** the tundra, the forests, and the grasslands.

    **c.** the tundra, the prairies, and the grasslands.

    **d.** the plateaus, the prairies, and the grasslands.

_____ 13. What are Europe's most important natural resources?

    **a.** oil, natural gas, and coal

    **b.** fertile soil, water, and fuels

    **c.** forests, natural gas, and coal

    **d.** minerals, fossil fuels, and solar energy

_____ 14. Because of Russia's size, harsh climate, and few rivers suitable for travel, the country has not developed its

    **a.** cultural resources.

    **b.** scientific resources.

    **c.** natural resources.

    **d.** communications resources.

Name _____ Date _____ Class _____

Europe and Russia: Physical Geography

**Test A** (*continued*)

## C. Critical Thinking

**Directions:** *Answer the following questions on the back of this paper or on a separate sheet of paper. (20 points)*

15. **Making Comparisons**  Compare how location and climate affect the shipping industry in both Europe and Russia. In your answer, consider the bodies of water located near each area.

16. **Recognizing Cause and Effect**  How has Russia's climate affected the population and economy of the country?

## D. Skill: Using a Precipitation Map

**Directions:** *Use the precipitation map below to answer the following questions. Write your answers in the blanks provided. (20 points)*

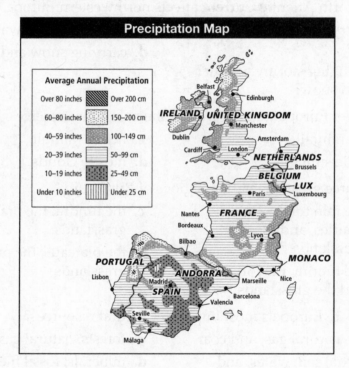

17. In general what does the map show? _____

18. Which areas have average rainfall of over 60 inches per year?

_____

19. Does Spain or the United Kingdom have the least rainfall overall?

_____

20. What do the cities of Paris, London, and Seville have in common?

_____

# Test B

## A. Key Terms

**Directions:** *Match the definitions in Column I with the terms in Column II. Write the correct letter in each blank. You will not use all the terms. (15 points)*

**Column I**

_____ 1. a body of land nearly surrounded by water

_____ 2. a large, raised area of mostly level land

_____ 3. an area on the dry, sheltered side of a mountain that receives little rainfall

_____ 4. Russian grasslands

_____ 5. an energy source developed from the remains of ancient plants and animals

**Column II**

a. fossil fuel

b. hydroelectric power

c. navigable

d. peninsula

e. permafrost

f. plateau

g. rain shadow

h. steppes

i. tributary

## B. Key Concepts

**Directions:** *Write the letter of the correct answer in each blank. (45 points)*

_____ 6. Which statement best compares the size of Europe with Russia?

    a. They are approximately the same size.

    b. Europe is a small continent and Russia is the largest country in the world.

    c. Both Europe and Russia are large continents.

    d. Russia is a medium-sized continent and Europe is a small country.

_____ 7. Which landform is shared by both Europe and Russia?

    a. the Alpine Mountain System

    b. the Central Uplands

    c. the North European Plain

    d. the West Siberian Plain

_____ 8. Two important rivers on the continent of Europe are

    a. the Ural and the Rhine.

    b. the Siberian and the Volga.

    c. the Volga and the Rhine.

    d. the Nile and the Volga.

## Test B (continued)

_____ 9. Northwestern Europe receives warm water from the Gulf of Mexico that is carried by the
    **a.** Pacific Ocean.
    **c.** South Atlantic Current.
    **b.** North Atlantic Current.
    **d.** Volga River.

_____ 10. In Europe, the areas west of mountains receive
    **a.** little sunlight.
    **c.** heavy rainfall.
    **b.** heavy winds.
    **d.** little rainfall.

_____ 11. The three great vegetation zones of Russia are
    **a.** the plains, the prairies, and the plateaus.
    **c.** the grasslands, the deserts, and the forests.
    **b.** the forests, the grasslands, and the marshes.
    **d.** the tundra, the forests, and the grasslands.

_____ 12. The most important natural resources of Western Europe are
    **a.** water, timber, and solar energy.
    **c.** fossil fuels, hydroelectric power, and solar energy.
    **b.** fertile soil, water, and fuels.
    **d.** coal, oil, and gas.

_____ 13. Why is most of Russia's industry west of the Ural Mountains?
    **a.** The natural resources cannot be mined in western Russia.
    **c.** The country's fossil fuels are on the continent of Asia.
    **b.** The Siberian rivers flow toward Russia's important cities.
    **d.** The country's reserves of iron ore are in the part of Russia that is on the continent of Europe.

_____ 14. How do Russia's harsh climate, size, and few navigable rivers affect its economic development?
    **a.** Russia is the richest nation on Earth.
    **c.** Russia can easily transport manufactured goods to Asia.
    **b.** Russia's natural resources are difficult to use.
    **d.** The land in Ukraine is hard to farm.

Europe and Russia: Physical Geography

**Test B** *(continued)*

## C. Critical Thinking

**Directions:** *Answer the following questions on the back of this paper or on a separate sheet of paper. (20 points)*

15. **Drawing Conclusions**  Think about the location of bodies of water surrounding Europe and Russia. How do you think the location affected trade between Europe and Russia and the rest of the world throughout history?

16. **Making Comparisons**  How do you think the climate and landforms of Europe and Russia have affected each area's population density?

## D. Skill: Using a Precipitation Map

**Directions:** *Use the precipitation map below to answer the following questions. Write your answers in the blanks provided. (20 points)*

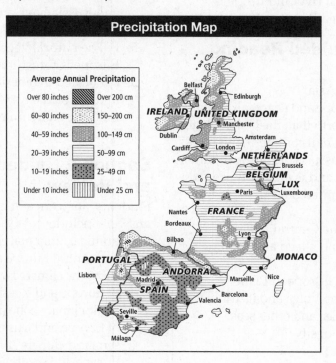

17. What is a precipitation map?

   _____

18. How many precipitation regions does Ireland have?  _____

19. What is the average rainfall per year for Madrid?

   _____

20. What does Belfast have in common with Cardiff and Manchester?

   _____

# Answer Key

## Section 1 Reading Readiness Guide

Students' answers will vary. Correct answers are:

1. T
2. F, Europe is a small continent with 47 different countries.
3. T
4. F, There are no physical barriers between Russia and the countries of Europe, so movement between these two regions has always been easy.
5. T
6. T
7. F, The longest river in Europe is Russia's Volga River.

## Section 1 Guided Reading and Review

1. Europe and Asia
2. Much of Europe and nearly all of Russia are farther north than the United States.
3. Europe is a small continent, but has 47 countries. Russia is the largest country in the world and is almost twice the size of the United States.
4. a peninsula
5. People use the Central Uplands to raise goats and sheep and to mine for minerals.
6. in the North European Plain
7. Canals link the Volga and its tributaries to the Baltic Sea and other seas.
8. population density
9. peninsula
10. plateau
11. tributary
12. navigable

## Section 1 Quiz

1. T
2. F, The average number of people living in an area is the population density.
3. F, A peninsula is nearly surrounded by water.
4. T

5. F, A navigable river is one that is usable for ship travel.
6. b
7. b
8. c
9. c
10. d

## Section 2 Reading Readiness Guide

Students' answers will vary. Correct answers are:

1. T
2. T
3. F, The northernmost areas of Europe and Russia have an arctic climate.
4. T
5. F, The natural vegetation for much of Europe is forest.
6. F, Located in Siberia, the largest forest in the world covers more than 4 million square miles.
7. T

## Section 2 Guided Reading and Review

Students' answers will vary for 1-8. Correct answers include:

1. humid continental climate zone (eastern and central Europe and western Russia)
2. subarctic climate zone (northern areas of Europe and Russia)
3. arctic climate zone (northernmost areas of Europe and Russia)
4. semiarid climate zone (southeastern Europe and southwestern Russia)
5. forests (northern Europe, Russia, and across Siberia)
6. grasslands (Northern European Plain and southwestern Russia)
7. tundra (northern parts of Europe and Russia)
8. Mediterranean (southern Europe)
9. rain shadow
10. steppes
11. tundra
12. permafrost

Europe and Russia: Physical Geography

## Answer Key (continued)

### Section 2 Quiz

1. a permanently frozen layer of ground below the top layer of soil
2. a cold, dry, treeless region covered with snow for more than half of the year
3. the area on the dry, sheltered side of a mountain that receives little rainfall
4. the grasslands of fertile soil suitable for farming in Russia
5. b
6. d
7. a
8. c
9. c
10. d

### Section 3 Reading Readiness Guide

Students' answers will vary. Correct answers are:
1. T
2. T
3. T
4. F, Eastern and Western Europe have similar resources.
5. F, Very fertile soil is the most important resource in Ukraine, a large country in Eastern Europe.
6. F, Russia has a huge variety of natural resources, but Russia's harsh climate, huge size, and few navigable rivers have made it difficult to turn the country's resources into wealth.
7. T

### Section 3 Guided Reading and Review

Students' answers will vary. Correct answers are:
1. fertile soil
2. water
3. fuels (coal, natural gas, oil)
4. hydroelectric power
5. fuels (coal, natural gas, oil)
6. fertile soil
7. iron ore
8. forest reserves

9. a type of rich, dust-like soil
10. the power generated by water-driven turbines
11. a source of energy that forms from the remains of ancient plants and animals

### Section 3 Quiz

1. F, Loess is a rich, dust-like soil.
2. T
3. F, Hydroelectric power is generated by water-driven turbines.
4. c
5. b
6. b
7. d
8. c

### Target Reading Skill

**Preview and Set a Purpose**
Answers will vary.

**Preview and Predict**
Answers will vary.

**Preview and Ask Questions**
Answers will vary.

### Word Knowledge

Definitions and/or examples will vary.

### Enrichment

Students' activities and reports will vary.

### Skills for Life

1. The map shows the average annual precipitation in Russia.
2. The key shows precipitation measurements in both inches and centimeters.
3. 20-39 inches (50-99 cm)
4. Moscow and Vladivostok receive similar amounts of precipitation each year.
5. Irkutsk, Magadan, Novosibirsk, Omsk, Rostov, Ufa, and Ulan-Ude all receive between 10 and 19 inches of precipitation per year.
6. west

## Answer Key (continued)

### Activity Shop Lab

1. It stays light all the time.
2. None. It is in darkness 24 hours a day. Hammerfest is in darkness because the northern part of Earth is tilted away from the sun, which prevents light from striking the Arctic region.
3. The tilt of Earth's axis. This is because in summer the Arctic is tilted toward the sun, exposing it to light 24 hours a day, and in winter it is tilted away from the sun. The rotation has far less effect on the amount of light that is received in the Arctic.
4. 24 hours; none; because the tilt of Earth affects the amount of light that is received in Hammerfest
5. Answers may vary. The Arctic would receive the same amount of light throughout the year and would have neither midnight sun nor total winter darkness. People would be far less affected by the changes of the seasons.
6. It would depend on whether Europe and Russia were facing toward or away from the sun. If they were facing away, they would never see the sun. If they were facing toward, they would always see the sun. There would be no night and day. Since the tilt of Earth would be the same, in summer the sun would be much stronger and in winter the sun would not strike the Arctic region.

### MapMaster Skills: Reading a Natural Vegetation Map

1. Answers will vary.
2. temperate grassland
3. coniferous forest
4. California
5. coniferous
6. Both have coniferous forests.

### Primary Sources and Literature Readings: The Endless Steppe

1. Answers will vary. Accept all reasonable answers.
2. Esther was surprised because the common view of Siberia is that it is icy, cold, and covered with snow.

### Writing Skills

**Doing Searches on the Internet**
Students' answers will vary.

**Preparing for Presentations**
Students' answers will vary.

### Vocabulary Development

1. j
2. e
3. a
4. l
5. i
6. d
7. k
8. c
9. h
10. f
11. b
12. g

Students' sentences will vary.

### Test A

| 1. h | 2. c | 3. i | 4. e | 5. b |
|------|------|------|------|------|
| 6. a | 7. d | 8. c | 9. a | 10. c |
| 11. c | 12. b | 13. b | 14. c | |

## Answer Key (continued)

15. Answers will vary. A possible answer: The continent of Europe juts out into the Atlantic Ocean. In addition, many smaller peninsulas provide bays and good harbors. The climate is milder in Europe than it is in Russia because Europe receives the benefit of the North Atlantic Current. Mild weather and good harbors have enabled Western European countries to become world leaders in the shipping industry. Russia lies on the Arctic Ocean. Because of the cold climate there, the water is frozen for most of the year and cannot be used for shipping.

16. Answers will vary. A possible answer: Although Siberia makes up 75 percent of Russian territory, only 20 percent of the people live there. This is because of the area's harsh climate. More people live in the western part of Russia because the climate is milder. There is also more industry in the western part, even though Siberia has many natural resources. The country's harsh climate has made it difficult to develop the natural resources to the east of the Ural Mountains.

17. average annual precipitation in the countries shown

18. northern part of Portugal, northwestern corner of Spain, several areas on the western coast of Ireland, areas in the northern tip of the United Kingdom, and a few small areas west of Lyon, France and on the border between France and Spain

19. Spain

20. precipitation regions which average 20–39 inches of rainfall per year

## Test B

| 1. d | 2. f | 3. g | 4. h | 5. a |
| 6. b | 7. c | 8. c | 9. b | 10. c |
| 11. d | 12. b | 13. d | 14. b | |

15. Answers will vary. A possible answer: Europe is a peninsula with many smaller peninsulas and bays that jut into the Atlantic Ocean. Because of the mild climate and good harbors, it was probably easy for Europeans to trade with other areas of the world by developing shipping routes. However, Russia lies on the Arctic Ocean, which is frozen for most of the year and can't be used for shipping. As a result, trade between Russia and the countries of Europe and Asia occurred via overland routes.

16. Answers will vary. A possible answer: Europe has a milder climate than Russia and its soil is fertile. Also, its location on a peninsula with many bays and harbors has provided easy access to other parts of the world, and its rivers can transport goods to and from many regions, allowing settlement there. As a result, Europe has a higher population density than most of the world. However, a region known as Siberia in eastern Russia makes up about 75 percent of Russian territory. Because of Siberia's poor soil and cold climate, only 20 percent of Russia's people live there. As a result, Russia has a lower population density than Europe.

17. A precipitation map shows the total amount of precipitation an area receives in a year.

18. three

19. 10–19 inches of rain per year

20. approximately 40–59 average inches of precipitation a year

Europe and Russia: Shaped by History
SECTION 1 Lesson Plan

# From Ancient Greece to the Middle Ages

*1 period, .5 block*

## Section Objectives

1. Learn how the heritage of ancient Greece influences life today.
2. Discover the glory of the ancient Roman Empire.
3. Learn about Europe in the Middle Ages.

## Vocabulary

• Middle Ages • democracy • city-state
• feudalism

## Local Standards

## Reading/Language Arts Objective

Reread to look for connections among words and sentences.

## PREPARE TO READ

**Build Background Knowledge**
Discuss how Greek and Roman cultures have influenced modern culture.
**Set a Purpose for Reading**
Have students evaluate statements on the *Reading Readiness Guide.*
**Preview Key Terms**
Teach the section's Key Terms.
**Target Reading Skill**
Introduce the section's Target Reading Skill of **rereading**.

## Targeted Resources

❏ **All in One Europe and Russia Teaching Resources**
• Reading Readiness Guide, p. 150 **L2**
• Reread or Read Ahead, p. 169 **L2**
❏ **Spanish Reading and Vocabulary Study Guide,** Section 1, pp. 14–15 **ELL L1**

## INSTRUCT

**The Greek Heritage**
Discuss ancient Greek influence on modern culture.
**The Glory of Ancient Rome**
Discuss the Roman Empire and its demise.
**Target Reading Skill**
Review **rereading**.
**Europe in the Middle Ages**
Discuss the changes that occurred during the Middle Ages.

## Targeted Resources

❏ **All in One Europe and Russia Teaching Resources,** Guided Reading and Review, p. 151 **L2**
❏ **Europe and Russia Transparencies,** Section Reading Support Transparency ER 35 **L2**
❏ **Teacher's Edition**
• For Advanced Readers, p. 40 **L3**
• For English Language Learners, p. 42 **L1**
❏ **Spanish Support,** Guided Reading and Review, p. 12 **ELL L2**

## ASSESS AND RETEACH

**Assess Progress**
Evaluate student comprehension with the section assessment and section quiz.
**Reteach**
Assign the Reading and Vocabulary Study Guide to help struggling students.
**Extend**
Assign a Small Group Activity.

## Targeted Resources

❏ **All in One Europe and Russia Teaching Resources**
• Section Quiz, p. 152 **L2**
• Small Group Activity, pp. 175–178 **L3**
❏ **Reading and Vocabulary Study Guide,** Section 1, pp. 16–18 **L1**
❏ **Spanish Support,** Section Quiz, p. 13 **ELL L2**

Section 1: From Ancient Greece to the Middle Ages
Europe and Russia: Shaped by History

# Reading Readiness Guide

## Anticipation Guide

How much do you think you know about ancient Greece and Rome, and about the Middle Ages in Europe? As your teacher reads the statements, mark whether you think each statement is true (T) or false (F) in the Me column. Then discuss your answers with your group and mark the group's decision in the Group column. As you read, look for information that will clarify whether the statements are true or false.

After you read the section, read the statements again and mark the After Reading column to indicate whether they are true or false.

| Before Reading | | Statements | After Reading |
|---|---|---|---|
| **Me** | **Group** | | |
| | | 1. The ancient Romans were Europe's first great philosophers, historians, poets, and writers. | |
| | | 2. In ancient times, Greece had more than a hundred city-states—cities with their own governments that were both cities and independent states. | |
| | | 3. During the "Golden Age" of Athens, democracy reached its highest point and the arts flourished. | |
| | | 4. One of ancient Rome's greatest gifts to the world was a system of written laws that protected all citizens. | |
| | | 5. Christianity became so strong in the Roman Empire that Constantine, a Roman emperor, outlawed the spread of Christianity and banned its practice. | |
| | | 6. The collapse of the Roman Empire in western Europe led to a time of security, order, and peace. | |
| | | 7. To bring about order, people in western Europe organized their societies with a political system called feudalism, where people had obligations based on their position in society. | |

Section 1: From Ancient Greece to the Middle Ages
Europe and Russia: Shaped by History

# Guided Reading and Review

## A. As You Read

**Directions:** *As you read Section 1, fill in the following chart with information about ancient Greece, ancient Rome, and Europe in the Middle Ages. Write two facts for each category.*

| Ancient Greece | |
|---|---|
| The growth of democracy and city-states | 1. |
| | 2. |
| **Ancient Rome** | |
| Pax Romana and Roman law | 3. |
| | 4. |
| **Europe in the Middle Ages** | |
| Feudalism | 5. |
| | 6. |

## B. Reviewing Key Terms

**Directions:** *Write the definitions for the following key terms in the blanks provided.*

7. Middle Ages

   _____

8. democracy

   _____

9. city-state

   _____

10. feudalism

    _____

Section 1: From Ancient Greece to the Middle Ages
Europe and Russia: Shaped by History

# Section Quiz

## A. Key Terms

**Directions:** *Read the statements below. If a statement is true, write T in the blank provided. If it is false, write F. Rewrite false statements on the back of this page to make them true.*

_____ **1.** The economic system called manorialism provided a basis for democracy.

_____ **2.** A Greek republic was both a city and an independent nation.

_____ **3.** The time between ancient and modern times is called the Middle Ages.

_____ **4.** A kind of government that citizens run themselves is called a dictatorship.

## B. Main Ideas

**Directions:** *Write the letter of the correct answer in each blank.*

_____ **5.** One important ancient Greek idea was a form of government called

    **a.** aristocracy.        **c.** absolute monarchy.

    **b.** dictatorship.        **d.** democracy.

_____ **6.** How did Alexander the Great help to spread Greek ideas?

    **a.** by conquest        **c.** by opening trade routes

    **b.** by exploration        **d.** by establishing schools

_____ **7.** An important contribution made by the ancient Romans to the modern world was

    **a.** the English language.        **c.** the spread of Islam.

    **b.** a system of written laws.        **d.** the idea of city-states.

_____ **8.** The Pax Romana was the period

    **a.** between the death of Alexander the Great and the building of the Roman Empire.

    **b.** between the fall of the Roman Empire and modern times.

    **c.** that began when the first Roman emperor took power and lasted 200 years.

    **d.** during which the Roman Empire was divided into two empires.

_____ **9.** After the collapse of the Roman Empire, European society was organized under a system called

    **a.** democracy.        **c.** feudalism.

    **b.** socialism.        **d.** communism.

_____ **10.** Under the feudal system, the people who farmed the land were

    **a.** landowners.        **c.** slaves.

    **b.** vassals.        **d.** serfs.

Europe and Russia: Shaped by History
SECTION 2 Lesson Plan

**Key**
**L1** Basic to Average
**L2** For All Students
**L3** Average to Advanced
**ELL** English Language Learners

# Renaissance and the Age of Revolution

🕐 *1 period, .5 block*

## Section Objectives
1. Discover what the Renaissance was like.
2. Examine the effects of increased trade and stronger rulers in the Renaissance.
3. Learn about revolutions in government and science in the 1600s and 1700s.

## Vocabulary
• Renaissance • monarch • revolution • colony

## Local Standards

## Reading/Language Arts Objective
Paraphrase to restate what you have read in your own words.

## PREPARE TO READ

**Build Background Knowledge**
Discuss how the invention of the printing press has influenced people's lives.

**Set a Purpose for Reading**
Have students evaluate statements on the *Reading Readiness Guide.*

**Preview Key Terms**
Teach the section's Key Terms.

**Target Reading Skill**
Introduce the section's Target Reading Skill of **paraphrasing**.

## Targeted Resources
❑ **All in One Europe and Russia Teaching Resources**
  • Reading Readiness Guide, p. 154 **L2**
  • Paraphrase, p. 170 **L2**
❑ **Spanish Reading and Vocabulary Study Guide,** Section 2, pp. 16–17 **ELL L1**

## INSTRUCT

**Glories of the Renaissance**
Discuss cultural and ideological changes that occurred during the Renaissance.

**More Trade, Stronger Rulers**
Discuss how overseas trade affected Europe.

**Target Reading Skill**
Review **paraphrasing**.

**Revolutions in Government**
Discuss the American and French Revolutions.

**Revolutions in Science**
Discuss the Scientific Revolution.

## Targeted Resources
❑ **All in One Europe and Russia Teaching Resources**
  • Guided Reading and Review, p. 155 **L2**
  • Enrichment, p. 173 **L3**
❑ **Europe and Russia Transparencies,** Section Reading Support Transparency ER 36 **L2**
❑ **Teacher's Edition**
  • For Less Proficient Readers, p. 47 **L1**
  • For Gifted and Talented, p. 47 **L3**
❑ **Spanish Support,** Guided Reading and Review, p. 14 **ELL L2**

## ASSESS AND RETEACH

**Assess Progress**
Evaluate student comprehension with the section assessment and section quiz.

**Reteach**
Assign the Reading and Vocabulary Study Guide to help struggling students.

**Extend**
Assign a literature reading.

## Targeted Resources
❑ **All in One Europe and Russia Teaching Resources,** Section Quiz, p. 156 **L2**
❑ **Reading and Vocabulary Study Guide,** Section 2, pp. 19–21 **L1**
❑ **Spanish Support,** Section Quiz, p. 15 **ELL L2**

Name _____ Date _____ Class _____

Section 2: Renaissance and the Age of Revolution
Europe and Russia: Shaped by History

# Reading Readiness Guide

## K–W–L

With your group, quickly preview this section, then brainstorm and list **what you already Know** about the Renaissance and revolutions in government and science in the first column of the chart below. In the second column, write what you **Want to know** or find out from reading the section.

After you read, review your notes and record **what you Learned** in the third column of the chart.

| What you already know | What you want to know | What you learned |
| --- | --- | --- |
| Example:<br>The Renaissance was a period of rebirth in learning and art. | Example:<br>Where and when did the Renaissance begin? | Example:<br>The Renaissance began in Italy in the 1300s and spread over the European continent. The Renaissance reached its peak in the 1500s. |
| | | |

Section 2: Renaissance and the Age of Revolution
Europe and Russia: Shaped by History

# Guided Reading and Review

## A. As You Read

**Directions:** *As you read Section 2, complete the following chart with information about Europe during the Renaissance and the Age of Revolution. Write supporting details for each main idea on the lines below.*

| Main Idea A |
| --- |
| Glories of the Renaissance |
| 1. |
| 2. |
| 3. |
| 4. |

| Main Idea B |
| --- |
| Revolutions in government and science |
| 5. |
| 6. |
| 7. |
| 8. |

## B. Reviewing Key Terms

**Directions:** *Write the key terms for the following definitions in the blanks provided.*

9. a period of European history that included the rebirth of interest in learning and art

_____

10. the ruler of a kingdom or empire, such as a king or queen

_____

11. a far-reaching change

_____

12. a territory ruled by another nation

_____

Section 2: Renaissance and the Age of Revolution
Europe and Russia: Shaped by History

# Section Quiz

## A. Key Terms

**Directions:** *Read the statements below. If a statement is true, write T in the blank provided. If it is false, write F. Rewrite false statements on the back of this page to make them true.*

_____ **1.** A far-reaching change is called a revolution.

_____ **2.** A monarch is the ruler of a kingdom or empire.

_____ **3.** The period when there was a rebirth of interest in learning and art is called the Reformation.

_____ **4.** A colony is a territory that rules itself.

## B. Main Ideas

**Directions:** *Write the letter of the correct answer in each blank.*

_____ **5.** Renaissance thinkers took a new approach to knowledge called
  **a.** mysticism.
  **b.** scholasticism.
  **c.** humanism.
  **d.** deism.

_____ **6.** European countries began exploring other lands because the rulers wanted
  **a.** more wealth.
  **b.** buyers for their goods.
  **c.** the support of the feudal lords.
  **d.** the support of the poor citizens.

_____ **7.** What was one result of exploration?
  **a.** Local lords became stronger.
  **b.** A middle class developed.
  **c.** Feudalism spread.
  **d.** Kings and queens lost power.

_____ **8.** France's Louis XIV was considered an absolute monarch because he had
  **a.** little power over his subjects.
  **b.** as much power as the nobles.
  **c.** total power over his subjects.
  **d.** as much power as the serfs.

_____ **9.** How did government in Europe change during the Age of Revolution?
  **a.** People paid higher taxes than they ever had before.
  **b.** Kings built strong armies.
  **c.** People questioned the power of their kings.
  **d.** Monarchs had more power.

_____ **10.** During the Scientific Revolution, scientists tested new ideas by using the
  **a.** humanistic method.
  **b.** scientific method.
  **c.** Renaissance ideal.
  **d.** Pax Romana.

Europe and Russia: Shaped by History
SECTION 3 Lesson Plan

**Key**

L1 **Basic to Average**
L2 **For All Students**
L3 **Average to Advanced**
ELL **English Language Learners**

# Industrial Revolution and Nationalism

⏱ *2 periods, 1.5 blocks (includes Skills for Life)*

## Section Objectives

1. Learn how the Industrial Revolution changed peoples' lives.
2. Examine how nationalism and war can be related.

## Vocabulary

• Industrial Revolution • textile • imperialism
• nationalism • alliance

## Local Standards

## Reading/Language Arts Objective

Summarize to help you better understand the text.

## PREPARE TO READ

**Build Background Knowledge**
Discuss ways that countries show nationalism.
**Set a Purpose for Reading**
Have students evaluate statements on the
*Reading Readiness Guide*.
**Preview Key Terms**
Teach the section's Key Terms.
**Target Reading Skill**
Introduce the section's Target Reading Skill of
**summarizing**.

## Targeted Resources

❑ **All in One Europe and Russia Teaching Resources**
• Reading Readiness Guide, p. 158 L2
• Summarize, p. 171 L2
❑ **Spanish Reading and Vocabulary Study Guide,** Section 3, pp. 18–19 ELL L1

## INSTRUCT

**The Industrial Revolution**
Discuss changes in Europe during and after the Industrial Revolution.
**Eyewitness Technology**
Discuss a textile mill.
**Target Reading Skill**
Review **summarizing**.
**A Century of War and Nationalism**
Discuss nationalism and World War I and II.

## Targeted Resources

❑ **All in One Europe and Russia Teaching Resources,** Guided Reading and Review, p. 159 L2
❑ **Europe and Russia Transparencies,** Section Reading Support Transparency ER 37 L2
❑ **Teacher's Edition**
• For English Language Learners, p. 57 L1
• For Special Needs Students, p. 58 L1
❑ **Spanish Support,** Guided Reading and Review, p. 16 ELL L2

## ASSESS AND RETEACH

**Assess Progress**
Evaluate student comprehension with the section assessment and section quiz.
**Reteach**
Assign the Reading and Vocabulary Study Guide to help struggling students.
**Extend**
Extend the lesson by assigning an Internet activity.

## Targeted Resources

❑ **All in One Europe and Russia Teaching Resources,** Section Quiz, p. 160 L2
❑ **Reading and Vocabulary Study Guide,** Section 3, pp. 22–24 L1
❑ **Spanish Support,** Section Quiz, p. 17 ELL L2

Section 3: Industrial Revolution and Nationalism
Europe and Russia: Shaped by History

# Reading Readiness Guide

## Anticipation Guide

How much do you think you know about the Industrial Revolution and the century of nationalism and war that followed? As your teacher reads the statements, mark whether you think each statement is true (T) or false (F) in the Me column. Then discuss your answers with your group and mark the group's decision in the Group column. As you read, look for information that will clarify whether the statements are true or false.

After you read the section, read the statements again and mark the After Reading column to indicate whether they are true or false.

| Before Reading | | Statements | After Reading |
|---|---|---|---|
| Me | Group | | |
| | | 1. The Industrial Revolution was a life-changing period when goods went from being made by hand to being made by machines in factories. | |
| | | 2. The first machines were invented in the United States to speed up the weaving of cloth products. | |
| | | 3. Machines were housed in large factories, and this new factory system brought about new inventions in machinery, transportation, and communication. | |
| | | 4. During the Industrial Revolution, cities grew rapidly and people lived in new, clean urban housing. | |
| | | 5. Unclean and crowded conditions in cities led to the rapid spread of diseases. | |
| | | 6. The late 1800s are called the Age of Imperialism, when European countries colonized much of Africa and parts of Asia. | |
| | | 7. Between 1900 and 1950, the force of nationalism played a part in preventing two world wars. | |

Section 3: Industrial Revolution and Nationalism
Europe and Russia: Shaped by History

# Guided Reading and Review

## A. As You Read

**Directions:** *As you read Section 3, answer the following questions in the spaces provided.*

1. How did the Industrial Revolution change the way goods were made?

   _____

2. What was the purpose of the first machines invented in Great Britain?

   _____

3. How did inventions bring about improvements in agriculture?

   _____

4. In what conditions did factory workers live and work?

   _____

   _____

5. Why did European governments become more aggressive abroad and want to establish more colonies?

   _____

   _____

6. Why are the late 1800s called the Age of Imperialism?

   _____

7. Which countries made up the Allies during World War II?

   _____

## B. Reviewing Key Terms

**Directions:** *Complete the sentences by writing the correct key terms in the blanks provided.*

8. Before the _____, people made what they needed, or bought it from a craftsperson or at a store for a high price.

9. A cloth product, such as woven cotton, is called a _____.

10. Beginning in the 1600s, many European nations followed the policy of _____, or taking over other countries and turning them into colonies.

11. The force of _____ helped cause World War I and World War II.

12. To protect themselves during World War I, nations made a(n) _____ with one another.

Section 3: Industrial Revolution and Nationalism
Europe and Russia: Shaped by History

# Section Quiz

## A. Key Terms

**Directions:** *Read the statements below. If a statement is true, write T in the blank. If it is false, write F. Rewrite false statements on the back of this page to make them true.*

_____ **1.** A textile is a cloth product.

_____ **2.** Nationalism is pride in one's country.

_____ **3.** The political and economic control over one country by another is called socialism.

_____ **4.** An alliance is an agreement between nations to protect one another.

_____ **5.** The period when products began to be made by machines in factories is called the Mechanical Revolution.

## B. Main Ideas

**Directions:** *Write the letter of the correct answer in each blank.*

_____ **6.** What was one way the Industrial Revolution changed life in Europe?

    **a.** People moved to small towns.

    **b.** People moved from cities to farms.

    **c.** People moved to large industrial centers to work in factories.

    **d.** People produced goods in their homes.

_____ **7.** As factory workers became more important to the nations' economies, European countries became

    **a.** less democratic.

    **b.** more revolutionary.

    **c.** more democratic.

    **d.** less imperialistic.

_____ **8.** European nations colonized other countries because they wanted

    **a.** markets and raw materials.

    **b.** more agricultural workers.

    **c.** more jobs for their citizens.

    **d.** higher wages for their workers.

_____ **9.** In 1914, fighting between two groups of countries started

    **a.** World War II.

    **b.** the Industrial Revolution.

    **c.** the Spanish-American War.

    **d.** World War I.

_____ **10.** The effort by countries to build a common European community is an example of

    **a.** destructive nationalism.

    **b.** imperialism.

    **c.** creative nationalism.

    **d.** monarchy.

Europe and Russia: Shaped by History
SECTION 4 Lesson Plan

**Key**
**L1** Basic to Average
**L2** For All Students
**L3** Average to Advanced
**ELL** English Language Learners

# Imperial Russia to the Soviet Union

🕐 *1 period, .5 block*

## Section Objectives
1. Discover how Russia built its empire.
2. Understand the fall of the Russian tsars.
3. Examine the rise and fall of the Soviet Union.
4. Learn the causes and effects of the Cold War.
5. Learn about the Russian Federation today.

## Vocabulary
• westernization • tsar • revolutionary
• communism

## Local Standards

## Reading/Language Arts Objective
Read ahead to help clarify an unfamiliar word or passage.

## PREPARE TO READ

**Build Background Knowledge**
Ask students to generate a list of words that describe Catherine the Great.
**Set a Purpose for Reading**
Have students evaluate statements on the *Reading Readiness Guide.*
**Preview Key Terms**
Teach the section's Key Terms.
**Target Reading Skill**
Introduce the section's Target Reading Skill of **reading ahead.**

### Targeted Resources
❑ **All in One Europe and Russia Teaching Resources**
• Reading Readiness Guide, p. 162 **L2**
• Reread or Read Ahead, p. 169 **L2**
❑ **Spanish Reading and Vocabulary Study Guide,** Section 4, pp. 20–21 **ELL L1**

## INSTRUCT

**Building a Vast Empire**
Discuss the Russian Empire.
**The Fall of the Tsars**
Discuss challenges Russia faced in the 1900s.
**Target Reading Skill**
Review **reading ahead.**
**The Rise and Fall of the Soviet Union**
Ask about Lenin, Stalin, and World War II.
**The Cold War**
Discuss the Cold War.
**The Russian Federation**
Discuss challenges of the Russian Federation.

### Targeted Resources
❑ **All in One Europe and Russia Teaching Resources,** Guided Reading and Review, p. 163 **L2**
❑ **Europe and Russia Transparencies,** Section Reading Support Transparency ER 38 **L2**
❑ **Teacher's Edition**
• For Advanced Readers, p. 65 **L3**
• For Less Proficient Readers, pp. 66, 67 **L1**
❑ **Spanish Support,** Guided Reading and Review, p. 18 **ELL L2**

## ASSESS AND RETEACH

**Assess Progress**
Evaluate student comprehension with the section assessment and section quiz.
**Reteach**
Assign the Reading and Vocabulary Study Guide to help struggling students.
**Extend**
Assign a literature reading.

### Targeted Resources
❑ **All in One Europe and Russia Teaching Resources,** Section Quiz, p. 164 **L2**
❑ **Reading and Vocabulary Study Guide,** Section 4, pp. 25–27 **L1**
❑ **Spanish Support,** Section Quiz, p. 19 **ELL L2**

Section 4: Imperial Russia to the Soviet Union
Europe and Russia: Shaped by History

# Reading Readiness Guide

## Anticipation Guide

How much do you think you know about Russian history—from its development as an empire in the Middle Ages to the formation of the Russian Federation today? As your teacher reads the statements, mark whether you think each statement is true (T) or false (F) in the Me column. Then discuss your answers with your group and mark the group's decision in the Group column. As you read, look for information that will clarify whether the statements are true or false.

After you read the section, read the statements again and mark the After Reading column to indicate whether they are true or false.

| Before Reading | | Statements | After Reading |
|---|---|---|---|
| Me | Group | | |
| | | 1. During the 1330s, Moscow was ruled by a prince who became one of the strongest rulers in the region. | |
| | | 2. In the 1540s, Ivan IV earned the name Ivan the Great for his fairness and generosity. | |
| | | 3. The Romanovs continued expanding Russian territory throughout the 1600s; they ruled Russia for more than 300 years. | |
| | | 4. Peter the Great brought Western European ideas and culture to Russia. | |
| | | 5. The idea of communism—sharing property and resources equally—appealed to many Russians, who had suffered terrible hardships under the tsars. | |
| | | 6. After World War II, the Cold War was a time of cooperation between the United States and the Soviet Union, which lasted from 1945 to 1991. | |
| | | 7. After the breakup of the Soviet Union, Russia changed its name to the Russian Federation, and made efforts to rebuild the communist-style economy. | |

Section 4: Imperial Russia to the Soviet Union
Europe and Russia: Shaped by History

# Guided Reading and Review

## A. As You Read

**Directions:** *As you read Section 4, complete the following table with information about Russian history. Write two details for each category.*

**Important Events in Russian History**

| 1200s–1300s | 1. |
| | 2. |
| 1400s–1500s | 3. |
| | 4. |
| 1600s–1700s | 5. |
| | 6. |
| 1800s | 7. |
| | 8. |
| 1900s before World War II | 9. |
| | 10. |
| 1900s after World War II | 11. |
| | 12. |

## B. Reviewing Key Terms

**Directions:** *Write the definitions for the following key terms in the blanks provided.*

**13.** westernization

_____

**14.** tsar

_____

**15.** revolutionary

_____

**16.** communism

_____

Section 4: Imperial Russia to the Soviet Union
Europe and Russia: Shaped by History

# Section Quiz

## A. Key Terms

**Directions:** *Read the statements below. If a statement is true, write T in the blank provided. If it is false, write F. Rewrite false statements on the back of this page to make them true.*

_____ 1. A Russian emperor is called a king.

_____ 2. When a country becomes more like Western Europe, it undergoes a process called westernization.

_____ 3. Soviets believed in capitalism, a theory that states a country's property and resources should be equally shared.

_____ 4. An idea that could cause the overthrow of a government is considered to be conservative.

## B. Main Ideas

**Directions:** *Write the letter of the correct answer in each blank.*

_____ 5. After the mass killing known as Bloody Sunday, Nicholas II was forced to
    **a.** leave Russia and live in Paris.
    **b.** free the serfs.
    **c.** disband the army.
    **d.** share his power with the Duma.

_____ 6. What was one result of the Russian Revolution?
    **a.** The Germans conquered Russia.
    **b.** The tsar gave up his throne.
    **c.** Russia entered World War I.
    **d.** People faced food and fuel shortages.

_____ 7. Why did many Russian people welcome communism?
    **a.** The merchants believed trade with the West would result.
    **b.** A new tsar would be appointed.
    **c.** The poor believed they would have a better standard of living.
    **d.** The nobles believed they could continue to live in luxury.

_____ 8. At the end of 1991, many of the former Soviet republics became
    **a.** part of a new western alliance.
    **b.** part of a new Soviet Union.
    **c.** independent nations.
    **d.** communist states.

Europe and Russia: Shaped by History
SECTION 5 Lesson Plan

**Key**

**L1** Basic to Average
**L2** For All Students
**L3** Average to Advanced
**ELL** English Language Learners

# The European Union

◄€► *4 periods, 2 blocks (includes Chapter Review and Assessment)*

## Section Objectives

**1.** Learn about the history of the EU.
**2.** Understand the purpose of the EU.
**3.** Examine the structure of the EU.
**4.** Find out what the future holds for the EU.

## Vocabulary

• euro • single market • foreign minister

## Local Standards

## Reading/Language Arts Objective

Reread or read ahead to help understand words and ideas in the text.

### PREPARE TO READ

**Build Background Knowledge**
Discuss the word *union*.
**Set a Purpose for Reading**
Have students evaluate statements on the *Reading Readiness Guide*.
**Preview Key Terms**
Teach the section's Key Terms.
**Target Reading Skill**
Introduce the section's Target Reading Skill of **rereading or reading ahead**.

### Targeted Resources

❏ **All in One Europe and Russia Teaching Resources**
  • Reading Readiness Guide, p. 166 **L2**
  • Reread or Read Ahead, p. 169 **L2**
❏ **Spanish Reading and Vocabulary Study Guide,** Section 5, pp. 22–23 **ELL** **L1**

### INSTRUCT

**History of the European Union**
Discuss the history of the European Union.
**What Does the European Union Do?**
Discuss goals and policies of the EU.
**Structure of the European Union**
Discuss the institutions responsible for making policy.
**Target Reading Skill**
Review **rereading or reading ahead**.
**Future of the European Union**
Ask questions about nations joining the European Union in the future.

### Targeted Resources

❏ **All in One Europe and Russia Teaching Resources,** Guided Reading and Review, p. 167 **L2**
❏ **Europe and Russia Transparencies,** Section Reading Support Transparency ER 39 **L2**
❏ **Teacher's Edition**
  • For Advanced Readers, p. 71 **L3**
  • For Special Needs Students, p. 72 **L1**
❏ **Spanish Support,** Guided Reading and Review, p. 20 **ELL** **L2**

### ASSESS AND RETEACH

**Assess Progress**
Evaluate student comprehension with the section assessment and section quiz.
**Reteach**
Assign the Reading and Vocabulary Study Guide to help struggling students.
**Extend**
Extend the lesson by assigning a map activity.

### Targeted Resources

❏ **All in One Europe and Russia Teaching Resources**
  • Section Quiz, p. 168 **L2**
  • Chapter Tests A and B, pp. 203–208, **ELL** **L2**
❏ **Reading and Vocabulary Study Guide,** Section 5, pp. 28–30 **L1**
❏ **Spanish Support**
  • Section Quiz, p. 21 **ELL** **L2**
  • Vocabulary Development, p. 23 **ELL** **L2**

# Reading Readiness Guide

## Anticipation Guide

How much do you think you know about the European Union? As your teacher reads the statements, mark whether you think each statement is true (T) or false (F) in the Me column. Then discuss your answers with your group and mark the group's decision in the Group column. As you read, look for information that will clarify whether the statements are true or false.

After you read the section, read the statements again and mark the After Reading column to indicate whether they are true or false.

| Before Reading | | Statements | After Reading |
|---|---|---|---|
| Me | Group | | |
| | | 1. The European Union began with a small group of six nations—Belgium, France, Italy, Luxembourg, the Netherlands, and West Germany. | |
| | | 2. The Maastricht Treaty established the European Union. | |
| | | 3. The Maastricht Treaty laid out a plan for the member nations to continue using their own money. | |
| | | 4. The currency of the European Union is called the *uno*. | |
| | | 5. Like the United States, the European Union is a federation of states. | |
| | | 6. Nations that belong to the European Union can trade freely with one another without having to pay taxes on international trade. | |
| | | 7. The majority of the European Union laws are passed by the European Parliament. | |

Section 5: The European Union
Europe and Russia: Shaped by History

# Guided Reading and Review

## A. As You Read

**Directions:** *As you read Section 5, answer the following questions in the spaces provided.*

1. Why did Robert Schuman, a French government official, propose a new organization called the European Coal and Steel Community?

   _____

   _____

2. What is the ECSC called today? How many countries belong?

   _____

3. What plan did the Maastricht Treaty make for the European Union's currency?

   _____

4. Which three nations in the EU did not adopt the euro?

   _____

5. What was the goal of the European Union when it was created?

   _____

   _____

6. What policy supports the EU's view that citizens of all member nations are equal?

   _____

7. What are the three main policy-making institutions of the European Union?

   _____

   _____

## B. Reviewing Key Terms

**Directions:** *Complete these sentences by writing the key terms in the blanks provided.*

8. By 2001, twelve countries had adopted the _____, which is the currency of the European Union.

9. The European Union has a _____, which means goods, services, and capital move freely without barriers.

10. A _____ is a government official who is in charge of a nation's foreign affairs, or relations with other nations.

Section 5: The European Union
Europe and Russia: Shaped by History

# Section Quiz

## A. Key Terms

**Directions:** *Define each of the key terms. Write your definitions on the back of this page.*

1. euro

2. single market

3. foreign minister

## B. Main Ideas

**Directions:** *Write the letter of the correct answer in each blank.*

_____ 4. The European Union had its origins in

    **a.** the Union of Soviet Socialist Republics.

    **b.** the United Nations.

    **c.** the European Coal and Steel Community.

    **d.** the French Community and the British Commonwealth.

_____ 5. What document did the members of the European Economic Community sign to create the European Union?

    **a.** the U.N. charter

    **b.** the Treaty of Versailles

    **c.** the Maastricht Treaty

    **d.** the North American Free Trade Agreement

_____ 6. What kind of money is used by most member nations of the European Union?

    **a.** the U.S. dollar

    **b.** the euro

    **c.** the British pound

    **d.** the Japanese yen

_____ 7. What documents do citizens of one EU nation need to travel and work in another EU nation?

    **a.** a visa

    **b.** a work permit

    **c.** a passport

    **d.** none of the above

_____ 8. The European Union is working to create

    **a.** major urban centers.

    **b.** stronger borders.

    **c.** a tariff-free region.

    **d.** a single country.

_____ 9. Which of the following does the European Union *not* handle?

    **a.** national defense policies

    **b.** policies on fighting crime

    **c.** policies on the environment

    **d.** policies on education

_____ 10. Which EU institution meets and debates in public?

    **a.** the European Summit

    **b.** the Council of the European Union

    **c.** the European Parliament

    **d.** all of the above

Europe and Russia: Shaped by History

# Target Reading Skill: Clarifying Meaning

## Reread or Read Ahead

Sometimes there may be something in your text that you do not understand. A sentence may have words you do not recognize. The main ideas may be difficult to grasp. When this happens, rereading can help. Rereading means to read something again. When you reread a sentence that has new words, you may see that clues to the definition are in the sentence. As you reread the sentence, ask yourself questions. What is the subject of each sentence? What action is taking place? Separating out these parts will help focus your rereading.

If you do not understand the main idea in a paragraph, reread the paragraph. Look for the details. If the details do not seem related to the main idea, look for connecting words or phrases that can help you understand the main idea.

Reading ahead is another tool you can use to help you understand. Sometimes a word is defined after its first use in a text. The main idea may be discussed, defined, and clarified in the following paragraphs. For example, you might read about a particular event in history, and the material under the next heading may give you more information about the event. Read ahead. Look at the next heading and subheadings in the section. They often provide clues to help you understand the information.

**Directions:** *Examine a section of your textbook that you just read. Then answer the following questions on a seperate sheet of paper.*

1. Were there any sentences that you did not understand? If so, write two of them.

2. Reread the sentences. What clues do you find that help you understand them better?

3. If there were no clues in the sentences, reread the paragraphs in which these sentences appear. What clues do you find in the paragraphs to help you understand?

4. Find a main heading in a section that has one or more subheadings below it. In your text, subheadings appear in bold blue type at the beginnings of paragraphs. Read the first paragraph under the main heading. Then, read ahead and preview the subheadings. Are there any subheadings that relate to the first paragraph? If so, read the information under the subheadings. What more did you learn about the information in the first paragraph? Did reading ahead help you understand the material?

Europe and Russia: Shaped by History

# Target Reading Skill: Clarifying Meaning

## Paraphrase

To paraphrase means to put something into your own words. After you read the material under one heading in a section, stop reading. Take a moment to paraphrase what you have just read. Putting what you have read into your own words is a very useful reading tool. It will help you clarify meaning. It will show you whether or not you understood what you read. Paraphrasing will also help you remember what you have read.

Paraphrasing does not mean writing a summary. It means saying or writing the information in your own words. If you cannot put what you have just read into your own words, you need to stop and reread the material. Try again to put it into your own words. Read the paragraph below:

> Scientists believe that over 200 million years ago, dinosaurs easily walked from Africa to South America. This is because Africa and South America were connected. About 190 million years ago, forces within our planet caused South America and Africa to move apart.

A sample paraphrase for this paragraph might be: "Scientists think dinosaurs moved from Africa to South America 200 million years ago when the two continents were connected. Then, 190 million years ago, South America and Africa were forced apart.

**Directions:** *Read a section of your text. Put what you have read into your own words. Begin with the main headings.*

1. Write each of the Reading Checks that appear in the section on the lines below. Next to each Reading Check question, write a question that paraphrases the Reading Check.

   _____

   _____

   _____

   _____

2. Choose two parts of this section that are of interest to you. In thirty words or less, paraphrase these two parts on the back of this page. When you have finished your paraphrases, read them over and use them to help you better understand the text.

Europe and Russia: Shaped by History

# Target Reading Skill: Clarifying Meaning

## Summarize

To summarize means to write a short statement of the main points of a section of the text. Summarizing is a tool that can help you clarify and remember what you have read. Writing a summary will also help you organize the concepts that you are learning.

When you summarize a section, you restate its main points. Because the summary is shorter than the text you are reading, you leave out the less important details. You must keep the main ideas or facts in the correct order. Using the headings and subheadings in the section will help you do this.

A summary, however, is not a paraphrase. A paraphrase is a simple restatement of ideas. A summary states the important ideas and details in the order presented in the text.

Read the following paragraph:

In 1903, the United States wanted to build a canal across the Isthmus of Panama, in the nation of Colombia. A canal would benefit American trade and the American navy. When Colombia refused permission to build a canal, President Theodore Roosevelt backed a revolt by the people of Panama. Once Panama was independent, it allowed the United States to build the Panama Canal.

A summary might read as follows:

In 1903, the United States wanted to build the Panama Canal to benefit trade and the navy. Colombia, which owned the land, refused, and the United States backed a Panamanian revolt. When Panama gained independence, the United States built the canal.

**Directions:** *Read this section of your textbook. Choose two main headings and write them on a separate sheet of paper. Then, on the same sheet of paper answer the following questions. Underneath each heading, write a brief summary of the material in that part.*

1. What key facts did you include in your summary?

2. How long is your summary compared to the text?

3. If individual people are listed in the section, which individuals did you include in your summary?

4. If particular dates are listed in the section, which dates did you include in your summary? Why did you select these?

Europe and Russia: Shaped by History

# Word Knowledge

**Directions:** *As your teacher reads the words, think about what each word might mean and mark the appropriate number in the Before Reading column.*

①= Know it    ②= Kind of know it    ③= Don't know it

After you have read and discussed the chapter, rate the words again in the After Reading column. Then write a definition or example for each word to help you clarify and remember the words.

| | Word | Rating | | Definition or Example |
| --- | --- | --- | --- | --- |
| | | **Before Reading** | **After Reading** | |
| **Section 1** | process, *n.* | | | |
| | rely, *v.* | | | |
| | collapse, *n.* | | | |
| **Section 2** | focus, *v.* | | | |
| | radical, *adj.* | | | |
| **Section 3** | policy, *n.* | | | |
| | invade, *v.* | | | |
| | generation, *n.* | | | |
| **Section 4** | reign, *n.* | | | |
| | reform, *n.* | | | |
| | withdraw, *v.* | | | |
| **Section 5** | legal, *adj.* | | | |
| | debate, *v.* | | | |

Europe and Russia: Shaped by History

# Enrichment

## Leonardo da Vinci: A Renaissance Man

**Directions:** *Read the following paragraphs about Leonardo da Vinci. Then, research one of the topics below, and prepare an oral or written report.*

Leonardo da Vinci ranks as one of the greatest painters of the Italian Renaissance. Two of his paintings were among the most famous in history—*Mona Lisa* and *The Last Supper*. The *Mona Lisa* is a portrait of a young woman, Lisa del Giocondo. The painting is famous for the mysterious smile on Lisa's face. The *Last Supper* portrays a scene from the New Testament of the Bible. It shows Jesus and the 12 apostles at the last meal they had together.

Leonardo was a sculptor as well as a painter. But Leonardo was not only a great artist, he was a genius in other fields as well. He was interested in many areas of science and kept notebooks of his scientific observations. Also, in his notebooks, he drew plans for inventions. Some of these inventions, such as a flying machine, would be created much later. Many of the drawings themselves are considered masterpieces of art. The wide range of intellectual interests and accomplishments that characterized Leonardo later gave rise to the term, *Renaissance man*. Today, we say a Renaissance man or woman is one who knows a great deal about both the arts and the sciences.

### Research Topics

- Characteristics of Leonardo's style in painting or sculpture
- Leonardo's drawings of machines and inventions
- Leonardo's life and work habits
- Leonardo's scientific observations

**Chapter and Section Support**

Europe and Russia: Shaped by History

# Skills for Life

## Problem Solving

**Directions:** *Read the following passage. Then, answer the questions that follow in the spaces provided.*

### Rumblings of Revolution

In 1894, Nicholas II became tsar. He would be the last Russian tsar. Russia was badly beaten in a war with Japan in 1904 and 1905, and unrest grew among peasants and workers. In 1905, thousands of workers in St. Petersburg marched to the Winter Palace. They wanted to appeal directly to the tsar for reforms. Troops stopped them and fired into the crowd, killing hundreds. This mass killing was known as Bloody Sunday.

Tsar Nicholas was forced to agree to establish the Duma, a kind of congress. The people elected its members. In theory, the Duma shared power with the tsar. In fact, the Duma had very little real power. Some progress toward reform was made, but many people wanted more.

1. Identify the problem Nicholas II faced as tsar of Russia.

   _____

   _____

2. Why do you think the solutions mentioned in the passage didn't work?

   _____

   _____

3. What might have been some possible solutions to the problem?

   _____

   _____

4. What kind of resources would each possible solution require? What might be the possible outcome or consequences for each solution?

   _____

   _____

   _____

5. What solution do you think is best? Explain why you think it is the best solution, and what its outcome would be.

   _____

   _____

   _____

Name _____ Date _____ Class _____

Europe and Russia: Shaped by History

# Small Group Activity

## Castle Mural

During feudal times, many people lived near castles. Each castle was built on a piece of land called a manor. Outside the castle were houses and farms that belonged to the lord of the manor. Serfs were people who lived on the land and worked for the lord. In this activity, you will work with a group to research information and illustrations about European castles from the Middle Ages. Then, you will draw a mural for a castle that includes information about the buildings.

### Background

During the Middle Ages in Europe, castles were a center of power and strength. In many places, the countryside was not safe. Lords struggled with each other and fought to control the lands around them. They built strong castles to protect themselves, their families, and the people who worked for them. These castles were often more than just a large house. They usually included open spaces and dwellings for workers, such as carpenters, masons, blacksmiths, and house workers. Most lords had knights too. Stables were used for animals. Perhaps most important, there was always a good supply of water inside the castle walls.

### Procedure

1. **Research information.** Read all the steps in this project. Then meet with your group to decide who will do each job. Look in the library for books and articles about castles, the Middle Ages in Europe, knights, and other related subjects. The more information and illustrations you find, the more detailed your mural can be.

2. **Draw the castle.** When your group has gathered information and illustrations, decide how to divide up the rest of the work. Before you begin, make a sketch of the castle in the space below.

© Pearson Education, Inc., publishing as Pearson Prentice Hall. All rights reserved.

Chapter and Section Support

Europe and Russia: Shaped by History

## Small Group Activity *(continued)*

Then use a large sheet of paper to make a detailed drawing. You might have some group members draw sections of the castle. Begin by sketching in the rough shapes of the buildings and walls. Be sure the paper is large enough to include interesting details and information. When the basic buildings are done, other students can add figures of people doing tasks such as getting water from a well, cooking food, feeding horses, and standing guard. If there is room, show the lands outside of the castle.

3. **Write the captions.** As details of the castle are drawn, write captions that explain what is happening. The captions can be done on separate pieces of paper and then glued to the mural. Be sure the captions are simple, neatly written, and easy to read. Include as much information as you can. Point out things most viewers might not notice. This will make the mural fun to look at and full of interesting information.

4. **Display the castle mural.** When your group has finished its castle mural, tack or tape it to the wall. As you look at all the murals, notice how they are similar and how they are different. Are they from different countries? Are they copies of real castles? Or are they combinations of several different castles? Use these murals as a way to compare life in the Middle Ages in Europe with life for students today.

# Small Group Activity: Teacher Page

## Castle Mural

### Content Objectives

- Students will learn about the architecture and function of European feudal castles and manors.
- Students will become aware of how people lived in the Middle Ages in Europe.

### Skill Objectives

- Drawing conclusions
- Writing for a purpose—explanation
- Locating information
- Organizing information

### Advance Preparation

Gather the following materials:

- large sheets of paper for murals
- pencils, markers, pens, and paints
- scissors, glue, and tape

**Suggested group size:** eight students

**Suggested time:** 20 minutes for researching information; 60 minutes for planning and making the mural and captions; 40 minutes for presenting and discussing murals

### Procedure

Divide the class into groups. Distribute student pages and have students begin to work on the project. You may wish to give a copy of the rubric for murals to each group.

As students begin to do research, explain that they can either copy one castle illustration or use several as the basis for their drawings. Encourage them to include as many details as possible. They can photocopy illustrations as they find them.

Help students decide on the final form for the castle. Once this has been established, they should be able to divide the work and complete each task. When students have finished their murals, invite them to discuss each one. You might use the following questions to begin the discussion:

- What things did you learn about life in the Middle Ages in Europe?
- Would you like to have lived during that time? Why or why not?
- Do people still do any of the activities shown in the castles?
- Do you think your group worked well as a team?

# Small Group Activity: Teacher Page

Castle murals will be evaluated according to the following rubric.

## Rubric for Castle Murals

| Grading Criteria | Excellent | Admirable | Acceptable |
|---|---|---|---|
| **Research** | Students find many sources of information about castles and life in the Middle Ages in Europe; they gather interesting facts and illustrations; they learn in detail about the construction, uses, and layout of European castles. | Students find several sources of information; they gather many good facts and illustrations about castles in Europe. | Students find some information about castles in Europe. |
| **Drawing the Murals** | Drawings are filled with details about many aspects of castle life; they show buildings, animals, people, and other important points both inside and outside the castle. | Drawings contain many details about castle life; they are accurate and include buildings and people. | Drawings show castle buildings and some details about life in the Middle Ages in Europe. |
| **Presentation** | Murals are beautiful to look at, clear, neatly drawn, and colorful; captions are full of interesting facts and easy to understand; the mural is both fun and educational. | Murals are well drawn and include many interesting details; the captions are clear and readable. | Murals are fairly well drawn, though some aspects could be improved; the captions are generally neat, but some are hard to relate to a specific part of the drawing. |
| **Teamwork** | Students work extremely well together as a team; each group member contributes and helps others with their work. | Students work together as a team and complete the job with enthusiasm. | Students work as a team, but some do more work than others. |

# Outline Map 14: Western Europe: Political

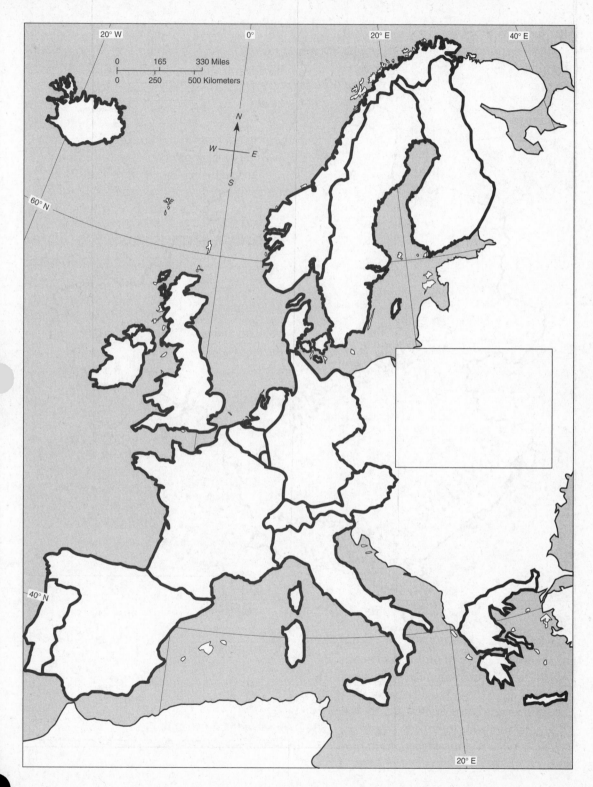

20° W    0°    20° E    40° E

0    165    330 Miles
0    250    500 Kilometers

N
W    E
S

60° N

40° N

20° E

Chapter and Section Support

Europe and Russia: Shaped by History

# Outline Map 17: Eastern Europe: Physical

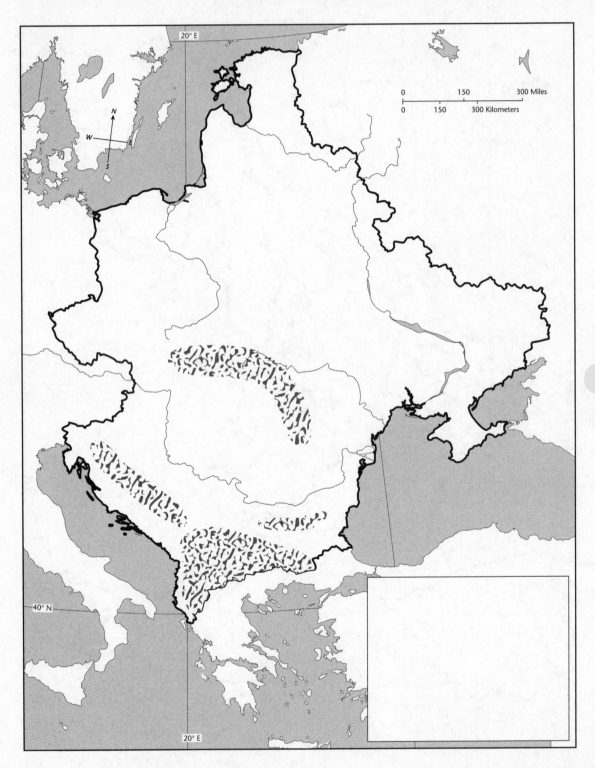

# Outline Map 18: Eastern Europe and Russia: Political

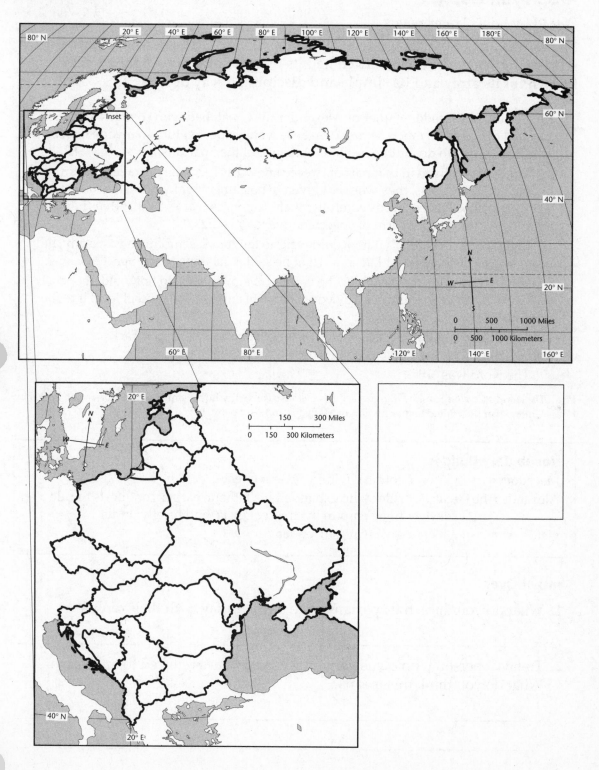

Chapter and Section Support

Europe and Russia: Shaped by History

# Primary Sources and Literature Readings

## A Spartan Reply

Retold by Louis Untermeyer

**Sparta was one of the great Greek city-states. These cities were self-contained with their own governments. Each had its own personality—Sparta being known for its army and its simple and disciplined way of life.**

King Philip of Macedon, father of Alexander the Great, had won so many victories and had captured so much territory that everyone expected him to invade Greece. This he planned to do, but he hesitated because of the Spartans.

The Spartans lived in that part of Greece known as Laconia. A brave and simple people, utterly fearless, they were not given to boasting or vain talk. They used few words and chose those words carefully; their sentences were so short that they were called "laconic," a form of speech native to Laconia.

Philip at last decided that he would wait no longer. Assembling a vast army, he brought it to the borders of Laconia. Then he sent a message to the Spartans.

"When I invade your country," he warned them, "if you do not yield at once, I will burn your villages and destroy your cities. If I enter Laconia I will level it to the ground."

The Spartans did not waste words or time. Their answer came back immediately, a truly laconic reply. It consisted of a single word.

The word was "IF!"

From *The World's Greatest Stories: Fifty-Five Legends that Live Forever* by Louis Untermeyer. Copyright © 1964 by Louis Untermeyer. Reprinted by permission of M. Evans and Company, Inc.

---

**Vocabulary Builder**

| | |
|---|---|
| Macedon | country within ancient Greece |
| Alexander the Great | ruler who expanded his father's earlier conquests to rule a huge empire in Greece, Persia, and briefly, India |
| yield | give way, surrender |

---

**Think It Over**

1. What do you think the Spartans were trying to say with their reply?

   _____

2. Today, a person who owns very little is sometimes referred to as spartan. What do you think this means?

   _____

   _____

Europe and Russia: Shaped by History

# Primary Sources and Literature Readings

## Storm in the State

by Alcaéus of Mytilène

**Big changes in your life can make you feel like you are caught in the middle of a storm. Poets have long used nature to describe human events, such as wars and political struggles. Alcaéus of Mytilène was a Greek nobleman. He was very involved in politics, sometimes fighting for change and sometimes fighting against it. Perhaps his poem comments on these changes.**

> I cannot understand how the winds are set
> against each other. Now from this side and now
> from that the waves roll. We between them
> run with the wind in our black ship driven,
> hard pressed and laboring under the giant storm.
> All round the mast-step washes the sea we shipped.
> You can see through the sail already
> where there are opening rents within it.
> The forestays slacken. . . .

From *Greek Lyrics* by Richard Lattimore. Copyright © 1949, 1955, and 1960 by Richard Lattimore. Reprinted by permission of the University of Chicago Press.

---

**Vocabulary Builder**

| | |
|---|---|
| mast-step | raised platform from which the mast of the ship rises |
| rents | tears |
| forestays | rope securing the forward mast to the ship's deck |
| slacken | weaken, lose tension |

---

**Think It Over**

1. What do you think Alcaéus is describing? What are some images he uses to paint his word picture?

   _____

   _____

2. If Alcaéus' ship is a symbol of the society in which he lived, what is happening to that society?

   _____

Europe and Russia: Shaped by History

# Primary Sources and Literature Readings

## Testing a Theory

A letter from Blaise Pascal

**About 150 years after Leonardo da Vinci's scientific experiments, Renaissance science was still moving forward. Scientists had developed new ways to test their ideas. One method was by repeated experiment. Here is a letter written by scientist and thinker Blaise Pascal, in which he asked his brother-in-law to help him test the idea that air has a different pressure as elevation increases.**

*November 15, 1647*

I am taking the liberty of interrupting you in your daily professional labors, and of bothering you with questions of physics, because I know that they provide rest and recreation for your moments of leisure…. The question concerns the well-known experiment carried out with a tube containing mercury, first at the foot and then at the top of a mountain, and repeated several times on the same day, in order to ascertain whether the height of the column of mercury is the same or differs in the two cases…. For it is certain that at the foot of the mountain the air is much heavier than at the top.

Quoted from *A Treasury of the World's Great Letters*, edited and compiled by M. Lincoln Schuster. Copyright © 1940 by Simon & Schuster, Inc. Copyright renewed 1968 by Simon & Schuster, Inc.

| **Vocabulary Builder** | |
| --- | --- |
| physics | the study of energy and matter |
| mercury | a liquid metallic element that reacts to changes in temperature or air pressure |
| ascertain | determine, figure out |

### Think It Over

1. What exactly was Pascal asking his brother-in-law to do? What can you conclude from this letter about the way science was conducted in the 1600s?

   _____

   _____

2. When reporting the successful proving of Pascal's theory, the brother-in-law later wrote that he was filled with "wonder and admiration." Why do you think he felt that way about Pascal's discovery?

   _____

   _____

# Primary Sources and Literature Readings

## A Child in Prison Camp

by Shizuye Takashima

**During World War II, when Canada was at war with Japan, Japanese Canadians were feared as possible enemies. The Canadian government sent them from their homes to camps where they stayed for several years. Here, Shizuye Takashima describes the experiences of her family in her journal.**

Japan is at war with the United States, Great Britain, and all the Allied Countries, including Canada, the country of my birth. My parents are Japanese, born in Japan, but they have been Canadian citizens for many, many years and have become part of this young country. Now, overnight, our rights as Canadians are taken away. Mass evacuation for the Japanese!

"All the Japanese," it is carefully explained to me, "whether we were born in Tokyo or in Vancouver are to be moved to distant places. Away from the west coast of British Columbia—for security reasons."

We must all leave—my sister Yuki, my older brother David, my parents, our relatives—all.

The older men are the first to go. The Government feels that my father, or his friends, might sabotage the police and their buildings. Imagine! I couldn't believe such stories, but there is my father packing just his clothes in a small suitcase.

Yuki says, "They are going to the foothills of the Rockies, to Tete Jaune. No one's there, and I guess they feel Father won't bomb the mountains."

The older people are very frightened. Mother is so upset; so are all her friends. I being only eleven, seem to be on the outside.

One March day, we go to the station to see Father board the train . . .

We have been waiting for months now. The Provincial Government keeps changing the dates of our evacuation, first from April, then from June, for different reasons: lack of trains, the camps are not ready. We are given another final notice. We dare not believe this is the one.

Mother is anxious. She has just received a letter from Father that he is leaving his camp with others; the families will be back together. I feel happy. He writes that he is located in one of the most beautiful spots in British Columbia. It's near a small village, 1800 feet above sea level. The Government wants the Japanese to build their own sanatorium for T.B. patients. I hear there are many Japanese who have this disease, and the high altitude and dry air are supposed to be good for them. I feel secretly happy, for I love the mountains. I shall miss the roaring sea, but we are to be near a lake. Yuki says, "They decided all the male heads of families are to rejoin their wives, but the single men stay." So, of course, David will remain in his camp far away.

We rise early, very early, the morning we are to leave. The city still sleeps. The fresh autumn air feels nice. We have orders to be at the Exhibition Grounds. The train will leave from there, not from the station where we said good-bye to Father and David. We wait for the train in small groups scattered alongside the track.

Chapter and Section Support

Europe and Russia: Shaped by History

## *Primary Sources and Literature Readings* (continued)

There is no platform. It is September 16. School has started. I think of my school friends and wonder if I shall ever see them again. The familiar mountains, all purple and splendid, watch us from afar. The yellowy-orange sun slowly appears. We have been standing for over an hour. The sun's warm rays reach us, touch a child still sleeping in its mother's arms, touch a tree, blades of grass. All seems magical. I study the thin yellow rays of the sun. I imagine a handsome prince will come and carry us all away in a shining, gold carriage with white horses. I daydream and feel nice as long as I don't think about leaving this city where I was born.

The crisp air becomes warmer. I shift my feet, restless. Mother returns; she has been speaking to her friend. "Everyone says we will have to wait for hours." She bends, moves the bundles at our feet: food, clothes for the journey. I am excited. This is my first train ride! Yuki smiles. She, too, feels the excitement of our journey. Several children cry, weary of waiting. Their mothers' voices are heard, scolding.

Now the orange sun is far above our heads. Yuki asks me if I am tired. I nod. "I don't feel tired yet, but I'm getting hungry." We haven't eaten since six in the morning. Names are being called over the loudspeaker. One by one, families gather their belongings and move toward the train. Finally ours is called.

Yuki shouts, "That's us!"

I shout, "Hooray!" I take a small bag; Yuki and Mother the larger ones and the suitcases. People stare as we walk toward the train. It is some distance away. I see the black, dull-colored train. It looks quite old. Somehow I had expected a shiny new one.

Yuki remarks, " I hope it moves. You never know with the Government."

Mother looks, smiles. "Never mind, as long as we get there. We aren't going on a vacation; we are being evacuated."

Bang . . . bang . . . psst . . . the old train gurgles, makes funny noises. I, seated by the window, feel the wheels move, stop, move, stop. Finally I hear them begin to move in an even rhythm slowly.

I look out the dusty window. A number of people still wait their turn. We wave. Children run after the train. Gradually it picks up speed. We pass the gray granaries, tall and thin against the blue Vancouver sky. The far mountains and tall pines follow us for a long time until finally they are gone.

Mother sits opposite; she has her eyes closed, her hands are on her lap. Yuki stares out the window. A woman across the aisle quietly dabs her tears with a white cloth. No one speaks.

From *A Child in Prison Camp* by Shizuye Takashima. Copyright © 1974 by Shizuye Takashima. By permission of Morrow Junior Books, a division of William Morrow & Company, Inc.

Europe and Russia: Shaped by History

## *Primary Sources and Literature Readings* (continued)

---

**Vocabulary Builder**

| | |
|---|---|
| Allied Countries | countries, including Canada and the United States, who fought against Germany, Japan, and Italy during World War II |
| evacuation | being removed from one's home |
| sabotage | lay a trap, damage |
| sanatorium | health clinic |
| T.B. | tuberculosis, a disease of the lungs |

---

### Think It Over

1. How did Shizuye feel about the evacuation? Why do you think she had so many different feelings?

   _____

   _____

   _____

2. In time of war, why might a government want to keep its coastline secure?

   _____

   _____

3. Was the confinement of the Japanese Canadians fair? Was it necessary? Why do you think so?

   _____

   _____

   _____

   _____

Chapter and Section Support

Europe and Russia: Shaped by History

# Primary Sources and Literature Readings

## A Letter from Napoleon's Army

by Count Philippe-Paul De Ségur

**In the early 1800s, Napoleon Bonaparte was the emperor of France. When he tried to invade Russia's city of Moscow, its residents burned the city and fled. Napoleon's army could get no supplies and had to retreat. They were caught in the bitter Russian winter, and many died of cold or starvation. This letter was written from the battlefield.**

*The Eighth of September*

Napoleon rode over the battlefield; there was never such a ghastly sight. Everything contributed to the horror of it: the gloomy sky, the cold rain, the violent gale, the houses in ashes, the plain torn up, littered with ruins and debris. On the horizon the melancholy foliage of the northern trees; soldiers wandering among the corpses, looking for food in the very knapsacks of their fallen comrades; dreadful wounds (Russian bullets were larger than ours); cold campfires without song or tale; a tragic silence!

Clustered round the standards were the few remaining officers, noncommissioned officers, and soldiers—barely enough to guard the eagle. Their clothing was torn by the violence of the struggle, black with powder, stained with blood. Yet, despite the rags, the misery and disaster, they still looked proud and let out shouts of triumph at the sight of the Emperor. The shouts, though, were rare and excited; for in this army, capable of self-analysis as well as enthusiasm, each individual was aware of the total situation. French soldiers are not easily deceived; and these wondered why, with so many Russians killed and wounded, there should be only eight hundred prisoners. It was by the number of prisoners that they judged success, since the dead attested to the courage of the defeated, rather than to a victory. If the survivors were able to retreat in such good order, proud and undaunted, what did the winning of one field matter? In this vast country, would the Russians ever lack for space on which to fight?

*The First Snowstorm*

On the sixth of November the sky became terrible; its blue disappeared. The army marched along wrapped in a cold mist. Then the mist thickened, and presently from this immense cloud great snowflakes began to sift down on us. It seemed as if the sky had come down and joined with the earth and our enemies to complete our ruin. Everything in sight became vague, unrecognizable. Objects changed their shape; we walked without knowing where we were or what lay ahead, and anything became an obstacle. While the men were struggling to make headway against the icy, cutting blast, the snow driven by the wind was piling up and filling the hollows along the way. Their smooth surfaces hid unsuspected depths which opened up treacherously under our feet. The men were swallowed up, and the weak, unable to struggle out, were buried forever.

Europe and Russia: Shaped by History

## *Primary Sources and Literature Readings* (continued)

The soldiers following them turned around, but the tempest whipped their faces with the snow falling from above or swept up from the earth, and seemed fiercely determined to oppose their progress. Russian winter in this new guise attacked them on all sides; it cut through their thin uniforms and worn shoes, their wet clothing froze on them, and this icy shroud molded their bodies and stiffened their limbs. The sharp wind made them gasp for breath, and froze the moisture from their mouths and nostrils into icicles on their beards…

But in front of them, all around them, everything was snow. The eyes of the men were lost in the immense, dreary uniformity. To their stricken imagination it was like a great white shroud that Nature was winding about the army. The only objects that stood out were the tall somber firs, graveyard trees, as we called them, with the funereal verdure, and the gigantic immobility of their black trunks, which completed a picture of universal mourning, a dying army in the midst of a dead nature.

Excerpts from *Napoleon's Russian Campaign* by Philippe-Paul de Ségur, translated by J. David Townsend. Copyright © 1958 by J. David Townsend. Reprinted by permission of Houghton Mifflin Company. All rights reserved.

---

**Vocabulary Builder**

| | |
|---|---|
| melancholy foliage | the trees of the far north are mostly evergreens with needles instead of leaves |
| standards | flags |
| noncommissioned officers | officers with less authority |
| attested to | was proof of |
| undaunted | unbeaten, unafraid |
| tempest | storm |
| guise | form |
| shroud | a cloth used to cover a corpse before burial |
| uniformity | sameness |
| stricken | weakened |
| funereal verdure | the bushes and trees seem very serious, like the mood at a funeral |
| immobility | inability to move |

---

**Think It Over**

1. Why were the French soldiers surprised there were only 800 Russian prisoners? What does this suggest about the outcome of the battle?

2. How did the geography of Russia help its soldiers? How did it hurt the French soldiers?

Europe and Russia: Shaped by History

# Primary Sources and Literature Readings

## Lenin's Deathbed Words

by Vladimir Lenin

**An important leader of the Bolshevik movement, Vladimir Lenin helped found the Soviet Union. There was a lot of fighting among different groups within the country as to how the new government should be run. As Lenin lay dying in the early 1920s, many people wanted to take over the power he would leave behind. In this postscript to a letter he wrote in January of 1924, Lenin warned the Soviet people about the danger he saw coming from one of those people, Josef Stalin.**

Postscript: Stalin is too rude, and this fault, entirely supportable in relations among us Communists, becomes insupportable in the office of General Secretary. Therefore, I propose to the comrades to find a way to remove Stalin from that position and appoint to it another man who in all respects differs from Stalin only in superiority—namely, more patient, more loyal, more polite and more attentive to comrades, less capricious, etc. This circumstance may seem an insignificant trifle, but I think that from the point of view of preventing a split and from the point of view of the relation between Stalin and Trotsky which I discussed above, it is not a trifle, or it is such a trifle as may acquire a decisive significance.

—Lenin

Quoted from *A Treasury of the World's Great Letters*, edited and compiled by M. Lincoln Schuster. Copyright © 1940 by Simon & Schuster, Inc. Copyright renewed 1968 by Simon & Schuster, Inc.

---

### Vocabulary Builder

| | |
|---|---|
| postscript | new text added on to the end of a letter, containing an idea thought of at the last moment |
| supportable | acceptable, supported by reason |
| comrades | members of the Communist party |
| capricious | likely to change his mind without warning or cause |
| trifle | a little and unimportant thing |
| Trotsky | another revolutionary, with whom Stalin was struggling for power |
| decisive | important in deciding |

---

## Think It Over

1. Lenin gives many reasons for disliking Stalin. What might be another reason for his attitude? _____

   _____

2. What reason does Lenin give for wanting Stalin removed?

   _____

   _____

Europe and Russia: Shaped by History

# Primary Sources and Literature Readings

## Kampf

by Josef Stalin

**Lenin warned the Soviet people about the danger of the leadership qualities and the desire for power of Josef Stalin. Lenin turned out to be right. Josef Stalin was a brutal dictator who killed and jailed many Soviets. The statement below suggests a little of his personality.**

"To choose one's victim, to prepare one's plans minutely, to stake an implacable vengeance, and then to go to bed…there is nothing sweeter in the world."

Quoted from *A Treasury of the World's Great Letters*, edited and compiled by M. Lincoln Schuster. Copyright © 1940 by Simon & Schuster, Inc. Copyright renewed 1968 by Simon & Schuster, Inc.

---

**Vocabulary Builder**

| | |
|---|---|
| minutely | considering even the tiniest detail |
| implacable | relentless; without any possible relief |
| vengeance | revenge |

---

**Think It Over**

1. What does Stalin's statement reveal about his personality?

   _____

   _____

   _____

   _____

2. What does this statement tell you about the type of leader he was?

   _____

   _____

   _____

   _____

Chapter and Section Support

Europe and Russia: Shaped by History

# Primary Sources and Literature Readings

## The Endless Steppe

by Esther Hautzig

**Esther Hautzig was born and spent her early years in Vilna, Poland. In 1939, the Soviet army, which was then fighting in World War II alongside the Germans, invaded Vilna. Esther and her family were exiled to Siberia, along with many others. Here, Esther describes the harsh lands to which they were sent.**

My first glimpse of Rubtsovsk was of a frontier village built around a large open square in straight lines, as if the muddy paths were laid out for ticktacktoe. Immediately surrounding the square were the market stalls, open wooden sheds. These were empty that day. Once again the loud-speaker crackled with authority; this time we were ordered to arrange ourselves in family groups in the square and await further instructions. Since families had clung to each other, this was done with dispatch.

The square was even hotter than the road, the sun being reflected from its cobblestones of all sizes and shapes. I stepped closer to my mother.

The flatness of this land was awesome. There wasn't a hill in sight; it was an enormous, unrippled sea of parched and lifeless grass.

"Tata, why is the earth so flat here?"

"These must be steppes, Esther."

"Steppes? But steppes are in Siberia."

"This is Siberia," he said quietly.

If I had been told that I had been transported to the moon, I could not have been more stunned.

"Siberia?" My voice trembled. "But Siberia is full of snow."

"It will be," my father said.

Siberia! Siberia was the end of the world, a point of no return. Siberia was for criminals and political enemies, where the punishment was unbelievably cruel, and where people died like flies. Summer or no summer—and who had ever talked about hot Siberia?—Siberia was the tundra and mountainous drifts of snow. Siberia was *wolves*.

I had been careless. I had neglected to pray to God to save us from a gypsum mine in Siberia.

From *The Endless Steppe* by Esther Hautzig. Copyright © 1968 by Esther Hautzig, published by HarperKeypoint, an imprint of HarperCollins Publishers.

Europe and Russia: Shaped by History

## *Primary Sources and Literature Readings* (continued)

**Vocabulary Builder**

| | |
|---|---|
| Tata | Papa or Father |
| steppes | flat, treeless plains |
| tundra | far northern lands, treeless and with permanently frozen subsoil |
| gypsum | a mineral used in making plaster |

**Think It Over**

1. What might it feel like to live in a place with no trees or hills?

   _____

   _____

   _____

   _____

2. Why was Esther so surprised to find it was hot in Siberia?

   _____

   _____

   _____

   _____

**Chapter and Section Support**

# Primary Sources and Literature Readings

## Whose Falkland Islands Are They?

by Prime Minister Margaret Thatcher

**The Falkland Islands are in the South Atlantic Ocean, off the coast of southern Argentina. They have been under British colonial rule since the 1830s, although Argentina also claimed the islands. In 1982, Argentina took the islands by force. The British sent troops to take the islands back. Some in Great Britain questioned this decision to use force. In this speech, British Prime Minister Margaret Thatcher justified her actions.**

In a series of measured and progressive steps, over the past weeks, our forces have tightened their grip on the Falkland Islands. They have retaken South Georgia. Gradually they have denied fresh supplies to the Argentine garrison.

Finally, by the successful amphibious landing at San Carlos Bay in the early hours of Friday morning, they have placed themselves in a position to retake the islands and reverse the illegal Argentine invasion.

By the skill of our pilots, our sailors, and those manning the Rapier missile batteries onshore, they have inflicted heavy losses on the Argentine air force—over fifty fixed-wing aircraft have been destroyed.

There have, of course, been tragic losses. You will have heard of the further attacks on our task force. HMS *Coventry* came under repeated air attack yesterday evening and later sank. One of our merchant marine ships, the *Atlantic Conveyor*, supporting the task force, was also damaged and had to be abandoned. We do not yet know the number of casualties, but our hearts go out to all those who had men in these ships.

Despite these grievous losses, our resolve is not weakened. . . .

It was eight weeks ago today that information reached us that the Argentine fleet was sailing towards the Falklands. . . .

And so, seven weeks to the day after the invasion, we moved to recover by force what was taken from us by force. It cannot be said too often: we are the victims, they are the aggressors.

As always, we came to military action reluctantly.

But when territory which has been British for almost 150 years is seized and occupied; when not only British land but British citizens are in the power of the aggressor—then we have to restore our rights and the rights of the Falkland Islanders.

There have been a handful of questioning voices raised here at home. I would like to answer them. It has been suggested that the size of the Falkland Islands and the comparatively small number of its inhabitants—some eighteen hundred men, women, and children—should somehow affect our reaction to what has happened to them.

To those—not many—who speak lightly of a few islanders beyond the seas and who ask the question "Are they worth fighting for?" let me say this: right and wrong are not measured by a head count of those to whom that wrong has been done. That would not be principle but expediency.

## *Primary Sources and Literature Readings* (continued)

And the Falklanders, remember, are not strangers. They are our own people. As the prime minister of New Zealand, Bob Muldoon, put it in his usual straightforward way, "With the Falkland Islanders, it is family."

When their land was invaded and their homes were overrun, they naturally turned to us for help, and we, their fellow citizens, eight thousand miles away in our much larger island, could not and did not beg to be excused.

We sent our men and our ships with all speed, hoping against hope that we would not have to use them in battle but prepared to do so if all attempts at a peaceful solution failed. When those attempts failed, we could not sail by on the other side.

And let me add this. If we, the British, were to shrug our shoulders at what has happened in the South Atlantic and acquiesce in the illegal seizure of those faraway islands, it would be a clear signal to those with similar designs on the territory of others to follow in the footsteps of aggression.

Surely we, of all people, have learned the lesson of history: that to appease an aggressor is to invite aggression elsewhere, and on an ever-increasing scale.

Other voices—again only a few—have accused us of clinging to colonialism or even imperialism. Let me remind those who advance that argument that the British have a record second to none of leading colony after colony to freedom and independence. We cling not to colonialism but self-determination.

Still others—again only a few—say we must not put at risk our investments and interests in Latin America; that trade and commerce are too important to us to put in jeopardy some of the valuable markets of the world.

But what would the islanders, under the heel of the invader, say to that?

What kind of people would we be if, enjoying the birthright of freedom ourselves, we abandoned British citizens for the sake of commercial gain?

Now we are present in strength on the Falkland Islands.

Our purpose is to repossess them. We shall carry on until that purpose is accomplished.

When the invader has left, there will be much to do—rebuilding, restoring homes and farms, and, above all, renewing the confidence of the people in their future.

Their wishes will need time to crystallize and, of course, will depend in some measure on what we and others are prepared to do to develop the untapped resources and safeguard the islands' future.

Madam Chairman, our cause is just.

It is the cause of freedom and the rule of law.

It is the cause of support for the weak against aggression by the strong.

Let us, then, draw together in the name, not of jingoism, but of justice.

And let our nation, as it has so often in the past, remind itself—and the world:

Nought shall make us rue,

If England to herself do rest but true.

By permission of Margaret Thatcher.

Europe and Russia: Shaped by History

## *Primary Sources and Literature Readings* (continued)

**Vocabulary Builder**

| | |
|---|---|
| measured | thought out carefully |
| garrison | army camp |
| amphibious landing | a military operation involving the landing of troops on a shore from ships |
| manning | running, operating |
| grievous | sad, causing grief |
| acquiesce | agree to, allow to happen |
| seizure | taking |
| appease | try to keep happy |
| colonialism/imperialism | the rule of one country over another that is far away |
| repossess | own or have again |
| crystallize | become firm and clear |
| untapped | not yet used |
| jingoism | fierce patriotism that supports aggressive and warlike foreign policy |
| nought | nothing |
| rue | regret |

**Think It Over**

1. What reasons did Margaret Thatcher give to justify her actions of sending troops to the Falkland Islands?

   _____

   _____

   _____

2. How did the physical geography affect Great Britain's attempt to protect the land and people of the Falkland Islands?

   _____

   _____

   _____

Europe and Russia: Shaped by History

# Primary Sources and Literature Readings

## Lords and Vassals

by Bishop Fulbert of Chartres

**Which do you think is a harder job, worker or boss? Perhaps each has its challenges. During medieval times, the bosses were the lords and the workers were called vassals. The feudal system defined a contract between the lord and his vassals. Both sides of the contract had duties to the other. This letter was written in 1020. It describes some of those duties.**

"He who takes the oath of fealty to his lord ought always to keep in mind these six things: what is harmless, safe, honorable, useful, easy, and practicable. *Harmless*, which means that [the vassal] ought not to injure his lord in his body; *safe*, that [the vassal] should not injure [the lord] by betraying his confidence [trust] or the defenses upon which he depends for security; *honorable*, that [the vassal] should not injure [the lord] . . . in matters that relate to [the lord's] honor; *useful*, that [the vassal] should not injure [the lord's] . . . property; *easy*, that [the vassal] should not make difficult that which his lord can do easily; and *practicable*, that [the vassal] should not make impossible for the lord that which is possible.

However, while it is proper that the faithful vassal avoid these injuries, it is not for doing this alone that he deserves his holding; for it is not enough to refrain from wrongdoing, unless that which is good is done also . . . . Therefore, . . . in the same six things referred to above he should faithfully advise and aid his lord, if he wishes to . . . be safe concerning his fealty which he has sworn.

The lord also ought to act toward his faithful vassal in the same manner in all these things. And if he fails to do this, he will be rightfully regarded as guilty of bad faith, just as the former [would be], if he should be found shirking . . . his obligations."

Written by Bishop Fulbert of Chartres, translated by Edward P. Cheney. Quoted in Frederic Austin Ogg, ed., *A Source Book of Medieval History*. New York: Cooper Square Publishers, 1907.

---

**Vocabulary Builder**

| | |
|---|---|
| oath of fealty | promise of loyalty |
| betraying his confidence | breaking his trust |
| shirking | avoiding, failing to fill |

---

**Think It Over**

1. What characteristic in people do you think the feudal system valued most? Why was this so important to that society?

2. How are the duties of lords and vassals to each other similar? How are they different?

# Writing Skills

## Writing Stories

Writing a story involves using your imagination to create a plot or a story line, characters, places, and many kinds of details. Some parts of the story can be based on real places and events, but the basic story must come from your imagination. Stories can range in length from a few pages to more than 1,000 pages. If you are interested in writing stories, you may want to start with shorter stories and work your way up to longer ones.

As with other forms of writing, story writing involves a purpose and an audience. Story writers generally have a target audience in mind. The audience may be young children, teens, or adults. Within those broad categories, the audience may be fans of science fiction, or romance novels, of historical novels, or of stories about animals. The story writer's purpose may be to inform, to amuse, to entertain, to inspire, or a combination of these and other purposes.

**Directions:** *Use you own life experiences as the basis for a short story. Choose one of the topics below, and think about how you could convert it into a short story. Use the spaces to identify your purpose and your audience. Then, describe the basic plot for your story, and list the characters you will include. When you are satisfied with your plan, use a separate sheet to write a first draft of your story.*

**Possible topics:**

■ What was the most exciting place you ever visited? Use it as the basis for a story.

■ Choose a natural disaster—such as a hurricane, a tornado, a volcano, or a flood—that you experienced or that people you know experienced. Write a story about that disaster.

■ Do you know someone who moved into your community from another country? Write a story about making friends with a person from a different cultural background.

Purpose of story:

_____

Audience:

_____

Basic plot: _____

_____

_____

Main characters (names and descriptions):

_____

_____

# Vocabulary Development

**Directions:** *The underlined words in the following sentences are important key terms for this chapter. On the back of this page or on a separate sheet of paper, write sentences of your own using the terms or forms of the terms. If necessary, look up the terms in your book's glossary.*

1. During the <u>Middle Ages</u>, religion provided a sense of security and community.

2. <u>Democracy</u> was a new idea for the ancient Greeks, who believed citizens should have a voice in their own government.

3. In the Greek <u>city-state</u> of Athens, citizens were either elected or chosen at random for government positions.

4. The political system called <u>feudalism</u> brought order and structure to European society after the collapse of the Roman Empire.

5. During the <u>Renaissance</u>, people re-examined ancient Greek and ancient Roman poetry, plays, ideas, buildings, and sculpture.

6. The powerful <u>monarch</u> of France, Louis XIV, lived an extremely luxurious lifestyle, which was paid for by taxes and trade.

7. In 1789 a violent <u>revolution</u> overthrew the French government.

8. A <u>colony</u> is a territory ruled by another nation, usually one far away.

9. The <u>Industrial Revolution</u> began in Great Britain, where the first machines were invented to speed up the process of weaving cloth.

10. The yarn in <u>textiles</u> is first spun, then dyed, and finally woven.

11. Beginning in the 1600s, many European governments became more aggressive abroad and followed the policy of <u>imperialism</u>.

12. At the start of the 1900s, Europeans were filled with feelings of <u>nationalism</u>.

13. In 1940, Germany, Italy, and Japan formed an <u>alliance</u> called the Axis Powers.

14. Peter the Great hired foreign professors, scientists, and advisors and encouraged <u>westernization</u> in Russia.

15. Ivan the IV called himself <u>tsar</u>, but he was called Ivan the Terrible by others.

16. The Russian government imprisoned Lenin for spreading <u>revolutionary</u> ideas.

17. Lenin promised <u>communism</u> would bring equality to Russians.

18. The European Union currency is the <u>euro</u>.

19. The European Union has a <u>single market</u> in which goods, services, and capital move freely across borders.

20. A <u>foreign minister</u> is a government official who is in charge of a nation's foreign affairs, or relations with other nations.

Chapter and Section Support

# Rubric for Assessing a Journal Entry

| Grading Criteria | Excellent | Acceptable | Minimal | Unacceptable |
|---|---|---|---|---|
| **Content** | Response to assigned topic thorough and well written, with varied sentence structure and vocabulary; opinions always supported with facts. | Response thoughtful and fairly well written; most opinions supported with facts. | Response adequately addresses some aspects of the assigned topic; opinions sometimes based on incorrect information. | Response consists of unsupported opinions only marginally related to topic. |
| **Idea Development** | Excellent use of examples and details to explore and develop ideas and opinions. | Good reliance upon examples and details to illustrate and develop ideas and opinions. | Incomplete development of ideas; details and examples not always relevant. | Ideas not clearly stated or developed. |
| **Organization** | Very logically organized; contains introduction, development of main idea (or ideas), and conclusion. | Contains introduction, some development of ideas, and conclusion. | Topics and ideas discussed somewhat randomly; entry may lack clearly defined introduction or conclusion. | Entry is unstructured. |
| **Mechanics** | Flawless spelling and punctuation. | Few or no spelling errors; some minor punctuation mistakes. | Several spelling and punctuation errors. | Many instances of incorrect spelling and punctuation. |

# Rubric for Assessing a Writing Assignment

| Grading Criteria | Excellent | Acceptable | Minimal | Unacceptable |
|---|---|---|---|---|
| Content | Clearly focused introduction; idea development interesting and sophisticated; supporting evidence detailed, accurate, and convincing; perceptive conclusion. | Introduction gives assignment direction; idea development clear; supporting evidence accurate; strong conclusion. | Introduction unclear; idea development uneven and simplistic; supporting evidence uneven; conclusion summarizes information in assignment. | Introduction incomplete, ineffective; idea development ineffective; supporting evidence vague, inaccurate, or missing; conclusion incomplete or missing. |
| Organization | Paragraph order reinforces content; strong topic sentences make content easy to follow; effective and varied transitions. | Logical paragraph order; clear topic sentences; clear and functional transitions. | Ineffective paragraph order; narrow or inaccurate topic sentences; few clear transitions. | Inconsistent paragraph order; topic sentences and transitions missing. |
| Mechanics | Flawless punctuation and spelling; varied and interesting sentence structure. | Few spelling and punctuation errors; sentence structure correct. | Some careless spelling and punctuation errors; some errors in sentence structure. | Many spelling and punctuation errors; many sentence fragments and run-ons. |

**Chapter and Section Support**

# Rubric for Assessing a Letter to the Editor

| Grading Criteria | Excellent | Acceptable | Minimal | Unacceptable |
|---|---|---|---|---|
| **Idea Development** | Takes a strong, well-defined position; presents appropriate reasons, supporting details, and facts. | Takes a clear position; presents some reasons and details, but does not fully develop argument. | Position not clearly stated; gives unrelated, unsupported general statements, reasons, and details; minimal facts used. | Does not take a clear position; ideas are undeveloped; no facts or details used to support position. |
| **Organization** | Contains topic sentence clearly related to position; well-developed paragraphs present ideas and details; transitions are used to enhance organization; strong conclusion evident. | Topic sentence is logical and comprehensive; paragraph order demonstrates clear plan; transitions are clear; conclusion restates position effectively. | Topic sentence blandly states position; paragraphs not ordered effectively; conclusion present but not developed. | No position or conclusion; paragraphs in no particular order; ideas not logically organized. |
| **Mechanics and Style** | Sentences interesting and varied; flawless punctuation and spelling; rich vocabulary. | Sentence construction correct and varied; a few punctuation and spelling errors; contains a few rich vocabulary words. | Sentence structure contains some variety, but is incorrect in places; careless errors in spelling and punctuation; weak use of language. | Sentences are repetitious; multiple errors in structure, spelling, and punctuation; weak and incorrect use of vocabulary. |
| **Presentation** | Neatly typed; contains date, correct addresses (return and destination), and signature. | Presented neatly; contains necessary elements. | Presented legibly; missing one or two necessary elements. | Difficult to read; lacking important elements, such as signature and return address. |

Europe and Russia: Shaped by History

# Test A

## A. Key Terms

**Directions:** *Match the phrases in Column I with the key terms in Column II. Write the correct letter in each blank. You will not use all the terms. (15 points)*

**Column I**

_____ 1. type of government citizens run themselves

_____ 2. a period of history in which there was a rebirth of interest in learning and art

_____ 3. an agreement between countries to protect one another

_____ 4. the process of becoming more like Western Europe

_____ 5. a political theory that states all the people should own the farms and factories

**Column II**

**a.** alliance

**b.** colony

**c.** communism

**d.** democracy

**e.** euro

**f.** feudalism

**g.** Renaissance

**h.** textile

**i.** westernization

## B. Key Concepts

**Directions:** *Write the letter of the correct answer in each blank. (45 points)*

_____ 6. One of ancient Rome's greatest contributions to the world was

    **a.** the idea of separate city-states.

    **b.** the concept of democracy.

    **c.** an organized system of written laws.

    **d.** a scientific way of gathering knowledge.

_____ 7. During the Middle Ages, society was organized according to a system called

    **a.** anarchy.

    **b.** feudalism.

    **c.** democracy.

    **d.** dictatorship.

_____ 8. Why did Europeans begin to explore other lands during the Renaissance?

    **a.** They wanted to tax other countries.

    **b.** They wanted to conquer other countries.

    **c.** They were searching for trading wealth.

    **d.** They wanted to spread their religion.

## Test A (continued)

_____ 9. During the Scientific Revolution, scientists based their theories on information they had

    **a.** tested.

    **b.** read about.

    **c.** learned in church.

    **d.** learned from the Romans.

_____ 10. One important result of the Industrial Revolution was the growth of

    **a.** wages paid to factory workers.

    **b.** family values.

    **c.** small farms.

    **d.** cities.

_____ 11. What was an effect of nationalism in Europe during the early 1900s?

    **a.** Countries learned to work together for the good of all Europe.

    **b.** Alliances between groups of nations resulted in World War I.

    **c.** Countries decided to adopt a common language.

    **d.** Countries formed a union to protect European political interests.

_____ 12. What themes appear in Russia's history?

    **a.** scientific discovery, industrial invention, economic growth

    **b.** slow westernization, global colonization, democratic growth

    **c.** expansion, harsh treatment of common people, slow westernization

    **d.** growing equality, enlightened rulers, influence in the West

_____ 13. What was one factor that led to the overthrow of Nicholas II?

    **a.** war with the United States

    **b.** the spread of dictatorship

    **c.** food and fuel shortages

    **d.** the freeing of the serfs

_____ 14. What happened as a result of the Russian civil war?

    **a.** Stalin called for a general election.

    **b.** Lenin created a democratic state.

    **c.** Lenin created the Union of Soviet Socialist Republics.

    **d.** The Soviet empire collapsed.

*Test A* (continued)

## C. Critical Thinking

**Directions:** *Answer the following questions on the back of this paper or on a separate sheet of paper. (20 points)*

15. **Making Comparisons** How were people governed during the Roman Empire and during the Middle Ages in Europe?

16. **Identifying Central Issues** Why were the 1600s and 1700s called the Age of Revolution? In your answer, name two revolutions that occurred during this time.

## D. Skill: Problem Solving

**Directions:** *Read the paragraph below. Then answer the questions on the lines provided. (20 points)*

For centuries, people have used devices such as dams, flood basins, and canals to control natural water sources. Recently, people have questioned whether or not they should build dams in particular areas. Although farmers living downstream from a dam might have water for irrigation, they would lose the silt deposits left by a moving river. Rivers might stop supporting living organisms, including fish. People along the river would lose a source of food and fertilizer. There is some evidence that building dams contributes to erosion in some areas. These are a few of the reasons why many people are thinking carefully before they build dams.

17. Describe the subject of this paragraph.

_____

18. What is one problem that can result from building a dam?

_____

19. How could building a dam affect the food supply of people living along the river?

_____

20. What problems can dams cause to the quality of farmland?

_____

Europe and Russia: Shaped by History

# Test B

## A. Key Terms

**Directions:** *Fill in the blanks in Column I by writing the letter of the correct key term from Column II. You will not use all the terms. (15 points)*

**Column I**

_____ 1. The political system that developed during the Middle Ages, under which people had obligations based on their position in society, was known as _____.

_____ 2. During the Age of _____, many European countries took over other nations and turned them into colonies.

_____ 3. The first Russian emperor, or _____, Ivan IV, was crowned in 1547.

_____ 4. Under _____, everyone is supposed to share the work equally and receive an equal share of the rewards.

_____ 5. The European Union is an example of a(n) _____, a system in which goods, services, and capital move freely without barriers.

**Column II**

a. alliance

b. communism

c. democracy

d. feudalism

e. Imperialism

f. monarch

g. revolution

h. single market

i. tsar

## B. Key Concepts

**Directions:** *Write the letter of the correct answer in each blank. (45 points)*

_____ 6. Alexander the Great spread Greek culture throughout the world by

    a. building universities.

    b. conquering other lands.

    c. establishing trade routes.

    d. making himself a Greek god.

_____ 7. What was one of the greatest contributions ancient Romans made to the world?

    a. a new educational system

    b. a new system of written, organized laws

    c. a new monetary system

    d. a new scientific method

Europe and Russia: Shaped by History

## Test B (continued)

_____ **8.** How were people governed during the Middle Ages in Europe?
- **a.** by feudal lords
- **b.** by democratically elected leaders
- **c.** by the emperor
- **d.** by the local serfs

_____ **9.** What statement best describes the political situation during the Renaissance?
- **a.** Feudalism declined as kings became richer and more powerful.
- **b.** Feudalism grew as kings became weaker.
- **c.** The middle class took control of the governments.
- **d.** The lower classes revolted and overthrew the monarchs.

_____ **10.** How did science change during the Age of Revolution?
- **a.** Scientists made very few scientific advancements.
- **b.** Scientists used experiments to test their theories.
- **c.** Scientists relied on theories, unsupported by facts.
- **d.** Scientists no longer used the scientific method.

_____ **11.** During the 1800s, the way goods were produced changed and resulted in the
- **a.** Pax Romana.
- **b.** Age of Revolution.
- **c.** Industrial Revolution.
- **d.** Age of Reason.

_____ **12.** Peter the Great changed Russia by
- **a.** refusing to pay taxes to the Mongols.
- **b.** freeing the serfs.
- **c.** bringing in Western European ideas and culture.
- **d.** conquering western Siberia.

_____ **13.** As a result of the mass killing known as Bloody Sunday, Tsar Nicholas II agreed to establish
- **a.** a Russian congress.
- **b.** an absolute monarchy.
- **c.** a free educational system.
- **d.** an improved judicial system.

_____ **14.** What form of government did Lenin bring to Russia?
- **a.** absolute monarchy
- **b.** constitutional monarchy
- **c.** democracy
- **d.** communism

Chapter and Section Support

Europe and Russia: Shaped by History

***Test B*** *(continued)*

## C. Critical Thinking

**Directions:** *Answer the following questions on the back of this paper or on a separate sheet of paper. (20 points)*

15. **Drawing Conclusions** Why do you think feudalism was an important part of people's lives during the Middle Ages in Europe? In your answer, briefly explain feudalism.

16. **Recognizing Cause and Effect** How did the Russian serfs' living conditions lead to opposition to the tsars? In your answer, describe the serfs' living conditions under the tsars.

## D. Skill: Problem Solving

**Directions:** *Read the paragraph below then, answer the questions on the lines provided. (20 points)*

For centuries, people have used devices such as dams, flood basins, and canals to control natural water sources. Recently, people have questioned whether or not they should build dams in particular areas. Although farmers living downstream from a dam might have water for irrigation, they would lose the silt deposits left by a moving river. Rivers might stop supporting living organisms, including fish. People along the river would lose a source of food and fertilizer. There is some evidence that building dams contributes to erosion in some areas. These are a few of the reasons why many people are thinking carefully before they build dams.

17. Where and why are dams built?

_____

18. Name two problems that can result from building a dam.

_____

_____

19. What is one benefit of dams?

_____

20. How could building a dam on a river affect farming along the river?

_____

# Answer Key

## Section 1 Reading Readiness Guide

Answers will vary. Correct answers are:

1. F, The ancient Greeks were Europe's first great philosophers, historians, poets, and writers.
2. T
3. T
4. T
5. F, Christianity became so strong that Constantine, a Roman emperor, became a Christian and encouraged the spread of Christianity. It became the official religion of the Roman Empire.
6. F, The collapse of the Roman Empire in western Europe led to a time of uncertainty, confusion, and warfare.
7. T

## Section 1 Guided Reading and Review

Students' answers for 1–6 will vary. Correct answers include:

1. Democracy was a new idea for the Greeks and it reached its highest point during Athens' Golden Age.
2. Ancient Greece had more than a hundred city-states. These city-states had several different kinds of government, and many of them were democracies.
3. The Pax Romana was a 200-year period of peace during which Rome was the most powerful state in Europe and the Mediterranean.
4. Roman law was based on written laws; it protected all citizens and influenced the legal systems of most European countries.
5. To bring order after the collapse of the Roman Empire, people in Western Europe developed feudalism to organize their societies.
6. In feudal society, the king held the highest position and provided

security for his kingdom. Noble landholders needed serfs and peasants to live on and work estates. The noble maintained order, enforced laws, and protected the peasants.

7. the time between ancient and modern times, about A.D. 500–1500
8. a kind of government in which citizens govern themselves
9. a city with its own government that was both a city and an independent state
10. a system in which people had obligations based on their position in society

## Section 1 Quiz

1. F, The economic system called manorialism provided a basis for feudalism.
2. F, A Greek city-state was both a city and an independent nation.
3. T
4. F, A kind of government that citizens run themselves is called a democracy.
5. d  6. a  7. b  8. c  9. c  10. d

## Section 2 Reading Readiness Guide

Examples will vary. Correct statements from the text should appear in the *What you learned* column.

## Section 2 Guided Reading and Review

Answers for 1–8 will vary. Correct answers include:

1. During the Renaissance, the wealthy had time to enjoy art and learning—and the money to support artists and scholars.
2. Renaissance thinkers re-examined and rediscovered the ideas, art, and literature of the ancient Greeks and Romans.

## Answer Key (continued)

3. Humanism affected every part of Renaissance life, and emphasized the importance of human nature and the abilities of human beings to change the world.

4. During the Renaissance, art was an important way to understand man, God, and nature.

5. People began questioning their governments, believing that kings should not have all the power.

6. The idea that people should have a say in government spread to North America and France. During the American Revolution, the colonists defeated the British and formed the independent nation of the United States. During the French Revolution, the French people overthrew their government.

7. Scientists began to observe nature closely and base their theories on facts instead of religious beliefs.

8. One of the greatest scientists of the Scientific Revolution was Isaac Newton, who invented calculus and created a set of laws about how planets move.

9. Renaissance
10. monarch
11. revolution
12. colony

## Section 2 Quiz

1. T
2. T
3. F, The period when there was a rebirth of interest in learning and art is called the Renaissance.
4. F, A colony is a territory ruled by another nation.
5. c  6. a  7. b  8. c  9. c  10. b

## Section 3 Reading Readiness Guide

Answers will vary. Correct answers are:
1. T

2. F, The first machines were invented in Great Britain to speed up the weaving of cloth products.
3. T
4. F, During the Industrial Revolution, cities grew rapidly and people lived in cramped, dirty housing.
5. T
6. T
7. F, Between 1900 and 1950, the destructive force of nationalism played a part in causing two world wars.

## Section 3 Guided Reading and Review

1. During the Industrial Revolution, goods went from being made by hand to being made by machines in factories.

2. The first machines were invented to speed up the weaving of textiles.

3. Food could be grown in large quantities by fewer people and transported quickly to supply factory workers in the cities.

4. They lived in cramped, dirty housing, where diseases spread rapidly. In the factories, workers were taken advantage of by owners and paid low wages.

5. They wanted colonies to supply the raw materials, such as cotton, wood, and minerals, industry needed. They also wanted markets for the goods produced.

6. European countries competed strongly for new colonies, colonizing most of Africa, Southeast Asia, and many South Pacific islands.

7. Great Britain, the Soviet Union, France, China, and the United States made up the Allies during World War II.

8. Industrial Revolution
9. textile
10. imperialism
11. nationalism
12. alliance

## Answer Key (continued)

### Section 3 Quiz

1. T
2. T
3. F, The political and economic control of one country by another is called imperialism.
4. T
5. F, The period in the 1800s when products began to be made by machines in factories is called the Industrial Revolution.
6. c  7. c  8. a  9. d  10. c

### Section 4 Reading Readiness Guide

Answers will vary. Correct answers are:

1. T
2. F, In the 1540s, Ivan IV earned the name Ivan the Terrible for his cruelty to those he conquered and to his own people.
3. T
4. T
5. T
6. F, After World War II, the Cold War was a time of tension between the United States and the Soviet Union, which lasted from 1945 to 1991.
7. F, After the breakup of the Soviet Union, Russia changed its name to the Russian Federation, which has made efforts to build a western-style economy.

### Section 4 Guided Reading and Review

Students' answers for 1–12 will vary. Correct answers include:

1. Mongol invaders from Asia swept in and conquered the Slavs living in the region that eventually became the Russian Empire.
2. By the 1330s, the prince of Moscow had become the strongest ruler in the region and Moscow conquered surrounding territory.

3. By the end of the 1400s, Moscow had freed itself entirely from Mongol rule.
4. In the 1540s, Ivan IV became the first tsar, or emperor, of the region. He was known as Ivan the Terrible for his cruelty.
5. In 1613, Michael Romanov became tsar and restored order to Russia.
6. When Peter the Great came to power in 1689, he brought Western European ideas and culture to Russia.
7. Napoleon and his French army invaded Russia in 1812.
8. In 1894, Nicholas II became the last Russian tsar.
9. In 1914, Russia entered World War I against Germany and the Russian people suffered severe food and fuel shortages.
10. Tsar Nicholas II was forced to give up his throne, and Lenin became the new leader of Russia, establishing a communist government.
11. After World War II, the United States and the Soviet Union were the world's two most powerful countries and relations between them were extremely tense.
12. The Soviet Union forces Eastern European countries to become communist and cut off contact with the West. The Soviets also tried to expand their power beyond Eastern Europe to Asia and Africa.
13. the adoption of western European culture
14. a Russian emperor
15. ideas that relate to or cause the overthrow of a government or other great change
16. a political system in which a country's property and resources belong equally to everyone

### Section 4 Quiz

1. F, A Russian emperor is called a tsar.
2. T

## Answer Key *(continued)*

3. F, Soviets believed in communism, a theory that says a country's property and resources should be equally shared.
4. F, An idea that could cause the overthrow of a government is considered to be revolutionary.
5. d  6. b  7. c  8. c

## Section 5 Reading Readiness Guide

Answers will vary. Correct answers are:
1. T
2. T
3. F, The Maastricht Treaty laid out the plan for European Union nations to adopt a single currency.
4. F, The European Union currency is called the euro.
5. F, Unlike the United States, the European Union is not a federation of states; it is a group of individual countries that have agreed to give certain powers to the EU.
6. T
7. T

## Section 5 Guided Reading and Review

1. He wanted European nations to work together to control their coal and steel industries.
2. Today, the ECSC is called the European Union. It has 25 member states.
3. The treaty laid out the plan for EU nations to adopt a single currency called the euro.
4. Denmark, Sweden, and the United Kingdom chose not to adopt the euro.
5. The goal of the EU was to make future wars impossible by binding together the people and governments of Europe.
6. Throughout the EU, people can move around freely without needing special visas or permits.

7. the European Parliament, the Council of the European Union, and the European Commission
8. euro
9. single market
10. foreign minister

## Section 5 Quiz

1. the official currency of the European Union
2. system in which goods, services, and capital move freely without barriers
3. a government official who is in charge of a nation's foreign affairs
4. c  5. c  6. b  7. d  8. c  9. a  10. b

## Target Reading Skill

### Reread and Read Ahead
Answers will vary.

### Paraphrase
Answers will vary.

### Summarize
Answers will vary.

## Word Knowledge

Students' definitions and/or examples will vary.

## Enrichment

Students' research topics and reports will vary.

## Skills for Life

Answers will vary.

## Primary Sources and Literature Readings

### A Spartan Reply
1. The Spartans are saying that Phillip should not count on entering their country, let alone conquering it.
2. It means they live a plain, simple life as the ancient Spartans did.

## *Answer Key* (continued)

### Storm in the State

1. On the surface, he is describing a ship caught and battered by a huge storm. It is generally believed the storm is a metaphor for political turmoil threatening the "ship of state." Images include the winds blowing from different directions, rolling waves on all sides, a ship at the mercy of these forces, with water pouring over its decks, a sail full of holes, and ropes loosening.
2. The society is being destroyed by opposing political forces.

### Testing a Theory

1. Pascal is asking his brother to help him do the experiment to find what effect altitude has on air pressure. Answers will vary. Students may suggest science was conducted by amateurs in those days, but that hypotheses were made and then confirmed by experiments that could be repeated with the same results, as is the case today.
2. Answers will vary. Accept all reasonable answers.

### A Child in Prison Camp

1. Shizuye feels upset at losing her rights and disbelief that the government finds her father threatening. She is secretly happy when she learns about rejoining her father and living in the mountains, but she will miss the sea and the city where she is born. She is excited about the journey.
2. Answers will vary.
3. Accept all reasonable answers.

### A Letter from Napoleon's Army

1. The soldiers were surprised because they thought they had won. The small number of prisoners suggested this was not the case. Most of the Russians had withdrawn to fight another day.
2. The immensity of the land gave the Russians room to fight and hide. They were more used to the climate than the French, who had no experience with heavy snow and ice.

### Lenin's Deathbed Words

1. Answers will vary. Possible answer: Lenin wants the new government to be run in a more civil and reasonable way than he feels Stalin will run it.
2. Answers will vary. Possible answer: Lenin feels that Stalin does not have the qualities of a good and trustworthy leader.

### Kampf

1. Answers will vary. Possible answer: Stalin seems to enjoy the planning and preparing of brutality.
2. Answers will vary. Possible answer: Stalin was scheming and devious.

### The Endless Steppe

1. Answers will vary. It may make you feel vulnerable and alone.
2. Esther is surprised because the common view of Siberia is that it is icy, cold, and covered with snow.

### Whose Falkland Islands Are They?

1. Thatcher's reasons were that the land belonged to Great Britain for 150 years and the people living there were British citizens. The Falkland Islands were being taken over by force and the people asked for help from Britain. Attempts at peaceful solutions failed. Ignoring the invasion would lead others to try to take over territory that didn't belong to them.
2. Because the Falklands are islands, Great Britain used a fleet of ships to transport and land troops. Also, airplanes were used to drive out invaders.

### Lords and Vassals

1. It valued duty and loyalty. This kept the workers and lords from harming one another.
2. They are the same, according to this document.

## Answer Key *(continued)*

### Writing Skills: Writing Stories
Students' answers will vary.

### Vocabulary Development
Students' sentences will vary.

### Test A
1. d  2. g  3. a  4. i  5. c
6. c  7. b  8. c  9. a  10. d
11. b  12. c  13. c  14. c

15. Answers will vary. A possible answer: During the Roman Empire, an emperor ruled the people according to a system of well-organized written laws. After the fall of the Roman Empire, however, there was no central government. This period was called the Middle Ages. During the Middle Ages, people were ruled by feudal lords who controlled local areas. These lords, who were loyal to a more powerful leader, or king, collected taxes, maintained order, and enforced the laws. The serfs who worked on the lords' manors could not leave without permission.

16. Answers will vary. A possible answer: During the 1600s and 1700s, far-reaching changes occurred in both government and science. Politically, it was the beginning of modern democracy as people began to question the absolute power traditionally held by monarchs. In the 18th century, there were revolutions in both America and France. There was also a Scientific Revolution, during which scientists learned to base their theories on facts that were tested via the scientific method.

17. how dams can affect areas surrounding them

18. Possible answers: Rivers would no longer deposit silt along their banks. Fish in a river could disappear. Land erosion could become a problem.

19. Rivers might stop supporting living organisms, including the fish people eat.

20. Soil wouldn't get silt deposits. Erosion might occur.

### Test B
1. d  2. e  3. i  4. b  5. h
6. b  7. b  8. a  9. a  10. b
11. c  12. c  13. a  14. d

15. Answers will vary. A possible answer: Feudalism was a method of organizing society when there was no central government. Under feudalism, leaders called lords, ruled the local areas and owned land called a manor. The people who worked on the land were called serfs and they depended on the lord for protection. Feudalism was important during this period because following the collapse of the Roman Empire, the powerful laws of the Roman government no longer protected people.

16. Answers will vary. A possible answer: Under the tsars, there were two groups of people: the very rich and the very poor. The serfs were very poor. They could not own land and they were under the control of the person whose land they worked. When the serfs complained about their living conditions, the tsar sent troops against them. Because they were unfairly treated, the serfs opposed the tsars, which eventually led to the Russian Revolution.

17. Dams are built along rivers and waterways to control natural water sources.

18. Possible answers: Rivers would no longer deposit silt along their banks. Fish in a river could disappear. Land erosion could become a problem.

19. Farmers living downstream from a dam would have their crops irrigated.

20. Farmers lose silt deposits left by a moving river. Also, there could be erosion and a loss of natural fertilizers.

Cultures of Europe and Russia
SECTION 1 Lesson Plan

# The Cultures of Western Europe

**Key**
**L1** Basic to Average
**L2** For All Students
**L3** Average to Advanced
**ELL** English Language Learners

⏱ *1 period, .5 block*

## Section Objectives

1. Find out how industry has led to the growth of cities and increased wealth.
2. Learn about the cultural centers of Western Europe.
3. Understand how open borders affect life in Western Europe.

## Vocabulary

• urbanization • immigrant

## Local Standards

## Reading/Language Arts Objective

Learn how to identify main ideas.

---

### PREPARE TO READ

**Build Background Knowledge**
Discuss countries in Western Europe and their capital cities.
**Set a Purpose for Reading**
Have students evaluate statements on the *Reading Readiness Guide.*
**Preview Key Terms**
Teach the section's Key Terms.
**Target Reading Skill**
Introduce the section's Target Reading Skill of **identifying main ideas**.

### Targeted Resources

❑ **All in One** **Europe and Russia Teaching Resources**
  • Reading Readiness Guide, p. 216 **L2**
  • Identify Main Ideas, p. 227 **L2**
❑ **Spanish Reading and Vocabulary Study Guide,** Section 1, pp. 25–26 **ELL** **L1**

---

### INSTRUCT

**Growth of Industry**
Discuss changes in industry after World War II.
**Centers of Culture**
Discuss cultural attractions and popular recreational activities.
**Target Reading Skill**
Review **identifying main ideas**.
**Open Borders**
Discuss travel in Europe.

### Targeted Resources

❑ **All in One** **Europe and Russia Teaching Resources**
  • Guided Reading and Review, p. 217 **L2**
  • Small Group Activity, pp. 233–236 **L3**
❑ **Europe and Russia Transparencies,** Section Reading Support Transparency ER 40 **L2**
❑ **Teacher's Edition**
  • For Advanced Readers, p. 86 **L3**
  • For Special Needs Students, p. 86 **L1**
❑ **Spanish Support,** Guided Reading and Review, p. 24 **ELL** **L2**

---

### ASSESS AND RETEACH

**Assess Progress**
Evaluate student comprehension with the section assessment and section quiz.
**Reteach**
Assign the Reading and Vocabulary Study Guide to help struggling students.
**Extend**
Assign an Enrichment activity.

### Targeted Resources

❑ **All in One** **Europe and Russia Teaching Resources,** Section Quiz, p. 218 **L2**
❑ **Reading and Vocabulary Study Guide,** Section 1, pp. 32–34 **L1**
❑ **Spanish Support,** Section Quiz, p. 25 **ELL** **L2**

---

Section 1: The Cultures of Western Europe
Cultures of Europe and Russia

# Reading Readiness Guide

## K–W–L

With your group, quickly preview the section then brainstorm and list **what you already Know** about Western European cultures in the first column of the chart below. In the second column, write what you **Want to know** or find out from reading the section.

   After you read, review your notes and record **what you Learned** in the third column of the chart.

| What you already know | What you want to know | What you learned |
| --- | --- | --- |
| Example: Most Western European countries are wealthy. | Example: What is Western European wealth based on? | Example: Their wealth is based on industry. Factories in Western Europe make consumer goods that are in great demand around the world. |
| | | |

Section 1: The Cultures of Western Europe
Cultures of Europe and Russia

# Guided Reading and Review

## A. As You Read

**Directions:** *As you read Section 1, fill in the following chart with facts about the development and cultures of Western Europe. Write two facts for each category.*

**The Development and Culture of Western Europe**

| | |
|---|---|
| Growth of Industry | 1. |
| | 2. |
| Centers of Culture | 3. |
| | 4. |
| European Union | 5. |
| | 6. |
| Immigrants | 7. |
| | 8. |
| Open Borders | 9. |
| | 10. |

## B. Reviewing Key Terms

**Directions:** *Write the definitions for the following key terms in the blanks provided.*

11. urbanization

_____

12. immigrant

_____

Chapter and Section Support

Name _____ Date _____ Class _____

Section 1: The Cultures of Western Europe
Cultures of Europe and Russia

# Section Quiz

## A. Key Terms

**Directions:** *Read the statements below. If a statement is true, write T in the blank provided. If it is false, write F. Rewrite false statements on the back of this page to make them true.*

_____ 1. In Western Europe, the growth of cities, or urbanization, increased after World War II.

_____ 2. A person who moves to one country from another is an immigrant.

## B. Main Ideas

**Directions:** *Write the letter of the correct answer in each blank.*

_____ 3. One important change that affected agriculture in Western Europe was
    **a.** more shipping routes.        **c.** better farm machines.
    **b.** more public schools.        **d.** decreases in soil quality.

_____ 4. How did the Industrial Revolution affect farmers in Western Europe?
    **a.** Farmers moved to the cities.        **c.** Farmers worked harder.
        **d.** Farmers became merchants.
    **b.** Farmers worked on large farms.

_____ 5. Today, most Western Europeans are
    **a.** farmers.        **c.** factory or service workers.
    **b.** merchants or farmers.        **d.** miners or factory workers.

_____ 6. What is the European Union's role in the arts?
    **a.** It does nothing to support the arts.        **c.** It funds programs to help cultural development.
    **b.** It discourages the arts.        **d.** It encourages cultural diffusion.

_____ 7. Most of France's immigrants come from
    **a.** Algeria.        **c.** Turkey.
    **b.** the former Yugoslavia.        **d.** India.

_____ 8. Which currency has been replaced by the euro?
    **a.** the French franc        **c.** the Italian lira
    **b.** the German mark        **d.** all of the above

Cultures of Europe and Russia
SECTION 2 Lesson Plan

**Key**
L1 Basic to Average
L2 For All Students
L3 Average to Advanced
ELL English Language Learners

# The Cultures of Eastern Europe

⏱ *2 periods, 1 block (includes Skills for Life)*

## Section Objectives

1. Learn about the different ethnic groups in Eastern Europe.
2. Understand the impact of foreign domination on the region.
3. Find out about ethnic conflict in Eastern Europe.
4. Learn about Eastern Europe's cultural centers.

## Vocabulary

• migration • ethnic group • dialect

## Local Standards

## Reading/Language Arts Objective

Learn how to identify supporting details in a text to help understand the main idea.

---

### PREPARE TO READ

**Build Background Knowledge**
Discuss the origins of different ethnic groups.
**Set a Purpose for Reading**
Have students evaluate statements on the *Reading Readiness Guide.*
**Preview Key Terms**
Teach the section's Key Terms.
**Target Reading Skill**
Introduce the section's Target Reading Skill of **identifying supporting details**.

### Targeted Resources

❑ **All in One Europe and Russia Teaching Resources**
  • Reading Readiness Guide, p. 220 L2
  • Identify Supporting Details, p. 228 L2
❑ **Spanish Reading and Vocabulary Study Guide,** Section 2, pp. 27–28 ELL L1

---

### INSTRUCT

**Eastern Europe's Ethnic Groups**
Discuss the Slavs.
**Target Reading Skill**
Review **identifying supporting details**.
**Foreign Domination**
**Ethnic Conflict**
Discuss conflicts in Czechoslovakia and Yugoslavia.
**European Centers of Culture**
Discuss the major cities of Prague and Budapest.

### Targeted Resources

❑ **All in One Europe and Russia Teaching Resources**
  • Guided Reading and Review, p. 221 L2
  • Skills for Life, p. 232 L2
❑ **Europe and Russia Transparencies,** Section Reading Support Transparency ER 41 L2
❑ **Teacher's Edition,** For Gifted and Talented, p. 96 L3
❑ **Spanish Support,** Guided Reading and Review, p. 26 ELL L2

---

### ASSESS AND RETEACH

**Assess Progress**
Evaluate student comprehension with the section assessment and section quiz.
**Reteach**
Assign the Reading and Vocabulary Study Guide to help struggling students.
**Extend**
Extend the lesson by assigning a Book Project.

### Targeted Resources

❑ **All in One Europe and Russia Teaching Resources**
  • Section Quiz, p. 222 L2
  • Book Project, pp. 80–82 L3
❑ **Reading and Vocabulary Study Guide,** Section 2, pp. 35–37 L1
❑ **Spanish Support,** Section Quiz, p. 27 ELL L2

---

Section 2: The Cultures of Eastern Europe
Cultures of Europe and Russia

# Reading Readiness Guide

## Anticipation Guide

How much do you think you know about the ethnic groups in Eastern Europe? As your teacher reads the statements, mark whether you think each statement is true (T) or false (F) in the Me column. Then discuss your answers with your group and mark the group's decision in the Group column. As you read, look for information that will clarify whether the statements are true or false.

After you read the section, read the statements again and mark the After Reading column to indicate whether they are true or false.

| Before Reading | | Statements | After Reading |
|---|---|---|---|
| Me | Group | | |
| | | 1. Because movement throughout much of Eastern Europe has always been easy, various groups have crossed through this region for thousands of years. | |
| | | 2. The Albanians migrated across Eastern Europe long ago and first lived in parts of present-day Poland, Slovakia, and Ukraine. | |
| | | 3. Today, descendants of Albanians make up most of Eastern Europe's ethnic groups. | |
| | | 4. Today, about ten Slavic languages are spoken in Eastern Europe, including Czech, Polish, and Russian. | |
| | | 5. About 90 percent of the people of Hungary belong to an ethnic group called the Magyars. | |
| | | 6. In 1993, the Czechs and Slovaks agreed to separate peacefully and form two countries—the Czech Republic and Slovakia. | |
| | | 7. Budapest got the nickname "Queen of the Rhine" because of the beauty of the Rhine River and the hills surrounding the city. | |

Section 2: The Cultures of Eastern Europe
Cultures of Europe and Russia

# Guided Reading and Review

## A. As You Read

**Directions:** *As you read Section 2, answer the following questions in the spaces provided.*

1. Why has movement always been easy throughout much of Eastern Europe?

   _____

2. What are some of the reasons for the frequent migration in Eastern Europe?

   _____

   _____

3. What happened to the Slavic language as the Slavs separated?

   _____

4. What are two important differences among Slavs? _____

   _____

5. What are the names of some other ethnic groups in Eastern Europe?

   _____

6. After World War II, what country influenced the Eastern European
   governments? _____

7. What decision did the leaders in Czechoslovakia make in 1993? Why did they
   make this decision? _____

   _____

8. Name some composers who lived and worked in Prague and Budapest.

   _____

## B. Reviewing Key Terms

**Directions:** *Complete these sentences by writing the correct key terms in the blanks provided.*

9. For thousands of years, various groups have entered or crossed through
   Eastern Europe. This movement from place to place is called

   _____.

10. A(n) _____ is a group of people who share the same
    ancestors, culture, language, or religion, which sets them apart from their
    neighbors.

11. Even though two Slavs may speak the same language, they may not speak the
    same _____.

Chapter and Section Support

Section 2: The Cultures of Eastern Europe
Cultures of Europe and Russia

# Section Quiz

## A. Key Terms

**Directions:** *If a statement is true, write T in the blank provided. If it is false, write F. Rewrite false statements on the back of this page to make them true.*

_____ 1. A regional version of a language is a dialogue.

_____ 2. People who share the same ancestors, culture, language, or religion are members of the same ethnic group.

_____ 3. For many years, there has been a migration throughout Eastern Europe.

## B. Main Ideas

**Directions:** *Write the letter of the correct answer in each blank.*

_____ 4. One reason people have moved throughout Eastern Europe is to search for
    **a.** a different climate.        **c.** new trade routes.
    **b.** natural resources.       **d.** new countries to conquer.

_____ 5. Two important differences among Slavs living in Eastern Europe are their
    **a.** ethnic backgrounds and religions.    **c.** ethnic backgrounds and languages.
    **b.** languages and religions.    **d.** religions and occupations.

_____ 6. Which of the following countries is mostly Slavic?
    **a.** Albania        **c.** Hungary
    **b.** Croatia        **d.** Romania

_____ 7. Which of the following makes up most of the population of Hungary?
    **a.** the Magyars       **c.** the Roma
    **b.** Germans        **d.** Albanians

_____ 8. Where did most of the Czechs live in Czechoslovakia?
    **a.** in Slovakia       **c.** in Bohemia and Moravia
    **b.** in Chechnya       **d.** in Belarus and Moldova

_____ 9. Why did students and writers protest communist rule in Czechoslovakia?
    **a.** low wages       **c.** required to work in factories
    **b.** government dictated material to study and write    **d.** wanted democratic government

_____ 10. Why did Czechoslovakia split into two separate nations in 1993?
    **a.** ethnic conflict       **c.** military treaty
    **b.** economic problems      **d.** disagreement about running government

Cultures of Europe and Russia
SECTION 3 Lesson Plan

# The Cultures of the Russian Federation

🕐 *3 periods, 1.5 block (includes Chapter Review and Assessment)*

## Section Objectives
1. Learn about Russia's ethnic groups.
2. Find out about the Russian culture and educational system.

## Vocabulary
• heritage • propaganda

## Local Standards

## Reading/Language Arts Objective
Learn how to identify implied main ideas to help remember the most important information.

## PREPARE TO READ

**Build Background Knowledge**
Ask students to discuss works of art that they like or dislike.
**Set a Purpose for Reading**
Have students evaluate statements on the *Reading Readiness Guide.*
**Preview Key Terms**
Teach the section's Key Terms.
**Target Reading Skill**
Introduce the section's Target Reading Skill of **identifying main ideas**.

## Targeted Resources

❑ **All in One Europe and Russia Teaching Resources**
  • Reading Readiness Guide, p. 224 **L2**
  • Identify Implied Main Ideas, p. 229 **L2**
❑ **Spanish Reading and Vocabulary Study Guide,** Section 3, pp. 29–30 **ELL L1**

## INSTRUCT

**Russia's Ethnic Groups**
Discuss ethnic groups in Russia.
**Target Reading Skill**
Review **identifying main ideas**.
**Eyewitness Technology**
Discuss the beginning of the space age.
**Russian Culture and Education**
Discuss art and education in Russia.

## Targeted Resources

❑ **All in One Europe and Russia Teaching Resources,** Guided Reading and Review, p. 225 **L2**
❑ **Europe and Russia Transparencies,** Section Reading Support Transparency ER 42 **L2**
❑ **Teacher's Edition,** For Special Needs Students, p. 105 **L1**
❑ **Spanish Support,** Guided Reading and Review, p. 28 **ELL L2**

## ASSESS AND RETEACH

**Assess Progress**
Evaluate student comprehension with the section assessment and section quiz.
**Reteach**
Assign the Reading and Vocabulary Study Guide to help struggling students.
**Extend**
Extend the lesson by assigning a literature reading.

## Targeted Resources

❑ **All in One Europe and Russia Teaching Resources**
  • Section Quiz, p. 226 **L2**
  • Chapter Tests A and B, pp. 247–252 **L2**
❑ **Reading and Vocabulary Study Guide,** Section 3, pp. 38–40 **L1**
❑ **Spanish Support**
  • Section Quiz, p. 29 **ELL L2**
  • Chapter Summary, p. 30 **ELL L2**
  • Vocabulary Development, p. 31 **ELL L2**

Section 3: The Cultures of the Russian Federation
Cultures of Europe and Russia

# Reading Readiness Guide

## K–W–L

With your group, quickly preview the section then brainstorm and list **what you already Know** about Russia's ethnic groups and culture in the first column of the chart below. In the second column, write what you **Want to know** or find out from reading the section.

After you read, review your notes and record **what you Learned** in the third column of the chart.

| What you already know | What you want to know | What you learned |
|---|---|---|
| Example: Most Russians belong to the ethnic group of Russian Slavs and speak the Russian language. | Example: Where do most Russian Slavs live? | Example: Most of them live in western parts of the Russian Federation. |

Section 3: The Cultures of the Russian Federation
Cultures of Europe and Russia

# Guided Reading and Review

## A. As You Read

**Directions:** *As you read Section 3, complete the following chart with details about the Russian Federation. Write two details for each category.*

**Details about Culture in the Russian Federation**

| Religion | 1. |
| | 2. |
| Ethnic Groups | 3. |
| | 4. |
| Culture | 5. |
| | 6. |
| St. Petersburg | 7. |
| | 8. |
| Education | 9. |
| | 10. |

## B. Reviewing Key Terms

**Directions:** *Write the definitions for the following key terms in the blanks provided.*

11. heritage

_____

12. propaganda

_____

Chapter and Section Support

Section 3: The Cultures of the Russian Federation
Cultures of Europe and Russia

# Section Quiz

## A. Key Terms

**Directions:** *Read the statements below. If a statement is true, write T in the blank provided. If it is false, write F. Rewrite false statements on the back of this page to make them true.*

_____ 1. Customs and practices passed from one generation to the next are a culture.

_____ 2. The only art allowed by the Soviet government was propaganda supporting communism.

## B. Main Ideas

**Directions:** *Write the letter of the correct answer in each blank.*

_____ 3. Most of the Russian people belong to which ethnic group?
   **a.** Russian Slavs                    **c.** Mongolians
   **b.** Armenians                        **d.** Yakuts

_____ 4. Many ethnic groups living in Russia
   **a.** are descended from the           **c.** speak languages other than
   Mongolians.                             Russian.
   **b.** live in the same village.        **d.** practice many different religions.

_____ 5. Which of the following is the largest religious group in the Russian Federation?
   **a.** Islam                            **c.** Russian Orthodox
   **b.** Buddhism                         **d.** Judiasm

_____ 6. In 1991, what former Soviet republic gained independence?
   **a.** the Russian Federation          **c.** the Neva
   **b.** Armenia                          **d.** Mongolia

_____ 7. How has the new Russian government tried to keep the country unified?
   **a.** by allowing ethnic groups        **c.** by giving ethnic groups the right
   the right to form their                 to rule themselves
   own countries
                                           **d.** by repressing Russian heritage
   **b.** by forming a new Soviet
   Union

_____ 8. Which of the following Russians composed classical music?
   **a.** Leo Tolstoy                      **c.** Wassily Kandinsky
   **b.** Peter Tchaikovsky                **d.** Yuri Gagarin

# Target Reading Skill: Identifying the Main Idea

## Identify Main Ideas

Since you cannot remember every detail of what you read, it is important that you identify the main ideas. The main idea of a section or paragraph is the most important point being made and the one you should remember.

The first thing to do to identify the main idea of a section in a textbook, for example, is to look at each heading and subheading in the section. The headings will give you a clue to the section's main idea. As you read the text that comes after each heading stop and ask yourself, "What is the main idea here?" Sometimes you will find that the main idea is stated in the first sentence or two of the paragraph. Other times, however, the main idea is more difficult to find. It is helpful to remember that details are facts in the paragraph that tell you more about the main idea. You can use the details provided to help determine the main idea.

Read the paragraph below:

**Preserving Habitat**
Many Westerners are working to preserve the land areas where black bears and other wild animals live. Parts of the West have been made into national parks, forests, and wilderness areas. In addition, logging companies are working to preserve the environment by planting new trees to replace the ones that have been cut down.

What is the main idea? If you guessed that the main idea was that people in the West are preserving land for wild animals, you are correct.

After you read a section, ask yourself, "What was the most important event?" "Who was the most important person described in the paragraph?" "What is this paragraph about?" After you have an answer to one of these questions, look for one sentence that expresses that idea. Then ask yourself, do the details in the section support this idea?

**Directions:** *Read the following paragraph. Underline the main idea and then write down three details that support it.*

The largest, wealthiest, and most influential city in the United States is New York City. More than 8 million people live there, making it one of the 10 largest cities in the world. New York is the center of fashion, publishing, and the arts in the United States. The headquarters of many of the country's wealthiest corporations are in New York. New York City's skyline is recognized by people around the world.

1. _____

2. _____

3. _____

**Chapter and Section Support**

Cultures of Europe and Russia

# Target Reading Skill: Identifying the Main Idea

## Identify Supporting Details

Identifying the main idea gives you the "big picture" in a paragraph or within a section of your textbook. Supporting details explain the main idea and help you understand it better. Supporting details provide facts, examples, and reasons.

In order to find the supporting details in a paragraph, you should first identify the main idea. You may wish to jot it down on a piece of paper using an outline format similar to the one below. Then, look for the supporting details and add them to your outline. Details support the main idea by telling the reader *what, where, why, how much,* and *how many.* Remember that Roman numeral I is the main idea of the paragraph. The letters that follow are the supporting details. They provide examples and facts to support the main idea.

Read the paragraph below and then complete the outline.

### Sailors of the Seventh Century

South Americans have been trading with the people of Mexico since at least A.D. 600. They sailed north from Ecuador, Colombia, and Peru on rafts. These adventurers traded not only goods such as tweezers and bells, but also skills and ideas. For example, they taught the people of Mexico how to make metal objects such as needles.

I. South Americans trade with Mexico [main idea]

   A. Trading since A.D. 600 [supporting detail]

   B. Traded goods such as tweezers and bells [supporting detail]

   C. _____

**Directions:** *Read the section in your textbook assigned by your teacher. Choose a subsection. Then, on a separate piece of paper, create an outline similar to the one above for each paragraph in the subsection.*

Cultures of Europe and Russia

# Target Reading Skill: Identifying the Main Idea

## Identify Implied Main Ideas

Identifying main ideas in your reading will help you remember the important points. One of the first steps in identifying main ideas is to look at each heading and subheading in the section. This will give you the "big picture."

Sometimes, the main idea is not stated in a single sentence. All the details in a paragraph may point to, or add up to, the main idea. In cases like this, we say that the main idea is implied, or suggested. It is up to you to put the details together and identify the main idea of the paragraph. As you read, ask yourself, "What is happening?" "What is this about?" The answer to these questions will lead you to the main idea.

**Directions:** *In the paragraphs below, the main idea is not stated in a single sentence. It is implied. Read the paragraph and see if you can identify the main idea from the choices below each paragraph.*

_____ 1. Early people gathered the seeds of the wild grains. People spent a lot of their time searching for food. However, about 10,000 years ago, people in Southwest Asia decided to try to plant wild wheat to tide them over. The first crop was poor. But farmers saved seeds from the best plants and tried again the next year. Their efforts led to today's domesticated wheat.

    **a.** Farming began when people planted grains.

    **b.** Wild grains are hard to grow.

    **c.** The domestication of today's wheat began 10,000 years ago.

    **d.** Gathering wild grain is hard.

_____ 2. The glaciers were over a mile in thickness. As the glaciers moved they changed the landscape. They dug deep trenches in the land. Water from the melting glaciers filled these trenches to produce the Great Lakes.

    **a.** Glaciers melt.

    **b.** Glaciers formed the Great Lakes.

    **c.** All lakes are formed from glaciers.

    **d.** Glaciers change the earth.

**Chapter and Section Support**

Name _____ Date _____ Class _____

Cultures of Europe and Russia

# Word Knowledge

**Directions:** *As your teacher reads the words, think about what each word might mean and mark the appropriate number in the Before Reading column.*

① = Know it ② = Kind of know it ③ = Don't know it

After you have read and discussed the chapter, rate the words again in the After Reading column. Then write a definition or example for each word to help you clarify and remember the words.

| | Word | Rating | | Definition or Example |
|---|---|---|---|---|
| | | **Before Reading** | **After Reading** | |
| **Section 1** | revolution, *n.* | | | |
| | scholar, *n.* | | | |
| | recreation, *n.* | | | |
| | exchange, *v.* | | | |
| **Section 2** | descendant, *n.* | | | |
| | conflict, *n.* | | | |
| | thrive, *v.* | | | |
| **Section 3** | unify, *v.* | | | |
| | intricate, *adj.* | | | |
| | campaign, *n.* | | | |

Cultures of Europe and Russia

# Enrichment

## Talk With Shakespeare

**Directions:** *The English writer William Shakespeare (1564–1616) wrote some of the greatest works of English literature. Shakespeare invented many words and well-known expressions such as "fair play" and "catch cold." Certain lines and passages from Shakespeare's works, like the ones below, have become famous and are often quoted. Read the following passages. What do you think they mean? On a separate sheet of paper, write a sentence saying what you think Shakespeare meant in each quotation.*

"A horse! A horse! My kingdom for a horse!"
from *Richard III*

"All that glitters is not gold."
from *The Merchant of Venice*

"How sharper than a serpent's tooth it is
To have a thankless child!"
from *King Lear*

"Some are born great, some achieve greatness,
and some have greatness thrust upon 'em."
from *Twelfth Night*

"All the world's a stage,
And all the men and women merely players."
from *As You Like It*

"Neither a borrower nor a lender be."
from *Hamlet*

"[First] to thine own self be true."
from *Hamlet*

From *The Complete Works of Shakespeare*, edited by David Bevington. Copyright © 1992 by HarperCollins Publishers Inc. Reprinted by permission of Addison-Wesley Educational Publishers Inc.

**Chapter and Section Support**

Cultures of Europe and Russia

# Skills for Life

## Supporting a Position

**Directions:** *Read the following excerpt from your textbook about Russia's educational system. Then, answer the questions in the spaces provided.*

After the fall of the Soviet Union, the Russian Federation continued free public schooling for children between ages 6 and 17. When students finish ninth grade, they can choose to continue their education in a secondary school or a vocational school. Secondary schools emphasize academic subjects such as mathematics and science, while the vocational schools prepare students for careers in industry and agriculture.

1. Imagine you are a ninth-grade student in Russia's school system. Would you decide to continue your education in a secondary school or in a vocational school? Write a statement to present to your parents summarizing the educational choice you believe would be best for your future.

   _____

   _____

   _____

2. Identify at least three reasons to support your position.

   _____

   _____

   _____

3. What additional reasons, details, and examples might support your position and strengthen the argument for your educational choice?

   _____

   _____

   _____

4. Rewrite your position in a logical and effective order.

   _____

   _____

   _____

Cultures of Europe and Russia

# Small Group Activity

## European and Russian Music

Throughout Europe and Russia, many different kinds of music can be heard. Each country and ethnic group has unique styles of traditional folk music. Also, many countries have long histories of classical music. Today there is a variety of popular musical forms, including jazz and music influenced by immigrants from around the world. In this activity, you will choose one country or ethnic group and explore either its classical or folk music. You will find recorded examples and information about the culture that produced the music and share these with the class.

### Background

There are too many different European musical forms to list here. You have probably heard European classical music. You may know some of the composers, such as Bach, Mozart, Beethoven, or Tchaikovsky. You also may have heard some types of folk music, such as Spanish flamenco or Polish polkas. These are just some varieties of music to explore. More traditional folk music styles have been passed from generation to generation for hundreds of years. Many of them are played for dancers, who often wear traditional costumes. One of the reasons European music is familiar is that it has strongly influenced American music. Most classical concerts include music by European composers. Many American folk and pop forms contain elements of folk songs that came from different parts of Europe.

### Procedure

1. **Find recordings and information.** Read all the steps in this project. Then, meet with your group to divide the jobs. To begin, group members can search for recordings of folk or classical music from Europe and Russia. Ask your librarian for help. You might also call a local music store and ask for suggestions. Try to find unusual examples that other students may not have heard. When you have found music you like, look for information about the culture from which it came. You may find what you need on the liner notes of the recordings. Or you may find it in encyclopedias and books from the library.

2. **Organize recordings and information.** Now that you have focused on one area, gather all the materials you have. You might take notes about the examples you would like to share. Work together to choose a presentation order. Jot down ideas on the back of this page or on a seperate sheet of paper.

Chapter and Section Support

## *Small Group Activity* (continued)

Discuss as a group how you would like to present your music. You might play
examples and then talk about each one. You can include information about
where the music is found, what instruments are used, whether it is used for
dance or ceremonies, and where students can find more examples. Look for
illustrations and photographs of instruments, traditional costumes, or folk
dancers. If you have chosen classical music, you can show photographs of an
orchestra, a chamber group, or a choir.

3. **Write the information.** Remember, you are going to make an oral presentation.
Each group member can take part by preparing a short speech about some part
of the music or culture. You can write down exactly what you will say or prepare
note cards that outline important points.

4. **Present your music.** When you are ready, share your music and information
with the class. Include photos and illustrations and as much interesting
background information as you can. When you play and listen to recordings, be
sure everyone is quiet and really listening. You might consider playing short
examples more than once. In this way, students will have a chance to get used to
music they may not have heard before.

# Small Group Activity: Teacher Page

## European and Russian Music

### Content Objectives

- Students will learn about music from different parts of Europe and Russia.
- Students will gain a deeper understanding of various European and Russian cultures.

### Skill Objectives

- Writing for a purpose—explanation
- Locating information
- Organizing information

### Advance Preparation

Gather the following materials:

- recordings of many types of European and Russian classical and folk music
- cassette, phonograph, or CD player

**Suggested group size:** six students

**Suggested time:** 40 minutes for finding recordings and researching; 40 minutes for preparing the presentation; 40 minutes for presenting and discussing the music

### Procedure

Divide the class into groups. Distribute the student pages and have students begin work on the project. You may wish to give a copy of the rubric for music presentations to each group.

You may wish to help students locate recordings. You can ask the students' families, the library, or local music stores for suggestions or examples. Some families may even have traditional costumes or dress from a region of Europe or Russia.

Encourage students to look for examples of music that are new to them. For example, few students have probably heard Bulgarian women singing, which is extremely beautiful and unusual. You might monitor the choices of each group to be sure the groups are not duplicating each other. In this way, the music presentations will be varied and interesting. During presentations, encourage students to listen carefully, without distractions.

When students have finished presenting the music, invite them to discuss what they have heard and learned. To help students get started, ask questions such as these:

- Have you heard any types of music for the first time? Which examples were new to you?
- What have you learned about European and Russian cultures from listening to their music?
- How well would you say your group worked together?

Cultures of Europe and Russia

# Small Group Activity: Teacher Page

Music presentations will be evaluated according to the following rubric.

## Rubric for Music Presentations

| Grading Criteria | Excellent | Admirable | Acceptable |
| --- | --- | --- | --- |
| **Research** | Students gather a large number of recordings from which to choose; they locate information about the music, instruments, culture, and history. | Students found a variety of recordings; they locate information about the music and culture; they use several different sources. | Students find some recordings of music from a country; they locate information about the music. |
| **Preparing the Presentation** | Students spend a great deal of time preparing their presentation; they choose music examples with purpose; they organize the information, order of speakers, and music well. | Students prepare for the presentation by carefully choosing music examples and organizing the information. | Students choose music examples and prepare information, but they could be more organized. |
| **Presentation** | Each piece of music is accompanied by interesting facts, information, and illustrations; students speak in a relaxed manner and are clearly familiar with their topic; the presentation flows easily from one section to the next. | Each piece of music is accompanied by interesting facts; students are organized and are easily understood. | Some music examples are accompanied by facts; students speak clearly, but could know more about the topic. |
| **Teamwork** | Group members work well together; they are able to reach agreement about important parts of the project; they help each other out and are enthusiastic about their work. | Group members work well together; each student does an important part of the project. | Group members work together; the group may have trouble agreeing about specific parts of the project. |

Cultures of Europe and Russia

# Primary Sources and Literature Readings

## Your Government Has Returned to You!

A speech by Václav Havel

**Communism didn't last very long as a way of government. By the late 1980s, the Soviet Union and its communist government were weakening. In 1990, the country of Czechoslovakia broke free of that influence. Writer Václav Havel was chosen to lead the new democratic government. He had been jailed three times for protesting the old government. Here is part of the speech he made as he took office.**

My dear fellow citizens, for forty years on this day you heard from my predecessors the same thing in a number of variations: how our country is flourishing, how many millions of tons of steel we produce, how happy we all are, how we trust our government, and what bright prospects lie ahead of us.

I assume you did not propose me for this office so that I, too, should lie to you.

Our country is not flourishing. The enormous creative and spiritual potential of our nation is being wasted. Entire branches of industry produce goods that are of no interest to anyone, while we lack the things we need. The state, which calls itself a workers' state, humiliates and exploits workers. Our outmoded economy wastes what little energy we have. A country that once could be proud of the educational level of its citizens now spends so little on education that it ranks seventy-second in the world. We have polluted our land, rivers, and forests, bequeathed to us by our ancestors; we now have the most contaminated environment in all of Europe. People in our country die sooner than in the majority of European countries....

You may ask what kind of republic I dream of. Let me reply: I dream of a republic that is independent, free, and democratic; a republic with economic prosperity yet social justice; a humane republic that serves the individual and therefore hopes that the individual will serve it in turn; a republic of well-rounded people, because without such people, it is impossible to solve any of our problems, whether they be human, economic, ecological, social, or political.

The most distinguished of my predecessors opened his first speech with a quote from Comenius [the great Czech educator of the seventeenth century]. Allow me to end my first speech with my own paraphrase of the same statement: My people, your government has returned to you!

*From Open Letters by Václav Havel. Copyright © 1991 by Václav Havel, published by Alfred A. Knopf, Inc.*

Chapter and Section Support

## *Primary Sources and Literature Readings* (continued)

**Vocabulary Builder**

| | |
|---|---|
| predecessors | those who came before |
| flourishing | thriving, succeeding |
| exploit | take advantage of, use without fair payment |
| outmoded | old-fashioned |
| bequeathed | left to us |
| prosperity | success |
| humane | fair and kind to all people |
| paraphrase | saying someone else's idea or words in your own words |

**Think It Over**

1. What do Václav Havel's comments suggest about the success of the communist revolution?

   _____

   _____

   _____

   _____

   _____

2. What was Václav Havel's dream for the republic under his leadership?

   _____

   _____

   _____

# Primary Sources and Literature Readings

## Lenin's Deathbed Words

by Vladimir Lenin

**An important leader of the Bolshevik movement, Vladimir Lenin helped found the Soviet Union. There was a lot of fighting among different groups within the country as to how the new government should be run. As Lenin lay dying in the early 1920s, many people wanted to take over the power he would leave behind. In this postscript to a letter he wrote in January of 1924, Lenin warned the Soviet people about the danger he saw coming from one of those people, Josef Stalin.**

Postscript: Stalin is too rude, and this fault, entirely supportable in relations among us Communists, becomes insupportable in the office of General Secretary. Therefore, I propose to the comrades to find a way to remove Stalin from that position and appoint to it another man who in all respects differs from Stalin only in superiority—namely, more patient, more loyal, more polite and more attentive to comrades, less capricious, etc. This circumstance may seem an insignificant trifle, but I think that from the point of view of preventing a split and from the point of view of the relation between Stalin and Trotsky which I discussed above, it is not a trifle, or is it such a trifle as may acquire a decisive significance.

—Lenin

Quoted from *A Treasury of the World's Great Letters*, edited and compiled by M. Lincoln Schuster. Copyright © 1940 by Simon & Schuster, Inc. Copyright renewed 1968 by Simon & Schuster, Inc.

---

**Vocabulary Builder**

| | |
|---|---|
| postscript | new text added on to the end of a letter, containing an idea thought of at the last moment |
| supportable | acceptable, supported by reason |
| comrades | members of the Communist party |
| capricious | likely to change his mind without warning or cause |
| trifle | a little and unimportant thing |
| Trotsky | another revolutionary, with whom Stalin was struggling for power |
| decisive | important in deciding |

**Chapter and Section Support**

---

**Think It Over**

1. Lenin gives many reasons for disliking Stalin. What might be another reason for his attitude? _____

_____

2. What reason does Lenin give for wanting Stalin removed?

_____

_____

# Primary Sources and Literature Readings

## Kampf

by Josef Stalin

**Lenin warned the Soviet people about the danger of the leadership qualities and the desire for power of Josef Stalin. Lenin turned out to be right. Josef Stalin was a brutal dictator who killed and jailed many Soviets. The statement below suggests a little of his personality.**

> "To choose one's victim, to prepare one's plans minutely, to stake an implacable vengeance, and then to go to bed…there is nothing sweeter in the world."

Quoted from *A Treasury of the World's Great Letters*, edited and compiled by M. Lincoln Schuster. Copyright © 1940 by Simon & Schuster, Inc. Copyright renewed 1968 by Simon & Schuster, Inc.

---

**Vocabulary Builder**

| | |
|---|---|
| minutely | considering even the tiniest detail |
| implacable | relentless; without any possible relief |
| vengeance | revenge |

---

**Think It Over**

1. What does Stalin's statement reveal about his personality?

   _____

   _____

2. What does this statement tell you about the type of leader he was?

   _____

   _____

Name _____  Date _____  Class _____

Cultures of Europe and Russia

# Primary Sources and Literature Readings

## Housekeeping in Russia Soon After the Revolution

by Marina Tsvetaeva

**Revolution is never easy, especially for families. At first, poet Marina Tsvetaeva supported the Russian Revolution. But in 1919, she wrote to her sister and described the hardships she and her young children were suffering. Her husband, Seryozha, was missing and may have been jailed or killed in the revolution.**

I live with Alya and Irina (Alya is six, Irina two) in our same flat opposite two trees in the attic room which used to be Seryozha's. We have no flour and no bread. Under my writing desk there are about twelve pounds of potatoes which is all that is left from the food 'lent' by my neighbours. These are the only provisions we have. I walk all over Moscow looking for bread. If Alya comes with me, I have to tie Irina to a chair, for safety. I feed Irina, then put her to bed. She sleeps in the blue armchair. There is a bed but it won't go through the door. I boil up some old coffee, and drink it, and have a smoke. I write. Alya writes or reads. There is silence for two hours; then Irina wakes up. We heat up what remains of the mashed goo. With Alya's help, I fish out the potatoes which remain, or rather have become clogged in the bottom of the samovar. Either Alya or myself puts Irina back to bed. Then Alya goes to bed. At 10 pm the day is over.

| Vocabulary Builder | |
|---|---|
| flat | apartment |
| provisions | supplies |
| samovar | a closed pitcher used in Russia to heat up food and drinks |

### Think It Over

1. According to the text, what hardships did the Russian family encounter after the revolution?

   _____

   _____

2. Although a revolution might be successful in overthrowing an old government and creating a new government, why do you think such hardships may occur?

   _____

   _____

   _____

Cultures of Europe and Russia

# Writing Skills

## Writing Plays

Writing a play involves using your imagination to create a plot, a cast of characters, and a script. Playwriting also involves describing stage sets and giving stage directions. That way, when the play is performed, the cast members will know exactly what is expected of them.

To write a play, the playwright needs a purpose and an intended audience. The audience may be a particular group, such as an elementary school or a senior citizens group. The playwright's purpose may be to amuse, to inform, to entertain, to inspire, to shock, or a combination of these or other purposes.

Plays involve spoken words. Therefore, when writing the script, the playwright needs to be able to mimic the way people speak. He or she also needs to construct the play so that it reveals the personalities of the characters through their actions and words and through the comments of other characters.

**Directions:** *Use a topic you feel strongly about as the basis for a play. Choose one of the topics below, and think about how you might convert it into a short play, or choose another topic. Use the spaces to identify your purpose and your audience. Then, describe the basic plot for your play, and list the characters who will take part. When you are satisfied with your plan, use a separate sheet of paper to write the first draft of your play.*

- You have become concerned about the amount of pollution in a nearby body of water. Write a play in which you deal with opposition in trying to protect the water supply.

- Your school has been asked to collect canned food for poor people in the community. Write a play in which students brainstorm ideas for a successful food collection drive.

- A park in your neighborhood has been closed after repeated acts of vandalism. Characters in your play are lobbying to have the park reopened.

- Your own idea: _____

  Purpose of play: _____

  Audience: _____

  Basic plot: _____

  _____

  _____

  Main characters (names and descriptions) _____

  _____

  _____

  _____

Cultures of Europe and Russia

# Vocabulary Development

**Directions:** *Match the key terms in the box with the definitions below. Write the correct letter in each blank. Then, write a sentence in the space provided using that term or the plural form of the term. If necessary, look up the terms in your textbook glossary.*

| | |
|---|---|
| **a.** urbanization | **e.** dialect |
| **b.** immigrant | **f.** heritage |
| **c.** migration | **g.** propaganda |
| **d.** ethnic group | |

_____ **1.** movement from place to place

_____

_____

_____ **2.** the spread of ideas designed to support a cause or hurt an opposing cause

_____

_____

_____ **3.** the customs and practices passed from one generation to the next

_____

_____

_____ **4.** the movement of populations toward cities

_____

_____

_____ **5.** a version of a language found only in a certain region

_____

_____

_____ **6.** a person who moves to one country from another

_____

_____

_____ **7.** a group of people who share the same ancestors, culture, language, or religion

_____

_____

# Rubric for Assessing a Writing Assignment

| Grading Criteria | Excellent | Acceptable | Minimal | Unacceptable |
|---|---|---|---|---|
| **Content** | Clearly focused introduction; idea development interesting and sophisticated; supporting evidence detailed, accurate, and convincing; perceptive conclusion. | Introduction gives assignment direction; idea development clear; supporting evidence accurate; strong conclusion. | Introduction unclear; idea development uneven and simplistic; supporting evidence uneven; conclusion summarizes information in assignment. | Introduction incomplete, ineffective; idea development ineffective; supporting evidence vague, inaccurate, or missing; conclusion incomplete or missing. |
| **Organization** | Paragraph order reinforces content; strong topic sentences make content easy to follow; effective and varied transitions. | Logical paragraph order; clear topic sentences; clear and functional transitions. | Ineffective paragraph order; narrow or inaccurate topic sentences; few clear transitions. | Inconsistent paragraph order; topic sentences and transitions missing. |
| **Mechanics** | Flawless punctuation and spelling; varied and interesting sentence structure. | Few spelling and punctuation errors; sentence structure correct. | Some careless spelling and punctuation errors; some errors in sentence structure. | Many spelling and punctuation errors; many sentence fragments and run-ons. |

# Rubric for Assessing a Student Poster

| Grading Criteria | Excellent | Acceptable | Minimal | Unacceptable |
|---|---|---|---|---|
| **Content** | Well-written text and carefully chosen visuals work together to illustrate and inform about poster subject. | Descriptive text and appropriate visuals work together to inform viewers. | Text contains inaccuracies, and some visual materials lack pertinence or impact. | Text scanty and inaccurate; visuals lack impact. |
| **Design** | Logical and easy to read; type and visuals neatly executed; layout complements the content. | Fairly logical; type and visuals mostly neat and easy to understand. | Somewhat disorganized; fails to complement content. | Disorganized; hastily and carelessly planned. |
| **Visual Appeal** | Pleasing use of color, shapes, symbols, and other graphic elements captures viewers' attention and interest. | Good use of color and eye-catching graphic elements. | Good ideas overshadowed by other elements that distract or give a cluttered appearance. | Little constructive use of color or graphic elements. |
| **Creativity** | Incorporates unique but pertinent ideas, design elements, visuals, or text that make the poster stand out. | Contains some unique or imaginative elements. | Contains some good, although not entirely original, elements. | No evidence of creativity. |

Chapter and Section Support

# Rubric for Assessing an Oral Presentation

| Grading Criteria | Excellent | Acceptable | Minimal | Unacceptable |
|---|---|---|---|---|
| **Preparation** | Gathers information from varied sources; makes note cards to use as cues during the presentation; creates attractive visual aids to illustrate the presentation. | Gathers information from three or four sources; prepares notes and visual aids to use during presentation. | Gathers information from one or two sources; writes presentation word-for-word as it will be given. | Gathers information from only one source; may not be able to complete task because of lack of preparation. |
| **Content** | Abundance of material clearly related to topic; points clearly made; varied use of materials. | Adequate information about the topic; many good points made; some variation in use of materials. | Some information not connected to the topic. | Information included has little connection to topic. |
| **Organization** | Information is well organized and logically ordered; argument easy to follow; conclusion clear. | Most information presented in logical order; argument generally clear and easy to follow. | Ideas loosely connected; organization and flow choppy and somewhat difficult to follow. | No apparent logical order of information in presentation. |
| **Speaking Skills** | Enthusiastic, poised, and confident during the presentation; uses complete sentences; speaks clearly. | Engaged during presentation; speaks mostly in complete sentences. | Little or no expression; enunciation not always clear; speaks mostly in sentence fragments. | Appears disinterested during presentation; hard to understand. |

Cultures of Europe and Russia

# Test A

## A. Key Terms

**Directions:** *Match the phrases in Column I with the key terms in Column II. Write the correct letter in each blank. You will not use all the terms. (15 points)*

**Column I**

_____ 1. the movement of populations to cities

_____ 2. a person who moves to one country from another

_____ 3. movement from place to place by a group

_____ 4. a different version of a language that can be found only in a certain region

_____ 5. customs and practices that are passed from one generation to the next

**Column II**

**a.** dialect

**b.** ethnic group

**c.** heritage

**d.** immigrant

**e.** migration

**f.** propaganda

**g.** urbanization

## B. Key Concepts

**Directions:** *Write the letter of the correct answer in each blank. (45 points)*

_____ 6. Two hundred years ago, most people in Western Europe worked as
   **a.** merchants.
   **b.** sailors.
   **c.** farmers.
   **d.** manufacturers.

_____ 7. What was one result of the Industrial Revolution?
   **a.** the development of small towns
   **b.** the growth of large farms
   **c.** the growth of large cities
   **d.** the increased need for farmworkers

_____ 8. Since World War II, how has the movement of people in Europe changed?
   **a.** Large numbers of people have left Western Europe.
   **b.** People have begun moving to Western Europe.
   **c.** People have left the large cities and moved to farms.
   **d.** People have moved to Eastern Europe and South Asia.

_____ 9. Although Slavs share the same customs, they have different
   **a.** languages and religions.
   **b.** cultures and economies.
   **c.** cultures and languages.
   **d.** religions and economies.

Cultures of Europe and Russia

## Test A *(continued)*

_____ **10.** Which of the following Eastern European countries does *not* have a Slavic majority?

    **a.** Poland          **c.** Albania

    **b.** Croatia        **d.** Slovenia

_____ **11.** What happened when Czechoslovakia divided in 1993?

    **a.** Many ethnic communities fought each other.

    **c.** The Magyars gained most of the land.

    **b.** Two new countries were peacefully formed.

    **d.** One part of the country joined Russia.

_____ **12.** What is one important way in which Russians are reconnecting with their past?

    **a.** by forming separate countries

    **c.** by practicing their religion

    **d.** by learning about Western culture

    **b.** by learning to read and write

_____ **13.** The largest ethnic group in Russia is the

    **a.** Mongolians.        **c.** Turks.

    **b.** Armenians.        **d.** Slavs.

_____ **14.** To keep the country unified, the new Russian government has allowed ethnic groups to

    **a.** rule themselves.

    **c.** form new countries.

    **b.** join forces with other Eastern European countries.

    **d.** join forces with Western European countries.

## C. Critical Thinking

**Directions:** *Answer the following questions on the back of this paper or on a separate sheet of paper. (20 points)*

**15. Recognizing Cause and Effect** What are two ways the Industrial Revolution affected the culture of Western Europe?

**16. Drawing Conclusions** When the Soviet Union fell apart in 1991, some non-Russian ethnic groups broke away to form their own countries. Why do you think this happened?

Cultures of Europe and Russia

*Test A* *(continued)*

## D. Skill: Supporting a Position

**Directions:** *Read the paragraph below and determine what your position is on whether or not the Russian Federation should remain unified or should allow its ethnic groups to form independent nations. Then, answer the questions that follow in the spaces provided. (20 points)*

The Soviet Union was made up of many republics. Each was the homeland of a large ethnic group. When the Soviet Union came apart, the non-Russian republics broke away and formed their own countries. However, other ethnic groups remained part of Russia, sometimes unwillingly. Many of them have called for more rights to rule themselves. Some have even called for independence. These efforts have brought much ethnic tension.

The government of the Russian Federation has tried to keep the country unified. It has given many ethnic groups the right to rule themselves. However, it must work hard to turn the nations' ethnic diversity into an asset, rather than a source of conflict.

17. Write a statement that summarizes your position on whether or not the Russian Federation should remain unified or should break into separate nations.

_____

_____

18. Using the information you learned from the chapter, give one detail, reason, or example that supports your position.

_____

_____

19. Give a second detail, reason, or example that backs up your position.

_____

_____

20. Summarize your position in a one-sentence conclusion.

_____

_____

_____

Chapter and Section Support

Cultures of Europe and Russia

# Test B

## A. Key Terms

**Directions:** *Fill in the blanks in Column I by writing the letter of the correct key term from Column II. You will not use all the terms. (15 points)*

**Column I**

_____ 1. A person who moves from one country to another is known as a(n) _____.

_____ 2. People who share things such as a culture, language, or religion are called a(n) _____.

_____ 3. People who speak the same language may be unable to understand each other if they each speak a different _____, or version of the language.

_____ 4. Customs and practices that are passed from one generation to the next form a culture's _____.

_____ 5. The Soviet government only approved art that supported their _____ campaign.

**Column II**

**a.** dialect

**b.** ethnic group

**c.** heritage

**d.** immigrant

**e.** migration

**f.** propaganda

**g.** urbanization

## B. Key Concepts

**Directions:** *Write the letter of the correct answer in each blank. (45 points)*

_____ 6. As a result of the Industrial Revolution, many people in Western Europe moved to

    **a.** large farms.           **c.** cities.

    **b.** America.            **d.** suburbs.

_____ 7. Since World War II, many people have moved

    **a.** from Europe to North Africa and Asia.        **c.** from Eastern Europe and South Asia to Western Europe.

    **b.** from Western Europe to the United States.        **d.** to Eastern Europe from Western Europe.

Cultures of Europe and Russia

## Test B (continued)

_____ **8.** How has the European Union made the movement of goods, ideas, and people easier?

    **a.** by increasing taxes

    **b.** by increasing the amount of imports

    **c.** by opening borders between member nations

    **d.** by ending taxes

_____ **9.** What are two major differences among Slavs in Eastern Europe?

    **a.** heritage and language

    **b.** language and religion

    **c.** culture and education

    **d.** language and dialect

_____ **10.** Which of the following Eastern European countries has a Slavic majority?

    **a.** Poland

    **b.** Hungary

    **c.** Albania

    **d.** Romania

_____ **11.** The Russian Orthodox religion and the Slavic ethnic group are two important parts of

    **a.** the Russian educational system.

    **b.** communism.

    **c.** the grasslands, the deserts, and the forests.

    **d.** Russia's heritage.

_____ **12.** After the breakup of the Soviet Union, some non-Russian ethnic groups wanted to form

    **a.** their own religion.

    **b.** separate countries.

    **c.** a permanent union with Russia.

    **d.** an alliance with Eastern Europe.

_____ **13.** Under communism, the government only allowed art that

    **a.** had been done during the Renaissance.

    **b.** reflected Western traditions.

    **c.** supported communism.

    **d.** supported the tsar.

_____ **14.** Under the education system of the old Soviet Union, the nation increased

    **a.** the number of religious schools.

    **b.** the high school dropout rate.

    **c.** the number of people who could read and write.

    **d.** the number of private schools.

Cultures of Europe and Russia

***Test B*** *(continued)*

## C. Critical Thinking

**Directions:** *Answer the following questions on the back of this paper or on a separate sheet of paper. (20 points)*

15. **Recognizing Cause and Effect** How do you think the location of Western European countries and the ease of movement between them has affected the cultures of the region?

16. **Drawing Conclusions** During Communist rule, many Eastern European countries kept their culture, religion, and art. However, the republic of the Soviet Union did not. Why do you think this was?

## D. Skill: Supporting a Position

**Directions:** *Read the passage below and determine your position on whether or not the European Union is a positive or negative influence on the cultures of Europe. Then answer the following questions in the spaces provided. (20 points)*

The goal of the European Union (EU) was to make future wars impossible by binding together the people and governments of Europe. It works to achieve that goal by cooperating to promote economic and social progress. The EU is a group of individual countries that have agreed to give certain powers to the European Union, however each nation remains an independent nation. The EU has been effective in opening trade between member nations, has helped stabilize economies, and has encouraged cultural exchange. However, there are some Europeans who feel that the EU is causing each member's nation to lose its cultural identity and uniqueness.

17. Write a statement that summarizes your position on whether or not the European Union is a positive or negative influence on the cultures of Europe.

_____

_____

18. Using the information you learned from the chapter, give one detail, reason, or example that supports your position.

_____

19. Give a second detail, reason, or example that backs up your position.

_____

20. Summarize your position in a one-sentence conclusion.

_____

_____

# Answer Key

## Section 1 Reading Readiness Guide

Students' examples will vary. Correct statements from the text should appear in the *What you learned* column.

## Section 1 Guided Reading and Review

Answers will vary for 1–10. Correct answers include:

1. During the Industrial Revolution, the need for factory workers grew and many people began moving to cities, where factories were located.
2. After World War II, the United States provided billions of dollars to help Western Europe recover from the war. With this help, the region's industries came back stronger than ever.
3. People travel to Western European cities to enjoy cultural attractions.
4. Most Western European cities are a mix of the old and the new, and each city is different from other cities.
5. The EU helps to support Europe's cultural community by organizing concerts, events, and conferences.
6. The EU finances programs that help people connect to their cultural heritage.
7. Since World War II, industry continued to expand and demand more workers; therefore, people from other countries began moving to Western Europe.
8. Most of the immigrants in Western Europe are from Eastern Europe, North Africa, South Asia, and Southwest Asia.
9. Travelers—as well as ideas, goods, and raw materials—can go from one country to another in a matter of hours.
10. The open exchange of ideas, goods, and money is an outcome of the EU, and has helped Western Europe thrive.

11. the movement of populations toward cities
12. a person who moves to one country from another

## Section 1 Quiz

1. T
2. T
3. c
4. a
5. c
6. c
7. b
8. d

## Section 2 Reading Readiness Guide

Answers will vary. Correct answers are:

1. T
2. F, The Slavs migrated across Eastern Europe long ago and first lived in parts of present-day Poland, Slovakia, and Ukraine
3. F, Today, descendants of Slavs make up most of Eastern Europe's ethnic groups.
4. T
5. T
6. T
7. F, Budapest got the nickname "Queen of the Danube" because of the beauty of the Danube and of the hills surrounding the city.

## Section 2 Guided Reading and Review

1. Because there are few mountains or other natural barriers in much of the region, movement has always been easy.
2. People moved to search for land with good natural resources, to escape enemies and danger, and to search for a better life.
3. Different Slavic languages developed. Today, about ten Slavic languages are spoken in Eastern Europe, including Czech, Polish, and Russian.

Cultures of Europe and Russia

## Answer Key (continued)

4. They speak different dialects and follow different religions, although most follow the Eastern Orthodox faith or Roman Catholicism.
5. Other ethnic groups include the Magyars, Romanians, Albanians, Roma, and Germans.
6. The Soviet Union influenced the governments of Eastern Europe following World War II.
7. The country divided into two new nations: the Czech Republic and Slovakia. They made this decision because the two groups disagreed about how to carry out the goals of the newly democratic country.
8. Antonín Dvorák, Wolfgang Mozart, Béla Bartók, and Franz List.
9. migration
10. ethnic group
11. dialect

## Section 2 Quiz

1. F, A different version of a language that can be found only in a certain region is a dialect.
2. T
3. T
4. b
5. b
6. b
7. a
8. c
9. d
10. d

## Section 3 Reading Readiness Guide

Students' examples will vary. Correct statements from the text should appear in the *What you learned* column.

## Section 3 Guided Reading and Review

Answers will vary for 1–10. Correct answers include:

1. The Russian Orthodox religion is a branch of Christianity that has been a powerful bond among many Russians for hundreds of years.
2. After the collapse of the Soviet Union, which tried to prevent people from practicing religion, people returned to religion in places of worship all across Russia.
3. More than 80 percent of Russian citizens belong to the ethnic group of Russian Slavs.
4. More than 60 other ethnic groups live in Russia, including Armenians, Mongolians, and Yakuts.
5. Russia has produced many great artists, including Tolstoy and Tchaikovsky.
6. After the collapse of the Soviet Union, the Russian people eagerly returned to their artistic traditions.
7. Founded by Peter the Great in 1703, St. Petersburg is an important center of Russian culture.
8. The Hermitage Museum houses one of the world's finest art collections of Russian, Asian, and European art.
9. After the fall of the Soviet Union, the Russian Federation continued free public schooling for children between ages 6 and 17.
10. When students finish ninth grade, they can choose to continue their education in a secondary school or a vocational school.
11. the customs and practices passed from one generation to the next
12. the spread of ideas designed to support a cause or hurt an opposing cause

## Section 3 Quiz

1. F, Customs and practices passed from one generation to the next are a heritage.
2. T
3. a

## *Answer Key* (continued)

**4.** c
**5.** c
**6.** b
**7.** c
**8.** b

# Target Reading Skill

### Identify Main Ideas
Students will underline the first sentence. Details will vary.

### Identify Supporting Details
Answers will vary.

### Identify Implied Main Ideas
1. c
2. b

# Word Knowledge
Definitions and/or examples will vary.

# Enrichment
Students' interpretations of quotations will vary.

# Skills for Life
Answers will vary, but should show a clear and thoughtful process of determining and supporting students' position.

# Primary Sources and Literature Readings

### Your Government Has Returned to You!
1. His comments suggest the communist revolution took the country into ruin by producing goods that were of no interest to anyone, while the people of the republic lacked the basic goods they needed; the state humiliated and exploited its workers; energy was wasted; little money was spent on education and, as a result, the country ranked seventy-second in the world; and their land, rivers, and forests are polluted.

2. Václav Havel's dream was of an independent, free, and democratic country with economic prosperity and social justice; a humane republic that serves the individual with the hope that the individual will serve in return; a republic of well-rounded people.

### Lenin's Deathbed Words
1. Answers will vary. Possible answer: Lenin wants the new government to be run in a more civil and reasonable way than he feels Stalin will run it.
2. Answers will vary. Possible answer: Lenin feels that Stalin does not have the qualities of a good and trustworthy leader.

### Kampf
1. Answers will vary. Possible answer: Stalin seems to enjoy the planning and preparing of brutality.
2. Answers will vary. Possible answer: Stalin was a scheming and devious leader.

### Housekeeping in Russia Soon After the Revolution
1. Answers will vary, but may include that food and living space were scarce.
2. Answers will vary, but may include that it takes time for changes in government policy to take place, as well as creating a stable economy.

# Writing Skills: Writing Plays
Answers will vary.

### Vocabulary Development
1. c
2. g
3. f
4. a
5. e
6. b
7. d

Students' sentences will vary.

Cultures of Europe and Russia

## Answer Key *(continued)*

### Test A

1. g    2. d    3. e    4. a    5. c
6. c    7. c    8. b    9. a    10. c
11. b    12. c    13. d    14. a

15. Answers will vary. A possible answer: As factories' need for workers grew, more people moved to cities from rural areas. This resulted in the growth of cities, which increased after World War II. Also, as industry developed after World War II, immigrants moved to Western Europe from other countries, bringing their cultures with them.

16. Answers will vary. A possible answer: The non-Russian ethnic groups speak languages other than Russian and follow different religions. Also, they live far from the heavily populated western areas. As a result, they probably are not closely tied to the culture and customs of Russian ethnic groups. This cultural diversity probably led to their decision to have their own homelands.

17. Answers will vary. A possible answer: The Russian Federation should remain unified because it can provide the services and security needed by all its citizens and is able to overcome ethnic conflict.

18. Answers will vary. A possible answer: The Russian Federation provides free public education.

19. Answers will vary. A possible answer: Only one ethnic group has actually fought to break away from the Russian Federation.

20. Answers will vary. A possible answer: The Russian Federation should remain a unified nation.

### Test B

1. d    2. b    3. a    4. c    5. f
6. c    7. c    8. c    9. b    10. a
11. d    12. b    13. c    14. c

15. Answers will vary. A possible answer: Because European countries are small and close together, it is easy for travelers to go from one country to another quickly. Also, many people are moving to Western European countries from Eastern Europe, North Africa, South Asia, and the Middle East. This ease of movement has enabled new ideas and cultures to be introduced into countries throughout the continent. As a result, cultures blend and change.

16. Answers will vary. A possible answer: The rulers of Eastern European countries did not enforce the idea of rejecting religion, traditions, and using art only as a form of propaganda. The Soviet Union leaders forced people to abandon their religions, and even took over places of worship for government business. Art was to be used as a tool to promote communism.

17. Answers will vary. A possible answer: The EU is a positive influence on the cultures of Europe.

18. Answers will vary. A possible answer: One of the goals of the EU is to support Europe's cultural community.

19. Answers will vary. A possible answer: The EU is making efforts to encourage cooperation among cultures as well as encouraging respect of individual cultures.

20. Answers will vary. A possible answer: The European Union affects the cultures of Europe in a positive way.

Western Europe
SECTION 1 Lesson Plan

# The United Kingdom: Democracy and Monarchy

🕐 *2 periods, 1 block (includes Country Databank)*

## Section Objectives
1. Examine the regions of the United Kingdom.
2. Learn about the UK's democratic heritage.
3. Find out how the United Kingdom combines democracy and monarchy.
4. Understand why trade is important to the UK.

## Vocabulary
• Parliament • representative • constitution
• constitutional monarchy

## Local Standards

## Reading/Language Arts Objective
Use context clues to clarify unfamiliar words and ideas.

---

### PREPARE TO READ

**Build Background Knowledge**
Ask students to discuss words having to do with the United Kingdom's government.
**Set a Purpose for Reading**
Have students evaluate statements on the *Reading Readiness Guide.*
**Preview Key Terms**
Teach the section's Key Terms.
**Target Reading Skill**
Introduce the section's Target Reading Skill of **using context clues.**

### Targeted Resources

❑ **All in One Europe and Russia Teaching Resources**
  • Reading Readiness Guide, p. 258 **L2**
  • Using Context Clues: Definition and Description, p. 277 **L2**
❑ **Spanish Reading and Vocabulary Study Guide,** Section 1, pp. 32–33 **ELL L1**

---

### INSTRUCT

**Regions of the United Kingdom**
Discuss the formation of Great Britain.
**Target Reading Skill**
Review **using context clues.**
**A Democratic Heritage**
Discuss democracy in the United Kingdom.
**A Changing Monarchy**
Discuss aspects of the British constitution.
**The Importance of Trade**
Discuss trade and the British colonies.

### Targeted Resources

❑ **All in One Europe and Russia Teaching Resources**
  • Guided Reading and Review, p. 259 **L2**
  • Enrichment, p. 281 **L3**
❑ **Europe and Russia Transparencies,** Section Reading Support Transparency ER 43 **L2**
❑ **Teacher's Edition,** For Advanced Readers, pp. 118, 126 **L3**
❑ **Spanish Support,** Guided Reading and Review, p. 32 **ELL L2**

---

### ASSESS AND RETEACH

**Assess Progress**
Evaluate student comprehension with the section assessment and section quiz.
**Reteach**
Assign the Reading and Vocabulary Study Guide to help struggling students.
**Extend**
Assign a Small Group Activity.

### Targeted Resources

❑ **All in One Europe and Russia Teaching Resources**
  • Section Quiz, p. 260 **L2**
  • Small Group Activity, pp. 283–286 **L2**
❑ **Reading and Vocabulary Study Guide,** Guide Section 1, pp. 42–44 **L1**
❑ **Spanish Support,** Section Quiz, p. 33 **ELL L2**

Section 1: The United Kingdom: Democracy and Monarchy
Western Europe

# Reading Readiness Guide

## K–W–L

With your group, quickly preview the section, then brainstorm and list **what you already <u>Know</u>** about the United Kingdom in the first column of the chart below. In the second column, write what you **<u>Want</u> to know** or find out from reading the section.

After you read, review your notes and record **what you <u>Learned</u>** in the third column of the chart.

| What you already know | What you want to know | What you learned |
|---|---|---|
| Example:<br>England is a region within the United Kingdom. | Example:<br>What are the other regions within the United Kingdom? | Example:<br>In addition to England, the other regions within the United Kingdom are Scotland, Wales, and Northern Ireland. |
| | | |

Section 1: The United Kingdom: Democracy and Monarchy
Western Europe

# Guided Reading and Review

## A. As You Read

**Directions:** *As you read Section 1, answer the following questions in the spaces provided.*

1. What four regions make up the United Kingdom?

   _____

2. What is the Magna Carta? What was its purpose? _____

   _____

3. What do elected officials do in the British Parliament?

   _____

4. What are the two houses of the British Parliament? Which governs the nation?

   _____

   _____

5. What purpose does the monarchy serve? _____

   _____

6. How is the British constitution different from the Constitution of the United
   States? _____

   _____

7. Why has trade always been important to the United Kingdom?

   _____

8. What factors have helped the United Kingdom become a leading member of
   the European Union? _____

   _____

## B. Reviewing Key Terms

**Directions:** *Complete these sentences by writing the key terms in the blanks provided.*

9. The United Kingdom's modern _____ is made up of the
   House of Lords and the House of Commons.

10. A _____ is a person who represents, or speaks for, a group of
    people.

11. The United Kingdom is now governed by a _____, which is a
    set of laws that describes how a government works.

12. The British government is a _____, or a government that
    limits the power of kings and queens.

Section 1: The United Kingdom: Democracy and Monarchy
Western Europe

# Section Quiz

## A. Key Terms

**Directions:** *Read the statements below. If a statement is true, write T in the blank provided. If it is false, write F. Rewrite false statements on the back of this page to make them true.*

_____ 1. A representative is a person who speaks for a group of people.

_____ 2. An absolute monarchy is a legal system that limits the power of the kings and queens.

_____ 3. A constitution is a set of laws that describes how a government works.

_____ 4. The National Congress is the lawmaking body of the United Kingdom.

## B. Main Ideas

**Directions:** *Write the letter of the correct answer in each blank.*

_____ 5. Which of the following regions includes Northern Ireland?
   **a.** England
   **b.** Great Britain
   **c.** the United Kingdom
   **d.** all of the above

_____ 6. How did the Magna Carta affect the development of democracy in Great Britain?
   **a.** It limited the power of nobles and gave the king more power.
   **b.** It freed the serfs.
   **c.** It forced the king to obey the laws of the land.
   **d.** It gave the people the right to vote.

_____ 7. Today, the British monarchy is limited by
   **a.** constitutional laws.
   **b.** colonial rulers.
   **c.** the country's traditions.
   **d.** the symbols of Britain's past.

_____ 8. Which of the following does *not* have a regional assembly?
   **a.** England
   **b.** Northern Ireland
   **c.** Scotland
   **d.** Wales

_____ 9. What is one way Britain's colonies enabled it to become an economic power?
   **a.** by providing goods made in factories
   **b.** by providing handmade products
   **c.** by trading their goods with the United States
   **d.** by providing raw materials

_____ 10. European Union member nations are trying to promote
   **a.** higher educational standards.
   **b.** tourism to European nations.
   **c.** trade and cooperation among its members.
   **d.** advanced technology.

Western Europe
SECTION 2 Lesson Plan

# France: Cultural Heritage and Diversity

🕐 *1.5 periods, .75 block*

## Section Objectives

1. Find out why the French take pride in their traditional culture.
2. Learn about growing cultural diversity in France.

## Vocabulary

• philosophy

## Local Standards

## Reading/Language Arts Objective

Use context clues to understand new words

---

### PREPARE TO READ

**Build Background Knowledge**
Have students learn about France using the Passport to the World CD-ROM.
**Set a Purpose for Reading**
Have students evaluate statements on the *Reading Readiness Guide.*
**Preview Key Terms**
Teach the section's Key Terms.
**Target Reading Skill**
Introduce the section's Target Reading Skill of **using context clues.**

### Targeted Resources

❑ **All in One Europe and Russia Teaching Resources**
   • Reading Readiness Guide, p. 262 **L2**
   • Using Context Clues: Compare and Contrast, p. 278 **L2**
❑ **Spanish Reading and Vocabulary Study Guide,** Section 2, pp. 34–35 **ELL** **L1**

---

### INSTRUCT

**Pride in French Culture**
Discuss various aspects of French culture.
**Country Profile**
Ask students to derive information from maps, charts, and graphs.
**Diversity in France**
Discuss how other cultures have influenced that of France.
**Target Reading Skill**
Review **using context clues.**

### Targeted Resources

❑ **All in One Europe and Russia Teaching Resources,** Guided Reading and Review, p. 263 **L2**
❑ **Europe and Russia Transparencies,** Section Reading Support Transparency ER 44 **L2**
❑ **Teacher's Edition**
   • For Gifted and Talented, p. 132 **L3**
   • For Advanced Readers, p. 136 **L3**
❑ **Spanish Support,** Guided Reading and Review, p. 34 **ELL** **L2**

---

### ASSESS AND RETEACH

**Assess Progress**
Evaluate student comprehension with the section assessment and section quiz.
**Reteach**
Assign the Reading and Vocabulary Study Guide to help struggling students.
**Extend**
Extend the lesson by assigning a research project.

### Targeted Resources

❑ **All in One Europe and Russia Teaching Resources,** Section Quiz, p. 264 **L2**
❑ **Reading and Vocabulary Study Guide,** Guide Section 2, pp. 45–47 **L1**
❑ **Spanish Support,** Section Quiz, p. 35 **ELL** **L2**

---

Section 2: France: Cultural Heritage and Diversity
Western Europe

# Reading Readiness Guide

## K–W–L

With your group, quickly preview this section, then brainstorm and list **what you already <u>K</u>now** about France and its cultural heritage in the first column of the chart below. In the second column, write what you <u>**W**</u>**ant to know** or find out from reading the section.

After you read, review your notes and record **what you <u>L</u>earned** in the third column of the chart.

| What you already know | What you want to know | What you learned |
|---|---|---|
| Example:<br>The French have made many contributions to the arts. | Example:<br>Who were some of the great French artists? | Example:<br>Eugène Delacroix and Claude Monet were two of the great French artists. |

Section 2: France: Cultural Heritage and Diversity
Western Europe

# Guided Reading and Review

## A. As You Read

**Directions:** *As you read Section 2, answer the following questions in the spaces provided.*

1. In what fields have the French made important contributions over the centuries?

    _____

2. What is the French Academy? How does it help preserve French culture?

    _____

    _____

3. What idea about government did the French philosopher Baron de Montesquieu introduce?

    _____

4. For what achievement is the French Impressionist artist Claude Monet known?

    _____

5. What features characterize Gothic architecture that developed in Paris during the 1100s?

    _____

    _____

6. Why is French culture changing?

    _____

    _____

7. From which regions of the world have many immigrants come to France in the past few decades?

    _____

    _____

## B. Reviewing Key Terms

**Directions:** *Write the definition for the following key term in the blank provided.*

8. philosophy

    _____

Section 2: France: Cultural Heritage and Diversity
Western Europe

# Section Quiz

## A. Key Terms

**Directions:** *Define the following key term. Write your definition in the space provided.*

1. philosophy _____

## B. Main Ideas

**Directions:** *Write the letter of the correct answer in each blank.*

_____ 2. Which statement best describes the relationship between French culture and the cultures of other countries?

    **a.** France is not affected by cultures of other countries.

    **b.** Other countries are not influenced by French culture.

    **c.** France no longer has cultural ties with other countries.

    **d.** France is committed to preserving traditional French culture.

_____ 3. The French Academy is an organization that makes rules about

    **a.** the use of French words.

    **b.** the education of French students.

    **c.** the laws affecting trade.

    **d.** the laws affecting taxes.

_____ 4. Who was the French philosopher who originated the idea that government should be divided into three branches?

    **a.** Baron de Montesquieu

    **b.** Jean-Jacques Rousseau

    **c.** Jacques-Louis David

    **d.** Eugène Delacroix

_____ 5. What style of architecture developed in and around Paris during the 1100s?

    **a.** French Provincial

    **b.** Gothic

    **c.** Romanesque

    **d.** neoclassical

_____ 6. For what was the Louvre Museum originally built?

    **a.** to be a cathedral

    **b.** to be a museum

    **c.** to be a palace

    **d.** to be a library

_____ 7. Immigrants to France have had a strong impact on

    **a.** the legal system.

    **b.** French culture.

    **c.** the educational system.

    **d.** trade with the United States.

_____ 8. Why did people from other countries move to France?

    **a.** to leave Eastern Europe

    **b.** to leave the United States

    **c.** to speak a new language

    **d.** to find work

Western Europe
SECTION 3 Lesson Plan

# Sweden: A Welfare State

🕐 *1.5 periods, .75 block*

**Key**
**L1** Basic to Average
**L2** For All Students
**L3** Average to Advanced
**ELL** English Language Learners

### Section Objectives
1. Learn about Sweden's welfare state.
2. Find out how Sweden became a welfare state.
3. Examine possible solutions to Sweden's economic problems.

### Vocabulary
• welfare state • national debt

### Local Standards

### Reading/Language Arts Objective
Learn to use context clues to determine how familiar words are being used in the text.

## PREPARE TO READ

**Build Background Knowledge**
Ask students to discuss benefits the government provides.
**Set a Purpose for Reading**
Have students evaluate statements on the *Reading Readiness Guide*.
**Preview Key Terms**
Teach the section's Key Terms.
**Target Reading Skill**
Introduce the section's Target Reading Skill of **using context clues.**

### Targeted Resources
❑ **All in One Europe and Russia Teaching Resources**
  • Reading Readiness Guide, p. 266 **L2**
  • Using Context Clues: General Knowledge, p. 279 **L2**
❑ **Spanish Reading and Vocabulary Study Guide,** Section 3, pp. 36–37 **ELL L1**

## INSTRUCT

**A Welfare State**
Discuss the welfare system in Sweden.
**Country Profile**
Ask students to discuss maps, charts, and graphs.
**Building a Welfare State**
Discuss changes in Sweden in the 1800s–1900s and how the country became a welfare state.
**Target Reading Skill**
Review **using context clues.**
**Problems and Solutions**
Discuss challenges that Sweden's government and businesses faced in the late 1900s.

### Targeted Resources
❑ **All in One Europe and Russia Teaching Resources,** Guided Reading and Review, p. 267 **L2**
❑ **Europe and Russia Transparencies,** Section Reading Support Transparency ER 45 **L2**
❑ **Teacher's Edition**
  • For Special Needs Students, p. 142 **L1**
  • For Gifted and Talented, p. 142 **L3**
❑ **Spanish Support,** Guided Reading and Review, p. 36 **ELL L2**

## ASSESS AND RETEACH

**Assess Progress**
Evaluate student comprehension with the section assessment and section quiz.
**Reteach**
Assign the Reading and Vocabulary Study Guide to help struggling students.
**Extend**
Assign a literature reading.

### Targeted Resources
❑ **All in One Europe and Russia Teaching Resources,** Section Quiz, p. 268 **L2**
❑ **Reading and Vocabulary Study Guide,** Guide Section 3, pp. 48–50 **L1**
❑ **Spanish Support,** Section Quiz, p. 37 **ELL L2**

Section 3: Sweden: A Welfare State
Western Europe

# Reading Readiness Guide

## Anticipation Guide

How much do you think you know about Sweden and its economy and history? As your teacher reads the statements, mark whether you think each statement is true (T) or false (F) in the Me column. Then, discuss your answers with your group and mark the group's decision in the Group column. As you read, look for information that will clarify whether the statements are true or false.

After you read the section, read the statements again and mark the After Reading column to indicate whether they are true or false.

| Before Reading: | | Statements | After Reading |
|---|---|---|---|
| **Me** | **Group** | | |
| | | 1. Sweden is a welfare state, which means the government provides many services and benefits either for free or for a very low cost. | |
| | | 2. When a Swedish worker retires, the government stops providing services to him or her. | |
| | | 3. Swedish people pay as much as 60 percent of their income in taxes to help pay for everyone's welfare benefits. | |
| | | 4. Sweden remained neutral during both World War I and World War II. | |
| | | 5. Today, Sweden is a democracy. | |
| | | 6. A political party, called the Social Democrats, created Sweden's welfare state. | |
| | | 7. Environmental pollution is the greatest challenge facing Sweden today. | |

Section 3: Sweden: A Welfare State
Western Europe

# Guided Reading and Review

## A. As You Read

**Directions:** *As you read Section 3, complete the following chart with details about Sweden. Write four facts for each main idea.*

| **Main Idea A** |
|---|
| Sweden is a welfare state. |
| 1. |
| 2. |
| 3. |
| 4. |

| **Main Idea B** |
|---|
| Sweden's welfare state has problems and possible solutions. |
| 5. |
| 6. |
| 7. |
| 8. |

## B. Reviewing Key Terms

**Directions:** *Complete these sentences by writing the key terms in the blanks provided.*

9. In a(n) _____, the government pays for many services and benefits so all of the country's citizens can live well.

10. Some Swedes think the country's _____ is too high, so the government has cut some spending and increased taxes.

Section 3: Sweden: A Welfare State
Western Europe

# Section Quiz

## A. Key Terms

**Directions:** *Read the statements below. If a statement is true, write T in the blank provided. If it is false, write F. Rewrite false statements on the back of this page to make them true.*

_____ **1.** A welfare state is a country in which many services are paid for by the government.

_____ **2.** The amount of money owed by a government is its gross national product.

## B. Main Ideas

**Directions:** *Write the letter of the correct answer in each blank.*

_____ **3.** Which of the following best describes the Swedish welfare system?
- **a.** It helps only the retired.
- **b.** It helps only needy people.
- **c.** It helps only working people.
- **d.** It is a "cradle-to-grave" system.

_____ **4.** How does the Swedish government pay for the benefits it provides?
- **a.** by lowering its debt
- **b.** by collecting high taxes
- **c.** by increasing its trade routes
- **d.** by joining the European Union

_____ **5.** What kind of government does Sweden have?
- **a.** an absolute monarchy
- **b.** a constitutional monarchy
- **c.** a democracy
- **d.** a dictatorship

_____ **6.** Many people left Sweden at the end of the 1800s because
- **a.** the country was poor.
- **b.** the government encouraged exploration of other lands.
- **c.** industry had grown too rapidly.
- **d.** the new farming methods were difficult to learn.

_____ **7.** After 1932, Sweden changed into
- **a.** a communist country.
- **b.** an absolute monarchy.
- **c.** a constitutional monarchy.
- **d.** a welfare state.

_____ **8.** What can businesses do to help solve Sweden's economic problems?
- **a.** move overseas
- **b.** hire immigrants who do not qualify for benefits
- **c.** increase efficiency to earn more
- **d.** switch from electricity to fossil fuels for power

Western Europe
SECTION 4 Lesson Plan

**Key**
**L1** Basic to Average
**L2** For All Students
**L3** Average to Advanced
**ELL** English Language Learners

# Italy: Northern and Southern Divisions

🕐 *2.5 periods, 1.25 blocks (includes Skills for Life)*

## Section Objectives

1. Discover that there is another country within Italy called Vatican City.
2. Understand why there are divisions between northern and southern Italy.

## Vocabulary

• basilica • manufacturing • land reform

## Local Standards

## Reading/Language Arts Objective

Use what you know about an unfamiliar word to confirm information given in context clues.

---

### PREPARE TO READ

**Build Background Knowledge**
Show a video and discuss the Roman influence in Italy today.
**Set a Purpose for Reading**
Have students evaluate statements on the *Reading Readiness Guide.*
**Preview Key Terms**
Teach the section's Key Terms.
**Target Reading Skill**
Introduce the section's Target Reading Skill of **using context clues.**

### Targeted Resources

☐ **All in One Europe and Russia Teaching Resources**
  • Reading Readiness Guide, p. 270 **L2**
  • Using Context Clues: General Knowledge, p. 279 **L2**
☐ **Spanish Reading and Vocabulary Study Guide,** Section 4, pp. 38–39 **ELL** **L1**

---

### INSTRUCT

**A Unifying Force**
Discuss the Vatican.
**Target Reading Skill**
Review **using context clues.**
**Country Profile**
Ask students to derive information from maps, charts, and graphs.
**Divisions Between North and South**
Discuss the differences between northern and southern Italy and the challenges they face.

### Targeted Resources

☐ **All in One Europe and Russia Teaching Resources**
  • Guided Reading and Review, p. 271 **L2**
  • Skills for Life, p. 282 **L2**
☐ **Europe and Russia Transparencies,** Section Reading Support Transparency ER 46 **L2**
☐ **Teacher's Edition**
  • For English Language Learners, p. 150 **L1**
  • For Less Proficient Readers, p. 152 **L1**
☐ **Spanish Support,** Guided Reading and Review, p. 38 **ELL** **L2**

---

### ASSESS AND RETEACH

**Assess Progress**
Evaluate student comprehension with the section assessment and section quiz.
**Reteach**
Assign the Reading and Vocabulary Study Guide to help struggling students.
**Extend**
Assign an Internet activity.

### Targeted Resources

☐ **All in One Europe and Russia Teaching Resources,** Section Quiz, p. 272 **L2**
☐ **Reading and Vocabulary Study Guide,** Guide Section 4, pp. 51–53 **L1**
☐ **Spanish Support,** Section Quiz, p. 39 **ELL** **L2**

Section 4: Italy: Northern and Southern Divisions
Western Europe

# Reading Readiness Guide

## Anticipation Guide

How much do you think you know about life in Italy? As your teacher reads the statements, mark whether you think each statement is true (T) or false (F) in the Me column. Then discuss your answers with your group and mark the group's decision in the Group column. As you read, look for information that will clarify whether the statements are true or false.

After you read the section, read the statements again and mark the After Reading column to indicate whether they are true or false.

| Before Reading: | | Statements | After Reading |
|---|---|---|---|
| Me | Group | | |
| | | 1. Vatican City is the capital of Italy. | |
| | | 2. The Vatican's art museums have priceless collections of religious art, as well as artwork from ancient Greece and Rome. | |
| | | 3. Most people living in Italy are ethnic Italians and there are few ethnic minorities. | |
| | | 4. In modern times, the region of southern Italy became a center of industry. | |
| | | 5. In the late 1800s, the two regions of Italy were united into one nation, and a standard form of the Italian language was introduced to help unify the people. | |
| | | 6. In the small towns of southern Italy, life is organized around the Church and family. | |
| | | 7. After World War II, the economy in both northern and southern Italy collapsed. | |

Section 4: Italy: Northern and Southern Divisions
Western Europe

# Guided Reading and Review

## A. As You Read

**Directions:** *As you read Section 4, complete the following chart with information about Italy. Write two facts for each category.*

**Facts About Italy**

| The Vatican | 1. |
| | 2. |
| Northern Italy | 3. |
| | 4. |
| Southern Italy | 5. |
| | 6. |
| Church and Family | 7. |
| | 8. |
| Economics and Politics | 9. |
| | 10. |

## B. Reviewing Key Terms

**Directions:** *Write the definitions for the following key terms in the blanks provided.*

**11.** basilica

_____

**12.** manufacturing

_____

**13.** land reform

_____

Section 4: Italy: Northern and Southern Divisions
Western Europe

# Section Quiz

## A. Key Terms

**Directions:** *Read the statements below. If a statement is true, write T in the blank provided. If it is false, write F. Rewrite false statements on the back of this page to make them true.*

_____ 1. Land reform is the process of dividing large properties into smaller ones.

_____ 2. A basilica is a government building.

_____ 3. Manufacturing is the process of turning raw materials into finished products.

## B. Main Ideas

**Directions:** *Write the letter of the correct answer in each blank.*

_____ 4. The Vatican is
    **a.** the headquarters of the Roman Catholic Church.
    **b.** a city.
    **c.** an independent country.
    **d.** all of the above

_____ 5. Painted by Michelangelo, the most famous ceiling in the world is located in
    **a.** St. Peter's Basilica.
    **b.** the Sistine Chapel.
    **c.** Milan.
    **d.** Locorotondo.

_____ 6. A very important part of Italian life that unites the people is
    **a.** Rome's ancient history.
    **b.** Roman Catholicism.
    **c.** the Vatican's art museum.
    **d.** St. Peter's Church.

_____ 7. Until the 1800s, Italy was made up of
    **a.** two countries.
    **b.** the Vatican and several small kingdoms.
    **c.** separate city-states and territories.
    **d.** one large empire.

_____ 8. The economy of northern Italy is based on
    **a.** forestry.
    **b.** mining.
    **c.** agriculture.
    **d.** manufacturing.

_____ 9. The economy of southern Italy is based on
    **a.** farming.
    **b.** manufacturing.
    **c.** trade.
    **d.** mining.

_____ 10. The government is trying to help the development of southern Italy by
    **a.** rebuilding factories.
    **b.** turning it into a separate country.
    **c.** increasing agricultural production.
    **d.** increasing taxes.

Teacher _____  Class _____  Date___  M T W T F

Western Europe
SECTION 5 Lesson Plan

**Key**
**L1** Basic to Average
**L2** For All Students
**L3** Average to Advanced
**ELL** English Language Learners

# Germany: A Unified Nation

⏱ *3.5 periods, 1.75 blocks (includes Chapter Review and Assessment)*

## Section Objectives
1. Learn about Germany's past.
2. Find out how Germany became reunited.

## Vocabulary
• Holocaust • reunification • standard of living

## Local Standards

## Reading/Language Arts Objective
Learn to use context clues in several paragraphs to determine the meaning of an unfamiliar word.

---

### PREPARE TO READ

**Build Background Knowledge**
Discuss the concept of the Berlin Wall with students.
**Set a Purpose for Reading**
Have students evaluate statements on the *Reading Readiness Guide*.
**Preview Key Terms**
Teach the section's Key Terms.
**Target Reading Skill**
Introduce the section's Target Reading Skill of **using context clues.**

### Targeted Resources

❑ **All in One Europe and Russia Teaching Resources**
 • Reading Readiness Guide, p. 274 **L2**
 • Using Context Clues: Compare and Contrast, p. 278 **L2**
❑ **Spanish Reading and Vocabulary Study Guide,** Section 5, pp. 40–41 **ELL L1**

---

### INSTRUCT

**Germany's Past**
Discuss World War I, World War II, the Cold War, and the fall of the Berlin Wall in Germany.
**Country Profile**
Ask students to derive information from maps, charts, and graphs.
**Target Reading Skill**
Review **using context clues.**
**Germany Reunited**
Discuss the effects of the fall of the Berlin Wall on Germany.

### Targeted Resources

❑ **All in One Europe and Russia Teaching Resources,** Guided Reading and Review, p. 275 **L2**
❑ **Europe and Russia Transparencies,** Section Reading Support Transparency ER 47 **L2**
❑ **Teacher's Edition**
 • For Gifted and Talented, p. 156 **L3**
 • For Less Proficient Readers, p. 159 **L1**
❑ **Spanish Support,** Guided Reading and Review, p. 40 **ELL L2**

---

### ASSESS AND RETEACH

**Assess Progress**
Evaluate student comprehension with the section assessment and section quiz.
**Reteach**
Assign the Reading and Vocabulary Study Guide to help struggling students.
**Extend**
Extend the lesson by assigning a research project.

### Targeted Resources

❑ **All in One Europe and Russia Teaching Resources**
 • Section Quiz, p. 276 **L2**
 • Chapter Tests A and B, pp. 300–305 **L2**
❑ **Reading and Vocabulary Study Guide,** Guide Section 5, pp. 54–56 **L1**
❑ **Spanish Support**
 • Section Quiz, p. 41 **ELL L2**
 • Vocabulary Development, p. 43 **ELL L2**

Section 5: Germany: A Unified Nation
Western Europe

# Reading Readiness Guide

## K–W–L

With your group, quickly preview the section, then brainstorm and list **what you already Know** about events in German history in the first column of the chart below. In the second column, write what you **Want to know** or find out from reading the section.

After you read, review your notes and record **what you Learned** in the third column of the chart.

| What you already know | What you want to know | What you learned |
|---|---|---|
| Example:<br>At the end of World War II, Germany was divided into two halves—East Germany and West Germany. | Example:<br>Which part of Germany was a democratic country—East or West? | Example:<br>West Germany was a democratic country and East Germany was communist. |
| | | |

# Guided Reading and Review

## A. As You Read

**Directions:** *As you read Section 5, answer the following questions in the spaces provided.*

1. What two events caused Germans to become desperate after Germany lost World War I?

   _____

2. Who became dictator of Germany in 1933? _____

3. What actions led to the start of World War II in 1939?

   _____

4. By the end of World War II, what had happened to Europe and millions of people? _____

5. How was Germany divided at the end of World War II?

   _____

   _____

6. What happened to Berlin when Germany was divided? In what country was Berlin located? _____

   _____

7. How did the life of an average West German compare with the life of an average East German? _____

   _____

8. What happened to the Berlin Wall on November 9, 1989?

   _____

9. How has the reunited Germany affected Germans in the east?

   _____

   _____

## B. Reviewing Key Terms

**Directions:** *Write the definitions for the following key terms in the blanks provided.*

10. Holocaust _____

11. reunification _____

12. standard of living _____

Section 5: Germany: A Unified Nation
Western Europe

# Section Quiz

## A. Key Terms

**Directions:** *Read the statements below. If a statement is true, write T in the blank provided. If it is false, write F. Rewrite false statements on the back of this page to make them true.*

_____ 1. The mass murder of six million Jews, during World War II, is called the Holocaust.

_____ 2. Germans in the east now enjoy a much better standard of living than they did under communism.

_____ 3. After the Berlin Wall was destroyed, Germany began the process of partition.

## B. Main Ideas

**Directions:** *Write the letter of the correct answer in each blank.*

_____ 4. What was one effect of World War I on Germany?
   a. People felt hopeful.            c. Prices fell.
   b. The economy collapsed.       d. The government lowered taxes.

_____ 5. Which of Hitler's actions led to the start of World War II?
   a. He promised to make Germany a great nation again.        c. He attacked neighboring countries and forced them to submit to German rule.
   b. He said Germans were a superior ethnic group.        d. He blamed Germany's economic problems on German Jews.

_____ 6. At the end of World War II, the Americans, British, French, and Soviets divided
   a. Germany into two parts.            c. Russia into two parts.
   b. East Germany into several regions.       d. West Germany into several regions.

_____ 7. The capital of West Germany was
   a. West Berlin.            c. Munich.
   b. Bonn.                   d. Hamburg.

_____ 8. What is one result of unifying East Germany and West Germany?
   a. Easterners are paying lower prices for homes.        c. West Germany has had to rebuild the economy of East Germany.
   b. Easterners have more jobs.        d. East and West Germans have free child care for the first time.

Western Europe

# Target Reading Skill: Using Context Clues

## Definition and Description

Many times when you read, you will come across a word you do not know. Sometimes you will need to use your textbook glossary or a dictionary to look up the meaning of the new word. Often, however, you can guess the meaning of the word from the words that surround it, or from context. When you figure out what a word means from its context, you are using context clues to determine meaning.

In your textbook, the definitions of new words are often provided for you, at least the first time the words appear. These words are also listed in the textbook glossary. The definition of the new word is usually described in words you know. A description is a paraphrase. The writer defines the new word using different, familiar words or ideas. Sometimes, the description is done within the text, in the same sentence with the new word. Other times, you need to read the sentences that come before and after the sentence with the new word. When you read a word that you do not know, look for a description or a definition.

For example, read the following sentence:

In Argentina, the Andes Mountains slope down to a fertile plain called the pampas, where raising livestock and growing wheat are the primary occupations.

The term *pampas* may be new to you. However, from context you can understand that the pampas is a fertile plain where livestock is raised and wheat is grown. When you cannot figure out the meaning from the description or from context, turn to the textbook glossary, the list of key terms that appears in each section, or a dictionary for help.

**Directions:** *Read the sentences that follow. In each sentence, underline the description of the word or words in bold type. Then, in the lines that follow the sentence, rewrite the definition in your own words.*

1. Today, a **cartographer,** a person who creates maps, needs to have advanced computer skills.

   _____

2. For nearly seven hundred years, Japan was ruled by **shoguns,** or military leaders, and powerful land-owning warriors known as the **samurai.**

   _____

   _____

3. When very poor families move to Mexico City and cannot afford to buy or rent a house, they may become squatters. A **squatter** is a person who settles on someone else's land without permission.

   _____

Chapter and Section Support

# Target Reading Skill: Using Context Clues

## Compare and Contrast

Many times when you read, you will come across a word you do not know. Often, you can guess the meaning of the new word from clues in the same sentence or from clues in the sentences before and after the sentence with the new word. When you use these clues to figure out meaning, you are using context clues to determine meaning.

Context clues include comparison and contrast. Writers often compare and contrast topics within the same sentence or within the same paragraph. Using these comparisons and contrasts can help you figure out the meaning of a new word. When a writer uses contrast, the meaning of a new term will usually be the *opposite* of the known words in the sentence. When a writer uses comparison, the meaning of a new term will usually have a *similar* meaning to the other words in the sentence or paragraph.

There are words that signal, or tell you to look for, comparison and contrast. Words that signal comparison, or similarities, include *also, in addition, similarly,* and *similar to.* Words that signal contrast include *although, but, on the other hand, yet, though, however,* and *not.*

For example:

> *Many Georgia citizens, in addition to* **philatelists,** *are collecting the new series of stamps featuring scenes from the state of Georgia.*

In this example, the words *in addition to* tell you that Georgia citizens and philatelists have something in common. From context, you can figure out that philatelists are people who collect stamps.

> *Some children are* **loquacious,** *but other children hardly talk at all.*

In this example, the word *but* signals a contrast. You may not know that *loquacious* means talkative, but from context, you can figure out that it is the opposite of "hardly talk at all."

As you read and come across new words and terms, pause and reread the sentence in which the word is used. Does a word or group of words with a similar meaning reveal the meaning of the new word? Can you guess its meaning from context clues?

**Directions:** *Look at the key terms from the section you are reading. On a separate sheet of paper, write a sentence for each key term. In the sentence, use the key term and include a contrast word or phrase, or a comparison word or phrase to help a reader figure out what the key term means. Underline both the key term and the signal word or phrase.*

# Target Reading Skill: Using Context Clues

## General Knowledge

Many times when you read, you will come across a word you do not know. Often, you can guess the meaning of the word from the words that surround it, or its context. When you figure out what a word means from its context, you are using context clues to determine meaning.

You can use what you already know about a subject to help you figure out the meanings of new words. You use your general knowledge to make an educated guess.

For example, read the sentence below. Then use what you already know about cities in the United States to determine the meaning of **megalopolis.**

Boston, New York City, Philadelphia, Baltimore, and Washington, D.C., lie close together, forming a **megalopolis** in the Atlantic Coastal Plain.

If you know that the cities listed are all major and important cities, you might guess correctly that a megalopolis is a huge city or large urban area.

As you read and come across new words, stop and reread the sentence in which the word is used. What do you already know about the subject? Can you guess the meaning of the new word from context clues?

**Directions:** *Read the following paragraph. Then use what you already know about families to write definitions for the words in bold type.*

Both you and your older sister want to go to a movie on Saturday night. Your parents had made plans to be out. Your parents say that at least one of you must stay home to take care of your baby brother. Your parents insist that you **negotiate** a solution to the problem. You discuss the issue with your sister and reach a **compromise.** You will go to the late afternoon movie, and your sister will go when you return.

negotiate

_____

_____

compromise

_____

_____

Western Europe

# Word Knowledge

**Directions:** *As your teacher reads the words, think about what each word might mean and mark the appropriate number in the Before Reading column.*

①= Know it    ②= Kind of know it    ③= Don't know it

After you have read and discussed the chapter, rate the words again in the After Reading column. Then write a definition or example for each word to help you clarify and remember the words.

| | Word | Rating | | Definition or Example |
|---|---|---|---|---|
| | | **Before Reading** | **After Reading** | |
| **Section 1** | exert, *v.* | | | |
| | symbol, *n.* | | | |
| | finance, *n.* | | | |
| **Section 2** | contribution, *n.* | | | |
| | standard, *n.* | | | |
| **Section 3** | benefit, *n.* | | | |
| | productive, *adj.* | | | |
| **Section 4** | influence, *n.* | | | |
| | abundant, *adj.* | | | |
| **Section 5** | theory, *n.* | | | |
| | superior, *adj.* | | | |
| | elimination, *n.* | | | |
| | aid, *v.* | | | |

# Enrichment

## Understanding British English

**Directions:** *The following passage points out some of the differences between the English language as it is spoken by Americans and the British. Read the passage and then on a separate sheet of paper give the British words for the American terms listed below the excerpt.*

Some years ago my wife and I spent a lovely April in the English countryside. We exchanged homes, automobiles, and languages with a British couple who hankered for a holiday in America.

We turned over to them our two-year-old condo in teeming California and flew off to their two-centuries-old farmhouse in Dorset....

As the month sailed along, the delightful part of the trade turned out to be the British language. It's really something like English, once you're onto it.

Learning started with the car. Our Buick at home had left-side steering, a windshield, hood, and fenders. Their Nissan in Dorset had right-side steering, a wind-screen, bonnet, and wings. It had a boot, not a trunk, a number plate rather than a license plate, and no horn but a wonderful hooter, handy for scattering sheep....

Our first meal at the local pub introduced us to jackets: baked potatoes in full skins, a meal in themselves. I discovered scones and coddled cream, and wondered how I'd ever again live without those marvels....

In the adverts [advertisements], what looked like a roast was labeled a joint. A tin of biscuits turned out to be a can of sweet crackers, and a jar of monkey nuts was full of peanuts. Crisps were potato chips, and chips were French fries. The sausages—that is, bangers—were delicious, done up on the farmhouse kitchen's ancient but efficient cooker....

From "Something Like English" by Wen Smith, *Saturday Evening Post*, November-December 1995. Reprinted by permission.

1. windshield

2. hood (of a car)

3. fenders

4. trunk (of a car)

5. license plate

6. horn (of a car)

7. baked potatoes in full skins

8. roast

9. sweet crackers

10. peanuts

11. potato chips

12. French fries

13. sausages

14. stove

Chapter and Section Support

Western Europe

## Skills for Life

### Using Visual Information to Write a Paragraph

**Directions:** *Study the following circle graph. Then, answer the questions in the spaces provided.*

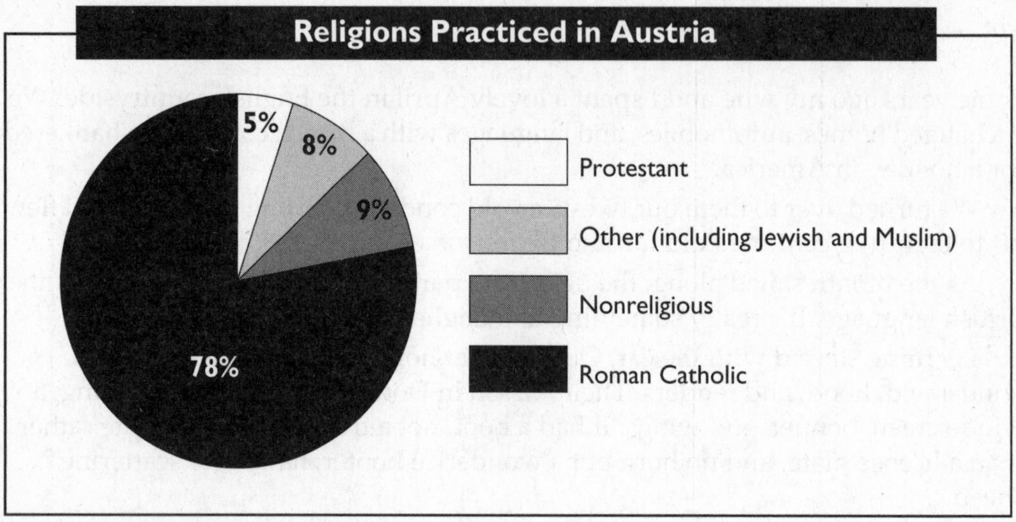

**Religions Practiced in Austria**

5%
8%
9%
78%

Protestant

Other (including Jewish and Muslim)

Nonreligious

Roman Catholic

1. What is the topic of the circle graph? What is the graph's purpose?

_____

_____

2. What are the key facts shown in the graph?

_____

_____

3. What religious faith do the majority of Austrians practice? What religious faiths are practiced by the minority of Austrians?

_____

4. What percentage of Austria's population is nonreligious?

_____

5. Write a brief paragraph that contains the major pieces of information you have learned from the circle graph. Include the conclusions you have drawn.

_____

_____

_____

_____

# Small Group Activity

## Comparing Types of Government

The United States government is strongly influenced by that of Great Britain. Even though the United States was formed by breaking way from Great Britain, we took many ideas and concepts from the British system. In this activity, you will research information about the governments in Great Britain and the United States. Then, you will make a table comparing the two systems and display it on a poster.

### Background

As you have read in the text, Great Britain is a constitutional monarchy. British kings and queens once held great power. Now they do not make laws or government decisions. They are symbols of the country's past. The government is run by a prime minister and Parliament. These are similar to the president and the Congress in the United States. Of course, we have no king or queen. While the systems are similar, there are differences. For example, members of Parliament generally serve for five years. In the United States, members of the House of Representatives serve two years and members of the Senate serve six years.

### Procedure

1. **Research information.** Read all the steps in this project. Then, meet with your group to decide who will do each job. Look in the library for books and articles about governments in Great Britain and the United States. You might divide your group in half and have each group research one country. Before you begin, choose the topics you would like to include. There are many possibilities, including how people vote, the role of political parties, how and when each system came into being, and how each has changed.

2. **Create the table.** Now make a table that contains the information you have gathered. Meet as a group and look over the facts you have found. Work together to create topics for your table. You can use the space below to list ideas. Remember, you are comparing the two systems. Each topic should have information for both countries.

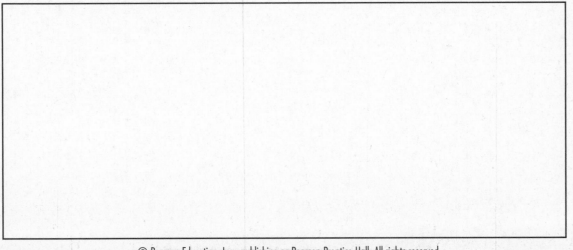

Western Europe

## Small Group Activity (continued)

3. **Make the table.** Because your table will be displayed on a poster, you will need a fairly large sheet of paper. Decide how you will work. You might draw the table on the poster paper itself. Or you can draw it on a separate sheet and glue it to the poster. Some students can make the table. Others can write the information that will go in the table. You can also include graphics on your poster. For example, you might draw or paint a flag, a royal crown, the U.S. capitol, or the White House in an appropriate place.

4. **Display the table.** When you have completed your poster, display it on a wall or bulletin board. Use the posters as a way to compare the two forms of government.

# Small Group Activity: Teacher Page

## Comparing Types of Government

### Content Objectives

- Students will learn about the governments of Great Britain and the United States.
- Students will learn how the British government influenced that of the United States.

### Skill Objectives

- Locating information
- Organizing information
- Recognizing cause and effect
- Drawing conclusions

### Advance Preparation

Gather the following materials:

- large sheets of paper or poster board
- pencils, markers, pens, and paints
- scissors and glue

**Suggested group size:** eight students

**Suggested time:** 40 minutes for researching information; 40 minutes for creating the tables and filling them in; 40 minutes for comparing the two governments

### Procedure

Divide the class into groups. Distribute student pages and have students begin to work on the project. You may wish to give a copy of the rubric for government tables to each group.

Help students think of topics for comparison. You might even have them look at the system of law in each country. For example, they may discover that the concept of legal precedent comes from the British system. You may need to explain this to students, but it is an idea they can probably grasp.

Encourage students to work neatly and carefully when they write in their tables. Point out that if they plan their tables well, they will have fewer problems.

When students have finished their posters, display them for the class. Invite students to discuss each one. To help students get started, ask questions such as:

- How are the governments of Great Britain and the United States similar and different?
- Why do you think the two systems are similar?
- Which system do you think works better? Why?
- Do you think your group worked well as a team?

# Small Group Activity: Teacher Page

Government tables will be evaluated according to the following rubric.

## Rubric for Government Tables

| Grading Criteria | Excellent | Admirable | Acceptable |
|---|---|---|---|
| **Research** | Students locate a large number of sources of information about both government systems; they are able to create many topics and have interesting and thoughtful points for each. | Students locate good sources of information about both government systems; they create a variety of topics for the table. | Students locate a few sources of information about both government systems; they create several topics. |
| **Making the Tables** | Students make a logical table that is clear and easy to understand; the topics are well organized and contain interesting facts; it is easy to compare the two forms of government by reading the table. | Students make a logical and clear table; it is well organized and contains details for each topic. | Students finish the work, but the table could have more topics and more information; some of the topics only have information for one government. |
| **Presentation** | Table is neatly drawn; the writing is clear and precise. Students have added illustrations for each topic; the table is interesting and attractive. | Table is well drawn and the writing is clear; it includes some illustrations. | Table is complete but could be drawn more neatly; some of the titles and information are hard to read. |
| **Teamwork** | Students make a good team from start to finish, they work together, supporting each other and sharing the work in an effective manner. | Students work as a team; they share jobs equally. | Students use teamwork and share most of the jobs; a few students tend to run the group. |

# MapMaster Skills

## Reading a Circle Graph

A circle graph enables you to compare parts with a whole. The complete circle represents all of something. Each section represents a percentage of the whole. Together, the sections add up to 100 percent. The circle graph below shows how the world's population is divided among different religions.

**Directions:** *Study the circle graph below, and answer the questions that follow. Then, draw your own circle graph.*

### Estimated Religious Population of the World

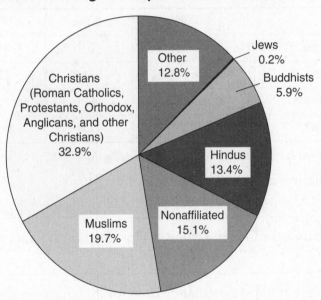

Source: *Encylopaedia Britannica Almanac, 2003*

1. What percentage of the world's population is Muslim? _____

2. What percentage is Jewish? _____

3. Which religious group has the most members? _____

4. Which religious group is the second largest? _____

5. Which is larger, the Buddhist population or the Hindu population? About how many times larger? _____

6. On a separate sheet, draw a circle graph that shows how the world's population is divided by region. Use the following figures: Africa 12.9%; North America 5.1%; Latin America and the Caribbean 8.6%; Asia 60.9%; Europe 12%; Oceania 0.5%. What does your circle graph tell you about the world's population distribution?

Chapter and Section Support

# MapMaster Skills

## Reading a Table

A table presents information in columns (up and down) and rows (across). It allows you to make comparisons and to analyze the information presented. A table is an efficient way of presenting information that needs to be analyzed. The table below presents population data for four countries in Central America.

**Directions:** *Study the table. Then, answer the questions that follow.*

## Population Data for Four Central American Countries

|  | Costa Rica | Panama | Honduras | Guatemala |
|---|---|---|---|---|
| Literacy Rate | 96% | 90% | 74% | 64% |
| Infant Mortality Rate (per 1,000 births) | 11 | 20 | 31 | 45 |
| Life Expectancy: Males | 74 | 73 | 67 | 64 |
| Life Expectancy: Females | 79 | 77 | 71 | 70 |
| Workers in Agriculture | 20% | 21% | 34% | 50% |

Source: *World Almanac and Book of Facts,* 2003; *CIA—The World Factbook,* 2002.

1. What information is shown in this table?

   _____

2. What are the infant mortality rates in Honduras and Guatemala?

   _____

3. In what way are the life expectancy data for all countries shown similar?

   _____

4. What is the relationship between literacy rate and infant mortality rate suggested by this table?

   _____

5. Identify another relationship suggested by the data in this table.

   _____

6. Identify the country on this table with the highest standard of living. Give reasons for your choice.

   _____

   _____

Name _____ Date _____ Class _____

Western Europe

# MapMaster Skills

## Reading a Line Graph

A line graph shows changes that take place over time. It has two axes. One measures time and the other measures quantity. The line graph below shows world population growth over a 350-year period. Different colors of shading indicate growth for developed and developing regions.

**Directions:** *Study the line graph below, and answer the questions that follow.*

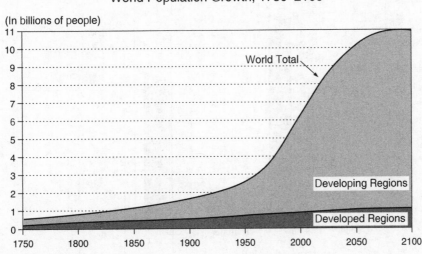

World Population Growth, 1750–2100

1. In which years was the rate of population growth greater—in the 1800s or the 1900s? _____

2. What is the total world population expected to be by the year 2100? _____

3. What was the world's population in 1950? _____

4. When was the world's population evenly divided between developed and developing regions? _____

5. On a separate sheet, draw a line graph that shows United States imports and exports, in billions of dollars, from 1970 to 1995. Use the following figures:

| Year | 1970 | 1975 | 1980 | 1985 | 1990 | 1995 |
|------|------|------|------|------|------|------|
| Imports | 40 | 99 | 245 | 345 | 495 | 743 |
| Exports | 43 | 108 | 221 | 213 | 394 | 584 |

What does your completed line graph tell you about imports and exports over that period?

_____

_____

# MapMaster Skills

## Reading a Bar Graph

A bar graph enables you to compare quantities of different things. Each bar stands for an amount of something. The longer the bar, the more there is of that item. The bar graph below compares exports and imports for four Mediterranean countries. You can use the scale on the left of the bar graph to estimate approximate quantities.

**Directions:** *Study the bar graph below, and answer the questions that follow.*

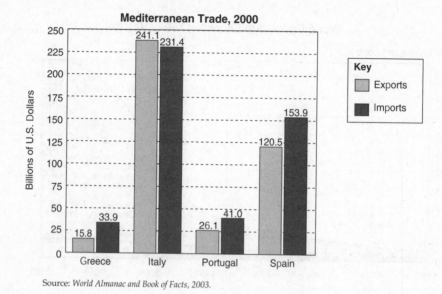

Source: *World Almanac and Book of Facts, 2003.*

1. Which country imported the most goods in 2000? _____

2. Which country exported the fewest goods in 2000? _____

3. Roughly how much did Portugal import and how much did it export in 2000?

   _____

4. Which country shows the greatest difference between the amount it imported and the amount it exported? _____

5. Draw a bar graph that compares average January and July temperatures in four cities on a separate sheet of paper. The scale on the left should start at 0°F and go to 100°F. Then, write one or two sentences describing a conclusion that can be drawn from your graph. The four cities to use to create your graph and their temperatures are as follows:

| Athens, Greece | January: | 48° | July: | 81° |
|---|---|---|---|---|
| Toronto, Canada | January: | 23° | July: | 69° |
| Auckland, New Zealand | January: | 66° | July: | 51° |
| Buenos Aires, Argentina | January: | 74° | July: | 50° |

# MapMaster Skills

## Reading a Timeline

A timeline shows the order in which events occur and the length of time between them. The timeline below shows events in the United Kingdom that were significant to the division of Ireland.

**Directions:** *Study the timeline and answer the questions that follow.*

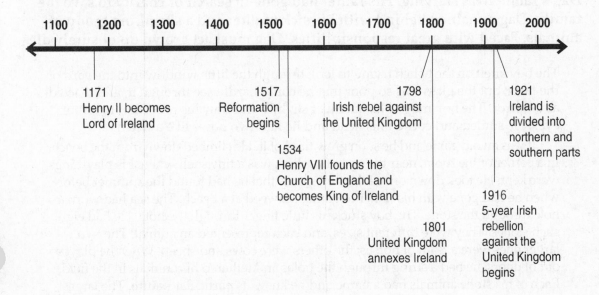

1. When did the Reformation begin?

   _____

2. How many years after the beginning of the Reformation did Henry VIII establish the Church of England?

   _____

3. How many years passed between the United Kingdom's annexation of Ireland and the division of Ireland?

   _____

4. When was Ireland divided into two parts?

   _____

5. On a separate sheet of paper, draw a timeline to illustrate significant events in the history of space exploration. Start with 1961, the year the first human traveled in space, and extend the timeline to the present day. Use an almanac to find dates and events. Then, select the most significant ones for your timeline. What does your timeline tell you about space exploration?

**Chapter and Section Support**

# Primary Sources and Literature Readings

## The Boy

From The Untold Tale

by Erik Christian Haugaard

**It was the mid-1600s. Denmark was at war with Sweden, and life in the countryside was harsh. In this story, the long northern winter had come, and Dag's family was starving. His father had gone in search of charity to save the family. Dag remained behind with his sick mother and a shrinking group of animals. Faced with great responsibilities, Dag must act grown up or surely die.**

The boy knelt on the bench trying to look through the little window into the yard of the farm; but the glass was so poor that he could hardly see through it, and it acted as a mirror. The boy moved his face just slightly and now his reflection had four eyes. He smiled and cocked his head and he had two noses like a witch.

It was an old game and he soon grew tired of it. He climbed down from the bench. In a corner of the room, near the open fireplace, was a tiny shelf where his playthings were kept. He took down one of the flint stones that he had found the summer before, when he had gone with his father to gather seaweed at a beach. The sea had worn a hole through the stone. The boy stuck his little finger through the hole. He had eight such stones. They were different sizes, and each represented an animal. The two larger ones were a team of horses; the others were cows and sheep. When he played out of doors, he tied a string through the holes and tethered his animals in the field. Each of his stone animals had a name and he knew its particular nature. The largest stone was a medallion; it was willful, liable to break its tether and run away.

He heard the barn door bang; it must have blown open. He knew that he ought to go out and shut it. He put his stones away but he remained in the room. He was afraid to go out to the stable, for he had been there in the morning and found the gelding dead. Its eyes had been all white.

He walked back to the table and sat down on the bench. He looked at his hands and carefully counted his fingers, as if he expected to have lost one. He broke the silence of the room by whispering, "Mother. . . " But the dying woman in the bed alcove did not hear him. He said the word again, a little louder; then he rose and tiptoed to the bed.

He stood still gazing at his mother; she appeared so small, as if she were a child now, too. He touched her cheek gently. She seemed cold to his touch, and yet her forehead was bathed in sweat. Slowly his mother opened her eyes and whispered his name. He shouted: "Mother!" But she turned her head towards the wall.

Again he heard the banging of the door and this time he went out to close it.

He need not have looked inside. He could just have closed the door and let the wooden latch fall into place. But once he had looked, he had had to enter. The young horse was still lying where it had fallen, its neck outstretched; all the bones of its body were visible through its skin. He could hear the breathing of the two cows who were still alive, but he did not dare approach them. He looked about for something to feed them. There was nothing, not even a handful of chaff. He noticed the straw roof, and the idea occurred to him of tearing out some straw and giving it to the cows.

## *Primary Sources and Literature Readings* (continued)

He climbed the ladder to the loft; it was empty, swept clean even of dust. With his hands, he tore at the roof. It was old and the straw crumbled into ragged bits. Carefully, he collected an armful, taking small amounts from several different places, in order not to destroy the roof.

He climbed down into the stable. Both cows were lying down. The boy divided the straw and put a bundle next to each cow's head. Neither of them made any attempt to rise; they were too weak to take any interest in dry dust.

When he came outside, the boy looked up at the blue sky; spring really was on its way. The icicles still hung from the eaves; but the sun had gained strength enough to make its warmth felt. The boy broke off a long, pointed icicle and sucked on it. He had not eaten since the day before; his father had made a gruel of barley before he had left for Elsinore. Dag wondered whether there might be something left in the pot; and even though he knew there wasn't, he returned to the house to look.

The pot was empty; he had scraped it himself that morning. He put a few sticks on top of the ashes that hid the embers and blew until they caught fire. He emptied water from the earthen pitcher into the iron pot, and hung the pot on the hook above the fire; though there was no reason to boil water, for he had nothing with which to make soup or gruel.

Thinking that his mother might want something to drink, he filled his father's tin cup with water. Her face was still turned towards the wall. He called to her and when she did not answer, he bent forward and touched her.

Her eyes told him that she was dead; they were like the cow's had been when she died: empty. He tried to put the cup down on the table carefully, but even though it was not filled to the brim, he spilled a little bit of the water. He dried it up with his sleeve. Tears ran from his eyes, but he cried soundlessly. Twice he called out: "Mother. . . Mother. . " But in the tone of his voice there was neither expectancy nor hope. Then he screamed: "Father!" and ran out of the house pursued by his own fear.

He ran quickly as he could past the two neighboring farms, that had been abandoned not long after New Year. When he reached the great forest, the sun was low on the horizon and the darkness of the woods frightened him. Reluctantly, he started back to the farm; but then he thought that he might have been wrong: that his mother might not be dead, and he started to run.

He entered the house out of breath. In the silence of the room, he could hear his own heart beating and he knew that he had not been mistaken. He did not walk to the alcove but to the fireplace. He looked into the iron pot; and since the water had boiled away, he filled it. With great care he rebuilt the fire. He did everything slowly, wanting it to take time.

He sat by the fire all night, waiting and listening for his father's footsteps. Once he heard an owl hooting. The sound came down through the chimney into the room; he closed his eyes and shuddered, although his father had told him that was not true that owls were the souls of dead people.

When the first gray light of morning came, he fell asleep on his little stool, his head resting in his hands. He slept until the middle of the morning when melting snow, falling from the roof into the yard, awakened him.

## *Primary Sources and Literature Readings* (continued)

Without looking around the room, he hurried outside. The sun was so bright that it almost blinded him, and the sky was clear. There were hardly any icicles hanging from the eaves; the smashed bits of once foot-long cones lay glistening on the ground. The boy ran down to the pond; the ice was so soft that he was able to make marks in it with a stick. Suddenly, as he stared at the lines he had been drawing in the ice, he felt certain that his father would not come back. He started to cry. Where was he to go? Who would help him? He looked over his shoulder towards the house; a little smoke was coming from the chimney. He had tried to pray during the night; but he knew only two prayers: the one you said before going to bed and the one of thanks recited before meals.

High above in the sky a lone swan was flying; Dag heard the beat of the wings. He dried his eyes and raised his head to look at it. "My father is dead," he said aloud. Then it was that it occurred to him to go and tell the King what had happened. His father had rented the land from the Crown, but the King was far away. "He doesn't know that we're starving!" the boy almost shouted. He—Dag—would tell King Christian of their misery and the King would help him. By some kind of miracle, the King would set all things right again; his mother and father would be alive and the mare and the gelding and cows would be well. Everything would be as it had been last summer—no! as it had been last spring, before the drought.

He ran back to the house to make himself ready for his journey. His first thought was to find something in which to carry his stones; then he decided to take only the best one, the stallion. A moment later he told himself that he was foolish, and he was so ashamed that he took all the stones and dumped them into the well.

He was wearing his warmest clothes and his boots. After finding his knitted cap, he looked around the room, though his glance carefully avoided the alcove bed. He wanted to take the large knife, but it had no sheath and he wondered how he could carry it. What he needed was a piece of rope, and when he found one, he tied it around his tunic and stuck the knife into it. His father's tin spoon fitted nicely beside the knife. He was determined to take the tin cup as well, but he did not want to carry it in his hand; finally, he shoved the cup inside his tunic. His father's staff—the one he used to drive the animals—stood by the door; the boy grabbed it and found that he was ready. He opened the door and hesitated; but finally, he lifted his head and forced himself to glance at the alcove bed.

"I will come back, Mother," he called aloud. Then he walked out into the sunlight and closed the door behind him. The boy stood in the middle of the farmyard holding the staff, which was twice his height, in his hand. He nodded to the house and to the barn, to say goodbye to them. Feeling that the moment was solemn, he dropped down on his knees in the wet snow and recited the prayer that he usually said before he got into bed. When he was almost finished, he remembered that he was wearing his cap, and he took it off. He was seven years old, Dag of King's Acre; and he was all alone.

A month later, the land was rented out again. A new farmer arrived with horses and cows. The body of Dag's mother was carried to the church at Gurre; and she was buried in the eastern part of the churchyard near the fence, farthest away from the church.

Name _____  Date _____  Class _____

Western Europe

## *Primary Sources and Literature Readings* (continued)

| | |
|---|---|
| **Vocabulary Builder** | |
| chaff | outer skin of grain such as wheat, left over after the seed has been removed by threshing |
| tunic | a very long shirt, which may be belted at the waist and worn over other clothes |

### Think It Over

1. How did Dag feel after his mother's death?

_____

_____

2. In what ways did Dag's experiences change him? How did he grow up?

_____

_____

_____

_____

# Writing Skills

## Writing to Inform and Explain

When you write to inform or explain a process, thing, or event, you must base your writing on well-organized facts.

The best way to do that is to research your topic and organize your data. First, discover the **who, what, when, where, why,** and **how** of a subject. Then, report your findings to the reader in a clear, organized way.

For example, you might write an essay to inform about an ancient culture. You discover that they played a kind of ball game in which the winner, not the loser, was sacrificed to the gods at the end of the game. A fascinating fact—a "**what**" in your essay. But why sacrifice the winner? And what other details—all the other "**Ws**" and the "**How**" listed above—can you provide to fully inform your reader?

The next step is to organize all the facts into logical sequence. If you are writing to explain a process, such as how to play a video game, for example, be sure to include all the steps in order. Leave out one, and your reader might not get past level one!

**Directions:** *Now practice writing to inform or explain by selecting one of the following topics or choosing one of your own. Do research, if necessary. Then, fill in the blanks below with your topic, purpose, audience, and key facts. On a separate sheet of paper, write your essay.*

- Write a summary of the best movie you saw this year, clearly explaining the plot.
- Explain to someone from out of town how to get from your home to your school.
- Write an informative article on an exciting vacation destination.
- Explain how to make a favorite dessert.
- Your own idea: _____

Topic: _____

Purpose in writing: _____

Audience: _____

Facts/details to include: _____

_____

_____

_____

Western Europe

# Vocabulary Development

**Directions:** *Match the key terms with the definitions below. Write the correct letter in each blank. Then write a sentence on the reverse side of the page that uses that term or the plural form of the term. If necessary, look up the terms in your textbook glossary.*

| | |
|---|---|
| **a.** Parliament | **h.** basilica |
| **b.** representative | **i.** manufacturing |
| **c.** constitution | **j.** land reform |
| **d.** constitutional monarchy | **k.** Holocaust |
| **e.** philosophy | **l.** reunification |
| **f.** welfare state | **m.** standard of living |
| **g.** national debt | |

_____ **1.** a system of ideas and beliefs

_____ **2.** a Roman Catholic church that has special, high status because of its age or history

_____ **3.** the process of becoming unified again

_____ **4.** the lawmaking body of the United Kingdom

_____ **5.** a government in which a monarch is the head of state but has limited powers

_____ **6.** the process of dividing large properties into smaller ones

_____ **7.** the level of comfort in terms of the goods and services people have

_____ **8.** a set of laws that describes how a government works

_____ **9.** the mass murder of six million Jews

_____ **10.** a person who represents, or speaks for, a group of people

_____ **11.** the amount of money a government owes

_____ **12.** the process of turning raw materials into finished products

_____ **13.** a country in which many services and benefits are paid for by the government

# Rubric for Assessing a Writing Assignment

| Grading Criteria | Excellent | Acceptable | Minimal | Unacceptable |
|---|---|---|---|---|
| **Content** | Clearly focused introduction; idea development interesting and sophisticated; supporting evidence detailed, accurate, and convincing; perceptive conclusion. | Introduction gives assignment direction; idea development clear; supporting evidence accurate; strong conclusion. | Introduction unclear; idea development uneven and simplistic; supporting evidence uneven; conclusion summarizes information in assignment. | Introduction incomplete, ineffective; idea development ineffective; supporting evidence vague, inaccurate, or missing; conclusion incomplete or missing. |
| **Organization** | Paragraph order reinforces content; strong topic sentences make content easy to follow; effective and varied transitions. | Logical paragraph order; clear topic sentences; clear and functional transitions. | Ineffective paragraph order; narrow or inaccurate topic sentences; few clear transitions. | Inconsistent paragraph order; topic sentences and transitions missing. |
| **Mechanics** | Flawless punctuation and spelling; varied and interesting sentence structure. | Few spelling and punctuation errors; sentence structure correct. | Some careless spelling and punctuation errors; some errors in sentence structure. | Many spelling and punctuation errors; many sentence fragments and run-ons. |

# Rubric for Assessing a Journal Entry

| Grading Criteria | Excellent | Acceptable | Minimal | Unacceptable |
|---|---|---|---|---|
| **Content** | Response to assigned topic thorough and well written, with varied sentence structure and vocabulary; opinions always supported with facts. | Response thoughtful and fairly well written; most opinions supported with facts. | Response adequately addresses some aspects of the assigned topic; opinions sometimes based on incorrect information. | Response consists of unsupported opinions only marginally related to topic. |
| **Idea Development** | Excellent use of examples and details to explore and develop ideas and opinions. | Good reliance upon examples and details to illustrate and develop ideas and opinions. | Incomplete development of ideas; details and examples not always relevant. | Ideas not clearly stated or developed. |
| **Organization** | Very logically organized; contains introduction, development of main idea (or ideas), and conclusion. | Contains introduction, some development of ideas, and conclusion. | Topics and ideas discussed somewhat randomly; entry may lack clearly defined introduction or conclusion. | Entry is unstructured. |
| **Mechanics** | Flawless spelling and punctuation. | Few or no spelling errors; some minor punctuation mistakes. | Several spelling and punctuation errors. | Many instances of incorrect spelling and punctuation. |

# Test A

## A. Key Terms

**Directions:** *Match the definitions in Column I with the key terms in Column II. Write the correct letter in each blank. You will not use all the terms. (15 points)*

**Column I**

_____ 1. a government in which a monarch is the head of state but has limited powers

_____ 2. a country in which many services and benefits are paid for by the government

_____ 3. a Roman Catholic church that has special, high status

_____ 4. the process of turning raw materials into finished products

_____ 5. the process of becoming unified again

**Column II**

**a.** basilica

**b.** constitutional monarchy

**c.** Holocaust

**d.** manufacturing

**e.** national debt

**f.** Parliament

**g.** representative

**h.** reunification

**i.** welfare state

## B. Key Concepts

**Directions:** *Write the letter of the correct answer in each blank. (45 points)*

_____ 6. Which of the following statements about British democracy is true?

    **a.** It grants the king great power.

    **b.** It began after World War II.

    **c.** Its roots go back hundreds of years.

    **d.** It has caused a national debt.

_____ 7. Great Britain's colonies provided the country with

    **a.** a new constitution and parliament.

    **b.** a welfare state.

    **c.** raw materials for its factories.

    **d.** manufactured goods to sell to the citizens.

_____ 8. Great Britain became a member of the European Union in order to improve its

    **a.** educational system.

    **b.** economy.

    **c.** relationship with its colonies.

    **d.** welfare system.

## Test A *(continued)*

_____ **9.** How did the French government react to the shortage of workers?

    **a.** It passed laws to encourage immigration.

    **b.** It passed laws to discourage immigration.

    **c.** It changed from a welfare state to a democracy.

    **d.** It became a welfare state.

_____ **10.** In order to fulfill its promise of a better life for all Swedes, the Social Democratic party changed the country into

    **a.** a welfare state.

    **b.** a multicultural country.

    **c.** an absolute monarchy.

    **d.** an agricultural nation.

_____ **11.** One drawback to Sweden's current benefit system is that people spend

    **a.** too many hours working.

    **b.** too much time waiting for benefits.

    **c.** all of their money on benefits.

    **d.** less money on goods because of high taxes.

_____ **12.** Compared with northern Italy, southern Italy is

    **a.** nationalistic and democratic.

    **b.** poor and very traditional.

    **c.** urban and religious.

    **d.** wealthy and modern.

_____ **13.** The Italian government has helped the development of the southern region by

    **a.** decreasing taxes throughout the nation.

    **b.** refusing to join the European Union.

    **c.** building roads and irrigation systems.

    **d.** decreasing the nation's foreign debt.

_____ **14.** What happened to Germany at the end of World War II?

    **a.** It was reunified.

    **b.** It joined the European Union.

    **c.** It was divided into two countries.

    **d.** It was governed by the United Nations.

## C. Critical Thinking

**Directions:** *Answer the following questions on the back of this paper or on a separate sheet of paper. (20 points)*

15. **Identifying Central Issues** What are two foreign influences on modern French culture?

16. **Recognizing Cause and Effect** What effect did World War II have on Germany? In your answer, address Germany's past and present situations.

Chapter and Section Support

**Test A** (continued)

## D. Skill: Using Visual Information to Write a Paragraph

**Directions:** *Use the table to answer the following questions. Write your answers in the spaces provided. (20 points)*

| Portugal: National Statistics 1995 and 2004 | | |
|---|---|---|
| **Category** | **1995** | **2004** |
| Total Population | 10,524,000 | 10,062,000 |
| Urban Population | 34% | 66% |
| Life Expectancy: Male | 72 years | 72.9 years |
| Life Expectancy: Female | 79 years | 80.1 years |
| Literacy Rate | 83% | 93% |
| Gross Domestic Product (GDP) | $93.7 billion | $182 billion |
| GDP Per Capita | $9,000 | $18,000 |

Source: *World Almanac 1995 and 2004*

17. How has the population changed according to the table?

_____

_____

18. What conclusion can you draw about Portugal's urban population?

_____

_____

19. How do you think the increase in Portugal's gross domestic product per capita has affected the population's standard of living?

_____

_____

20. Write a short paragraph that uses the information in the table and the conclusions you have drawn.

_____

_____

_____

_____

# Test B

## A. Key Terms

**Directions:** *Fill in the blanks in Column I by writing the letter of the correct term from Column II. You will not use all the terms. (15 points)*

**Column I**

_____ 1. A person who represents, or speaks for, a group of people is called a(n) _____.

_____ 2. The form of government in the United Kingdom is a(n)_____.

_____ 3. Many services are paid for by the government in a _____.

_____ 4. During the Industrial Revolution, _____, or turning raw materials into finished products, became an important part of the economy of many European countries.

_____ 5. The mass murder of six million Jews during World War II is called the _____.

**Column II**

a. constitutional monarchy

b. Holocaust

c. national debt

d. manufacturing

e. Parliament

f. representative

g. reunification

h. standard of living

i. welfare state

## B. Key Concepts

**Directions:** *Write the letter of the correct answer in each blank. (45 points)*

_____ 6. What two things helped make Britain a democracy?

a. raising taxes and providing benefits

b. unification of Scotland and Wales

c. Parliament and representatives

d. the changing of the guard and the crown jewels

_____ 7. In Great Britain, the constitution limits the power of the

a. monarchy.

b. Magna Carta.

c. absolute monarchy.

d. welfare state.

## Test B (continued)

_____ 8. Because Great Britain is an island, it has limited
    **a.** educational facilities.      **c.** harbors.
    **b.** trade routes.      **d.** natural resources.

_____ 9. French culture has changed since World War II because
    **a.** children of immigrants are considered French citizens.      **c.** immigrants have arrived from former French colonies.
    **b.** people speak only French when doing business.      **d.** the government has refused to join the European Union.

_____ 10. In order to pay for their benefits, Swedish citizens must pay
    **a.** high taxes.      **c.** all educational expenses.
    **b.** all medical costs.      **d.** retirement benefits.

_____ 11. What is one solution to Sweden's economic problems?
    **a.** spend more money on education      **c.** increase taxes for all citizens and businesses
    **b.** increase the national debt      **d.** make better use of the country's natural resources

_____ 12. Italy's history is closely linked with the history of the
    **a.** Catholic Church.      **c.** fashion industry.
    **b.** Slavic people.      **d.** monarchy.

_____ 13. What statement best describes the economy of northern Italy?
    **a.** The region is the center of the lumber industry.      **c.** The region is an agricultural center.
    **b.** The region is a manufacturing center.      **d.** The region is the center of the fishing industry.

_____ 14. What happened to Germany at the end of World War II?
    **a.** The country was reunited.      **c.** The country joined the European Union.
    **b.** The country was divided.      **d.** The country was governed by the United States.

## C. Critical Thinking

**Directions:** *Answer the following questions on the back of this paper or on a separate sheet of paper. (20 points)*

15. **Expressing Problems Clearly** What are some of the problems faced by Sweden because of the country's benefits program?

16. **Making Comparisons** Compare the problems faced by northern and southern Italy to those faced by a reunited Germany?

Name _____ Date _____ Class _____

Western Europe

## Test B *(continued)*

## D. Skill: Using Visual Information

**Directions:** *Use the graphs to answer the following questions. Write your answers in the spaces provided. (20 points)*

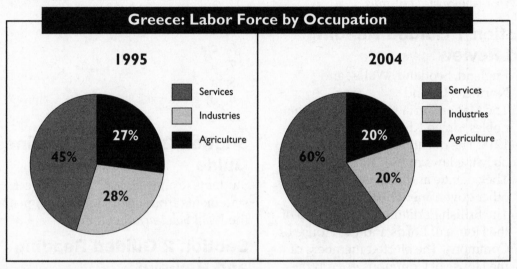

**Greece: Labor Force by Occupation**

**1995**

- Services
- Industries
- Agriculture

45%   27%   28%

**2004**

- Services
- Industries
- Agriculture

60%   20%   20%

Source: Central Intelligence Agency, *The World Factbook 2003*

17. What do the circle graphs show? _____

_____

18. Between 1995 and 2004, in which type of occupation was the greatest increase?

_____

19. What conclusion can you draw that explains what may have caused the decrease in the agriculture labor force in 2004?

_____

_____

20. Write a short paragraph that uses the information in the circle graphs and the conclusions you have drawn.

_____

_____

_____

_____

_____

Western Europe

# Answer Key

## Section 1 Reading Readiness Guide

Students' examples will vary. Correct statements from the text should appear in the *What you learned* column.

## Section 1 Guided Reading and Review

1. England, Scotland, Wales, and Northern Ireland
2. The Magna Carta is a document that nobles forced King John to sign in 1215. The document required kings to obey the laws of the land.
3. They debate and discuss laws and other government business.
4. The British Parliament is made up of the House of Lords and the House of Commons. The elected members of the House of Commons govern the nation.
5. The monarchy serves as an important symbol of Britain's past and also helps to unify the British people.
6. The Constitution of the United States is one written document of a set of laws describing how the government works. The British constitution is not one written document, but is made up of laws passed by Parliament, significant court decisions, and certain legal practices. Parliament can change the constitution as necessary.
7. The United Kingdom is an island nation with limited natural resources. Therefore, it must trade with other nations for natural resources.
8. Its expertise in such areas as shipping and finance, plus easier access to European markets, have helped the UK become a leading member of the EU.
9. Parliament
10. representative
11. constitution
12. constitutional monarchy

## Section 1 Quiz

1. T
2. F, A constitutional monarchy is a legal system that limits the power of the kings and queens.
3. T
4. F, Parliament is the lawmaking body of the United Kingdom.
5. c
6. c
7. a
8. a
9. d
10. c

## Section 2 Reading Readiness Guide

Students' examples will vary. Correct statements from the text should appear in the *What you learned* column.

## Section 2 Guided Reading and Review

1. Over the centuries, the French have made important contributions to art, religion, music, literature, and philosophy.
2. The French Academy is an organization that determines which words are officially accepted as part of the French language. It helps preserve French culture by preventing the French language from changing too much.
3. He introduced the idea that government should be divided into three branches.
4. He developed new techniques for painting light and shadow.
5. Gothic architecture is characterized by high ceilings, thin walls, and the use of columns and arches.
6. The cultures of other nations are influencing French culture more and more.
7. In the past few decades, many immigrants have come to France from northern and southern Africa and Southeast Asia.
8. a system of ideas and beliefs

## *Answer Key* (continued)

### Section 2 Quiz

1. a system of ideas and beliefs
2. d
3. a
4. a
5. b
6. c
7. b
8. d

### Section 3 Reading Readiness Guide

Students' answers will vary. Correct answers are:

1. T
2. F, When a Swedish worker retires, the government provides them with a monthly payment, which nearly equals the pay they received when they were working.
3. T
4. T
5. F, Today, Sweden is a constitutional monarchy.
6. T
7. F, Paying for the welfare system is the greatest challenge facing Sweden today.

### Section 3 Guided Reading and Review

Students' answers will vary for 1–8. Correct answers include:

1. The government provides benefits to all citizens for affordable health care, education, vacation pay, and retirement.
2. To pay for benefits, the government collects very high taxes—as much as 60% of income.
3. Food, clothing, and other consumer goods are expensive and heavily taxed.
4. The political party called the Social Democrats created Sweden's welfare state.

5. The national debt is high because the government had to borrow money to continue paying for the benefits of the welfare system.
6. Sweden has an aging population, which means there is less tax money to continue paying for benefits.
7. Government needs to reduce benefits and cut spending.
8. Businesses need to earn more and are developing methods of faster production.
9. welfare state
10. national debt

### Section 3 Quiz

1. T
2. F, The amount of money owed by a government is its national debt.
3. d
4. b
5. b
6. a
7. d
8. c

### Section 4 Reading Readiness Guide

Students' answers will vary. Correct answers are:

1. F, Vatican City is an independent city-state located within Rome, the capital of Italy.
2. T
3. T
4. F, In modern times, northern Italy became a center of industry. Southern Italy has always been heavily agricultural.
5. T
6. T
7. F, After World War II, the economy in Italy boomed, particularly in northern Italy. The agriculture-based economy of southern Italy failed to thrive, and many southern Italians headed north.

## Answer Key *(continued)*

### Section 4 Guided Reading and Review

Students' answers will vary for 1–10. Correct answers include:

1. Vatican City, also known as the Vatican, is an independent city-state located in Rome, the capital of Italy.
2. The Vatican is the world headquarters of the Roman Catholic Church.
3. Northern Italy was influenced by invaders from Western Europe and the region's city-states became bustling cities.
4. Northern Italy became a center of industry. Milan is typical of northern Italian cities, where abundant minerals, fast rivers, and a developed economy have brought wealth to the area.
5. In southern Italy, feudal kingdoms dominated, with large numbers of peasants working the land. As a result, southern Italy has always been heavily agricultural.
6. Most people in southern Italy follow a more traditional way of life, living in rural areas and making a living by farming or fishing.
7. The Roman Catholic Church is important to almost all Italians.
8. In the small towns of the south, life is organized around the larger family of the Church and the smaller family in the home.
9. After World War II, Italy's economy boomed, primarily in the north because of its large cities and industrial centers.
10. The Northern League wants to turn northern Italy into a separate country.
11. a Roman Catholic church that has special, high status because of its age or history
12. the process of turning raw materials into finished products
13. the process of dividing large properties into smaller ones

### Section 4 Quiz

1. T
2. F, A basilica is a Roman Catholic church that has special, high status because of its age or history.
3. T
4. d
5. b
6. b
7. c
8. d
9. a
10. c

### Section 5 Reading Readiness Guide

Students' examples will vary. Correct statements from the text should appear in the *What you learned* column.

### Section 5 Guided Reading and Review

1. The German government had to pay billions of dollars as punishment for attacking other countries. At the same time, the German economy collapsed.
2. Adolf Hitler
3. Hitler ordered attacks on neighboring countries and forced them to submit to German rule.
4. By the end of World War II, Europe was in ruins. The Germans had forced countless Jews, Gypsies, Slavs, and others into brutal prison camps, where millions of people were murdered.
5. The American, British, and French joined their sections to create the Federal Republic of Germany—a democratic country known as West Germany. The Soviet Union created a communist system in East Germany.
6. West Berlin became part of West Germany; East Berlin became part of East Germany. The Berlin Wall divided the two halves of the city. The entire city was actually located in East Germany.

## Answer Key *(continued)*

7. The average West German had a much better life than the average East German.
8. People began to destroy the hated wall, taking it apart piece by piece.
9. Germans in the east now enjoy a much higher standard of living than they did under communism.
10. the mass murder of six million Jews
11. the process of becoming unified again
12. the level of comfort in terms of the goods and services that people have

## Section 5 Quiz

1. T
2. T
3. F, After the Berlin Wall was destroyed, Germany began the process of reunification.
4. b
5. c
6. a
7. b
8. c

## Target Reading Skill

### Definition and Description
Answers will vary but should include a correct definition of the word.

### Compare and Contrast
Answers will vary.

### General Knowledge
Answers will vary but should include correct definitions of the bold-faced words.

## Word Knowledge
Students' definitions and/or examples will vary.

## Enrichment

1. wind-screen
2. bonnet
3. wings
4. boot
5. number plate
6. hooter

7. jackets
8. joint
9. biscuits
10. monkey nuts
11. crisps
12. chips
13. bangers
14. cooker

## Skills for Life

1. The topic of the graph is Religions Practiced in Austria. The graph's purpose is to show what percentages of the population practice the major religions.
2. The key facts are the specific breakdown by percentages of each category.
3. Majority: Roman Catholic; Minority: Protestant, Jewish, and Muslim
4. 9%
5. Students' paragraphs will vary.

## MapMaster Skills

### Reading a Circle Graph

1. 19.7 %
2. 0.2 %
3. Christians
4. Muslims
5. The Hindu population is more than twice as large as the Buddhist population.
6. Students' graphs should be clear and accurate. Asia has the largest population distribution, and Oceania has the smallest.

### Reading a Table

1. The table shows literacy rate, infant mortality rate, life expectancy for men and women, and percentage of agricultural workers in Costa Rica, Panama, Honduras, and Guatemala.
2. 31 per 1,000 in Honduras, 45 per 1,000 in Guatemala
3. In each country, women have a higher life expectancy than men.

## *Answer Key* (continued)

4. Table suggests that a higher literacy rate is related to a lower infant mortality rate.
5. Answers will vary but may include: higher literacy rate is related to higher life expectancy, a higher infant mortality rate is related to a shorter life expectancy, a higher infant mortality rate is related to a larger percentage of agricultural workers.
6. Students may assume that Costa Rica has the higher standard of living because it scores the best on every measure in the table.

### Reading a Line Graph
1. in the 1900s
2. 11 billion people
3. about 2.5 billion people
4. around 1800
5. Students should note the widening gap between imports and exports.

### Reading a Bar Graph
1. Italy
2. Greece
3. Portugal imported approximately $41 million and exported approximately $26.1 million.
4. Spain
5. Students' graphs and conclusions will vary.

### Reading a Timeline
1. 1517
2. 17 years after
3. 120
4. 1921
5. Students' timelines and conclusions will vary.

## Primary Sources and Literature Readings: The Boy
1. Dag felt sad and frightened.
2. Dag's experiences turn him into an adult. After his father leaves, he begins to take more responsibility. He looks for ways to feed the cows and tries to care for his mother. Later, he comes to accept that his parents are dead, and he makes plans to leave and live on his own.

## Writing Skills: Writing to Inform and Explain
Answers will vary, depending on the topic chosen.

## Vocabulary Development
1. e
2. h
3. l
4. a
5. d
6. j
7. m
8. c
9. k
10. b
11. g
12. i
13. f

Students' sentences will vary.

## Test A
1. b    2. i    3. a    4. d    5. h
6. c    7. c    8. b    9. a    10. a
11. d    12. b    13. c    14. c
15. Answers will vary. A possible answer: One foreign influence on French culture is the many people who have moved to France from the French colonies since World War II. In addition, when France joined the European Union, immigrants from other European countries moved there looking for work. A second influence is foreign film, television, and radio, which bring additional foreign ideas to France.

Western Europe

## Answer Key *(continued)*

16. Answers will vary. A possible answer:
World War II divided Germany.
When the Allies defeated Germany,
they divided the country. There was a
democratic country called West
Germany. The Soviet Union installed
a communist system in East Germany.
Eventually, the two Germanys were
reunited, but because each country
had grown accustomed to a different
style of government, differences
between the two sides still exist today.
Westerners are accustomed to more
freedom and economic opportunities.
Easterners are accustomed to things
like free child care and guaranteed
jobs.

17. Answers will vary. A possible answer
includes: The total population of
Portugal has decreased between 1995
and 2004, but the percentage of the
population in urban communities has
nearly doubled.

18. Answers will vary. A possible answer
includes: Portugal's urban population
has nearly doubled due to the fact that
more people are leaving rural
communities and are moving to the
cities to find jobs.

19. Answers will vary. A possible answer
includes: The increase of the GDP per
capita has most likely improved the
standard of living for most of the
population of Portugal.

20. Answers will vary, but should be
supported by the information in the
table.

## Test B

1. f    2. a    3. i    4. d    5. b
6. c    7. a    8. d    9. c    10. a
11. d   12. a   13. b   14. b
15. Answers will vary. A possible answer:
The country's economy has stalled.
Because people pay such high taxes,

they spend less money on clothing,
food, and other goods. The
government faces budgetary
problems because in order to pay for
the welfare benefits, it has had to
borrow money. As a result, the
national debt has gotten out of
control.

16. Answers will vary. Like West and East
Germany, northern Italy and southern
Italy have been linked throughout
history. Yet, the ways of life in
northern and southern Italy set the
areas apart. Northern Italy is a
manufacturing center; southern Italy
is mostly agricultural. Also, northern
Italy has more money than southern
Italy. Northern Italy is paying for
some of southern Italy's
modernization. West Germany and
East Germany were two separate
countries until recently. East Germany
was a communist nation; West
Germany was a democracy. Their
political differences set them apart.
Since reunification, Germany has
spent millions of dollars rebuilding
the economy of what was East
Germany. Former East Germans have
lost some of the economic benefits
they enjoyed under communism, such
as free child care and cheap housing.

17. the workforce of Greece by occupation
in 1995 and 2004

18. services

19. Answers will vary. A possible answer
includes: Because of improvements in
agricultural technology, fewer people
are needed in that industry and
therefore there is a lower percentage
of the labor force in agriculture.

20. Answers will vary, but should be
supported by the information in the
circle graphs.

Eastern Europe and Russia
SECTION 1 Lesson Plan

**Key**
**L1** Basic to Average
**L2** For All Students
**L3** Average to Advanced
**ELL** English Language Learners

# Poland: Preserving Tradition Amidst Change

🕒 *2 periods, 1 block (includes Country Databank)*

## Section Objectives

1. Find out about Polish traditions.
2. Learn about economic changes that have taken place in Poland since the collapse of communism.
3. Understand Poland's future challenges.

## Vocabulary

• shrine • capitalism • entrepreneur

## Local Standards

## Reading/Language Arts Objective

Compare and contrast to help you sort out and analyze information.

---

### PREPARE TO READ

**Build Background Knowledge**
Discuss traditions in students' communities.
**Set a Purpose for Reading**
Have students evaluate statements on the *Reading Readiness Guide*.
**Preview Key Terms**
Teach the section's Key Terms.
**Target Reading Skill**
Introduce the section's Target Reading Skill of **comparing and contrasting**.

### Targeted Resources

❑ **All in One Europe and Russia Teaching Resources**
  • Reading Readiness Guide, p. 314 **L2**
  • Compare and Contrast, p. 329 **L2**
❑ **Spanish Reading and Vocabulary Study Guide,** Section 1, pp. 43–44 **ELL** **L1**

---

### INSTRUCT

**Tradition in Poland**
Discuss the major religions in Poland and how language links the Polish people.
**Great Economic Changes**
Ask about how the transition from communism to capitalism improved Poland's economy.
**Target Reading Skill**
Review **comparing and contrasting**.
**Future Challenges**
Discuss how Poland is repairing its damaged environment and reducing unemployment.

### Targeted Resources

❑ **All in One Europe and Russia Teaching Resources**
  • Guided Reading and Review, p. 315 **L2**
  • Using the Map Key, p. 341 **L2**
❑ **Europe and Russia Transparencies,** Section Reading Support Transparency ER 48 **L2**
❑ **Teacher's Edition**
  • For Special Needs Students, pp. 167, 177 **L1**
  • For Less Proficient Readers, pp. 169, 179 **L1**
❑ **Spanish Support,** Guided Reading and Review, p. 44 **ELL** **L2**

---

### ASSESS AND RETEACH

**Assess Progress**
Evaluate student comprehension with the section assessment and section quiz.
**Reteach**
Assign the Reading and Vocabulary Study Guide to help struggling students.
**Extend**
Ask students to create a timeline on the collapse of communism in Poland.

### Targeted Resources

❑ **All in One Europe and Russia Teaching Resources,** Section Quiz, p. 316 **L2**
❑ **Reading and Vocabulary Study Guide,** Section 1, pp. 58–60 **L1**
❑ **Spanish Support,** Section Quiz, p. 45 **ELL** **L2**

---

Name _____ Date _____ Class _____

Section 1: Poland: Preserving Tradition Amidst Change
Eastern Europe and Russia

# Reading Readiness Guide

## Anticipation Guide

How much do you think you know about Poland before and after the fall of communism? As your teacher reads the statements, mark whether you think each statement is true (T) or false (F) in the Me column. Then, discuss your answers with your group and mark the group's decision in the Group column. As you read, look for information that will clarify whether the statements are true or false.

After you read the section, read the statements again and mark the After Reading column to indicate whether they are true or false.

| Before Reading: | | Statements | After Reading |
|---|---|---|---|
| Me | Group | | |
| | | 1. Poland has been controlled at different times by Russia, Germany, and Austria. | |
| | | 2. After World War II, Polish people lived for several decades under a harsh communist government. | |
| | | 3. Polish Orthodox religious life has been at the center of Polish tradition for centuries. | |
| | | 4. The communists banned the Polish language and today the majority of Poles speak Russian. | |
| | | 5. Like most former communist countries, Poland made the change gradually from communism to capitalism. | |
| | | 6. With the collapse of the communist government, many foreigners began to invest their money in Poland. | |
| | | 7. During the communist era, factories caused terrible pollution, which destroyed much of the forests in southern Poland and increased rates of diseases, such as cancer. | |

Section 1: Poland: Preserving Tradition Amidst Change
Eastern Europe and Russia

# Guided Reading and Review

## A. As You Read

**Directions:** *As you read Section 1, answer the following questions in the spaces provided.*

1. What happened in Poland in 1989? in 2003? _____

_____

2. What role has Catholicism played in Poland for centuries?

_____

3. How is the Polish language a cultural tie that unites Poles?

_____

_____

4. What dramatic changes did Polish leaders make to help with the transition
   from communism to capitalism?

_____

_____

5. How did private businesses begin in Poland's cities after the end of communist rule?

_____

_____

6. Why was the change to a capitalist economy harder for farmers than for most
   other Poles?

_____

_____

7. What are two major challenges Poland still faces today?

_____

## B. Reviewing Key Terms

**Directions:** *Complete these sentences by writing the key terms in the spaces provided.*

8. The church on top of the holy hill of Grabarka is an example of a
   _____, or holy place, in Poland.

9. Since the end of the communist government in Poland, the country has
   adopted _____, in which businesses are privately owned.

10. A(n) _____ is a person who develops original ideas in order to
    start new businesses.

Section 1: Poland: Preserving Tradition Amidst Change
Eastern Europe and Russia

# Section Quiz

## A. Key Terms

**Directions:** *Read the statements below. If a statement is true, write T in the space provided. If it is false, write F. Rewrite false statements on the back of this page to make them true.*

_____ 1. Under communism, businesses are privately owned.

_____ 2. An entrepreneur is a person who develops original ideas in order to start new businesses.

_____ 3. You can visit holy places, which are also called mosques, all over Poland.

## B. Main Ideas

**Directions:** *Write the letter of the correct answer in each blank.*

_____ 4. How did Poland change politically after World War II?

    **a.** It became a democracy.    **c.** It became Orthodox.

    **b.** It became a communist nation.    **d.** It became a monarchy.

_____ 5. One tradition that remains strong in Polish culture is

    **a.** the belief in the Roman Catholic Church.    **c.** the use of modern farm equipment.

    **b.** the use of the Russian language.    **d.** the use of the English language in schools.

_____ 6. What language did the communists force Polish schoolchildren to learn?

    **a.** Hungarian    **c.** English

    **b.** Russian    **d.** German

_____ 7. Under the new government, the biggest change in Poland has been in the country's

    **a.** culture.    **c.** educational system.

    **b.** transportation system.    **d.** economy.

_____ 8. How has the Polish economic system changed since communism ended?

    **a.** The government took control of prices.    **c.** Poland has brought in more foreign investment.

    **b.** The government made sure prices for farm produce remained high.    **d.** Poland has reduced the number of privately owned businesses.

Eastern Europe and Russia
SECTION 2 Lesson Plan

# Five Balkan Nations: A Region Tries to Rebuild

🕐 *1.5 periods, .75 block*

## Section Objectives

1. Identify the groups of people who live in the Balkans.
2. Understand how Yugoslavia was created and how it broke up.
3. Identify issues that these Balkan nations face in the future.

## Vocabulary

• civil war • secede • embargo • economic sanctions

## Local Standards

## Reading/Language Arts Objective

Make comparisons to find out how two or more situations are alike.

---

### PREPARE TO READ

**Build Background Knowledge**
Show the section video and discuss land mines.
**Set a Purpose for Reading**
Have students evaluate statements on the *Reading Readiness Guide*.
**Preview Key Terms**
Teach the section's Key Terms.
**Target Reading Skill**
Introduce the section's Target Reading Skill of **making comparisons.**

### Targeted Resources

❏ **All in One** **Europe and Russia Teaching Resources**
• Reading Readiness Guide, p. 318 **L2**
• Make Comparisons, p. 330 **L2**
❏ **Spanish Reading and Vocabulary Study Guide,** Section 2, pp. 45–46 **ELL** **L1**

---

### INSTRUCT

**Land of Many Peoples**
Discuss the Slavic groups in the Balkans.
**Target Reading Skill**
Review **making comparisons.**
**The Creation of Yugoslavia**
Discuss the history of the government.
**Yugoslavia Breaks Up**
Discuss war and conflict in Yugoslavia.
**The Region's Future**
Discuss Slobodan Milosevic and the Balkans.

### Targeted Resources

❏ **All in One** **Europe and Russia Teaching Resources**
• Guided Reading and Review, p. 319 **L2**
• Reading a Political Map, p. 343 **L2**
❏ **Europe and Russia Transparencies,** Section Reading Support Transparency ER 49 **L2**
❏ **Teacher's Edition,** For Special Needs Students, p. 184 **L1**
❏ **Spanish Support,** Guided Reading and Review, p. 46 **ELL** **L2**

---

### ASSESS AND RETEACH

**Assess Progress**
Evaluate student comprehension with the section assessment and section quiz.
**Reteach**
Assign the Reading and Vocabulary Study Guide to help struggling students.
**Extend**
Assign an Enrichment activity.

### Targeted Resources

❏ **All in One** **Europe and Russia Teaching Resources,** Section Quiz, p. 320 **L2**
❏ **Reading and Vocabulary Study Guide,** Section 2, pp. 61–63 **L1**
❏ **Spanish Support,** Section Quiz, p. 47 **ELL** **L2**

---

Section 2: Five Balkan Nations: A Region Tries to Rebuild
Eastern Europe and Russia

# Reading Readiness Guide

## Anticipation Guide

How much do you think you know about the Balkan nations in Southeastern Europe? As your teacher reads the statements, mark whether you think each statement is true (T) or false (F) in the Me column. Then, discuss your answers with your group and mark the group's decision in the Group column. As you read, look for information that will clarify whether the statements are true or false.

After you read the section, read the statements again and mark the After Reading column to indicate whether they are true or false.

| Before Reading: | | Statements | After Reading |
|---|---|---|---|
| Me | Group | | |
| | | 1. The Balkans include Serbia and Montenegro, Bosnia and Herzegovina, Macedonia, Croatia, Slovenia, Albania, Romania, Bulgaria, Greece, and European Turkey. | |
| | | 2. Five Balkan countries—Serbia and Montenegro, Bosnia and Herzegovina, Macedonia, Croatia, and Slovenia—used to make up the nation of Czechoslovakia. | |
| | | 3. For hundreds of years, the Ottoman Empire, based in Turkey, ruled much of the Balkans. | |
| | | 4. Formed in 1918, Yugoslavia emerged from the old Ottoman Empire as the first new Balkan nation and joined many ethnic and religious groups. | |
| | | 5. After World War II, Josip Broz Tito strictly ruled Yugoslavia according to communist principles and broke ties with anti-communist nations. | |
| | | 6. After Tito's death in 1980, Yugoslavia's government and economy became unstable and civil wars erupted among various ethnic groups. | |
| | | 7. The United States and Europe increased trade to the Balkan region to support the government of Slobodan Milosevic. | |

Section 2: Five Balkan Nations: A Region Tries to Rebuild
Eastern Europe and Russia

# Guided Reading and Review

## A. As You Read

**Directions:** *As you read Section 2, answer the following questions in the spaces provided.*

1. Why did much of Sarajevo lay in ruins ten years after the 1984 Winter Olympics?

   _____

2. Which five Balkan countries used to make up the nation of Yugoslavia?

   _____

   _____

3. What are the two largest ethnic groups in the five Balkan countries that used to be the nation of Yugoslavia?

   _____

   _____

4. What cultural differences separate the five Balkan countries whose ethnic groups speak related languages?

   _____

   _____

5. What are the three major religions of these five Balkan countries?

   _____

6. When was Yugoslavia created? When did it become a communist state?

   _____

7. How did Tito's death and the collapse of communism make Yugoslavia's problems worse?

   _____

   _____

8. What three changes were included in Macedonia's newly adopted constitution?

   _____

   _____

   _____

## B. Reviewing Key Terms

**Directions:** *Write the definitions for the following key terms in the spaces provided.*

9. civil war _____

10. secede _____

11. embargo _____

12. economic sanctions _____

# Section Quiz

## A. Key Terms

**Directions:** *Define each of the following key terms. Write your definitions on the back of this paper.*

1. secede
2. economic sanctions
3. embargo
4. civil war

## B. Main Ideas

**Directions:** *Write the letter of the correct answer in each blank.*

_____ 5. After World War II, the political system of Yugoslavia became
    **a.** communist.
    **b.** democratic.
    **c.** an absolute monarchy.
    **d.** socialist.

_____ 6. What did Tito do that put him in conflict with Stalin?
    **a.** He changed Yugoslavia to a capitalist economic system.
    **b.** He tried to take control of the Soviet Union.
    **c.** He maintained trading relations with Western countries.
    **d.** He sold inferior goods to the Soviet Union.

_____ 7. What caused the war in Bosnia and Herzegovina?
    **a.** economic problems
    **b.** tensions among ethnic groups
    **c.** high taxes
    **d.** language differences

_____ 8. Who was the Yugoslavian president who tried to increase Serbia's power in 1989?
    **a.** Josef Stalin
    **b.** Vojislav Kostunica
    **c.** Josip Broz Tito
    **d.** Slobodan Milosevic

_____ 9. After peace treaties were signed in the mid-1990s to end the fighting in Yugoslavia,
    **a.** Yugoslavia joined the European Union.
    **b.** tensions continued.
    **c.** all of Yugoslavia was reunited.
    **d.** peacekeeping forces left the region.

_____ 10. What did Macedonia do to ease tensions between ethnic Macedonians and Albanians?
    **a.** It banned the use of the Albanian language.
    **b.** It banned Albanians from government jobs.
    **c.** It forced Albanians to move back to Albania.
    **d.** It made Albanian an official language.

Eastern Europe and Russia
SECTION 3 Lesson Plan

**Key**
**L1** Basic to Average
**L2** For All Students
**L3** Average to Advanced
**ELL** English Language Learners

# Ukraine: Independence and Beyond

◄ *2.5 periods, 1.25 blocks (includes Skills for Life)*

## Section Objectives

1. Understand how Ukraine's history has been shaped by foreign rule.
2. Explain the major issues that Ukrainians have faced since independence.
3. Describe life in Ukraine today.

## Vocabulary

• chernozem • collective

## Local Standards

## Reading/Language Arts Objective

Compare and contrast different points in history to understand how a nation changed over time.

---

## PREPARE TO READ

**Build Background Knowledge**
Discuss how independence affected Ukraine.
**Set a Purpose for Reading**
Have students evaluate statements on the *Reading Readiness Guide.*
**Preview Key Terms**
Teach the section's Key Terms.
**Target Reading Skill**
Introduce the section's Target Reading Skill of **comparing and contrasting.**

## Targeted Resources

❏ **All in One Europe and Russia Teaching Resources**
  • Reading Readiness Guide, p. 322 **L2**
  • Compare and Contrast, p. 329 **L2**
❏ **Spanish Reading and Vocabulary Study Guide,** Section 3, pp. 47–48 **ELL** **L1**

---

## INSTRUCT

**A History of Occupation**
Discuss Ukraine's relationship with the Soviet Union.
**Target Reading Skill**
Review **comparing and contrasting.**
**Independence Brings Challenges**
Ask about changes after independence.
**Life in Ukraine**
Discuss life in Ukraine before and after independence and the nation's future.

## Targeted Resources

❏ **All in One Europe and Russia Teaching Resources**
  • Guided Reading and Review, p. 323 **L2**
  • Small Group Activity, pp. 335–338 **L3**
❏ **Europe and Russia Transparencies,** Section Reading Support Transparency ER 50 **L2**
❏ **Teacher's Edition**
  • For English Language Learners, p. 191 **L1**
  • For Advanced Readers, p. 193 **L3**
❏ **Spanish Support,** Guided Reading and Review, p. 48 **ELL** **L2**

---

## ASSESS AND RETEACH

**Assess Progress**
Evaluate student comprehension with the section assessment and section quiz.
**Reteach**
Assign the Reading and Vocabulary Study Guide to help struggling students.
**Extend**
Assign an Internet activity.

## Targeted Resources

❏ **All in One Europe and Russia Teaching Resources,** Section Quiz, p. 324 **L2**
❏ **Reading and Vocabulary Study Guide,** Section 3, pp. 64–66 **L1**
❏ **Spanish Support,** Section Quiz, p. 49 **ELL** **L2**

---

Section 3: Ukraine: Independence and Beyond
Eastern Europe and Russia

# Reading Readiness Guide

## Anticipation Guide

How much do you think you know about the history of Ukraine? As your teacher reads the statements, mark whether you think each statement is true (T) or false (F) in the Me column. Then, discuss your answers with your group and mark the group's decision in the Group column. As you read, look for information that will clarify whether the statements are true or false.

After you read the section, read the statements again and mark the After Reading column to indicate whether they are true or false.

| Before Reading: | | Statements | After Reading |
|---|---|---|---|
| Me | Group | | |
| | | 1. For hundreds of years, Ukraine's vast natural resources have attracted traders. | |
| | | 2. Germany ruled Ukraine between the late 1700s and 1991. | |
| | | 3. Ukraine, which was once one of Europe's largest grain-producing regions, became known as the breadbasket of Europe. | |
| | | 4. Soviet rulers took land away from Ukrainian farmers and created huge government-controlled farms called collectives. | |
| | | 5. In 1991, Ukraine won its independence from the Soviet Union. | |
| | | 6. Today, much of Ukraine's soil and water has been cleaned of the poisons from the explosion at the Chernobyl nuclear plant. | |
| | | 7. The city of Kharkiv is Ukraine's busiest industrial center today. | |

Section 3: Ukraine: Independence and Beyond
Eastern Europe and Russia

# Guided Reading and Review

## A. As You Read

**Directions:** *As you read Section 3, answer the following questions in the spaces provided.*

1. In 1990, how did the Ukrainian people protest the Soviet Union's control of their country?

_____

2. What are two reasons why Ukraine has had a history of being invaded and ruled by others?

_____

_____

3. Why was Ukraine known as the breadbasket of Europe?

_____

4. What happened to most Ukrainian farmers under Soviet rule?

_____

_____

5. When did Ukraine win its independence from the Soviet Union?

_____

6. Why was Ukrainian made the official language of the newly independent country?

_____

7. What happened at Chernobyl in 1986? What were some of its effects?

_____

_____

8. What changes has independence brought to Ukrainian life?

_____

_____

## B. Reviewing Key Terms

**Directions:** *Complete these sentences by writing the key terms in the spaces provided.*

9. Ukraine's farmland is so productive because more than half of the country is covered by a rich, black soil called _____.

10. Under Soviet rule, a Ukrainian farmer could be forced to give up his land and work on a(n) _____, which was a government-controlled farm.

Section 3: Ukraine: Independence and Beyond
Eastern Europe and Russia

# Section Quiz

## A. Key Terms

**Directions:** *Read the statements below. If a statement is true, write T in the space provided. If it is false, write F. Rewrite false statements on the back of this page to make them true.*

_____ **1.** Chernobyl is a rich, black soil.

_____ **2.** A huge government-owned farm is called a cooperative.

## B. Main Ideas

**Directions:** *Write the letter of the correct answer in each blank.*

_____ **3.** What is one reason why other countries have invaded Ukraine throughout its history?
  **a.** trade routes
  **b.** natural resources
  **c.** position as a world leader
  **d.** strong army

_____ **4.** The country that ruled Ukraine from the late 1700s to 1991 was
  **a.** Poland.
  **b.** Germany.
  **c.** Czechoslovakia.
  **d.** Russia.

_____ **5.** Which statement best describes the relationship between Ukraine and the Soviet Union?
  **a.** The Soviet Union used Ukraine's natural resources.
  **b.** The Soviet Union let Ukraine keep its goods.
  **c.** The Soviet Union encouraged Ukraine to become independent.
  **d.** The Soviet Union did not change Ukrainians' lives.

_____ **6.** What happened in the 1930s as a result of Soviet policies?
  **a.** People moved from cities to work on collectives.
  **b.** Ukraine became independent.
  **c.** Millions of Ukrainians died of hunger.
  **d.** The Ukrainian economy recovered from depression.

_____ **7.** A nuclear explosion in 1986 affected the Ukrainian environment by
  **a.** causing floods.
  **b.** poisoning the soil.
  **c.** increasing food production.
  **d.** lowering the temperature.

_____ **8.** Ukraine's busiest industrial center is
  **a.** Kharkiv.
  **b.** Kiev.
  **c.** Chernobyl.
  **d.** Lviv.

Eastern Europe and Russia
SECTION 4 Lesson Plan

**Key**
**L1** Basic to Average
**L2** For All Students
**L3** Average to Advanced
**ELL** English Language Learners

# Russia: A Huge Country Takes a New Path

🕒 *3.5 periods, 1.75 blocks (includes Chapter Review and Assessment)*

## Section Objectives

1. Investigate the changes that capitalism has brought to Russia.
2. Understand the cultural traditions that have endured throughout Russia.
3. Identify the issues challenging the Russians.

## Vocabulary

• investor • inflation

## Local Standards

## Reading/Language Arts Objective

Identify contrasts to find out how two things are different.

---

## PREPARE TO READ

**Build Background Knowledge**
Discuss the effects of capitalism on Moscow.
**Set a Purpose for Reading**
Have students evaluate statements on the *Reading Readiness Guide.*
**Preview Key Terms**
Teach the section's Key Terms.
**Target Reading Skill**
Introduce the section's Target Reading Skill of **identifying contrasts.**

## Targeted Resources

❑  **Europe and Russia Teaching Resources**
  • Reading Readiness Guide, p. 326 **L2**
  • Identify Contrasts, p. 331 **L2**
❑ **Spanish Reading and Vocabulary Study Guide,** Section 4, pp. 49–50 **ELL** **L1**

---

## INSTRUCT

**Emerging Capitalism**
Discuss the dissolution of the Soviet Union.
**Cultural Traditions Continue**
Discuss old and new cultural traditions.
**Target Reading Skill**
Review **identifying contrasts.**
**Uniting a Vast Nation**
Discuss changes in Russia after the dissolution of the Soviet Union.

## Targeted Resources

❑ **All in One Europe and Russia Teaching Resources,** Guided Reading and Review, p. 327 **L2**
❑ **Europe and Russia Transparencies,** Section Reading Support Transparency ER 51 **L2**
❑ **Teacher's Edition,** For Advanced Readers, p. 203 **L3**
❑ **Spanish Support,** Guided Reading and Review, p. 50 **ELL** **L2**

---

## ASSESS AND RETEACH

**Assess Progress**
Evaluate student comprehension with the section assessment and section quiz.
**Reteach**
Assign the Reading and Vocabulary Study Guide to help struggling students.
**Extend**
Assign a Literature Reading.

## Targeted Resources

❑ **All in One Europe and Russia Teaching Resources**
  • Section Quiz, p. 328 **L2**
  • Chapter Tests A and B, pp. 351–356 **L2**
❑ **Reading and Vocabulary Study Guide,** Section 4, pp. 67–69 **L1**
❑ **Spanish Support**
  • Section Quiz, p. 51 **ELL** **L2**
  • Vocabulary Development, p. 53 **ELL** **L2**

---

Section 4: Russia: A Huge Country Takes a New Path
Eastern Europe and Russia

# Reading Readiness Guide

## Anticipation Guide

How much do you think you know about Russia and the changes capitalism has brought to this large nation? As your teacher reads the statements, mark whether you think each statement is true (T) or false (F) in the Me column. Then, discuss your answers with your group and mark the group's decision in the Group column. As you read, look for information that will clarify whether the statements are true or false.

  After you read the section, read the statements again and mark the After Reading column to indicate whether they are true or false.

| Before Reading: | | Statements | After Reading |
|---|---|---|---|
| Me | Group | | |
| | | 1. When the Soviet Union first collapsed, investors came from many different countries to make money in Moscow. | |
| | | 2. Most Russians today earn large salaries and have a high standard of living. | |
| | | 3. Corruption is a problem, and criminal gangs often force business owners to pay them money. | |
| | | 4. In the 1990s, large numbers of Russians lost their life savings when banks failed and inflation soared. | |
| | | 5. Siberia is the cultural center of the nation, where art, theater, and dance thrive. | |
| | | 6. In the early 2000s, Russia's capitalist economy weakened and collapsed. | |
| | | 7. Russia depends too heavily on the sale of its natural resources and needs to create new jobs. | |

Name _____ Date _____ Class _____

Section 4: Russia: A Huge Country Takes a New Path
Eastern Europe and Russia

# Guided Reading and Review

## A. As You Read

**Directions:** *As you read Section 4, answer the following questions in the spaces provided.*

1. What transition did Russia struggle to make after the Soviet Union collapsed?

   _____

2. Why did business boom in Moscow when the Soviet Union first collapsed?

   _____

3. With the switch to capitalism, what have many average Russians been able to do?

   _____

4. What happened to large numbers of Russians in the 1990s?

   _____

5. How has free enterprise changed life in Siberia?

   _____

   _____

6. What cultural traditions have continued in Moscow?

   _____

7. What is life like in rural Siberia?

   _____

   _____

8. What economic problems does Russia still face?

   _____

   _____

## B. Reviewing Key Terms

**Directions:** *Write the definitions for the following key terms in the blanks provided.*

9. investor

   _____

10. inflation

    _____

Section 4: Russia: A Huge Country Takes a New Path
Eastern Europe and Russia

# Section Quiz

## A. Key Terms

**Directions:** *Read the statements below. If a statement is true, write T in the blank provided. If it is false, write F. Rewrite false statements on the back of this page to make them true.*

_____ **1.** Recession is an increase in the general level of prices.

_____ **2.** An investor is someone who spends money to start a business.

## B. Main Ideas

**Directions:** *Write the letter of the correct answer in each blank.*

_____ **3.** Which economic system replaced the communist system in Russia?
  **a.** socialist
  **b.** free market
  **c.** dictatorship
  **d.** welfare

_____ **4.** Why have people from other countries come to Moscow since the fall of communism?
  **a.** to invest money in businesses
  **b.** to work for government-owned companies
  **c.** to transport goods to Siberia
  **d.** to work on government-owned farms

_____ **5.** What is a problem that affects many Russians today?
  **a.** illiteracy
  **b.** corruption
  **c.** free enterprise
  **d.** overcrowding

_____ **6.** Life expectancy in Russia is
  **a.** very high for a developed country.
  **b.** about the same as other developed countries.
  **c.** very low for a developed country.
  **d.** rising due to improvements in health care.

_____ **7.** What is one way life in Siberia has changed since the fall of communism?
  **a.** All workers are guaranteed a job.
  **b.** Few people can buy their own homes.
  **c.** People are worried about losing their jobs.
  **d.** People cannot invest in the companies where they work.

_____ **8.** Which statement best describes life in Siberian villages today?
  **a.** It is similar to life in most Russian cities.
  **b.** Living conditions are very primitive.
  **c.** It is similar to life in many Eastern European cities.
  **d.** Living conditions are very modern.

Eastern Europe and Russia

# Target Reading Skill: Comparing and Contrasting

## Compare and Contrast

Comparing and contrasting will help you to sort out and analyze information while you read. When you compare, look for similarities. For example, you and your relatives may look similar. When you contrast, you look for differences. For example, you may be very outgoing, while a friend is shy. The difference between your personalities is a contrast.

Compare and contrast while you read. First, identify a topic to use to compare and contrast two subjects or ideas. If you were reading a passage about Spain, you might compare and contrast Barcelona and Madrid. Next, choose categories to compare and pinpoint similarities and differences. Is each city small or large? Are the cities located inland or on the coast? Finally, draw a conclusion. For example, you might conclude that the two Spanish cities have more differences than similarities.

An easy way to compare and contrast two items is with a Venn diagram. Where the circles intersect, list how the two things are alike. Inside the separate part of each circle, list how the two things are different.

**Directions:** *Read the section assigned by your teacher. Find two subjects, items, or ideas to compare and contrast. Fill in the Venn diagram below, using information from the section. Then, draw a conclusion based on your comparison.*

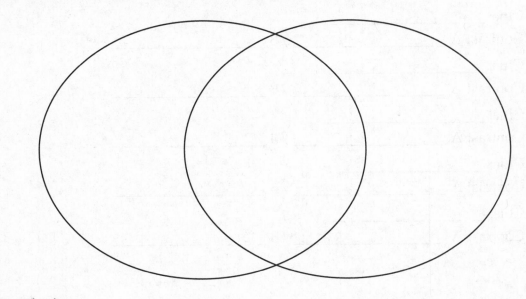

**Conclusion:**

_____

_____

Eastern Europe and Russia

# Target Reading Skill: Comparing and Contrasting

## Make Comparisons

As you know, when you compare, you look for how things are alike or similar. It is often easier to understand something that is not familiar by comparing it to something with which you are familiar.

When you are reading, look for words that compare two things. Words that end in -er and -est often signal a comparison.

### Examples

1. Texas is big**ger** than Maine.

   In this sentence two states are compared.

2. Asia is the larg**est** continent.

   This sentence compares Asia to all of the continents.

   There are other word clues that are used to make comparisons. As you read, look for the following word clues: *also, as well as, equally, like, just as, in the same way, both, as did, too, likewise, resemble, same as, similar to, same, more, less.*

**Directions:** *Read the section assigned by your teacher. Look for the word clues that are used to make comparisons. Write the word clue on the lines below and identify the items being compared.*

1. Clue: _____
   Contrast A _____ /B _____

2. Clue: _____
   Contrast A _____ /B _____

3. Clue: _____
   Contrast A _____ /B _____

4. Clue: _____
   Contrast A _____ /B _____

5. Clue: _____
   Contrast A _____ /B _____

Eastern Europe and Russia

# Target Reading Skill: Comparing and Contrasting

## Identify Contrasts

As you have learned, when you contrast, you look for differences between things or events. When you read, contrasting will help you see and understand differences. It will also help you understand why things are different. Contrasting is one way of sorting out and analyzing what you read.

To identify contrasts, first look for the main topic of the paragraph or section that you are reading. Look for information that shows differences. For example, suppose you are reading about Paris and Washington, D.C., the capital cities of France and the United States. You will see that the cities are located on different continents. In the information about these two cities, other categories for comparison will be given. How do the beginnings of the two cities differ? Is the population of the two cities similar or different? What about geography? After you contrast the information presented in the text, you might conclude that the two cities are alike in many ways. They are, however, very different. There are words that you can look for that signal contrasts. These signal words include: *different, although, yet, unlike, but, as opposed to, however, instead, while, despite, on the other hand, differs, different from,* and *in contrast to.* If you see one of these word clues, then you know that you are reading a contrast.

**Directions:** *Read the section assigned by your teacher. Look for the contrast clues listed above. On the lines below, write the contrast clue, then write the two things that are being contrasted.*

1. Clue: _____
   Contrast A _____ /B _____

2. Clue: _____
   Contrast A _____ /B _____

3. Clue: _____
   Contrast A _____ /B _____

4. Clue: _____
   Contrast A _____ /B _____

5. Clue: _____
   Contrast A _____ /B _____

Name _____ Date _____ Class _____

Eastern Europe and Russia

# Word Knowledge

**Directions:** *As your teacher reads the words, think about what each word might mean and mark the appropriate number in the Before Reading column.*

(1) = Know it    (2) = Kind of know it    (3) = Don't know it

After you have read and discussed the chapter, rate the words again in the After Reading column. Then write a definition or example for each word to help you clarify and remember the words.

| | Word | Rating | | Definition or Example |
|---|---|---|---|---|
| | | **Before Reading** | **After Reading** | |
| **Section 1** | unique, *adj.* | | | |
| | transition, *n.* | | | |
| | invest, *v.* | | | |
| **Section 2** | principle, *n.* | | | |
| | prevent, *v.* | | | |
| **Section 3** | consume, *v.* | | | |
| | publish, *v.* | | | |
| | contaminate, *v.* | | | |
| | produce, *n.* | | | |
| **Section 4** | dissolve, *v.* | | | |
| | enforce, *v.* | | | |
| | status, *n.* | | | |
| | resolve, *v.* | | | |

Eastern Europe and Russia

# Enrichment

## The Destruction of Sarajevo

**Directions:** *Read the two paragraphs below. Then, complete the activity that follows.*

Sarajevo is the capital of Bosnia and Herzegovina. Before the civil war, Sarajevo was a city of great beauty, charm, and culture. Many Muslims lived in Sarajevo, and the city had a strong Muslim character. It had many mosques, wood houses with richly decorated interiors, and a Turkish marketplace. The surrounding mountains provided not only beautiful scenery, but excellent skiing as well. The 1984 Winter Olympic Games were held in Sarajevo, and many visitors fell in love with the city and its friendly people.

Before the war, Sarajevo was not only beautiful, it was also a city where different ethnic groups lived together peacefully. The destruction of Sarajevo was tragic in many ways. In the book *Love Thy Neighbor*, a writer named Peter Maass writes: "There is a tradition in Sarajevo that people of different religions visit one another on religious holidays. On Christmas, the Pelzls' Muslim and Serb friends would come by for a visit. In turn, the Pelzls would visit their Muslim friends on the first day of Ramadan, the Muslim holy month, and visit their Serb friends on Orthodox Christmas, which falls in January."

## Activity

Work in a small group to research the geography, history, and culture of Sarajevo. Prepare a poster display describing the city before and after the war.

Eastern Europe and Russia

# Skills for Life

## Identifying Frame of Reference

**Directions:** *Read the passage from an article about the life of Iva Dvorakova, a young person in the Czech Republic. Then, in the spaces provided, write answers to the questions.*

Since Communist rule was overthrown in 1989, . . . life is different for Prague teenagers. From 1945 to 1989, the country was controlled by the Communist Party, which largely decided what you could read or watch and where you could travel or work. . . .

For Iva, the freedom to travel means that her family can take frequent ski trips. Freedom of thought means she can read, watch, or listen to whatever she wants. Her favorite novel, for example, John Steinbeck's *East of Eden*, was banned under Communist rule, along with most other Western art and literature. . . .

Iva's family has also benefited from the country's switch from a government-controlled economy to capitalism. When private enterprise became legal, her father went into business as a real estate developer. Now her family is part of Prague's emerging middle class.

For Iva, that means an allowance of 250 crowns (about $9) a month. She spends it on treats—"I love chocolates!" she says—or on movies. Although her country is known for fine filmmaking, her favorite movie is *Forrest Gump*. . . .

**1.** What is the main idea of the passage?

_____

_____

**2.** What qualifications and/or experiences have influenced Iva's frame of reference?

_____

_____

**3.** How might Iva's frame of reference have influenced her choice of John Steinbeck's *East of Eden* as her favorite novel?

_____

_____

**4.** How might Iva's age affect her opinion of freedom? Why might her opinion be different from that of a middle-aged or an elderly person?

_____

_____

**5.** Draw a conclusion about Iva's frame of reference.

_____

_____

# Small Group Activity

## Chernobyl—Report on a Disaster

Chernobyl was just one of hundreds of nuclear power plants built in Europe and Russia during the late 1900s. The accident there was a terrifying reminder of the possible dangers of nuclear power. Imagine you have been asked by the United Nations to conduct a study of Chernobyl. In this activity, you will work with your group to find out what happened in 1986, and how the accident affects the land and people of Ukraine today. You can also report on nuclear power in Europe, Russia, or the United States in general: how and where it is used, and what steps are being taken to avoid similar disasters in the future.

### Background

As you have learned, in April 1986 the nuclear power plant at Chernobyl overheated and leaked. Extremely poisonous radioactive clouds spread over a huge area. Thousands of square miles of Ukraine were eventually contaminated. This land may not be usable for a hundred years or more. Two hundred fifty people died; more than 30 died immediately. Many more suffered radiation poisoning over the following years. Towns were abandoned. The effects were not only felt in Ukraine. Radioactive particles were found as far away as Sweden. At one time, nuclear power was seen as the answer to energy needs for the world. For many reasons, this idea has come into question. You will prepare and present a report that answers these questions:

- Why did the accident at Chernobyl happen?
- What were the effects of the accident?
- What are the effects today on the area?
- How can a similar disaster be prevented in other places?

### Procedure

1. **Research information.** Read all the steps in this project. Meet as a group to decide what jobs need to be done. You might begin by choosing the sources of information you will seek. You can use up-to-date encyclopedias, magazine and newspaper articles from the time, and other articles about nuclear power. Ask your librarian for help in finding sources. At this time, you should also figure out what form your report will take. It could be a written report, an oral report, or a combination of both.

2. **Organize information.** As you gather information, be sure to keep track of your sources. If you need to return to a particular article, this will save a lot of time. You should also keep a record of your sources for each point. Look for photographs and illustrations to use. You may find charts or tables that explain the accident at Chernobyl or nuclear power in general.

## *Small Group Activity* (continued)

3. **Write the report.** When you have gathered information, organize it into main topics. Use the chart below to help you. Include important details for each main idea. Put them in the most logical order. Then write the report including graphics. Be sure you have covered the questions as completely as possible.

| |
|---|
| **Main Idea 1:** _____<br>Important details: |
| **Main Idea 2:** _____<br>Important details: |
| **Main Idea 3:** _____<br>Important details: |
| **Main Idea 4:** _____<br>Important details: |

4. **Present the report.** When you have finished the report, make a presentation. Work as a group to share your findings. Remember, the United Nations has asked you to draw some conclusions about what took place and how future disasters can be avoided. Be sure to address these issues. When all reports have been presented, discuss their strong and weak points as a class.

# Small Group Activity: Teacher Page

## Chernobyl—Report on a Disaster

### Content Objectives

- Students will learn about the accident at the Chernobyl nuclear power plant in Ukraine.
- Students will gain a deeper understanding about nuclear power and its pros and cons.

### Skill Objectives

- Writing for a report
- Locating information
- Organizing information
- Expressing problems clearly
- Recognizing cause and effect
- Distinguishing facts from opinions
- Drawing conclusions

### Advance Preparation

Gather sources of information on the Chernobyl nuclear disaster.

**Suggested group size:** six students

**Suggested time:** 40 minutes for researching information; 60 minutes for organizing and writing the report; 40 minutes for presentation and discussion (This may vary depending upon the format students choose.)

### Procedure

Divide the class into groups. Distribute the student pages and have students begin work on the project. You may wish to give a copy of the rubric for Chernobyl reports to each group.

You may need to help students find sources of information about Chernobyl. The librarian can help find magazines from the period of the accident on microfilm or microfiche. If you have access to the Internet, you will likely find sources there as well. You might remind students they are writing a report for the United Nations. Help them use an appropriate style for a formal report.

When students have finished their reports, invite them to discuss each one. To help students get started, ask questions such as these:

- What have you learned from your research about the accident at Chernobyl?
- What effects still exist today in Ukraine from the accident?
- Do you think nuclear power plants are a good source of energy? Why or why not?
- How well did your group share work on this project?

# Small Group Activity: Teacher Page

Reports will be evaluated according to the following rubric.

## Rubric for Chernobyl Reports

| Grading Criteria | Excellent | Admirable | Acceptable |
|---|---|---|---|
| **Research** | Students find a wide variety of sources for their reports; they locate information and images about the accident, the current situation, and the future of nuclear power. | Students find several sources for their reports; they locate information about the accident itself and the current situation. | Students find some information for their reports; most of what they find describes the accident. |
| **Writing the Reports** | Students include a great deal of information relating to the topic; their reports are well organized and give clear conclusions about what happened, what is currently happening, and how similar accidents can be avoided in the future; the writing style is appropriate for a formal report. | Students include details on the topic; their reports are well organized and easy to understand; they draw strong conclusions about what happened and what is currently happening; the writing style is appropriate for a formal report. | Students include some information on the topic; their reports could be better organized; they explain what happened in 1986, but could draw more conclusions; the writing style could be more consistent. |
| **Presentation** | Oral reports are well spoken, capture the interest of the audience, and are easy to understand; written reports are neat, and include illustrations and other graphics. | Oral reports are well spoken and easy to understand; written reports are neat and include illustrations. | Oral reports are spoken clearly, but could be better organized; written reports include basic facts and information, but are a bit sloppy. |
| **Teamwork** | Groups work very well together; they make decisions together and work enthusiastically as a team on all parts of the report. | Groups work as a team, make decisions together, and share most of the research, writing, and presentation. | Groups work together on most parts of the report, but some members do more than others. |

Name _____ Date _____ Class _____

Eastern Europe and Russia

# Activity Shop Interdisciplinary

## Plan a New Railroad Line

Siberia, the vast Asian region of Russia, has many natural resources, but it has few transportation routes. The region's major rail line, the Trans-Siberian Railroad, was completed in 1905. The route is thousands of miles long, but it covers only a part of Siberia. An addition to the rail line would make it easier for people to move throughout the region.

### Purpose

In this activity, you will plan a new branch of the Trans-Siberian Railroad. As you work on the activity, you will learn about Siberia's resources.

### 1. Draw a Resource Map

A new rail line in Siberia would transport some of the region's many natural resources to other parts of Russia. Look in an encyclopedia for information on Siberia and Russia.

   **a.** Make a list of Siberian natural resources below. Use a separate sheet of paper if necessary.

   **b.** Write down the main uses of each resource.

   **c.** Draw a small symbol, or picture, to represent each resource.

| Siberian Natural Resources | Uses | Symbols |
|---|---|---|
| | | |
| | | |
| | | |
| | | |
| | | |
| | | |
| | | |

Then draw a map of Siberia on a separate piece of paper and put the symbols on the map to show where these resources can be found.

Eastern Europe and Russia

## Activity Shop Interdisciplinary *(continued)*

### 2. Make a Circle Graph

Money to build a new rail line will come from towns and cities along the line, the Siberian regional government, and from the Russian national government. Using the percentages below, create a circle graph on a separate sheet of paper to show how money would be contributed.

- Cities and towns        15%
- Regional government   32%
- National government   53%

### 3. Decide on a Route

Look at some maps of Siberia, including your natural resources map. Then, decide where you think a new rail line should run.

    **a.** Write down a list of cities and towns the route might pass through.

_____

_____

_____

_____

    **b.** Write the distances between the cities and towns on the list above.

    **c.** Figure out the total distance of the route. _____

    **d.** Finally, circle the places where the line will start and end, using the list above.

### 4. Write a Proposal

Write a proposal to persuade the national government to build a new rail line in Siberia. Start with a brief history of the Trans-Siberian Railroad. Then, tell where the new rail line will run, what purpose it will serve, and how the project will be paid for.

### 5. Write a Railroad Song

Once a new rail line is built, people need to hear about it. Write a song that will advertise the new railroad. In your song lyrics, describe the features of the new train. Tell about the resources and wildlife of Siberia.

### 6. Analysis and Conclusion

On a separate sheet of paper, write a summary explaining what you've learned from planning and proposing the railroad extension. Be sure to answer the following questions in your summary:

    **a.** What have you learned about the geography of Siberia and its mineral resources?

    **b.** What did you learn about writing an effective proposal and song?

# MapMaster Skills

## Using the Map Key

A map key explains what the symbols, shading, and colors on a map represent.
Symbols range from simple dots and circles that represent cities and capitals to tiny
drawings that represent types of manufacturing and industry or agriculture.
Shading and colors are used to show elevation, population density, political
divisions, and so on. The map key for the map of China below uses a combination
of shading and drawings to represent economic activity and resources.

**Directions:** *Study the map and the map key. Then, answer the questions that follow on a
separate sheet of paper.*

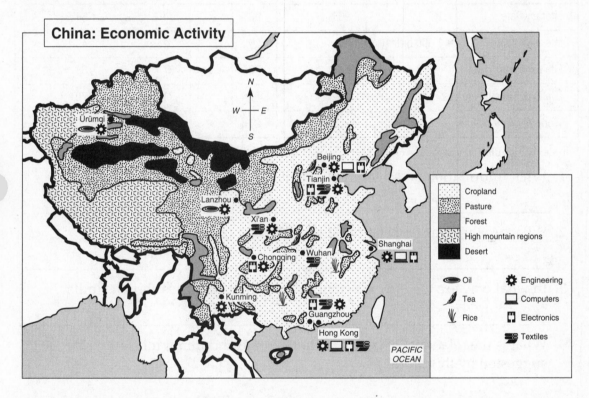

China: Economic Activity

1. How many different types of shading are represented on the map key?

2. What symbol is used to represent oil?

3. Which part of China is least developed economically?

4. Describe the economic activity and resources around Beijing.

5. Based on the map, which city in China has the most varied manufacturing and
   industry?

6. Why does the map use a combination of shadings and drawings to show
   economic activity and resources?

Name _____ Date _____ Class _____

Eastern Europe and Russia

# MapMaster Skills

## Reading a Table

A table presents information in columns (up and down) and rows (across). It allows you to make comparisons and to analyze the information presented. A table is an efficient way of presenting information that needs analyzing. The table below presents population data for four countries in Central America.

**Directions:** *Study the table. Then, answer the questions that follow.*

## Population Data for Four Central American Countries

|  | Costa Rica | Panama | Honduras | Guatemala |
|---|---|---|---|---|
| Literacy Rate | 96% | 90% | 74% | 64% |
| Infant Mortality Rate (per 1,000 births) | 11 | 20 | 31 | 45 |
| Life Expectancy: Males | 74 | 73 | 67 | 64 |
| Life Expectancy: Females | 79 | 77 | 71 | 70 |
| Workers in Agriculture | 20% | 21% | 34% | 50% |

Source: *World Almanac and Book of Facts,* 2003; *CIA: The World Factbook,* 2002.

1. What information is shown in this table?

    _____

2. What are the infant mortality rates in Honduras and Guatemala?

    _____

3. In what way are the life expectancy data for all countries shown similar?

    _____

4. What is the relationship between literacy rate and infant mortality rate suggested by this table?

    _____

5. Identify another relationship suggested by the data in this table.

    _____

6. Identify the country on this table with the highest standard of living. Give reasons for your choice.

    _____

    _____

Eastern Europe and Russia

Chapter and Section Support

# DK Compact Atlas of the World Activity: Reading a Political Map

Your teacher will tell you which map in the *Compact Atlas of the World* to use for this activity. Review the population key in the left-hand margin of the page. You may also wish to refer to the Key to Map Symbols at the front of the atlas.

1. How are the borders of countries shown on your map?

_____

2. How is color used on your map?

_____

3. If islands are depicted on your map, how can you tell to what country they belong?

_____

4. If there is a red dot within a square next to the name of a city, what do you know about that city?

_____

5. The map uses different styles of type to convey information. Turn to the Key to Map Symbols at the front of your atlas. Which cities use all capital letters? What features are labeled in an *italic* type style?

_____

6. The map you have been assigned is a combination political and physical map. That means some features on your map belong to political maps and other features belong to physical maps. Which of the features on your map might not be found on a physical map?

## Outline Map Activity

Using the Outline Map provided by your teacher, label each country or state in the region you are studying. Locate and label the capital of each country or state, using symbols appropriate to the estimated population. Include other political features as necessary. Make sure to include a map key that identifies the symbols you are using on your map.

# Outline Map 18:
# Eastern Europe and Russia: Political

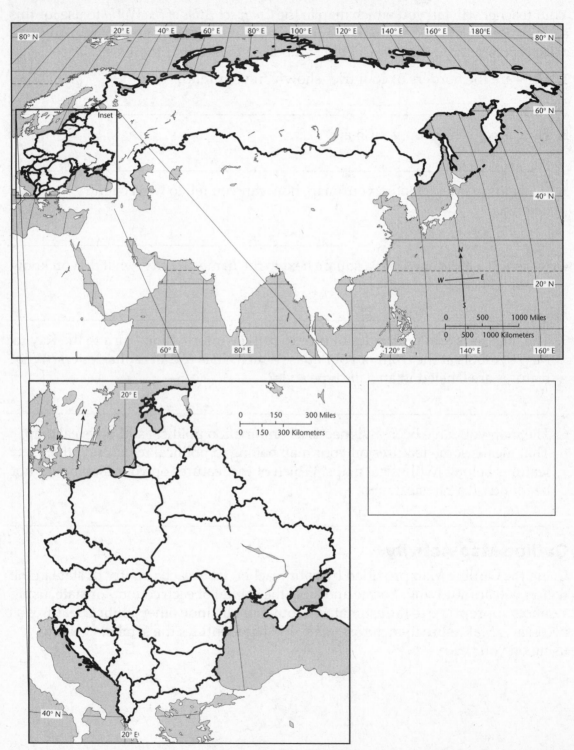

Name _____ Date _____ Class _____

# Primary Sources and Literature Readings

## Housekeeping in Russia Soon After the Revolution

by Marina Tsvetaeva

**Revolution is never easy, especially for families. At first, poet Marina Tsvetaeva supported the Russian Revolution. But in 1919, she wrote to her sister and described the hardships she and her young children were suffering. Her husband, Seryozha, was missing and may have been jailed or killed in the revolution.**

I live with Alya and Irina (Alya is six, Irina two) in our same flat opposite two trees in the attic room which used to be Seryozha's. We have no flour and no bread. Under my writing desk there are about twelve pounds of potatoes which is all that is left from the food 'lent' by my neighbours. These are the only provisions we have. I walk all over Moscow looking for bread. If Alya comes with me, I have to tie Irina to a chair, for safety. I feed Irina, then put her to bed. She sleeps in the blue armchair. There is a bed but it won't go through the door. I boil up some old coffee, and drink it, and have a smoke. I write. Alya writes or reads. There is silence for two hours; then Irina wakes up. We heat up what remains of the mashed goo. With Alya's help, I fish out the potatoes which remain, or rather have become clogged in the bottom of the samovar. Either Alya or myself puts Irina back to bed. Then Alya goes to bed. At 10 pm the day is over.

---

**Vocabulary Builder**

| | |
|---|---|
| flat | apartment |
| provisions | supplies |
| samovar | a closed pitcher used in Russia to heat up food and drinks |

---

**Think It Over**

1. According to the text, what hardships did the Russian family encounter after the revolution?

   _____

   _____

2. Although a revolution might be successful in overthrowing an old government and creating a new government, why do you think such hardships may occur?

   _____

   _____

Eastern Europe and Russia

# Vocabulary Development

**Directions:** *Match the key terms in the box with the definitions below. Write the correct letter in each space. Then write a sentence in the space provided that uses that term or the plural form of the term. If necessary, look up the terms in your textbook glossary.*

---

**a.** shrine       **e.** embargo       **i.** investor

**b.** capitalism       **f.** economic sanctions       **j.** inflation

**c.** entrepreneur       **g.** chernozem       **k.** civil war

**d.** secede       **h.** collective

---

_____ **1.** a ban on trade

_____

_____ **2.** someone who spends money on improving a business in the hope of making more money

_____

_____ **3.** a person who develops original ideas in order to start new businesses

_____

_____ **4.** rich, black soil

_____

_____ **5.** an increase in the general level of prices when the amount of goods and services remains the same

_____

_____ **6.** a holy place

_____

_____ **7.** a huge government-controlled farm

_____

_____ **8.** an economic system in which businesses are privately owned

_____

_____ **9.** actions to limit trade with nations that have violated international laws

_____

_____ **10.** leave a group, especially a political group or a nation

_____

_____ **11.** a war between groups of people within the same nation

_____

# Rubric for Assessing a Bar Graph

| Grading Criteria | Excellent | Acceptable | Minimal | Unacceptable |
|---|---|---|---|---|
| **Graph Elements** | Contains an x-axis and y-axis; has appropriate and concise title and labels. | Contains an x-axis and y-axis, a title, and labels. | Missing either x-axis or y-axis; some labels are missing; incomplete title. | Bars have no consistent x-axis or y-axis; many labels are missing; no title. |
| **Content** | Contains accurate, complete, and pertinent information. | Information meets criteria of assignment; few or no inaccuracies. | Contains some inaccuracies. | Does not include required items; information is inaccurate. |
| **Mechanics** | Evidence of care is shown in measuring bars, which show precise information. | Bars are correctly sized in relation to one another. | All but one or two bars are correctly sized. | Bars are incorrectly sized. |
| **Visual Appeal** | Very colorful and clean looking; labels are very easy to read; creative use of graphics connected to content. | Some color; most labels are easy to read. | Limited use of color; some labels are hard to read. | Limited or no use of color; labels are very difficult to read. |

# Rubric for Assessing a Newspaper Article

| Grading Criteria | Excellent | Acceptable | Minimal | Unacceptable |
|---|---|---|---|---|
| Content | Thorough, factual, and vividly written; answers five journalistic questions: *Who, Where, What, When,* and *How.* | Factual and competently written; answers five journalistic questions. | Contains minor factual errors; answers most journalistic questions. | Contains many errors and inaccuracies; answers only one or two journalistic questions. |
| Research | Excellent and thorough use of research data and interview materials to explore and develop ideas; all sources documented. | Good use of research data and interview materials to illustrate and develop ideas and opinions; all sources documented. | Faulty use of interview and research materials; some irrelevant quotations and data used; some sources not reliable or not documented. | Interview and research not completed. |
| Organization | Contains intriguing and attention-grabbing introduction, logically sequenced paragraphs, and decisive conclusion. | Contains introduction, development, and conclusion. | Topics and ideas discussed somewhat randomly; article may lack clearly defined introduction or conclusion. | No organizational framework apparent. |
| Mechanics | Flawless spelling, punctuation, and use of language. | Few or no spelling errors; some minor punctuation and usage mistakes. | Several spelling errors and minor punctuation and usage mistakes. | Many misspelled words, punctuation errors, and language usage problems. |

# Rubric for Assessing a Timeline

| Grading Criteria | Excellent | Acceptable | Minimal | Unacceptable |
|---|---|---|---|---|
| **Entry Choice** | Great care taken in selection of timeline entries; most significant events, those that show historical pattern, or those that show cause-and-effect relationship selected. | Selections meet assignment criteria; few inaccuracies. | Includes required number of entries; some inaccuracies. | Does not include required number of entries. |
| **Scale and Sequence** | Scale consistent and accurate; increments marked; all entries in sequence and placed with care. | Scale accurate; increments marked; entries in sequence. | Scale roughly drawn; increments fairly accurately marked; some entries out of sequence. | No apparent scale; increments not marked; many entries out of sequence. |
| **Mechanics** | Flawless. | Few mechanical errors. | Some errors in spelling and dates. | Many errors in spelling and dates. |
| **Visual Presentation** | Visually striking; very effective in communicating historical information. | Clear and uncluttered. | Legible. | Illegible and messy. |

# Rubric for Assessing a Writing Assignment

| Grading Criteria | Excellent | Acceptable | Minimal | Unacceptable |
|---|---|---|---|---|
| **Content** | Clearly focused introduction; idea development interesting and sophisticated; supporting evidence detailed, accurate, and convincing; perceptive conclusion. | Introduction gives assignment direction; idea development clear; supporting evidence accurate; strong conclusion. | Introduction unclear; idea development uneven and simplistic; supporting evidence uneven; conclusion summarizes information in assignment. | Introduction incomplete, ineffective; idea development ineffective; supporting evidence vague, inaccurate, or missing; conclusion incomplete or missing. |
| **Organization** | Paragraph order reinforces content; strong topic sentences make content easy to follow; effective and varied transitions. | Logical paragraph order; clear topic sentences; clear and functional transitions. | Ineffective paragraph order; narrow or inaccurate topic sentences; few clear transitions. | Inconsistent paragraph order; topic sentences and transitions missing. |
| **Mechanics** | Flawless punctuation and spelling; varied and interesting sentence structure. | Few spelling and punctuation errors; sentence structure correct. | Some careless spelling and punctuation errors; some errors in sentence structure. | Many spelling and punctuation errors; many sentence fragments and run-ons. |

# Test A

## A. Key Terms

**Directions:** *Fill in the blanks in Column I by writing the letter of the correct key term from Column II. You will not use all the terms. (15 points)*

**Column I**

_____ 1. People open and run their own businesses under the system of _____.

_____ 2. An action to limit trade with nations that have violated international laws is called a(n) _____.

_____ 3. A rich, black soil called _____ covers half of Ukraine.

_____ 4. Russia is now a country where an American _____ might spend money improving a business.

_____ 5. The Russian economy has been hurt by _____, or an increase in the general level of prices.

**Column II**

a. chernozem
b. collective
c. capitalism
d. economic sanctions
e. embargo
f. inflation
g. investor
h. secede
i. shrine

## B. Key Concepts

**Directions:** *Write the letter of the correct answer in each blank. (45 points)*

_____ 6. For centuries, the center of Polish tradition has been the
a. government.
b. Catholic Church.
c. Greek Orthodox Church.
d. university system.

_____ 7. Since the fall of communism, Poland has adopted an economic system in which
a. the government owns and runs most businesses.
b. foreign countries own and run all the businesses.
c. people own and run most of the businesses.
d. Eastern European countries own and run all the businesses.

## Test A (continued)

_____ 8. How has Polish life changed since the fall of the communist government?

    a. Foreigners have been afraid to invest there.

    c. There is very little unemployment.

    b. The government supports high prices for farm produce.

    d. People have access to more consumer goods.

_____ 9. While most Serbs belong to the Christian Orthodox Church, most Bosnians practice

    a. Judaism.

    c. Islam.

    b. Roman Catholicism.

    d. Buddhism.

_____ 10. What was a chief cause of the war in Bosnia and Herzegovina?

    a. Treaties were violated.

    b. There were tensions among different ethnic groups.

    c. No one country wanted to take control of the region.

    d. A popular leader was assassinated.

_____ 11. Other countries have invaded Ukraine because of the country's

    a. natural resources.

    c. foreign trade routes.

    b. excellent universities.

    d. location in Europe.

_____ 12. When the Soviet Union ruled Ukraine, individual farms were replaced with

    a. schools.

    c. collectives.

    b. large markets.

    d. factories.

_____ 13. Many people in Ukraine suffered serious health problems because of

    a. the lack of meat and milk in their diet.

    c. the breakdown of the national health system.

    b. the nuclear accident at Chernobyl.

    d. an invasion by Soviet forces.

_____ 14. Which statement best describes life in Moscow?

    a. No one maintains any traditional ways.

    c. All the people live as their ancestors did.

    b. Capitalism has brought changes, but Russian traditions still remain.

    d. Communism is helping people adapt to new ways.

**Test A** *(continued)*

## C. Critical Thinking

**Directions:** *Answer the following questions on the back of this paper or on a separate sheet of paper. (20 points)*

15. **Making Comparisons** How is life in the Polish countryside different from life in the cities? In your answer, explain what probably accounts for this difference.

16. **Drawing Conclusions** Why do you think Ukraine wanted its independence from the Soviet Union?

## D. Skill: Identifying Frame of Reference

**Directions:** *Read the passage below, which is an excerpt from a speech made by Václav Havel, the first democratic president of Czechoslovakia. Then, in the space provided, answer the questions that follow. (20 points)*

> Our country [Czechoslovakia] is not flourishing. The enormous creative and spiritual potential of our nation is being wasted. Entire branches of industry produce goods that are of no interest to anyone, while we lack the things we need.... Our outmoded economy wastes what little energy we have. A country that once could be proud of the education level of its citizens now spends so little on education that it ranks seventy-second in the world. We have polluted our land, rivers, and forests... [so] we now have the most contaminated environment in all of Europe....
>
> You may ask what kind of republic I dream of [as leader of Czechoslovakia]. Let me reply: I dream of a republic that is independent, free, and democratic; a republic with economic prosperity yet social justice; a republic of well rounded people, because without such people, it is impossible to solve any of our problems....
>
> —Václav Havel

17. What is the main idea of the passage?

_____

18. What is the writer's position?

_____

19. What is the tone of the passage?

_____

20. Briefly explain the writer's frame of reference.

_____

_____

# Test B

## A. Key Terms

**Directions:** *Match the definitions in Column I with the key terms in Column II. Write the correct letter in each blank. You will not use all the terms. (15 points)*

**Column I**

_____ 1. a holy place

_____ 2. an economic system in which businesses are privately owned

_____ 3. rich, black soil

_____ 4. a huge, government-controlled farm

_____ 5. someone who spends money on improving a business in the hope of getting more money

**Column II**

a. chernozem

b. collective

c. capitalism

d. economic sanctions

e. embargo

f. inflation

g. investor

h. secede

i. shrine

## B. Key Concepts

**Directions:** *Write the letter of the correct answer in each blank. (45 points)*

_____ 6. Two important Polish traditions are

    a. Greek Orthodoxy and Polish collective farms.

    b. Greek Orthodoxy and the Polish language.

    c. Polish Catholicism and the Polish language.

    d. Polish Catholicism and the Russian language.

_____ 7. How has the Polish economy changed since the fall of the communist government?

    a. Collective farms were built.

    b. A socialist system was adopted.

    c. People own and run their own businesses.

    d. The foreign debt was paid.

_____ 8. Serbs, Croats, and Bosniaks have different

    a. spoken languages.

    b. religions.

    c. economies.

    d. educational systems.

_____ 9. War started in Bosnia and Herzegovina because of

    a. the bombing of Belgrade.

    b. the military overthrow of the government.

    c. tensions among different ethnic groups.

    d. economic problems in Russia.

## Test B (continued)

_____ 10. Throughout its history, Ukraine's location and natural resources have attracted
     **a.** investors.
     **b.** invaders.
     **c.** merchants.
     **d.** scholars.

_____ 11. One important economic change made by the Soviets in Ukraine was the creation of
     **a.** small family farms.
     **b.** a free enterprise system.
     **c.** trade routes with the West.
     **d.** large collectives.

_____ 12. The accident at Chernobyl affected the environment by
     **a.** filling the air with radioactive materials.
     **b.** causing serious floods.
     **c.** lowering the temperature of the atmosphere.
     **d.** causing serious droughts.

_____ 13. Which statement best describes life in Siberia today?
     **a.** Life in many Siberian villages is similar to life in American suburbs.
     **b.** Life in many Siberian villages is still very traditional.
     **c.** Life in Siberian villages has been changed by the free enterprise system.
     **d.** Life in Siberian villages is similar to life in Moscow.

_____ 14. Although Moscow has been changed by the free market system, many people there are still influenced by
     **a.** Russian traditions.
     **b.** the Slavic educational system.
     **c.** the Siberian language.
     **d.** Ukrainian agricultural methods.

## C. Critical Thinking

**Directions:** *Answer the following questions on the back of this paper or on a separate sheet of paper. (20 points)*

15. **Expressing Problems Clearly** What are three differences among Bosnians, Croats, and Serbs that contributed to the conflict in Bosnia and Herzegovina?

16. **Distinguishing Fact From Opinion** Give two facts and two opinions about life in Siberia.

Eastern Europe and Russia

**Test B** *(continued)*

## D. Skill: Identifying Frame of Reference

**Directions:** *Read the passage below, which is an excerpt from a speech made by Václav Havel, the first democratic president of Czechoslovakia. Then, in the space provided, answer the questions that follow. (20 points)*

> Our country [Czechoslovakia] is not flourishing. The enormous creative and spiritual potential of our nation is being wasted. Entire branches of industry produce goods that are of no interest to anyone, while we lack the things we need.... Our outmoded economy wastes what little energy we have. A country that once could be proud of the education level of its citizens now spends so little on education that it ranks seventy-second in the world. We have polluted our land, rivers, and forests... [so] we now have the most contaminated environment in all of Europe....
>
> You may ask what kind of republic I dream of [as leader of Czechoslovakia]. Let me reply: I dream of a republic that is independent, free, and democratic; a republic with economic prosperity yet social justice; a republic of well rounded people, because without such people, it is impossible to solve any of our problems....
>
> —Václav Havel

17. What is the main idea of the passage?

_____

18. Do you think the speaker is qualified to make these statements?

_____

19. What word could you use to describe the tone of the passage?

_____

20. Do you think the speaker is giving a fair picture of the situation? Why or why not?

_____

_____

_____

_____

# Answer Key

## Section 1 Reading Readiness Guide

Students' answers will vary. Correct answers are:

1. T
2. T
3. F, Catholicism has been at the center of Polish tradition for centuries.
4. F, The communists did not ban the Polish language, which is spoken by the majority of the population today.
5. F, Poland changed almost overnight from communism to capitalism.
6. T
7. T

## Section 1 Guided Reading and Review

1. In 1989, the communist government fell and Poles regained their freedom. In 2003, Poland voted to join the European Union.
2. It has been at the center of Polish tradition for centuries.
3. It is spoken by the majority of the population and gives them pride in their heritage. As a Slavic language, it also links the nation to other Slavic nations in Eastern Europe.
4. They ended the government's control over prices. They froze taxes and wages. Then, a year later, they set up a stock market.
5. At first, traders set up booths in the streets. Slowly, some traders earned enough money to take over stores the government had once owned. Now, more than two million businesses are run by entrepreneurs.
6. Under communism, the government always bought regular amounts of produce and meat from farmers, providing them with a reliable income. After communism, prices dropped, and sales were no longer guaranteed.
7. Poland faces the challenge of cleaning up terrible pollution caused during communist rule and the challenge of a high unemployment rate.
8. shrine
9. capitalism
10. entrepreneur

## Section 1 Quiz

1. F, Under capitalism, businesses are privately owned.
2. T
3. F, You can visit holy places, which are also called shrines, all over Poland.
4. b
5. a
6. b
7. d
8. c

## Section 2 Reading Readiness Guide

Students' answers will vary. Correct answers are:

1. T
2. F, Five Balkan countries—Serbia and Montenegro, Bosnia and Herzegovina, Macedonia, Croatia, and Slovenia—used to make up the nation of Yugoslavia.
3. T
4. T
5. F, After World War II, Josip Broz Tito ruled Yugoslavia according to communist principles, but he also had good relations with anti-communist countries.
6. T
7. F, The United States and Europe placed economic sanctions on Yugoslavia and held Slobodan Milosevic responsible for the violence that had occurred in the region.

*Answer Key* (*continued*)

## Section 2 Guided Reading and Review

1. Civil war shattered the grand city of Sarajevo and broke up the nation of Yugoslavia.
2. Serbia and Montenegro, Bosnia and Herzegovina, Macedonia, Croatia, and Slovenia.
3. the Serbs and Croats
4. These groups, such as the Serbs and Croats, speak related languages, but use different alphabets to write Serbo-Croatian. Religion also separates groups that speak the same language.
5. Most Serbs, Montenegrins, and Macedonians belong to the Eastern Orthodox Church. Croats and Slovenes are mainly Roman Catholic. Bosniaks are mainly Muslim.
6. It was formed in 1918. It became a communist state in 1945, when World War II ended.
7. The economy and government became unstable. Some republics wanted to govern themselves. Tensions rose among ethnic groups and bitter civil wars erupted in some republics.
8. The newly adopted constitution made Albanian an official language of the nation, increased Albanians' access to government jobs, and removed language in the constitution that had made Albanians second-class citizens.
9. a war between groups of people within the same nation
10. to leave a group, especially a political group or a nation
11. a ban on trade
12. actions to limit trade with nations that have violated international laws

## Section 2 Quiz

1. to leave a group, especially a political group or a nation
2. actions to limit trade with nations that have violated international laws

3. a ban on trade
4. a war between groups of people within the same nation
5. a
6. c
7. b
8. d
9. b
10. d

## Section 3 Reading Readiness Guide

Students' answers will vary. Correct answers are:

1. F, For hundreds of years, Ukraine's vast natural resources have attracted invaders.
2. F, Russia, and later the Soviet Union, ruled Ukraine between the late 1700s and 1991.
3. T
4. T
5. T
6. F, Today, much of Ukraine's soil and water is still poisoned, and it may take as long as a hundred years to repair the damage.
7. T

## Section 3 Guided Reading and Review

1. They formed a human chain from Kiev to Lviv, covering 300 miles.
2. Ukraine is located between Europe and Russia. It also has vast natural resources, which invaders wanted to control.
3. because it produced so much grain
4. Their land was taken away from them to create collectives. Most farmers were forced to become workers on these collectives.
5. in 1991
6. The Ukrainian people believe that speaking Ukrainian could tie the country together and free it from its Soviet past.

## *Answer Key* (continued)

7. An explosion at a nuclear power plant filled the air with radioactive materials. Some people died and others developed serious health problems. More than 100,000 people had to be moved away from the area. Much of Ukraine's soil and water is still poisoned today because of the explosion at Chernobyl.
8. There are many parks, stores, and restaurants in cities such as Kiev. Newsstands sell newly published papers and magazines. Farmers sell their own produce at local markets.
9. chernozem
10. collective

## Section 3 Quiz

1. F, Chernozem is a rich, black soil.
2. F, A huge government-owned farm is called a collective.
3. b
4. d
5. a
6. c
7. b
8. a

## Section 4 Reading Readiness Guide

Students' answers will vary. Correct answers are:
1. T
2. F, Salaries are still low for Russian workers and about 25% of all Russians live in poverty.
3. T
4. T
5. F, Moscow is the cultural center of the nation, where art, theater, and dance thrive.
6. F, In the early 2000s, Russia's capitalist economy showed signs of strengthening.
7. T

## Section 4 Guided Reading and Review

1. It struggled to make the transition from communism to a free market economy.
2. Business boomed because investors came from many different countries to make money in Moscow.
3. Many have been able to start their own businesses, open small factories, fix up their apartments, and travel.
4. Large numbers of Russians lost their life savings when banks failed and inflation rose to high levels.
5. Siberians worry about losing their jobs or farms because now neither their jobs nor crop prices are guaranteed. But they also are able to buy their own homes and make their own decisions.
6. Moscow continues to be the cultural center of the nation, where art, theater, and dance thrive. Even the tradition of picnicking in the snow is still practiced.
7. Many homes have no running water, and sometimes the wells freeze in the winter. Siberians have adapted to life in their frigid climate. People live in log houses, where large stoves are used for both cooking and heating.
8. Russia's economic problems include corruption, struggling banks, and dependency on sales of its natural resources.
9. someone who spends money on improving a business in the hope of making more money
10. an increase in the general level of prices when the amount of goods and services remains the same

## Section 4 Quiz

1. F, Inflation is an increase in the general level of prices.
2. F, An investor is someone who spends money on improving a business.
3. b

## Answer Key *(continued)*

4. a
5. b
6. c
7. c
8. b

## Target Reading Skill

### Compare and Contrast
Answers will vary.

### Make Comparisons
Answers will vary.

### Identify Contrasts
Answers will vary.

## Word Knowledge
Students' definitions and/or examples will vary.

## Enrichment
Students' posters will vary.

## Skills for Life
Students' answers will vary.
1. Since Communist rule was overthrown, life is different for teenagers living in Prague.
2. She is a teenager, and she and her family have experienced life before and after communist rule in the Czech Republic.
3. Under communist rule, Western literature, including Steinbeck's *East of Eden*, was banned. Now, Iva is free to choose what she wishes to read.
4. As a teenager, she might see freedom as a collection of exciting choices; under communism, there were no choices. A middle-aged person or an elderly person might feel more fear with freedom because of economic struggles.
5. Students' conclusions will vary.

## Activity Shop Interdisciplinary
Answers will vary.

## MapMaster Skills

### Using a Map Key
1. Five different shadings are represented on the map.
2. a pool of oil
3. The western half is the least developed economically.
4. Answers may include that Beijing is near cropland and some pastures; tea is grown nearby; other activities include engineering, computers, and electronics.
5. Based on the map, Hong Kong has the most varied manufacturing and industry.
6. Shadings show large areas; drawings are better for smaller locations.

### Reading a Table
1. The table shows literacy rate, infant mortality rate, life expectancy for men and women, and percentage of agricultural workers in Costa Rica, Panama, Honduras, and Guatemala.
2. 31 per 1,000 in Honduras, 45 per 1,000 in Guatemala
3. In each country, women have a higher life expectancy than men.
4. The table suggests that a higher literacy rate is related to a lower infant mortality rate.
5. Answers will vary, but may include: higher literacy rates are related to higher life expectancy; a higher infant mortality rate is related to a shorter life expectancy; a higher infant mortality rate is related to a larger percentage of agricultural workers.
6. Students may assume that Costa Rica has the higher standard of living because it has the highest literacy rate.

### DK Compact Atlas of the World: Reading a Political Map
1. Borders are shown as gold lines.
2. Color is used to differentiate countries.
3. There may be a curved border or the country to which they belong may be identified within parentheses below the name of the island.

## *Answer Key* (continued)

4. It is a national capital of more than 500,000 people.

5. A capital city is identified with capital letters. Physical features such as mountains, rivers, and deserts are labeled in italics.

6. Features that might not be found on physical maps include the use of color for different countries, names of cities, population symbols for cities, disputed borders, and sovereignty of islands.

## Primary Sources and Literature Readings: Housekeeping in Russia Soon After the Revolution

1. Answers will vary, but may include that food and living space were scarce.

2. Answers will vary, but may include that it takes time for changes in government policy to take place as well as creating a stable economy.

## Vocabulary Development

1. e
2. i
3. c
4. g
5. j
6. a
7. h
8. b
9. f
10. d
11. k

Students' sentences will vary.

## Test A

1. c
2. e
3. a
4. g
5. f
6. b

7. c
8. d
9. c
10. b
11. a
12. c
13. b
14. b

15. Answers will vary. A possible answer: In the countryside, traditions remain strong, but the economy is not good. Polish Catholicism has been at the center of Polish tradition, and the Polish language has also stood the test of time, but without government assistance, many farmers are struggling. Young people are moving out of the countryside to search for jobs. The cities show the strongest evidence of the new Poland. Small businesses have been started all over Warsaw, and their owners are beginning to make good money. People are moving into the cities looking for opportunity. Since the cities are more likely to be influenced by foreign economies and cultural influences, the lifestyle there is probably less traditional.

16. In the 1930s, Soviet rulers took land away from Ukrainian farmers and forced them to work on government-controlled farms called collectives. The collectives sent all of their produce to the government and gave very little food to their workers, resulting in millions of Ukrainians dying of hunger. Soviet rulers also made Russian the official language of Ukraine, replacing Ukrainian. As a result, Ukrainians wanted independence both to end the harsh Soviet rule that had led to so many deaths and to restore Ukrainian culture, including the use of the Ukrainian language.

## Answer Key *(continued)*

17. Czechoslovakia has many problems. Havel is dedicated to improving the economy, education, and environment. He is hopeful that a "free" Czechoslovakia can solve these problems.
18. Change is necessary in Czechoslovakia
19. serious and hopeful
20. Answers will vary. A possible answer: Havel had seen the negative changes that occurred under communist rule, and is most likely giving an accurate picture of the situation.

## Test B

1. i
2. c
3. a
4. b
5. g
6. c
7. c
8. b
9. c
10. b
11. d
12. a
13. b
14. a
15. Answers will vary. A possible answer: Although the groups speak Serbo-Croatian, the Serbs and the Croats use different alphabets for this language. Also, while most Serbs belong to the Christian Orthodox Church, most Croats are Roman Catholics, and most Bosnians are Muslims. Another difference is that the Serbs were in control of the government of Yugoslavia and the Croats and Bosnians were not in control.
16. Answers will vary. A possible answer: Facts: Many of the factories in Siberia are outdated. Many Siberian homes have no running water. Opinions: Life is difficult in Siberia. Life in Siberia is not as satisfying as life in Moscow.
17. Czechoslovakia is not flourishing, but that with Havel's leadership and the people of Czechoslovakia, change is possible
18. Answers will vary. A possible answer: Václav Havel was the president and a citizen of Czechoslovakia. He is qualified to make these statements about the country.
19. Answers will vary. Possible answers include: emotional, angry, hopeful, honest
20. Answers will vary. A possible answer: The people of Czechoslovakia would know if Havel was not telling the truth, so he is likely to be giving a fair picture of the situation.

Europe and Russia

# Final Exam A

## A. Key Terms

**Directions:** *Fill in the blanks in Column I by writing the letter of the correct key term from Column II. You will not use all the terms. (15 points)*

**Column I**

_____ 1. A treeless plain where grasses and mosses grow is called _____.

_____ 2. The practice of one country turning another into a colony is called _____.

_____ 3. A person who moves from one country to another is a(n) _____.

_____ 4. Governments have to limit their _____, or the amount of money the government owes.

_____ 5. A rich, black soil called _____ is found in Ukraine.

**Column II**

a. capitalism

b. chernozem

c. economic sanctions

d. immigrant

e. imperialism

f. manufacturing

g. national debt

h. tundra

i. westernization

## B. Key Concepts

**Directions:** *Write the letter of the correct answer in each blank. (45 points)*

_____ 6. More than half of Europe is covered by the

a. Central Uplands.

b. Alpine Mountain System.

c. Northwestern Highlands.

d. North European Plain.

_____ 7. Two of Russia's most important resources are

a. fossil fuels and iron ore.

b. loess and water.

c. hydroelectric power and loess.

d. fossil fuels and water.

_____ 8. Early European explorers searched for new routes to

a. Russia and Ukraine.

b. rich lands in other parts of the world.

c. the Arctic Ocean.

d. the Central Uplands.

## Final Exam A (continued)

_____ 9. How did the Industrial Revolution change the way of life in Europe in the 1800s?
- **a.** Large farms developed.
- **b.** Cities grew quickly.
- **c.** People returned to their farms.
- **d.** Wages rose quickly.

_____ 10. Which statement best describes the direction of human movement since World War II?
- **a.** Many people left Western Europe.
- **b.** Many people moved to South Asia.
- **c.** Many people moved to Eastern Europe.
- **d.** Many people moved to Western Europe.

_____ 11. Today the Slavs of Eastern Europe have different
- **a.** languages and customs.
- **b.** religions and languages.
- **c.** religions and customs.
- **d.** customs and ethnic backgrounds.

_____ 12. Which of the following countries served as one of the first models for modern democracy?
- **a.** Italy
- **b.** Russia
- **c.** Yugoslavia
- **d.** Great Britain

_____ 13. In order to give Swedish citizens a better life, the government changed the country into a(n)
- **a.** agricultural country.
- **b.** welfare state.
- **c.** communist state.
- **d.** absolute monarchy.

_____ 14. Many countries have invaded Ukraine because of the area's
- **a.** location on the Atlantic.
- **b.** climate.
- **c.** natural resources.
- **d.** manufacturing centers.

## C. Critical Thinking

**Directions:** _Answer the following questions on the back of this paper or on a separate sheet of paper. (20 points)_

15. **Identifying Central Issues** How did the existence of different ethnic groups contribute to the war in Bosnia and Herzegovina?

16. **Making Comparisons** Compare the economic changes made by the Soviets in Ukraine with the economic changes made by the government of Sweden.

*Final Exam A* (continued)

## D. Skill: Using a Precipitation Map

**Directions:** *Use the precipitation map below to answer the following questions. Write your answers in the blanks provided. (20 points)*

### Precipitation Map

**Average Annual Precipitation**

| | |
|---|---|
| Over 80 inches | Over 200 cm |
| 60–80 inches | 150–200 cm |
| 40–59 inches | 100–149 cm |
| 20–39 inches | 50–99 cm |
| 10–19 inches | 25–49 cm |
| Under 10 inches | Under 25 cm |

Belfast
Edinburgh
IRELAND    UNITED KINGDOM
Manchester
Dublin                    Amsterdam
Cardiff    London
NETHERLANDS
Brussels
BELGIUM
LUX
Paris    Luxembourg
Nantes    FRANCE
Bordeaux
Lyon
Bilbao
MONACO
PORTUGAL
ANDORRA    Nice
Lisbon    Marseille
Madrid    Barcelona
SPAIN    Valencia
Seville
Málaga

Final Exams

17. What information does the key on this map provide?

_____

18. How many precipitation regions does Spain have?

_____

19. On this map is there another city that is in the same precipitation region as Valencia?

_____

20. What do Lisbon, Barcelona, Marseille, Nice, Nantes, Amsterdam, Edinburgh, and Dublin have in common?

_____

# Final Exam B

## A. Key Terms

**Directions:** *Match the definitions in Column I with the terms in Column II. Write the correct letter in each blank. You will not use all the terms. (15 points)*

**Column I**

_____ 1. a body of land nearly surrounded by water

_____ 2. a treeless plain where grasses and mosses grow

_____ 3. a government official who is in charge of a nation's foreign affairs

_____ 4. the move toward cities

_____ 5. someone who moves from one country to another

**Column II**

a. chernozem

b. collective

c. foreign minister

d. immigrant

e. investor

f. migration

g. peninsula

h. tundra

i. urbanization

## B. Key Concepts

**Directions:** *Write the letter of the correct answer in each blank. (45 points)*

_____ 6. Two major physical features of Russia are the
  a. North European Plain and the West Siberian Plain.
  b. North European Plain and Alpine Mountains.
  c. Northwestern Highlands and the Alpine Mountain System.
  d. West Siberian Plain and the Central Uplands.

_____ 7. The warm waters and winds of the Atlantic Ocean bring
  a. harsh weather to southern Europe.
  b. mild weather to northwestern Europe.
  c. mild weather to eastern Russia.
  d. harsh weather to northern Russia.

_____ 8. Why did feudalism play an important role in the Middle Ages?
  a. It increased the power of the serfs and the farmers.
  b. It limited the power of the lords in the local areas.
  c. It organized society when there was no central government.
  d. It enabled people to have a written code of laws.

_____ 9. The Industrial Revolution changed life across Europe by encouraging people to
  a. return to their villages.
  b. work in factories in the cities.
  c. work on large, government-owned farms.
  d. move to farms in other countries.

## Final Exam B (continued)

_____ 10. What statement best describes the direction of human movement since World War II?

a. Many people left Western Europe.

b. Many people moved to Eastern Europe.

c. Many people moved to Western Europe.

d. Many people moved to South Asia.

_____ 11. How has Great Britain's status as an island nation influenced its political development?

a. It is now a constitutional monarchy.

b. It built a large empire to provide its factories with raw materials.

c. It has a Parliament whose members can make laws.

d. It became a welfare state.

_____ 12. Compared to Southern Italy, Northern Italy is very

a. poor.

b. modern.

c. traditional.

d. religious.

_____ 13. Two important traditions in Poland are

a. Catholicism and the welfare state.

b. Islam and the Polish language.

c. Greek Orthodoxy and the Russian language.

d. Catholicism and the Polish language.

_____ 14. Why was Ukraine forced to become part of the Soviet Union?

a. The Soviet Union agreed to provide the region with food.

b. Ukraine needed the Soviet Union's natural resources.

c. The Soviets wanted to control the area's natural resources.

d. The Soviets had been invaded by the Ukrainians in the past.

## C. Critical Thinking

**Directions:** *Answer the following questions on the back of this paper or on a separate sheet of paper. (20 points)*

15. **Drawing Conclusions** How do you think the location and physical features of Europe and Russia have affected the population densities of these two areas? In your answer explain what population density is.

16. **Identifying Central Issues** Why were the 1600s and 1700s called the Age of Revolution? In your answer, describe two revolutions that happened during this time.

## *Final Exam B* (continued)

## D. Skill: Using a Precipitation Map

**Directions:** *Use the precipitation map below to answer the following questions. Write your answers in the blanks provided. (20 points)*

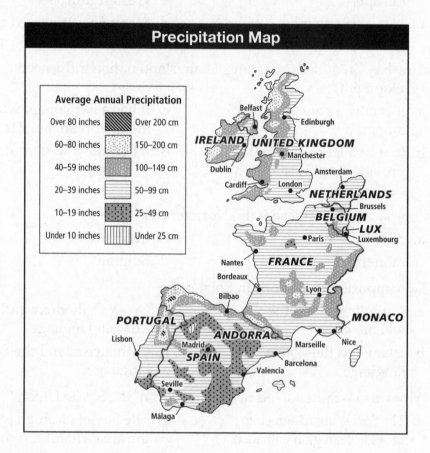

17. What does a precipitation map show?

_____

18. What do the cities of Belfast, Cardiff, and Bilbao have in common?

_____

19. Does Madrid or London have the highest average rainfall per year?

_____

20. Does Amsterdam or Seville have the least amount of average rainfall per year?

_____

# Answer Key

## Final Exam A

1. h
2. e
3. d
4. g
5. b
6. d
7. a
8. b
9. b
10. d
11. b
12. d
13. b
14. c
15. Answers may vary. A possible answer: The tensions among different ethnic groups, the Serbs, Croats, and Bosnians, led to a long and bitter war. When the Serbs controlled the government of Yugoslavia, the other ethnic groups wanted to form their own countries to rule themselves. But the groups distrusted each other and no group wanted to live in a country ruled by people of another ethnic group. This situation probably developed because the political leaders didn't reduce tensions and emphasized the religious and ethnic differences between the people who lived in the region.
16. Answers may vary. A possible answer: The economic changes made under the Soviet rule of Ukraine were very harsh. Ukrainian industries grew, but farmers were forced to work on large government-owned collectives instead of on individually owned farms. All the crops went to the government, and millions of Ukrainians died of hunger as a result. In Sweden, however, the government worked to provide benefits to the people by creating a welfare state. To pay for these services, the government collected high taxes.

17. The key provides average annual precipitation figures.
18. six
19. no
20. They are all coastal cities in the same precipitation region.

## Final Exam B

1. g
2. h
3. c
4. i
5. d
6. a
7. b
8. c
9. b
10. c
11. b
12. b
13. d
14. c
15. Answers may vary. A possible answer: Population density is the average number of people living in an area. Europe has a much higher population density than most of the world due to its mild climate, rich farmland, and water access. Because the continent of Europe forms a peninsula, its harbors and bays have enabled countries to trade with other lands throughout history. A major landform in Europe, the North European Plain, has productive farmland. Because of Europe's location, warm water and winds bring mild weather to much of northwestern Europe. Russia, however, has a much lower population density. Russia lies on the Arctic Ocean, which is frozen for most of the year and cannot be used for shipping. Also, few people can live in the vast plains and mountains of eastern Russia, where the soil is poor and the climate is very harsh.

Europe and Russia

## Answer Key *(continued)*

16. Answers may vary. A possible answer: During this period, there were revolutions in government and science. People began questioning the power of their governments and the English king was overthrown when he refused to share power with Parliament. The idea that the people, not their king or queen, should decide which type of government was best for them also spread to the American colonies and to France. In the French Revolution, the people overthrew the monarchs. In the Scientific Revolution, scientists began to base their theories on careful observation of the natural world. One result of this new approach was the development of the scientific method, in which ideas are tested with experiments and observations.

17. It shows the average amount of rainfall in a particular place.

18. All are in precipitation regions which receive 40–59 average inches of rain per year.

19. London

20. Neither, both are in the same precipitation region.

# Notes

# Notes

# Notes

# Transparency Planner

## To the Teacher

This Transparency Planner is a visual Table of Contents for *Europe and Russia Transparencies*, which accompanies the Prentice Hall World Studies program. *Europe and Russia Transparencies* offers color transparencies, section reading support transparencies, and blank graphic organizer transparencies to enrich your lessons and help students make connections. You can use this convenient set of thumbnails to review the full array of transparencies and decide which ones best fit your daily lessons.

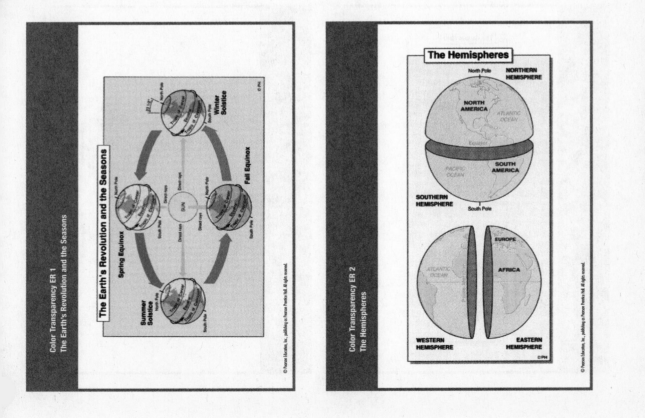

Color Transparency ER 5
The World: Continents and Oceans (B)

Color Transparency ER 6
Some Major Cities of the World (0)

Color Transparency ER 3
The Global Grid

Color Transparency ER 4
Map Projections

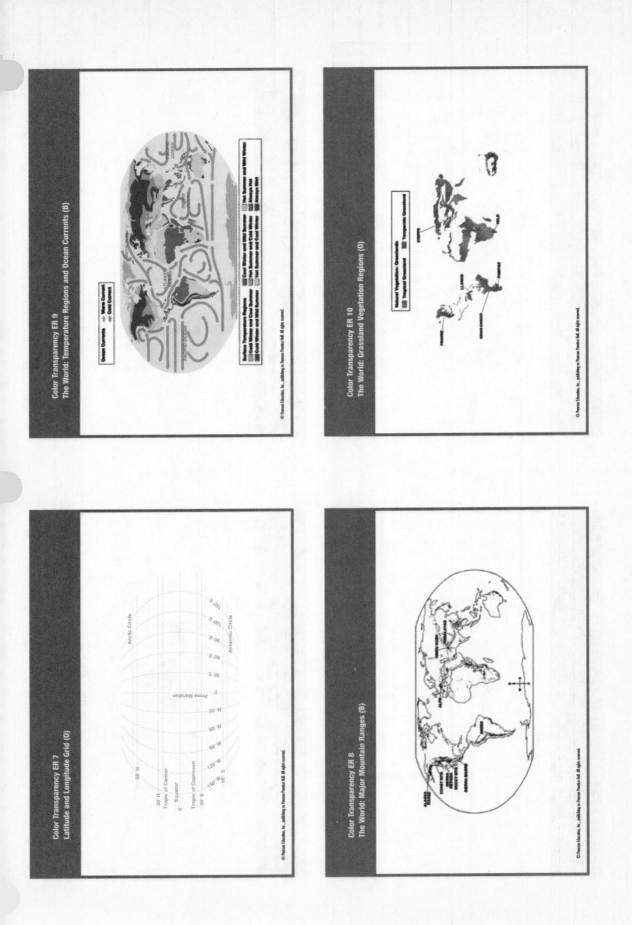

Color Transparency ER 9
The World: Temperature Regions and Ocean Currents (B)

Color Transparency ER 10
The World: Grassland Vegetation Regions (O)

Color Transparency ER 7
Latitude and Longitude Grid (O)

Color Transparency ER 8
The World: Major Mountain Ranges (B)

Transparency
Planner

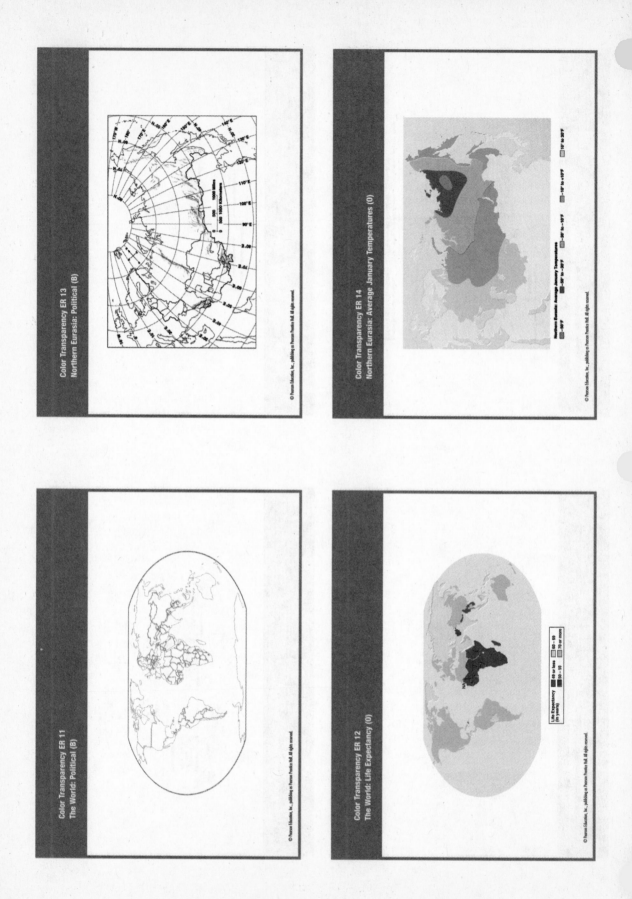

Color Transparency ER 11
The World: Political (B)

© Pearson Education, Inc., publishing as Pearson Prentice Hall. All rights reserved.

Color Transparency ER 12
The World: Life Expectancy (O)

Life Expectancy
(in years)
40 or less
50 – 59
60 – 69
70 or more

© Pearson Education, Inc., publishing as Pearson Prentice Hall. All rights reserved.

Color Transparency ER 13
Northern Eurasia: Political (B)

500   1000 Miles
0   500 1000 Kilometers

© Pearson Education, Inc., publishing as Pearson Prentice Hall. All rights reserved.

Color Transparency ER 14
Northern Eurasia: Average January Temperatures (O)

Northern Eurasia: Average January Temperatures
–50°F
–50° to 30°F
–30° to 10°F
–10° to 10°F
10° to 20°F

© Pearson Education, Inc., publishing as Pearson Prentice Hall. All rights reserved.

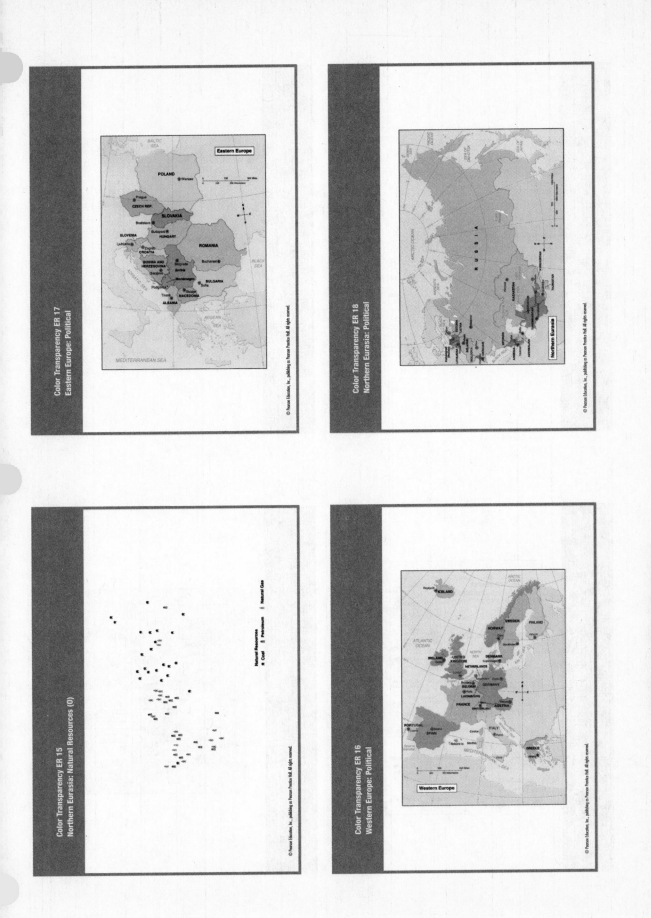

Color Transparency ER 17
Eastern Europe: Political

Color Transparency ER 18
Northern Eurasia: Political

Color Transparency ER 15
Northern Eurasia: Natural Resources (O)

Color Transparency ER 16
Western Europe: Political

Transparency Planner

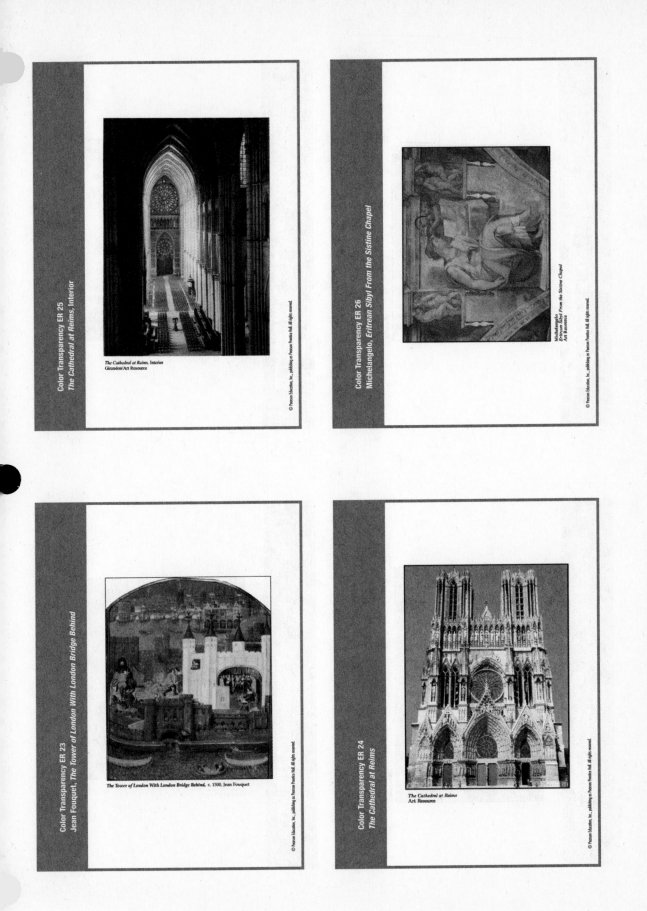

Color Transparency ER 25
*The Cathedral at Reims, Interior*

The Cathedral at Reims, Interior
Giraudon/Art Resource

Color Transparency ER 26
Michelangelo, *Eritrean Sibyl From the Sistine Chapel*

Michelangelo
*Eritrean Sibyl From the Sistine Chapel*
Art Resource

Color Transparency ER 23
Jean Fouquet, *The Tower of London With London Bridge Behind*

The Tower of London With London Bridge Behind, c. 1500, Jean Fouquet

Color Transparency ER 24
*The Cathedral at Reims*

The Cathedral at Reims
Art Resource

**Transparency Planner**

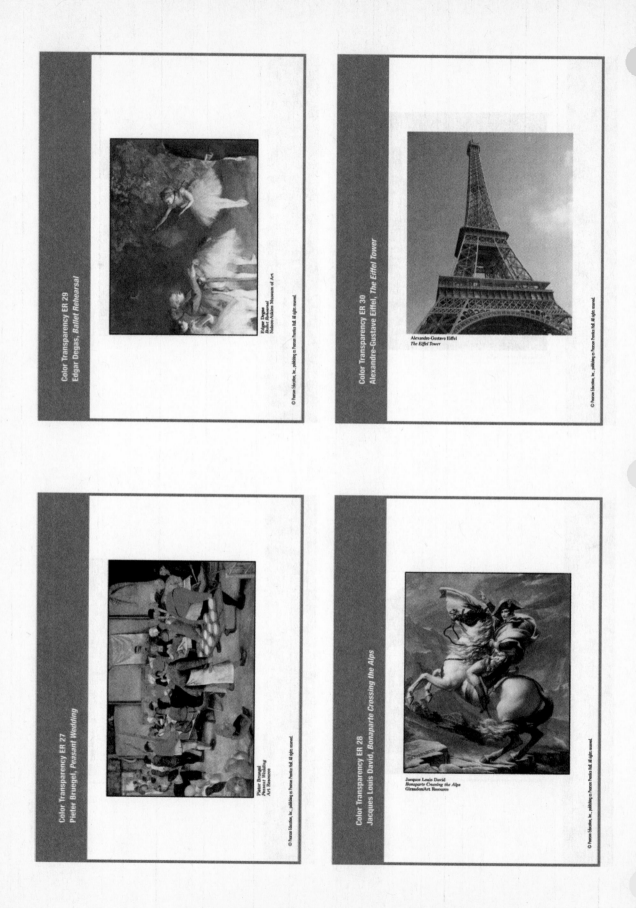

Color Transparency ER 29
Edgar Degas, *Ballet Rehearsal*

Edgar Degas
*Ballet Rehearsal*
Nelson-Atkins Museum of Art

Color Transparency ER 30
Alexandre-Gustave Eiffel, *The Eiffel Tower*

Alexandre-Gustave Eiffel
*The Eiffel Tower*

Color Transparency ER 27
Pieter Bruegel, *Peasant Wedding*

Pieter Bruegel
*Peasant Wedding*
Art Resource

Color Transparency ER 28
Jacques Louis David, *Bonaparte Crossing the Alps*

Jacques Louis David
*Bonaparte Crossing the Alps*
Giraudon/Art Resource

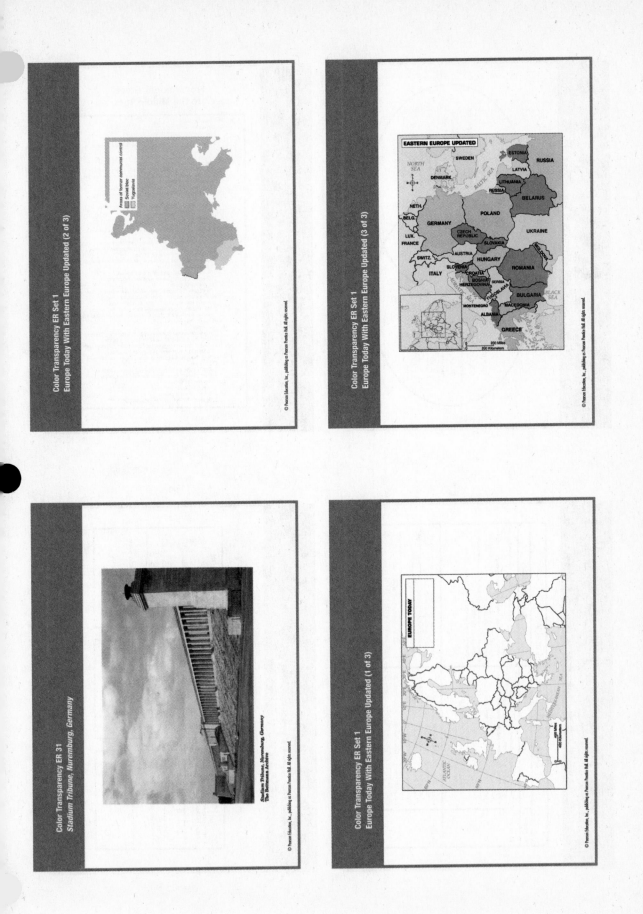

Color Transparency ER Set 1
Europe Today With Eastern Europe Updated (2 of 3)

© Pearson Education, Inc., publishing as Pearson Prentice Hall. All rights reserved.

Color Transparency ER Set 1
Europe Today With Eastern Europe Updated (3 of 3)

EASTERN EUROPE UPDATED

© Pearson Education, Inc., publishing as Pearson Prentice Hall. All rights reserved.

Color Transparency ER 31
*Stadium Tribune, Nuremburg, Germany*
*The Bettmann Archive*

© Pearson Education, Inc., publishing as Pearson Prentice Hall. All rights reserved.

Color Transparency ER Set 1
Europe Today With Eastern Europe Updated (1 of 3)

EUROPE TODAY

© Pearson Education, Inc., publishing as Pearson Prentice Hall. All rights reserved.

Transparency
Planner

## Natural Resources of Europe and Russia

**Europe**
- Rich, fertile soil
- Abundant water
- Oil, natural gas, coal
- Iron ore

**Europe and Russia**
- Fossil fuels
- Iron ore
- Ample and powerful rivers

**Russia**
- Cobalt, chrome, copper, and gold
- World's largest reserves of natural gas, iron ore and forests
- One of the world's five leading oil producers
- One-third world's coal reserves
- Abundant fishing

## From Ancient Greece to the Middle Ages

I. The Greek heritage
  A. Democracy
    1. Created concept of democracy.
    2. Democracies found in many city-states.
    3. Citizens were free-born males whose fathers were Athenian citizens.
    4. Every Athenian citizen voted on laws and policies.
  B. Golden Age of Athens (479–431 B.C.)
    1. The study of arts, literature, and philosophy flourished.
    2. Invented today's scientific way of gathering knowledge.
  C. Spread of Greek Ideas.
    1. Alexander the Great conquered many lands.
    2. Established Greek cities, language, and ideas around empire.
    3. Greek culture linked entire Mediterranean world.
II. The glory of ancient Rome
  A. Pax Romana
    1. Began in 27 B.C. and lasted about 200 years.
    2. Rome: most powerful state in Europe and Mediterranean.
  B. Roman law
    1. Roman lawmakers wrote laws down, which were brought together and put into an organized system.
    2. Protected the rights of all citizens.
    3. Modern laws and government are based on Roman law.
  C. Beginnings of Christianity
    1. Romans allowed some religious freedom.
    2. Emperor Constantine encouraged Christianity.
  D. The decline of Rome
    1. To defend the empire more soldiers were needed; taxes were increased causing the economy to suffer.
    2. Empire was too large to govern; split in two.
    3. The eastern empire remained strong, but the western empire continued to weaken until it collapsed in A.D. 476
III. Europe in the Middle Ages
  A. Feudalism
    1. A political system that developed to bring order to society.
    2. King was highest; provided security to kingdom.
    3. Nobles provided knights and foot soldiers; allowed serfs to farm, but kept most of crops and income.
    4. Serfs were bound to the land, but slaves could be sold.
  B. Christianity
    1. Gave people a sense of security and community.
    2. Most people's lives centered around the Church.
  C. Europe begins to change
    1. Over time, trade increased.
    2. Towns grew into cities.
    3. By the 1400s, life centered around cities.

## Europe and Russia: Land and Water

| Region | Land Forms | Bodies of Water |
| --- | --- | --- |
| Europe | - Small continent: a peninsula in Atlantic Ocean<br>- Ural Mountains are Europe–Asia boundaries<br>- Northwestern Highlands are old mountains, good for timber and little farming<br>- North European Plain covers over half of Europe, has productive farmland<br>- Central Uplands made up of mountains and plateaus, good for livestock and mining<br>- The Alpine Mountain System includes high mountains with some small-scale farming | - Good harbors allow shipping industry to be world leaders<br>- Rhine River runs from Switzerland through Netherlands into North Sea; connected to Europe by canals and tributaries<br>- Danube is second longest river, runs from western Germany to the Black Sea<br>- Contains few lakes compared to other regions |
| Russia | - Stretches over the continents of Europe and Asia<br>- Shares the North European Plain with Europe<br>- East of the Ural Mountains is Siberia with 75% of the land in Russia, and only 20% of the people<br>- West Siberian Plain is largest in world and is low and marshy<br>- Central Siberian Plateau meets East Siberian Uplands with mountains, plateaus, and volcanoes | - Much of Russia lies on Arctic Ocean; frozen most of year and cannot be used for shipping<br>- Volga River, longest in Europe, runs through western Russia to Caspian Sea; freezes during winter<br>- Has large number of lakes<br>- Lake Baikal is world's largest and deepest freshwater lake; nearly 400 miles long, average width of 30 miles, reaches depth of 5,315 feet |

## Europe and Russia: Climate and Vegetation

**FACTOR**
- Areas near oceans or seas
- Areas far from ocean (Siberia)
- North Atlantic Current carries warm water
- Winds and ocean currents carry moisture
- Mountains affect rainfall
- Mediterranean Sea

**CLIMATE**
- Fairly mild weather
- Extreme weather (subarctic climate)
- Warm water and winds bring mild weather to northwestern Europe
- Fairly wet climate in Western Europe
- Areas west of mountains receive heavy rain fall; areas to the east have lighter rainfall
- Mediterranean climate has hot, dry summers and mild, rainy winters

**VEGETATION**
- Forests or grasslands
- Tundra and forests
- Forests and grasslands
- Forests and grasslands
- Forests and grasslands
- Trees, scrub, and smaller plants

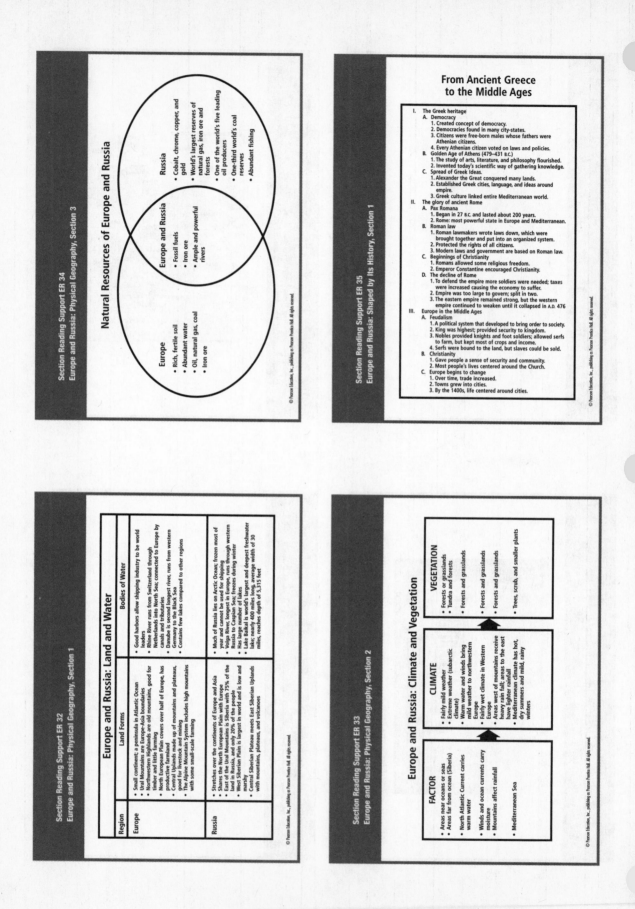

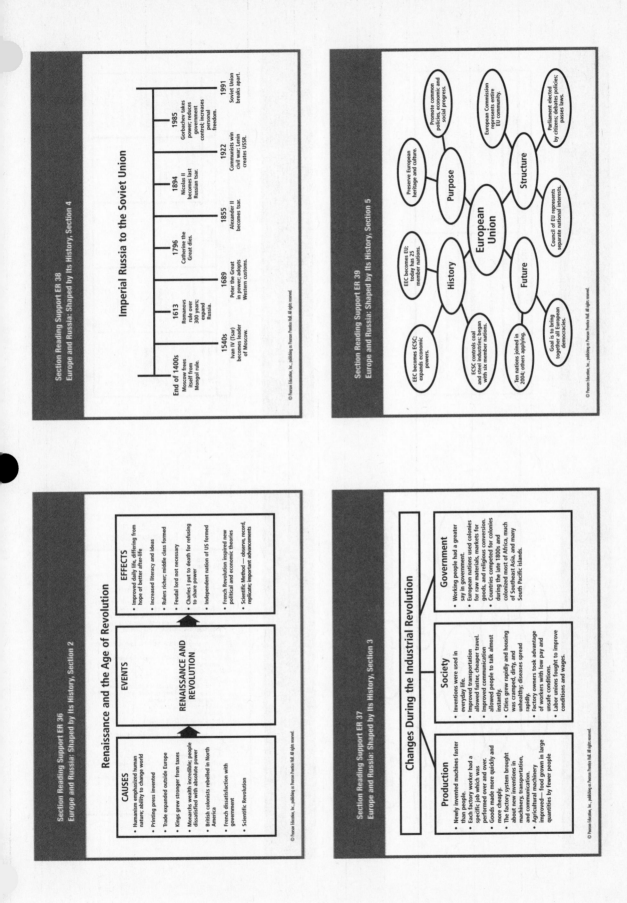

Transparency
Planner

## Cultural Expression

| Soviet Union | Russia |
|---|---|
| • Soviet Union tried to prevent people from practicing religion<br>• Comprised of individual republics, each with an ethnic group forming the majority population<br>• The work of many great artists came to a halt under communism; art was to serve political purpose | • Churches reopened across Russia<br>• Some non-Russian ethnic groups broke away; formed own countries; some have called for more rights; fighting only with Chechens<br>• People returned to artistic traditions and created new art |

## Events in British History

| Early years | 1500s | 1700s | 1800s | 1900s |
|---|---|---|---|---|
| • Romans ruled England 2000 years ago.<br>• Roman Empire falls; small kingdoms arise.<br>• Kingdom of Wessex unifies England into a nation by 800s.<br>• Magna Carta signed in 1215. | • Wales officially becomes part of England.<br>• Trade allows British to begin building a large empire. | • England and Scotland join; name changed to Great Britain. | • Great Britain takes control of Ireland.<br>• The empire covers six continents, becomes world economic power. | • Southern Ireland gains independence.<br>• After World War II, most British colonies seek independence.<br>• UK joins EU in 1973.<br>• End of 1990s, Parliament shifts some lawmaking power to regional assemblies.<br>• Hong Kong returned to China in 1997. |

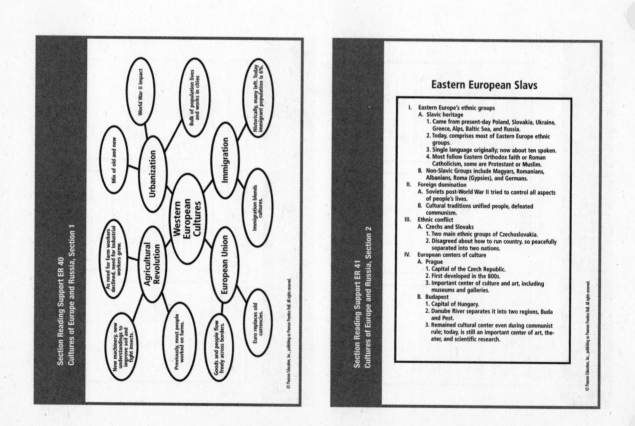

## Eastern European Slavs

I. Eastern Europe's ethnic groups
  A. Slavic heritage
    1. Came from present-day Poland, Slovakia, Ukraine, Greece, Alps, Baltic Sea, and Russia.
    2. Today, comprises most of Eastern Europe ethnic groups.
    3. Single language originally; now about ten spoken.
    4. Most follow Eastern Orthodox faith or Roman Catholicism, some are Protestant or Muslim.
  B. Non-Slavic Groups include Magyars, Romanians, Albanians, Roma (Gypsies), and Germans.
II. Foreign domination
  A. Soviets post-World War II tried to control all aspects of people's lives.
  B. Cultural traditions unified people, defeated communism.
III. Ethnic conflict
  A. Czechs and Slovaks
    1. Two main ethnic groups of Czechoslovakia.
    2. Disagreed about how to run country, so peacefully separated into two nations.
IV. European centers of culture
  A. Prague
    1. Capital of the Czech Republic.
    2. First developed in the 800s.
    3. Important center of culture and art, including museums and galleries.
  B. Budapest
    1. Capital of Hungary.
    2. Danube River separates it into two regions, Buda and Pest.
    3. Remained cultural center even during communist rule; today, is still an important center of art, theater, and scientific research.

## Life in Italy

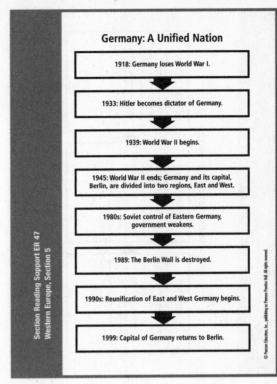

**Northern Italy**
- City-states became centers of industry.
- More prosperous than southern Italy through developed economy.
- Home to most manufacturing industries (cars, planes, leather goods, plastics).
- Cities are a mixture of old and new.
- Proposal to form separate country; support has diminished.

**Northern and Southern Italy**
- Most Italians are Catholic.
- Few ethnic minorities.
- Strong family ties are common.

**Southern Italy**
- Feudal kingdoms common.
- Coast supports agricultural products.
- Church is hub of life in small towns.
- After World War II, migration to northern Italy for jobs.
- Land reform, roads, and irrigation help economy; still lags behind the north.

---

## Germany: A Unified Nation

1918: Germany loses World War I.

1933: Hitler becomes dictator of Germany.

1939: World War II begins.

1945: World War II ends; Germany and its capital, Berlin, are divided into two regions, East and West.

1980s: Soviet control of Eastern Germany, government weakens.

1989: The Berlin Wall is destroyed.

1990s: Reunification of East and West Germany begins.

1999: Capital of Germany returns to Berlin.

---

## French Culture

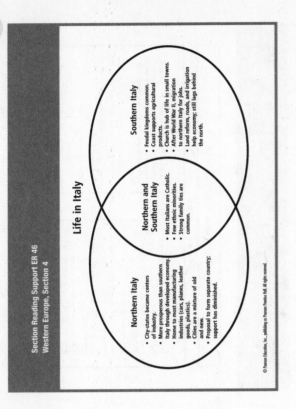

**Cultural Heritage**

**Influence of Immigrants**

- French Academy decides which words are officially accepted; protects French language from too much change.
- Important philosophies, which influence other nations, begin in France.
- French artists, composers, writers, and fashion designers create works that influence the world.
- French architecture leads in design.
- French cooking considered among the best in the world.

- French language borrows words from U.S., Germany, and other cultures.
- Immigrants have been welcomed in France since mid-1800s; since 1950s the largest group of immigrants has come from Algeria.
- Large groups of immigrants came in 1970s; French economy weakened; tensions were created over jobs.
- Debate continues as large number of North Africans immigrate, and the presence of Asian, Arab, and African culture is prominent; France makes adjustments to benefit from a diverse population.

---

## Sweden's Welfare State

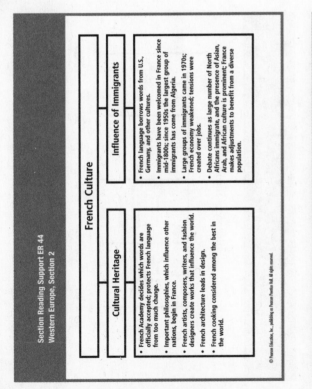

**Benefits**

**Economic Challenges**

- Many services are free or low cost.
- Cradle-to-grave system.
- Parents paid to stay home to care for infants.
- Childcare provided at a reduced cost.
- Education, books, and lunches are free.
- Citizens have free or inexpensive health care.
- Workers receive paid vacation and sick time.
- Retired workers receive monthly payments.

- Taxes are highest in Europe—as much as 60% of their income.
- In 1980s, people bought fewer goods because of high taxes; economy slowed.
- Companies less productive than in other nations, partly due to long vacations.
- Borrowed money to pay benefits; national debt grew; government increased taxes and cut spending.
- Highest ratio of retired people in world; fewer workers paying taxes; less money to pay for benefits.
- Voters against reduced spending for some benefits in 1990s.
- Businesses may become more productive using American or other methods.

**Transparency Planner**

## Ukraine: Natural Resources

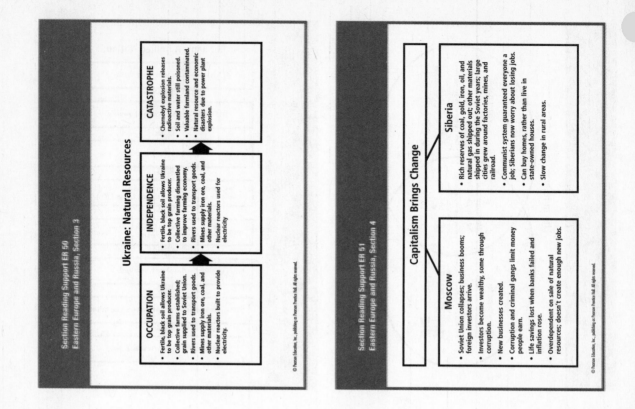

**OCCUPATION**
- Fertile, black soil allows Ukraine to be top grain producer.
- Collective farms established; grain supplied to Soviet Union.
- Rivers used to transport goods.
- Mines supply iron ore, coal, and other materials.
- Nuclear reactors built to provide electricity.

**INDEPENDENCE**
- Fertile, black soil allows Ukraine to be top grain producer.
- Collective farming dismantled to improve farming economy.
- Rivers used to transport goods.
- Mines supply iron ore, coal, and other materials.
- Nuclear reactors used for electricity

**CATASTROPHE**
- Chernobyl explosion releases radioactive materials.
- Soil and water still poisoned.
- Valuable farmland contaminated.
- Natural resource and economic disasters due to power plant explosion.

## Capitalism Brings Change

**Moscow**
- Soviet Union collapses; business booms; foreign investors arrive.
- Investors become wealthy, some through corruption.
- New businesses created.
- Corruption and criminal gangs limit money people earn.
- Life savings lost when banks failed and inflation rose.
- Overdependent on sale of natural resources; doesn't create enough new jobs.

**Siberia**
- Rich reserves of coal, gold, iron, oil, and natural gas shipped out; other materials shipped in during the Soviet years; large cities grew around factories, mines, and railroad.
- Communist system guaranteed everyone a job; Siberians now worry about losing jobs.
- Can buy homes, rather than live in state-owned houses.
- Slow change in rural areas.

## Poland: Tradition Amidst Change

I. Tradition in Poland
  A. Catholicism
    1. Communist government tried to discourage.
    2. Today, most Poles are Catholic.
    3. Pope is Polish; made world aware of Poland's struggles.
  B. Polish Orthodox shrines are visible all over Poland.
  C. Polish banned in the past, now spoken by majority of population.
II. Economic changes after communism
  A. Capitalism evolved quickly.
  B. Foreigners began to invest money in Poland.
  C. Entrepreneurs evolved with freedom to find ways to make money.
  D. Greater access to consumer goods.
  E. Changes in farm life
    1. Under communism farms privately owned; government regularly bought produce.
    2. After communism, prices dropped, no guarantees; farmers became innovated.
III. Future challenges
  A. Pollution
    1. Under communism, coal-mining and steel production cause terrible pollution; forests destroyed; increase in disease.
    2. After communism, leaders try to repair damage to environment.
  B. Unemployment
    1. Under communism people guaranteed jobs.
    2. Today, unemployment high; many move to other European countries for jobs.
    3. Under communism, farmers have reliable income.
    4. Today, farmers struggle; many change jobs or methods.

## History of Yugoslavia

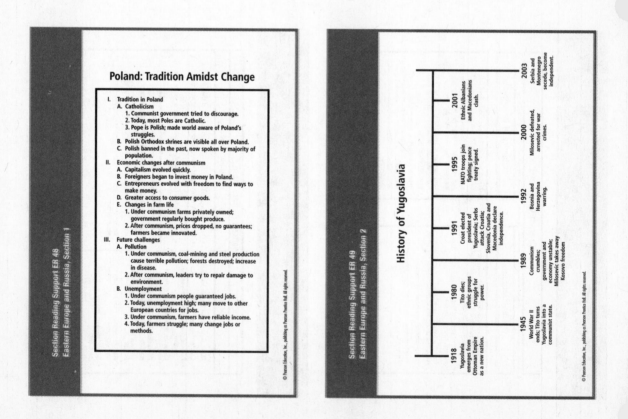

**1918** Yugoslavia emerges from Ottoman Empire as a new nation.

**1945** World War II ends; Tito turns Yugoslavia into a communist state.

**1980** Tito dies; ethnic groups struggle for power.

**1989** Communism crumbles; government and economy unstable; Milosevic takes away Kosovo freedom

**1991** Croat elected president of Yugoslavia; Serbs attack Croatia; Slovenia, Croatia and Macedonia declare independence.

**1992** Bosnia and Herzegovina warring.

**1995** NATO troops join fighting; peace treaty signed.

**2000** Milosevic defeated, arrested for war crimes.

**2001** Ethnic Albanians and Macedonians clash.

**2003** Serbia and Montenegro secede, become independent.

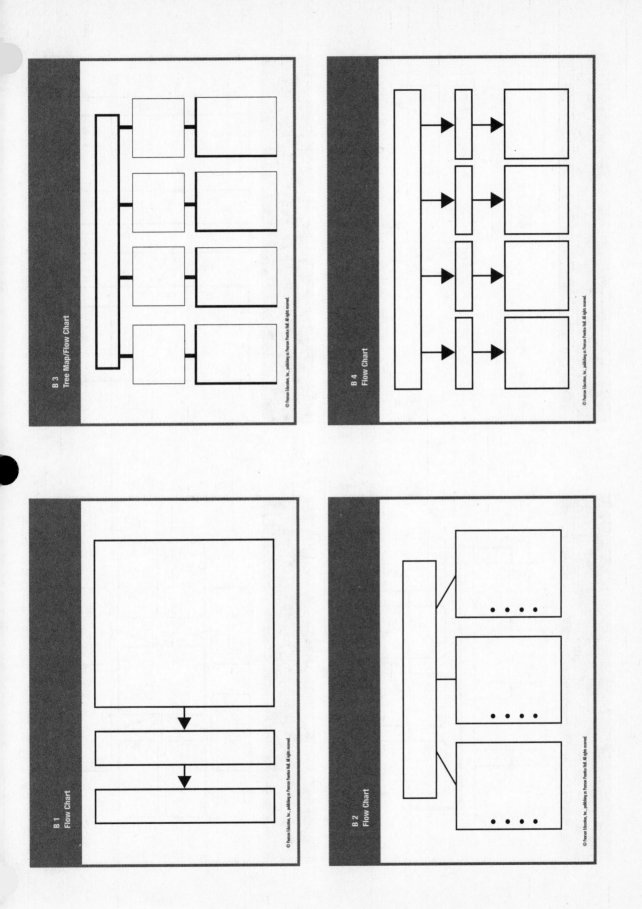

**Transparency Planner**

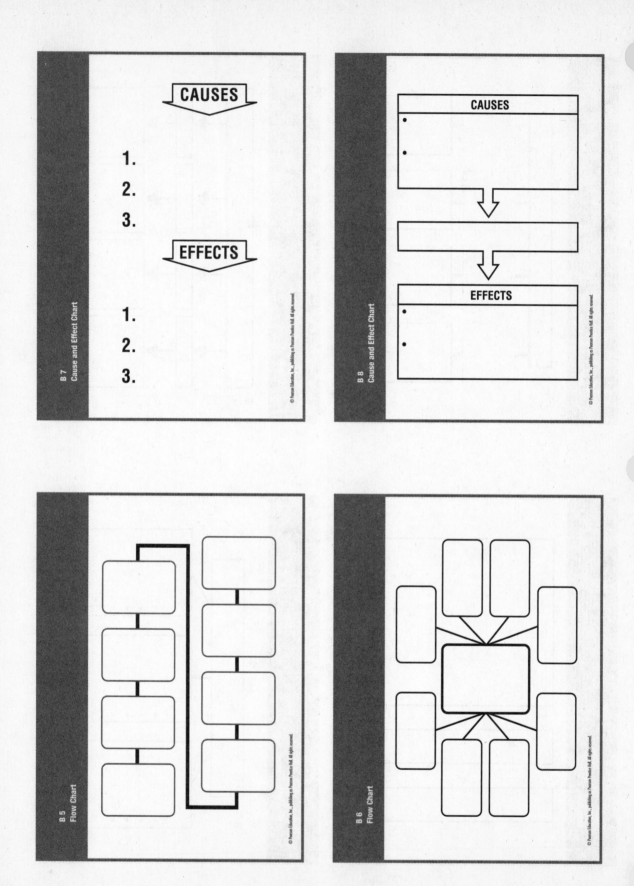

**CAUSES**

1.

2.

3.

**EFFECTS**

1.

2.

3.

B 7
Cause and Effect Chart

**CAUSES**
- 
- 

**EFFECTS**
- 
- 

B 8
Cause and Effect Chart

B 5
Flow Chart

B 6
Flow Chart

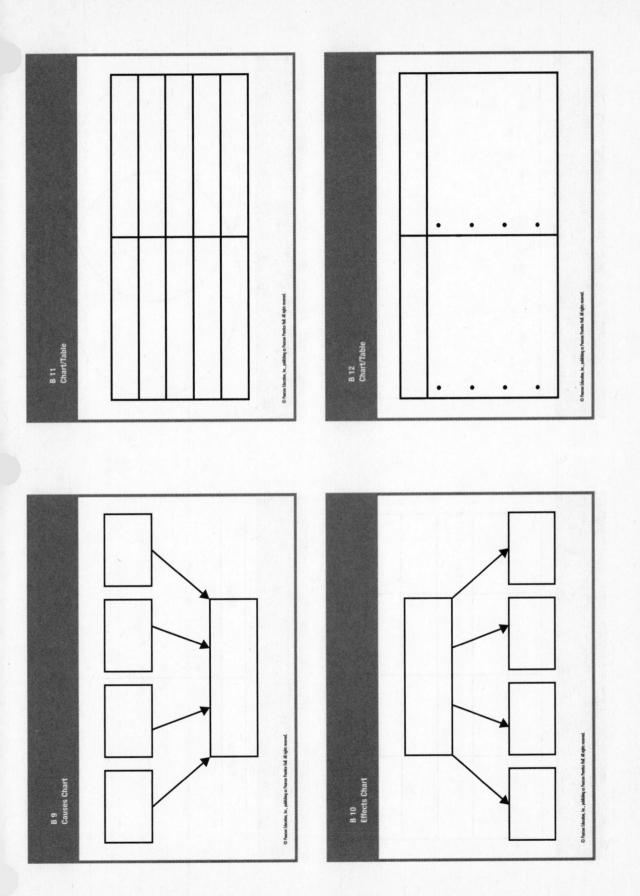

B 11
Chart/Table

B 12
Chart/Table

B 9
Causes Chart

B 10
Effects Chart

Transparency Planner

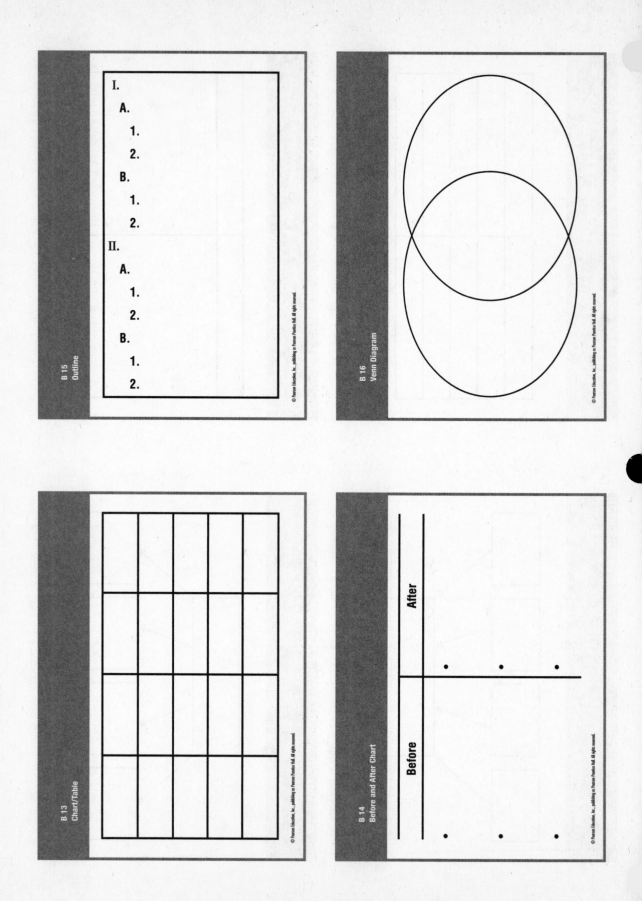

B 15
Outline

I.
  A.
    1.
    2.
  B.
    1.
    2.
II.
  A.
    1.
    2.
  B.
    1.
    2.

B 16
Venn Diagram

B 13
Chart/Table

B 14
Before and After Chart

Before     After

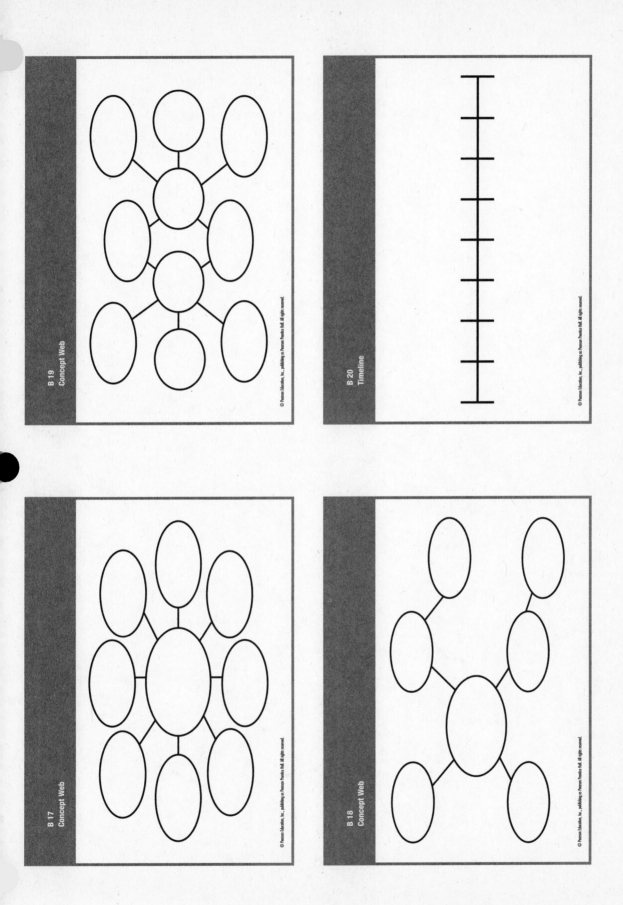

B 19
Concept Web

B 20
Timeline

B 17
Concept Web

B 18
Concept Web

Transparency
Planner